AF576584

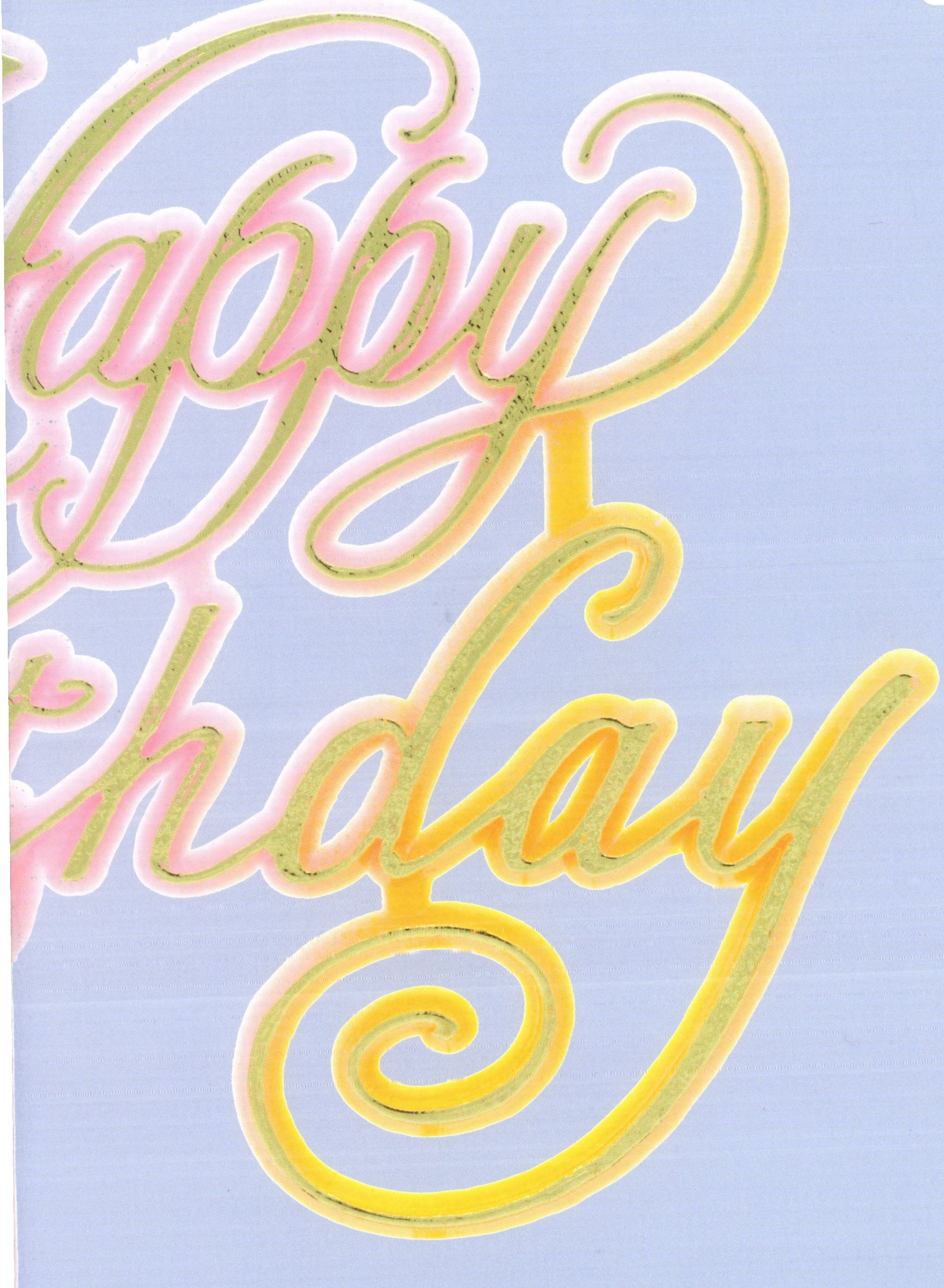

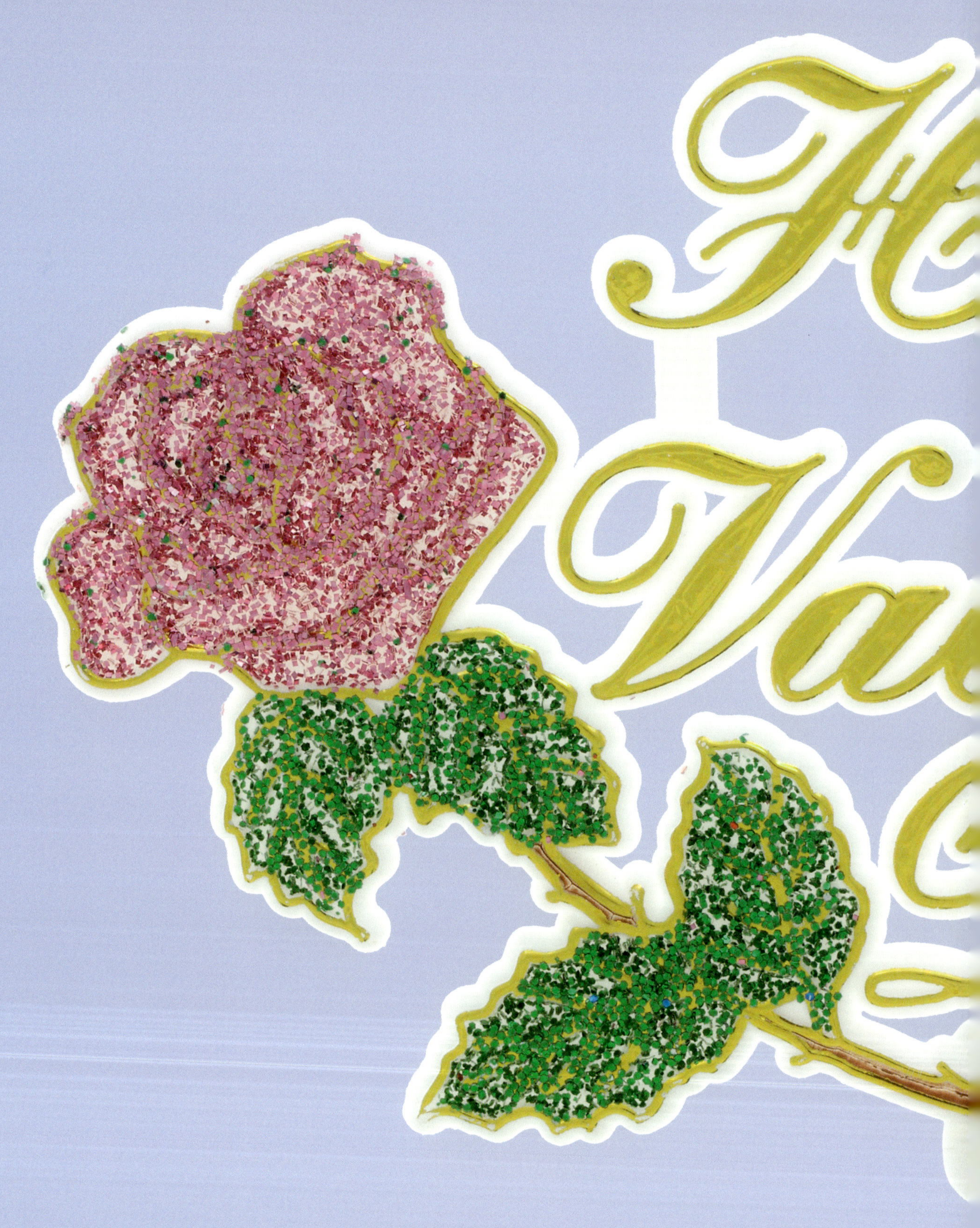

appy

lentine's

Day

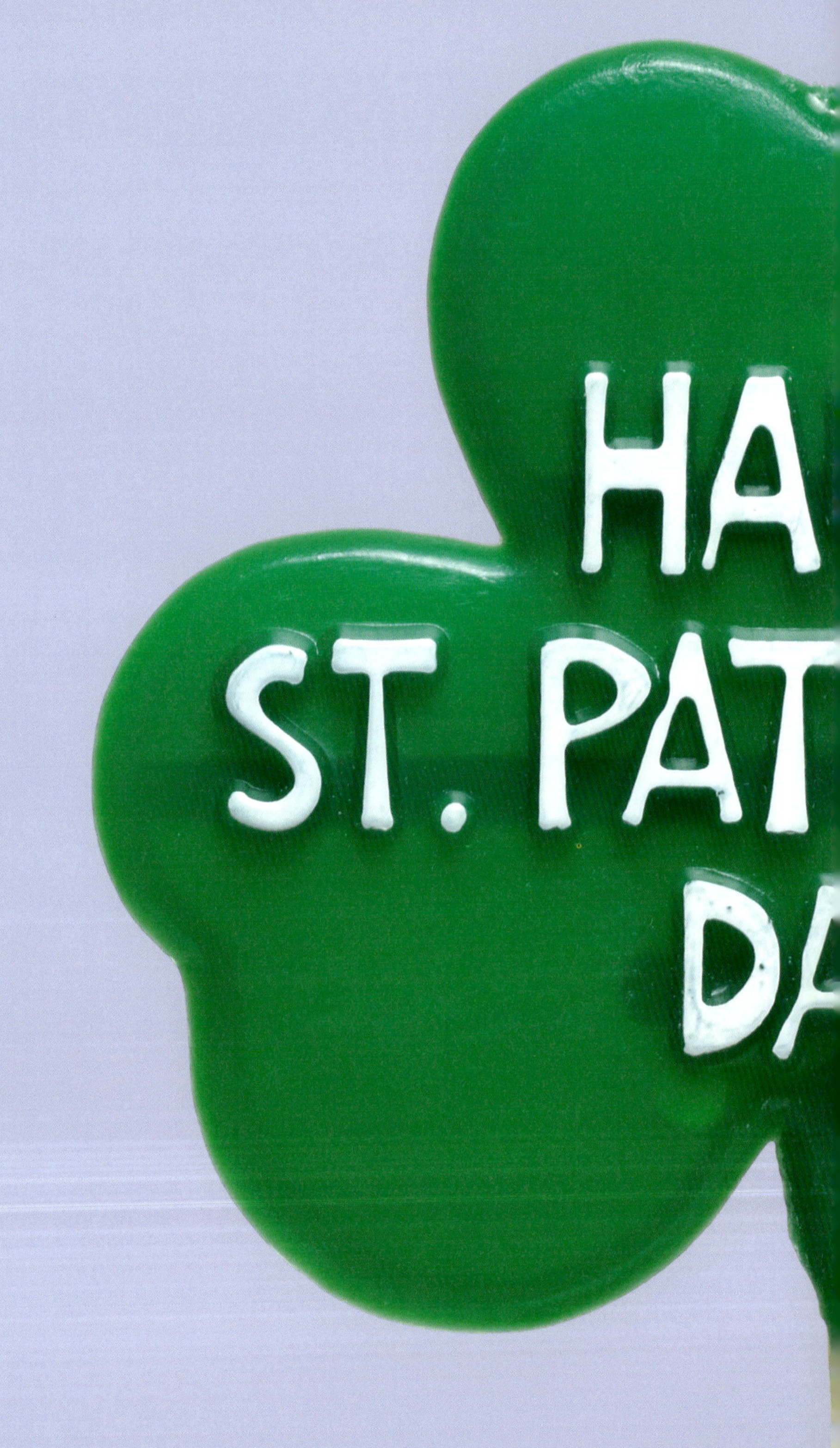
HA
ST. PAT
DA

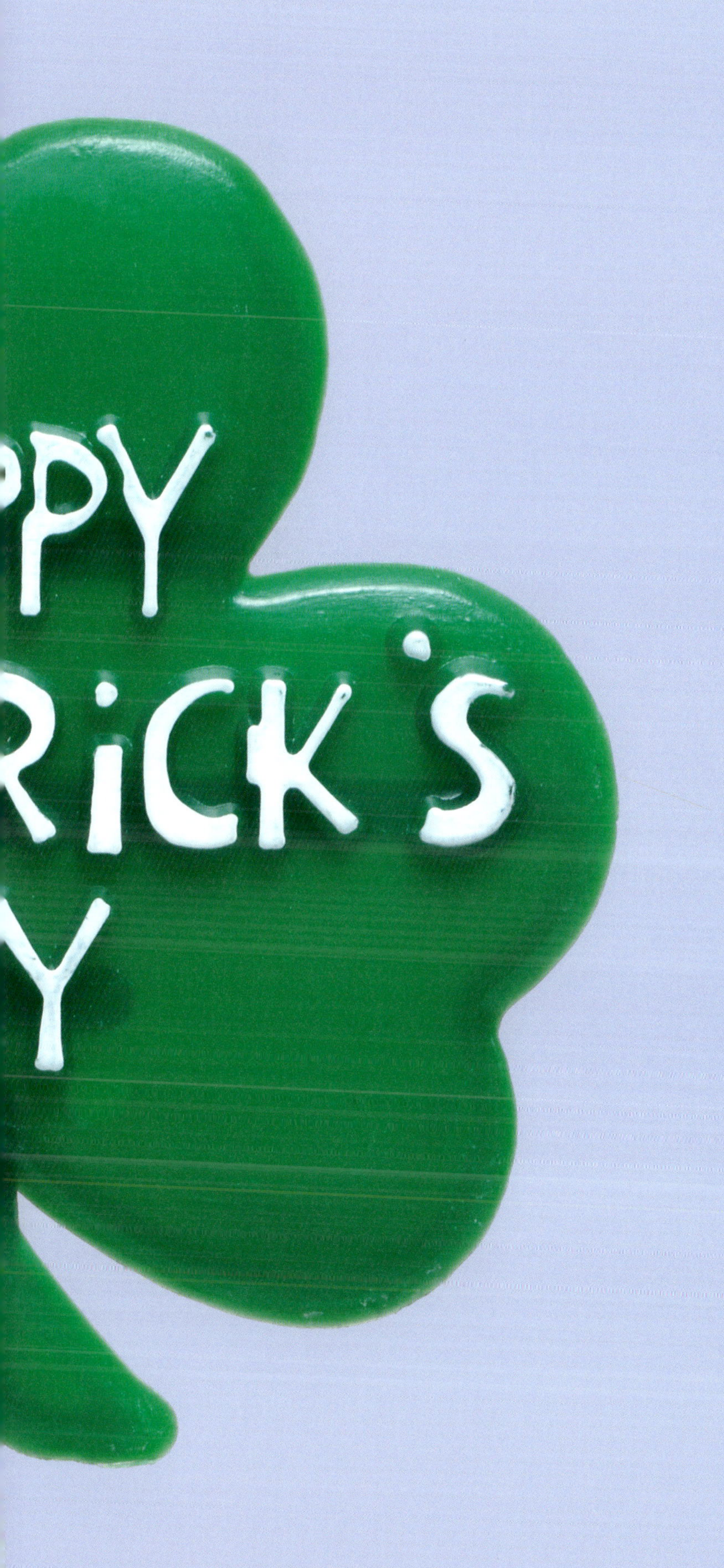
PPY
RICK'S
Y

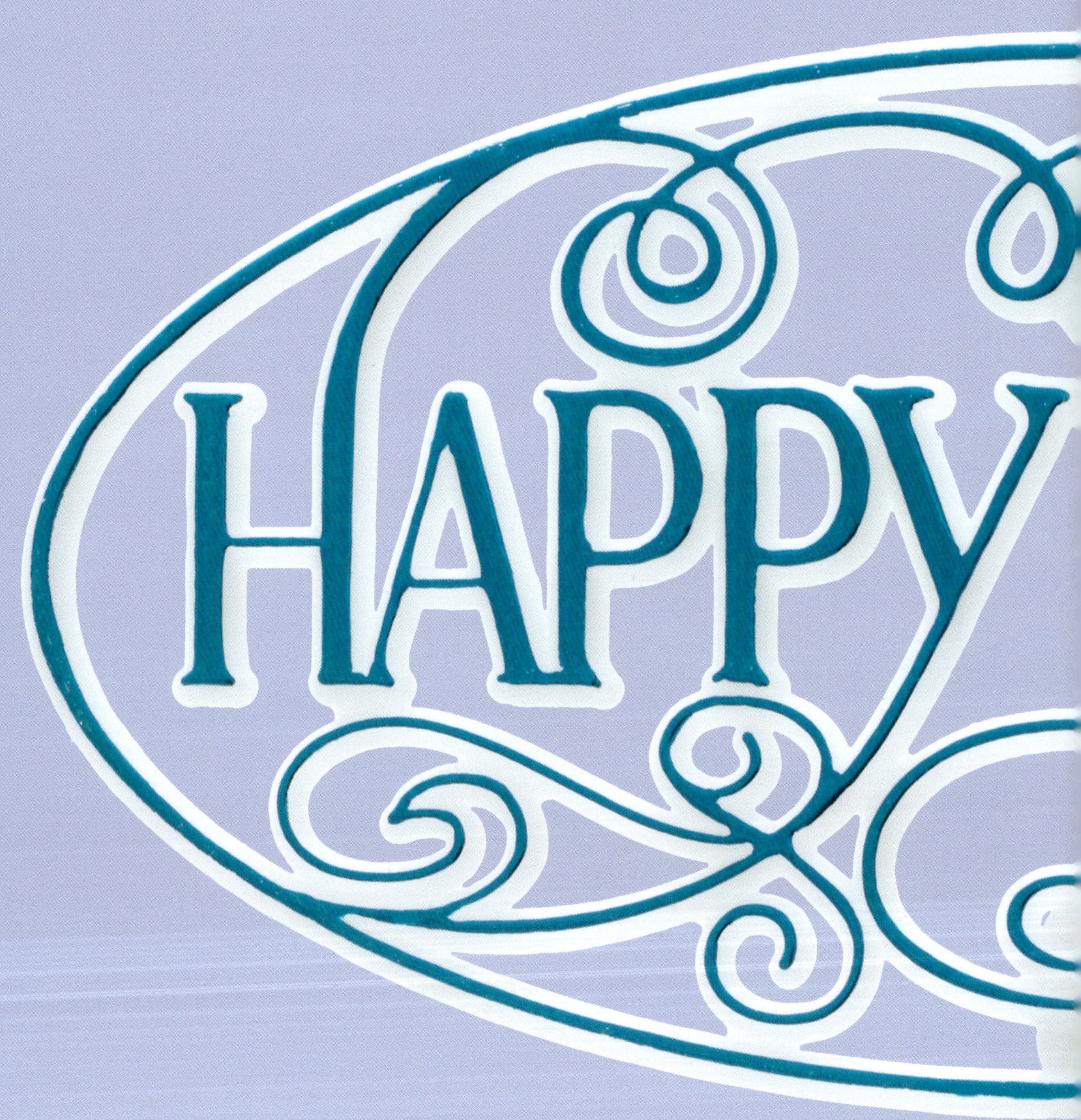
HAPPY

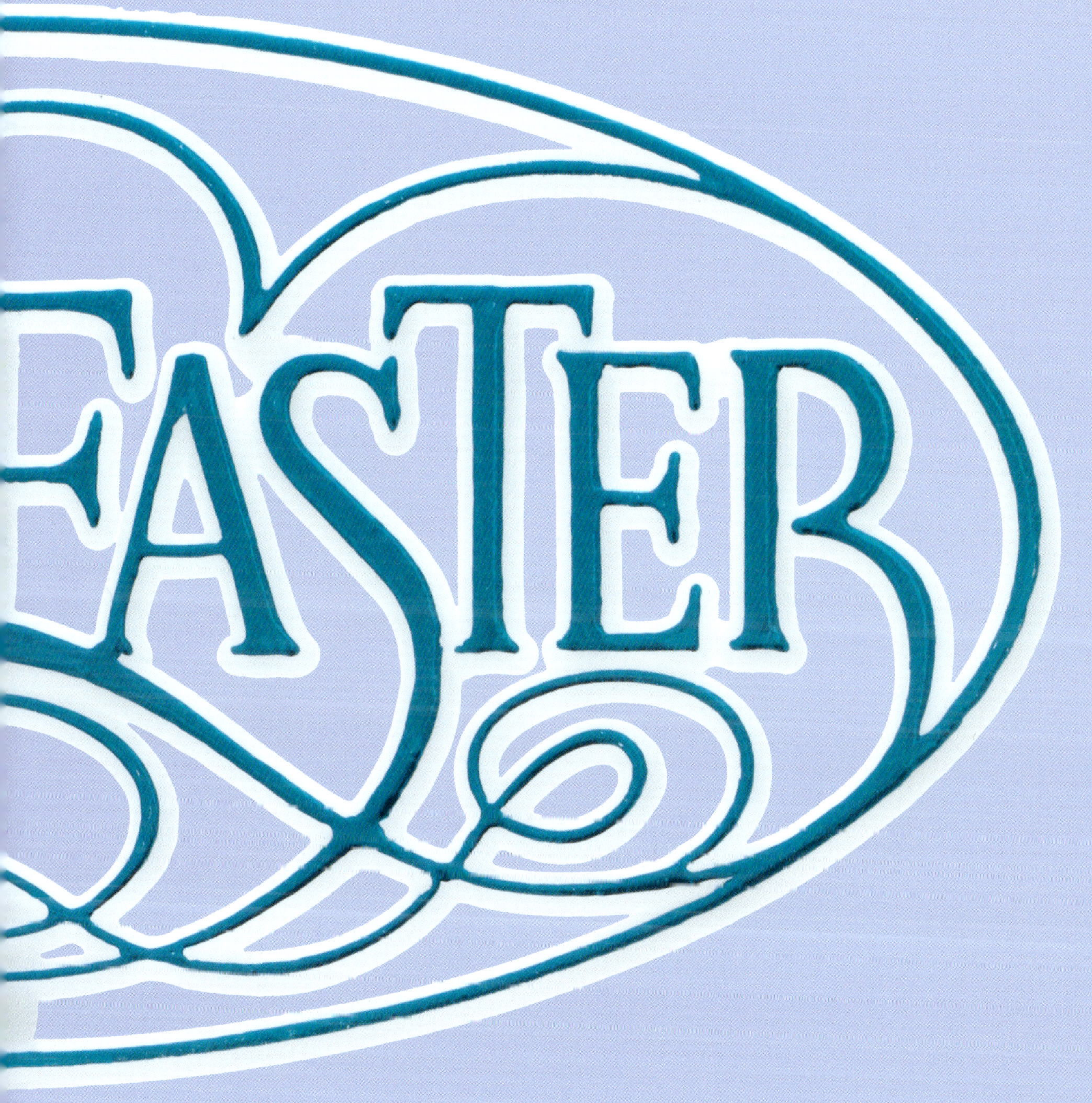
EASTER

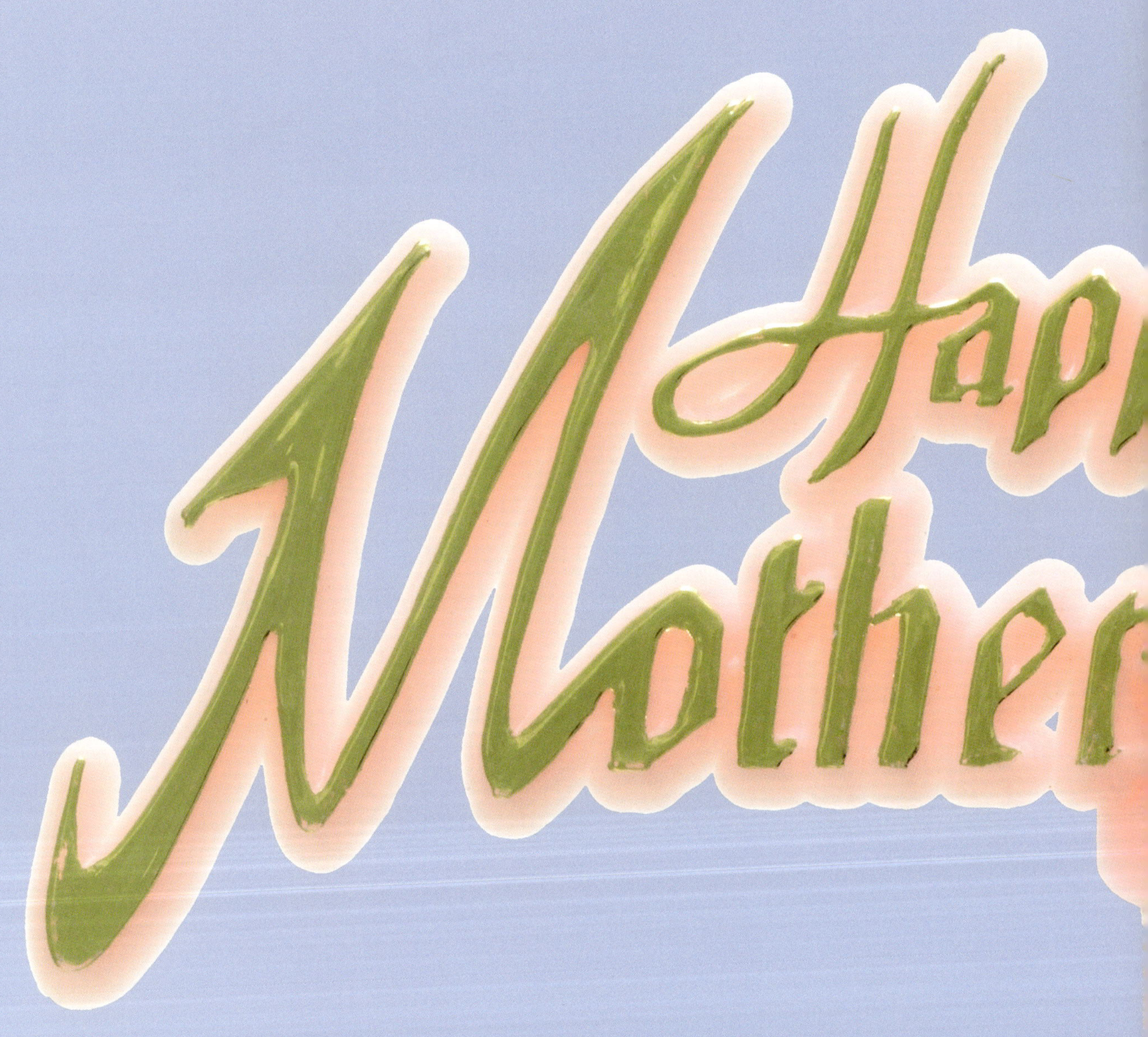

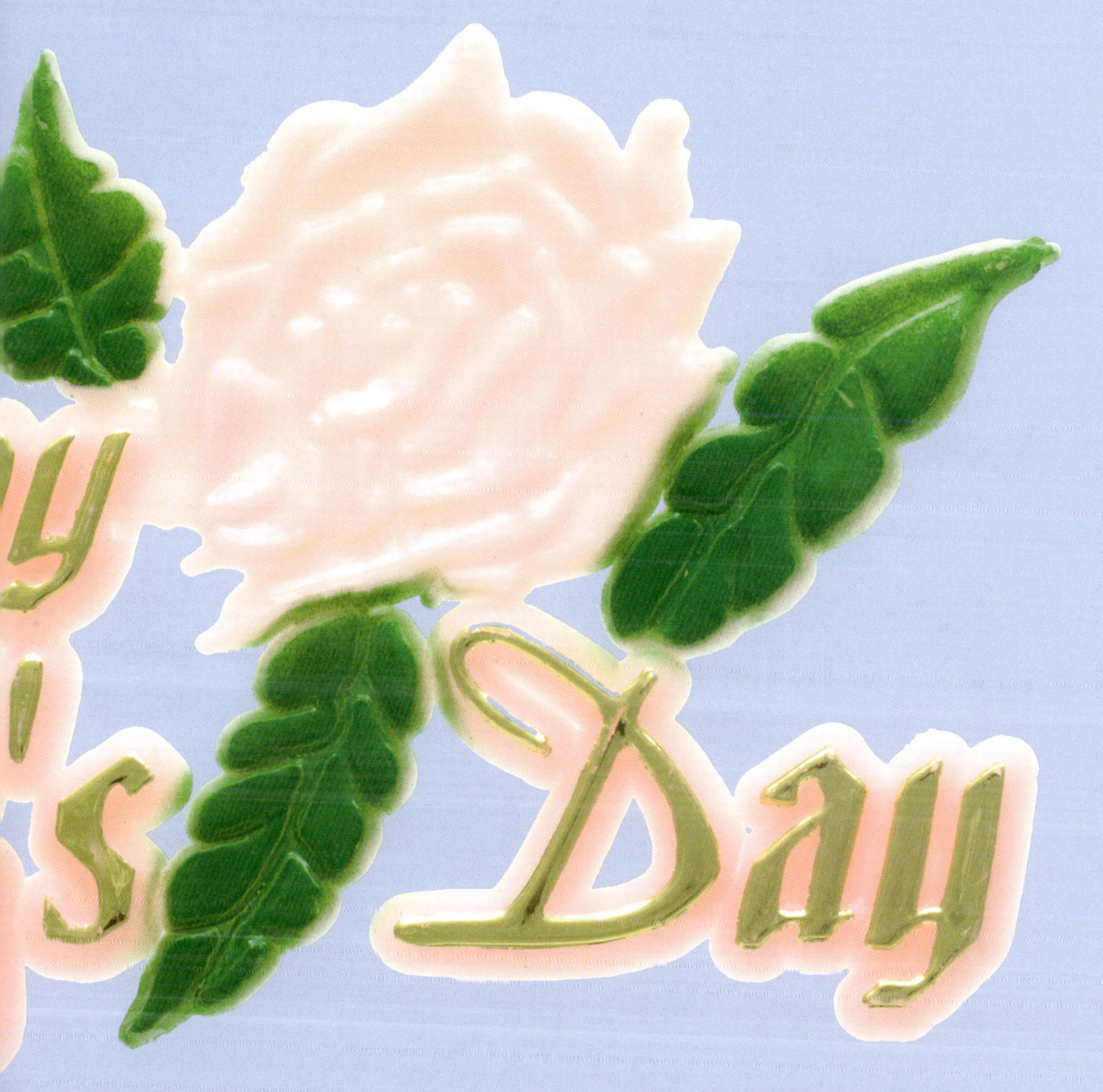
Day

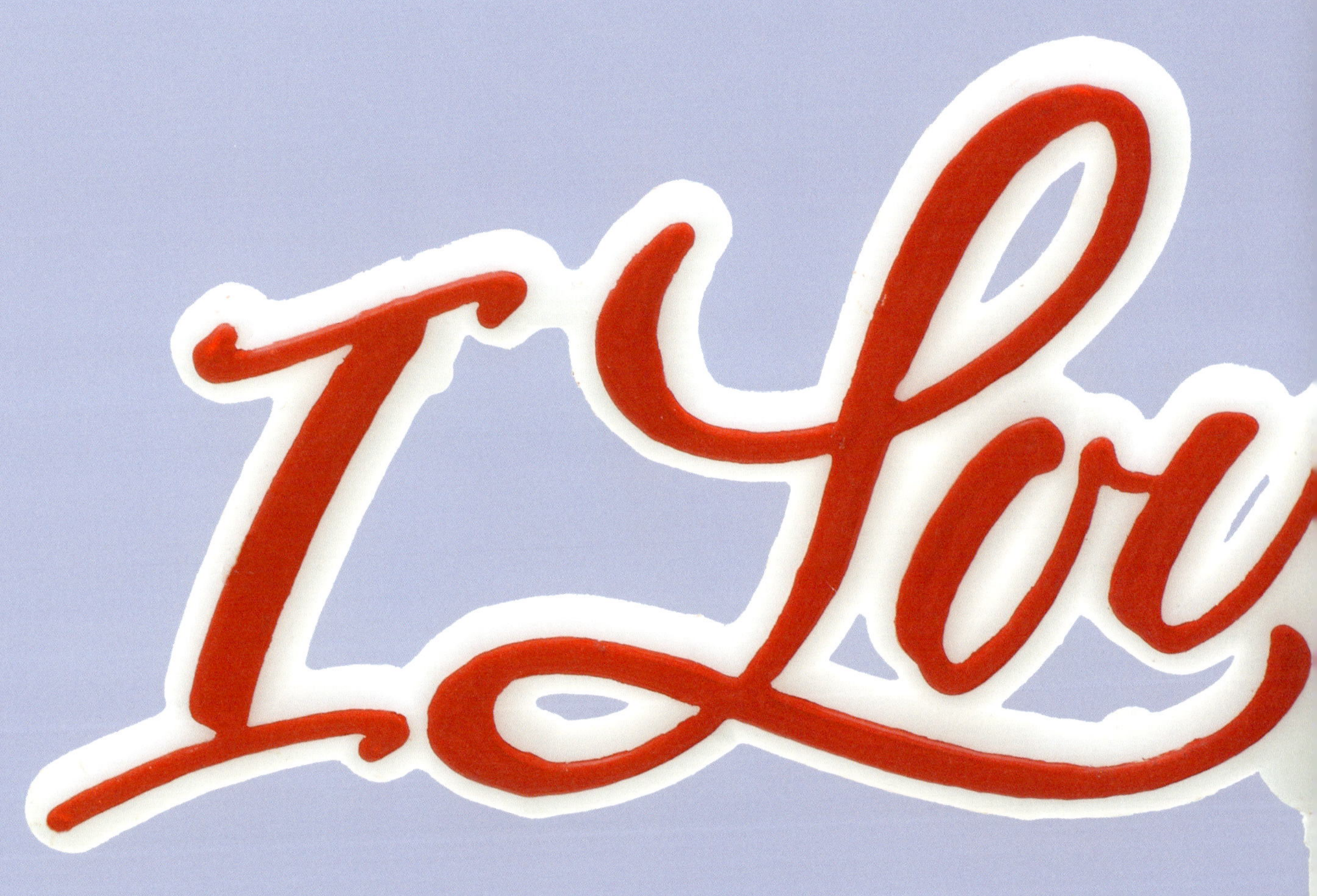
I Lo

You

Happy Together

NEW YORK & THE OTHER WORLD

PHOTOGRAPHS BY

JAN CHRISTIAAN BRAUN

ESSAYS BY

HOWARD GARDNER

AND

ROBERT STORR

STICHTING OVER HOLLAND

All photographs
are memento mori.
To take a photograph
is to participate
in another person's
(or thing's)
mortality, vulnerability,
mutability.

SUSAN SONTAG, ON PHOTOGRAPHY, 1977

JAN CHRISTIAAN BRAUN

Introduction

Rambling through New York one day, I ended up at a cemetery in Queens, which I visited with the idea of being able to photograph the American flag in a special setting. Instead, however, my attention was caught by a festively adorned gravestone with a striking wish: "Happy Birthday in Heaven." And so began the series *Happy Together: New York & The Other World.*

A record of loving and, above all, creative expressions by New Yorkers from almost every cultural background, in cemeteries in the Bronx, Brooklyn, Manhattan, Queens and Staten Island, *Happy Together* is a selection of photographs of 144 decorated graves, some of them appearing several times in different manifestations. The 150 photographs document the passage of a calendar year in the more recent and so more "lively" sections of the cemeteries. Decorations may announce the start of a new season, or may celebrate holidays such as St. Valentine's Day, St. Patrick's Day, Easter, Mother's and Father's Day, the Fourth of July, Halloween, Thanksgiving, Christmas, and of course birthdays. Others are simply free creations. They usually have a short life: some are cleared away by cemetery authorities after a certain period, others are rearranged or replaced altogether as relatives and friends of the dead mark the next festive occasion. Some, though, are left until they succumb to the New York weather.

The exposure time for all of the photographs in the *Happy Together* series totaled 0.6325825 seconds.

December 31, 2006

HOWARD GARDNER

Shock and Recognition

In modern Western eyes, Jan Christiaan Braun's amazing photographs of a gross (144) of decorated graves elicit both shock and recognition.* We are shocked by the incongruity of informal messages and vivid, colorful bric-a-brac in the solemn setting of a cemetery. But that shock is accompanied by recognition of a deep human impulse: the desire to remain in contact with beloved family and friends who have died.

* In 1943, the American literary critic Edmund Wilson published a collection of essays called *The Shock of Recognition.*

As perceivers we are most attracted—and at times transfixed—by displays that cut across familiar traditional categories. Unicorns and griffins are more arresting than dogs and songbirds; rainbows compel our attention more than hailstorms or sunny afternoons. The trickster, the wise fool, the knowing child, the helmsman who ferries dead souls across the River Styx—these are the figures who populate myths and steal scenes, whether in live theaters or on the cinema screen. As the anthropologist Claude Lévi-Strauss wrote, such representatives of liminal categories are "good to think with." His intellectual descendant Dan Sperber points out that these uncanny symbolic figures are evocative—that is, rather than being readily classifiable (and hence both easy to ignore and easy to forget), they call us back repeatedly to ponder deeply, to evoke long-buried memories, and to stimulate invention, anxiety, even obsession.

Incongruity adds to the appeal of some works of graphic art: the anorexic slimness of Giacometti's figures no less than the opulence of Rubens's (not to mention the disproportions of the Venus of Willendorff); the harshness of many of Picasso's women as contrasted with the lushness of Renoir's; the preternatural youth of Balthus's nudes juxtaposed to the unabashed age of Lucian Freud's. We are transfixed by the bestiary of Hieronymus Bosch no less than by that of James Ensor. How much ink has been spilled over the enigmatic smile of the Mona Lisa, the perplexing squiggles of Jackson Pollock, the strange individuals and estranged couples in Edward Hopper's melancholy scenes? In our own mundane lives we may seek stability and familiarity, but we make our multiple return visits to art for stimulation and evocation.

Not surprisingly, then, I find most arresting, most shocking, among Braun's subjects those stones and scenes that cut across our normal categorical scheme. Routine flowers, clichéd quotations, do not compel attention. What attracts the eye and mind is a T-shirt stretched across a headstone, lawn chairs alongside flags on the gravesite, and signs and icons imported from the worlds of commerce, government, or pop culture. What haunts the viewer is on the one hand the concatenation of happy faces, cartoon characters, and beach paraphernalia and on the other the knowledge that the burial of the dead more customarily engenders tears, sobriety, and silence on the part of the survivors.

It is said that one of the first signs of the emergence of genuine human beings—representatives of *Homo sapiens* whom we would recognize as belonging to our own kind—is the impulse to bury the dead and to mark the spot of interment. The flowers and beads that decorate 50,000- or even 100,000-year-old graves suggest to us that we are dealing not with a smart ape but with an all-too-human fellow creature. Over space and time, the decorations of burial plots tell us: "This is someone who was valued. That person is gone. We the survivors want to proclaim our love, our respect, our memories."

By the time of the great ancient empires, this impulse had become full-blown, even excessive to our contemporary sensibilities—though perhaps not to the former shah of Iran or the current leader of North Korea. The sovereigns of Egypt, Persia, China, and Meso-America were buried with enormous pomp. Their tombs were jam-packed with precious items, and all too often with their own family members or servants, who—virginal or not—were sacrificed to accompany the dead. The apparent message to the departed: "You are dead but you are not really dead. We are providing all of the creature comforts you could possibly want, and surrounding you with those whom you most value. You will prosper in the afterlife."

In the modern era, death has become less a part of everyday life, and our burials tend to be demure. Individuals die in hospitals, not at home; burial occurs quite quickly; whether or not we believe in an afterlife, the gravestone tends toward the matter-of-fact: name, date of birth, date of death. We think of Arthur Conan Doyle, writer turned spiritualist, who spent his declining years attempting to communicate with the dead, as belatedly whacko.

Yet if we are to believe the founding sociologist Emile Durkheim (himself a forefather of Lévi-Strauss and Sperber), every known society has hosted a belief in a human spirit or soul that exists apart from corporeal reality—and thus can be assumed to persist even after the body is dust. Today in Mexico, millions celebrate the Day of the Dead, when the spirit of the deceased is said to return. Today in Japan, at the Obon Buddhist festival, thousands welcome such spirits back for three days. But this blatant defiance of death is not part of the modal North American sensibility, least of all in putatively modern or even post-modern New York City. This uncanny state of affairs is challenged in the decorated graves captured by Braun in the city's five boroughs.

Death is literally irrevocable: the dead can no longer be called. The gravestones portrayed in the following pages reject this irrevocability. They represent the efforts of the survivors to converse with the dead, to appeal to them, appease them, maintain dialogue with them. And the bereaved do not perform these activities quietly, in dreams or prayers, or formally, at a séance; instead they do so publicly and visibly, at predictable (seasonal) and unpredictable ("just thinking of you") times, so that what they do can be seen not only by the dead but also by the passerby, even by the passerby with camera in hand.

From a human perspective this desire for dialogue is unsurprising—and this is the recognition about which I spoke initially. After all, the first impulses of infant and mother are to communicate with one another. Much of early development entails mastery of various means of communication: gestures, facial expressions, words, songs. Those experiences that we treasure—moments of relaxation with loved ones, celebration of important events, attendance at artistic or athletic performances—are marked by conversations conducted in words or in some other symbolic form. Indeed, we classify as odd those persons and situations bereft of communication: the autistic child, enforced silence at school as a punishment for misbehavior, monasteries dedicated to meditation or vows of silence. And most of us have difficulty comprehending those religious rites that preclude vocal or other symbolic forms of communication.

Death represents Nature's decisive effort to cut off communication and dialogue. One may speak to the dead but, at least to normal perception, the dead do not respond. (This is why brain death is often more decisive for doctors than cessation of the heartbeat.) Our shock in viewing Braun's photographs arises because we feel that we are eavesdropping on efforts to continue this communication even when it has apparently become one-sided. The impulse is easy to understand; the reality proves unexpected.

Communication consists of a medium and a message. Much great art consists of communication with an afterlife—consider Dante's messages to the famous and infamous who preceded him, or the letters of Saul Bellow's character Moses Herzog to his artistic predecessors. What we see in Braun's photographs of the gravestones of ethnically diverse New York are efforts by ordinary people, having available to them the ordinary tools of communication, to participate in this universal creative process.

The messages are touching and human: Get Well Soon, Happy Birthday in Heaven, Christmas in Heaven, Thinking of You on Mother's Day. They entail some events and ideas that would be familiar to the deceased and some that would be novel: the thoughts—lofty and banal— that we all have and would wish to share with someone who has died, as achingly recalled by Joan Didion in *The Year of Magical Thinking*. What strikes the perceiver, though—and what clearly caught Braun's wickedly perceptive eye—are the media employed. There aren't many packaged materials, like the sincere but saccharine Hallmark cards, or the signs for $10 a pop. These men and women have created their own memorial messages, using their own creations or pastiching and collaging them together from the iconography and iconology of our time. Who would have thought that the graveyards of Queens and the Bronx would be invaded or garlanded by characters from the cinema, Walt Disney style? By the icons of television? The teams of professional and amateur sports? The flags of the patriots and the Patriots? And this with a fullness, a colorfulness, and an arrangement of icons and messages that is often overwhelming.

To be sure, these grave decorators of graves are not artists in either the traditional sense—they neither establish nor join any atelier—or a contemporary one: thoughts of agents, galleries, or reviews would strike them as bizarre. It is better to think of them as bricoleurs, handymen who assemble their messages from the most available materials, both physically and in their mental museums. And what do these assemblages tell us about their particular provenance: life in the United States at the start of the twenty-first century? We see the roles played by the mass media, holidays both secular and religious, cute figures in cartoons, emblems of sports teams, symbols of patriotism. We see even more vividly the appeal of syncretism—ready, almost unconscious juxtapositions of images and icons in a dizzying range of the sacred and the profane. We see the upbeat, optimistic sentiments that have always struck European visitors to America. I also glimpse the lure of "reality," as in "reality television"—our bricoleurs are unembarrassed about displaying publicly their mourning and their celebration. I suspect that they take a certain pride in their displays—and after the initial shock, they might well be proud to recognize their images immortalized in a handsome volume.

Ultimately, we viewers of Braun's collection experience shock *and* recognition because the creators of these graveyard messages share some of the accoutrements and motivations of artists: the gravestone is their paper, their canvas, their material. Outsider artists of a kind, often European or Latin American in country of origin but contemporary North American in boldness and sensibility, they are creating their cherished works in a public setting to commemorate those whom they most esteem: their departed loved ones. Of course artists create for their audiences—in this case those who pass by no less than those who have passed away. But in both the first instance and the last analysis, artists create for themselves—because they have potent inspirations and feelings, a medium in which to express them, and the desire to place them in the public sphere so that their handiwork can be seen.

God creates human beings and then, when their time is over, calls them to their grave and perhaps to some form of existence beyond it. As humans, we have a strong impulse—which some restrain more than others—to continue to communicate with the deceased. Many of us do so privately, but in the graveyards of New York, some of our fellow human beings have chosen to communicate publicly. We are fortunate that Braun has recognized and made available through photographs this extraordinary world.

HOWARD GARDNER
IS A PSYCHOLOGIST WHO TEACHES AT HARVARD UNIVERSITY.
AMONG HIS MANY BOOKS ARE *ART, MIND AND BRAIN*,
MULTIPLE INTELLIGENCES, *CHANGING MINDS*, AND *GOOD WORK*.

ROBERT STORR

Here Below

The only certainties in life, so the saying goes, are death and taxes. Relatively speaking, though, for those with political clout and/or the sufficient means, taxes are negotiable: specially tailored statutes, clever accountants, and shrewd lawyers can defer the otherwise inevitable rendering unto Caesar, substantially reducing the burden or even virtually eliminating it altogether. And those with no access to power or expertise can always simply cheat, giving the common man at least gambler's odds on beating the house.

But no amount of leverage or wiliness can beat the reaper. That ineluctable reality is the simultaneously merry and macabre lesson of medieval and Renaissance renditions of the Dance of Death—notably that of Hans Holbein—in which kings, nobles, bishops, friars, soldiers, merchants, peasants, and bawdy women cavort with the grinning skeletal harvester of souls; the same cavalcade of souls that crosses the horizon in Ingmar Bergman's film *The Seventh Seal*.

This festive romp is ambiguously situated between before and after. It does not depict the manner of dying, since, except when mercifully sudden, that process is almost invariably miserable and even violent. For good reason, then, most people fear dying more than death itself. We nevertheless fend off extinction with greater energy than the things that make it likely; the evergreen allure of war, drink, smoking, high-risk sex, and high-speed cars is proof enough of that. Indeed many thrill-seekers regularly court death, though whether they do so for the sake of dangerous pleasures or for the pleasure of danger alone is open to question. To the extent that the latter is the primary motive, they are rehearsing their ultimate encounter with eternity by running a calculated risk of hastening it. Such existential gambling is said by those addicted to it to make them feel more alive.

Those less inclined to tempt fate must take their word for it, since it is not necessarily true that life becomes more precious when and where death threatens, only that it becomes more vivid by contrast. At a certain point, however, Thanatos may so enthrall a person that premonitions of the penultimate moment before succumbing to lifelessness are eclipsed by an exquisite morbidity, an attempt to imagine a hereafter—whether heavenly, hellish, or some inchoate state of nonbeing in which the soul has miraculously survived. Alternatively this death wish may simply express a craving for release, for the disembodiment of consciousness, or, where consciousness is hell on earth, for its merciful obliteration.

A fixation with life in extremis, or with passage into the afterlife, is the stuff of Romantic art in all its historically varied and culturally diverse forms. Romanticism's pervasive, dare one say undying appeal frankly affirms that such obsessions are not just neurotic but signs of an innate predisposition—even a healthy curiosity—characteristic of everyone born to die. It is not just our awareness of mortality that separates us from animals but our fascination with it. To be mesmerized by one's worst fears, a little in love with death, is to be human.

While mourning is likewise riven with ambivalence, a more-or less-anxious anticipation of our own death is utterly different from a survivor's anguished coping with death's irreversible claim on someone important to him or her. I have chosen the seemingly neutral adjective "important" precisely to avoid alternatives like "cherished" or phrases like "dear departed." Worst of all names for the deceased is "the loved one." As far back as 1948, in appreciation of its richly euphemistic awfulness, Evelyn Waugh used it as the title of his comic novel about the funeral business, but unfortunately it remains the undertaker's term of choice for a corpse and the homogenizing label preferred by police and politicians for accident and crime victims or for casualties of natural disasters and unnatural wars.

Incidentally, the constant references in the media and elsewhere in the public domain to "tragic death" have dulled language equally by confusing bad luck with fate, suffering that befalls people through forces and factors beyond their ken with suffering that befalls them precisely as a result of their own misunderstandings or misdeeds, as in plays from *Antigone* to *Hamlet* to *Death of a Salesman*. The crux of tragedy lies not in the misfortune of bystanders caught in a drama not of their making but in the death of those who, having failed to comprehend their destiny, nevertheless have fulfilled it by pursuing ends or ideas at odds with reality and by trusting too much in free will. The death of innocents—that is, of pure victims—inspires pathos; tragedy entails heroic error, the price of which is a loss of innocence. Confusion surrounding these terms is the taproot of sentimentality, and when that confusion is deliberately manipulated in situations where careful distinctions regarding the protagonists' intentions and actions should be stipulated and underscored, it is also the essence of propaganda.

Meanwhile, many people who die are unloved and some are unlovable. What makes their passing "important," perhaps abidingly painful, is the definitive foreclosure of opportunities to know them more fully or maybe to know them at all. Also canceled is any chance at reconciliation, despite all that one might know. So when mourning the frequently evoked relative we never met, the father who checked out early, the mother who tormented us in some indescribable way for some unfathomable reason, the sister or brother who was mean or, simply, more powerful, better looking, better loved, but who held us at arm's length and is gone too, we lament not "the loved one"—and at the grave's edge, decorum forbids us to speak of "the loathed or resented one"—but a vital, disquieting presence that has become a haunting absence, a formerly contingent, now petrified and permanently sited source of unease.

How many rites of remembrance are of this conflicted order is a secret well kept in most families. It may be hidden by one member from another, by the entire unit from the wider world, or by itself from itself, as a whole. But by and large the dead are enshrined by positive feelings, no matter the degree to which those feelings are also willed ones. And as the event of dying recedes and the subtle specifics of the life led begin to blur in shared recollection, the primary role and personal quirks of the deceased stand out more prominently, just as the nose, ears, and other distinguishing features of the aged become more pronounced as time goes by, naturally caricaturing their faces and bodies. In the long run, death edits collective memory of the dead, and all that remains of those who, in the words of the hymn, have "gone before" are names and dates in the back pages of family bibles, on family trees or genealogical listings, and on stones in the cemetery.

Of course not every culture inters its dead. Burial at sea is a common custom among sailors, but also among islanders in different parts of the world and in different periods of history. Elsewhere and in many eras, adherents of religions such as Zoroastrianism have practiced "sky burial," leaving bodies out in the open to be picked clean by birds of prey. In a gesture of quotidian commemoration, some groups recycle bones as decoration or utensils; certain Buddhists shear off the tops of the crania of dead monks and use these shallow vessels for ceremonial drinking, pouring the liquid from the space formerly occupied by the original owner's brain. Among those cultures that do bury their dead in the earth, not all erect monuments above ground, much less ornament them or celebrate rituals in their vicinity. But cemeteries are the principal resting places of the dead in Western societies, and for vast numbers of people, more or less regular visits to the graveyard constitute a filial duty, an indispensable source of solace, or a basis for pleasurable fellow feeling. Typically it is the cemetery that provides a primary locus for the task of mourning. One may pray for the dead in a church or synagogue, but one must also summon them, whereas in a field of markers they summon the mourner, and are right under foot. The cemetery also allows survivors to forestall complete separation through routines designed to normalize what has in fact become an entirely one-sided relationship.

In those societies that build and preserve cemeteries, differences of faith, culture, and history must still be taken into account. Those favored by the Gothic spirit are steeped in mystery, like the Jewish cemetery in Prague, with its wildly titling headstones, and the predominantly Catholic cemeteries full of elaborately carved mausoleums, such as La Recollecta in Buenos Aires or Père Lachaise in Paris. Periodically someone may come to lay flowers; in Père Lachaise it is as likely to be grizzled fans at the tomb of Doors singer Jim Morrison as old Marxist militants at the wall in a far corner where defenders of the Paris Commune of 1871 were lined up and shot by counterrevolutionary soldiers, incidentally reminding us that even amidst crucifixes and weeping angels some of the tenants were fervently anticlerical if not atheist. In the main, though, the grand old necropolises are unchanging, except for the ever-so-slow filling in of spaces reserved within these otherwise anachronistic compounds for a dwindling elite of future generations.

Not so the modern American cemetery. There, architecture and ornament are on the whole more modest. Although many plots are marked by rudimentary crosses and fences, or by austere stone blocks that barely rise above the level of the earth, standard-model headstones are fairly massive slabs. Like cars produced on Detroit assembly lines for the working and middle classes, they come in a range of tones and hues (black, white, gray, and shades of salmon pink, liver red, and orange-yellow ocher are most popular) and a variety of finishes (from smooth or mirror polished to artfully chipped and rusticated in the Rock of Ages mode), and they allow for customized accessories or add-ons such as in-the-round or bas-relief carvings of religious figures and symbols, engraved versions of familiar sacred iconography, the occasional emblematic image (commonly the Star and Stripes, or, in New York of late, the Twin Towers) or portrait (lately an eerie brand of snapshot-derived photorealism has emerged, with among its more eye-catchingly lurid examples the near-life-sized likenesses of gangsters that have begun to crop up in graveyards catering to recently fallen Scarfaces), scrolls for names and dates, and sometimes bronze attachments such as angels and flower-holders.

Where extravagance enters the picture is in the temporary decorations deposited on these generally unremarkable monuments by family members and others. When visitors come often, the decorations they leave often follow the cycle of the seasons—as if those annual passages still mattered to the deceased, as they do to the survivors. They also grant license to sentiments and impulses that surpass and in some cases contradict the conventional practices of mourning, striving instead to establish a running dialogue in social and psychological registers that are concealed from the rest of the world by the normal funeral regimen that with lugubrious ceremony forever relocates bodies from the city of the living to the city of death, where few but bereaved intimates venture.

A notable exception to the latter rule is Jan Christiaan Braun, who for the past eighteen months has been exploring the cemeteries of New York City, taking pictures of what he has found. Braun is a Dutchman with a keen interest in contemporary art. His bimonthly trips to the United States have provided the occasion for regular sidebar excursions to burying grounds in the outer boroughs of the city, where most New Yorkers with plans to stick around forever end up. This somewhat eccentric form of tourism might seem a symptom of a macabre temperament, but its accidental origins partly remove that stigma. Having retired comfortably from his earlier business, Braun spends his days in New York making the rounds of the galleries and museums. He also walks—and more than just a few blocks; in recent years his constitutionals have taken him the width and breadth of not only Manhattan but also Brooklyn and large stretches of Queens, Staten Island, and the Bronx. Mapping his itineraries in advance, he will set out at a remote jumping-off point reached by bus or subway and hike to a convenient transit junction, return to his midtown Manhattan hotel room, and pick up the next time precisely where he left off. Moving through neighborhoods populated by Americans of every imaginable extraction, he is keenly aware that he is and always will be a stranger in this country, though in many places he can "pass" and in virtually all his enthusiasm and sly humor put people at their ease.

By nature alert and methodical, Braun determined after several of these hikes that observation required selectivity and discipline. Seeking such a focus, he became interested in the ubiquity of the Stars and Stripes—one of those things, so Jasper Johns said, that "the mind already knows"—as a motif in vernacular decoration. Of course not everyone who knows something sees it with the same eyes, and Johns's genius was to capitalize on that fact and to radically destabilize a symbol that those who took it for granted merely saluted. Then, in case the rigid flatness and texturally shifting layers of his flags weren't lesson enough in the Cold War 1950s and '60s, he did the same thing to the map of America, something else "the mind already knows" from school and the road atlas—remember this was the hour of Jack Kerouac and rebel nomadism. So, after turning the "red white and blue" United States into red, blue, yellow, and turgid grays, Johns blurred national and regional borders, making here and there, them and us, indeterminate.

Naturally Johns's fascination with the map and flag are those of an insider. Braun's interest was that of a foreigner, an Amsterdamer in latter-day New Amsterdam—broadly sympathetic to but not blindly uncritical of the people whose customs he set out to scrutinize. And insofar as his object of study was the flag, significantly at the moment he began his quest its omnipresence partly stemmed form the patriotic mood of a country that felt itself besieged after September 11, 2001, and a city that had been deeply wounded on that day and was still in shock. In these circumstances flag-waving was both spontaneous and strategic, both a symbol of genuine popular public sentiment and a political device for leading the nation to war against an ill-defined enemy. With this social and historical backdrop, Braun, who always carries a camera, began to take pictures of flags—in gas station windows, on graffiti-covered walls, on billboards, in all the myriad places where they were emblazoned. Graveyards, it turned out, were among these, and Braun's detour into the vast acreage colonized by New York's most permanent residents began the project documented in this book.

A few words about labels, specifically "art" and "artist." Although much of modernism has been devoted to questioning the substance if not the legitimacy of these terms, they remain in use, as if we all agreed what they signified and who was entitled to award themselves or their work such designation. To avoid overt prejudice, make allowances for the exceptional, and grant dispensation to our offbeat enjoyments, we create special categories of art and artists by adding adjectives like "primitive" (now taboo though still a common usage), "eccentric," "vernacular," and so on. Overall, the status of such "outsiders" is determined by their actual or presumed remoteness from "high" culture, and thus the label usually entails an element of condescension, suggesting that as extraordinary as their work may be, in some basic sense "they know not what they do," or perhaps why they really do it or what it really means.

There is another term, equally prejudicial, for those of whom such things cannot be said: "amateur." At best, as the word's French origin indicates, the amateur is considered a gifted "lover" of an art form practiced as an avocation rather than a fully accredited vocation—in short, a dedicated dilettante. At worst the amateur is seen as a hobbyist. But in the face of arresting images from an unfamiliar or unexpected source—in this instance photographs taken while abroad by a well-to-do art world insider, working for his own interest, with no pretensions about his nonetheless considerable talent—such rubrics and distinctions create more problems than they solve, since they do nothing to explain why the person who made these photographs was stopped in his tracks by something he saw in passing, and why the viewer, unaware of why he took them or of who he might be, is likewise awakened to a fresh understanding of a subject normally pushed to the edge of consciousness, not only because of its banality but because of the disquiet it stirs up. Nor, finally, does such language make it easier to grasp how the viewer comes to understand that the photographs' effectiveness, regardless of the professional standing of the photographer, is predicated on a tangible, consistent, and carefully thought-out aesthetic. Like the German team of Bernd and Hilla Becher and many of their students and followers, Braun is a taxonomist of situations and people, and the considered stylelessness of his style is the key to its anthropological effectiveness.

So let us set these worries aside and content ourselves to be that viewer, while from time to time looking over the photographer's shoulder at the wider horizons of the land of the dead to which he has brought us. The first thing we notice is how orderly that land is. The reason is the same as in all real estate developments: to maximize the use of space so as to make room for as many paying tenants as possible, while also simplifying management of the site, which is somebody's long-term investment. Graves are in effect subterranean condominiums with a private garden on top and a communal garden all around. In the aggregate they constitute a subdivision, for while the graveyards that Braun has reconnoitered nest on great tracts inside the New York city line, they are less urban than suburban, mixing gridded and serpentine streets, generally similar-sized plots, and similar styles of "architecture," which alternate like tract houses and mostly come from a handful of pattern books, as do their counterparts in the land of the living. If cemeteries such as Green-Wood in Brooklyn have some romantic vistas and unique nineteenth- and early-twentieth-century structures, the average American graveyard resembles the average American housing scheme, from which in fact it drains much of its population. A mortuary Levittown with golf course lawns and foliage, it is a bedroom community for the "big sleep" or, as even more hardboiled types than Raymond Chandler have called it, the dirt nap, though that wise-guy turn of phrase still manages despite everything to hold out the prospect of suddenly waking up in the mid-afternoon of mid-eternity.

The same resemblance holds true for the cemetery's changing aspects. Urbanites and suburbanites in this country like to dress up their homes for special occasions, at any rate a great many do. Come Valentine's Day, Easter, Halloween, Thanksgiving, Christmas, or a signal day on the family calendar—a birth or birthday, a marriage, a retirement, and of course a death—appropriate decorations, and sometimes apparently inappropriate or at least unpredictable ones, suddenly erupt on and often all over the façades of houses and the green spaces in front of them. At Christmas and Hanukkah in brownstone neighborhoods in New York, in areas where single-family houses separated by driveways predominate or where grander homes sit on a grassy acre, you will find individual dwellings, even entire blocks, competitively festooned from the roof to the sidewalk with hanging lights numbering in the hundreds, along with plastic figures of all kinds, from "old-timey" ensembles (carolers, Santa Claus and his reindeer) to cartoon heros past and present (from Disney's Mickey Mouse to Disney-fied versions of Doctor Seuss's nefarious Grinch and Tim Burton's Jack Skellington). Frequently mechanized and miked, they may sing songs (ventriloquizing Perry Como or Nat King Cole from the other world) or laugh ("Ho, ho, ho") until the plug is pulled early in the new year. Halloween, another prime season for tricking out the house, brings the dark side of Americana to the fore: for the benefit of costumed revelers, mostly under age, home-owners plant tombstones on the lawn, hang witches from the eaves and spider webs in the windows, and put electrified jack-o-lanterns on the porch or front steps— and if, in descending order from sadistic to comic, their taste runs to *The Texas Chainsaw Massacre*, Freddy Krueger, or *Scary Movie*, they may also scatter novelty-shop masks and rubber body-parts around the scene. Needless to say, most of the ornaments of this kind that don't come from novelty shops come from Hong Kong or China by way of Wal-Mart, with the consequence that an over-the-top industrial cuteness leavens their sinister symbolism.

Now back to the "real thing"—the local necropolis—where you would think that death would be no joke. Yet right in the center of one plot photographed by Braun stands a Halloween skeleton that obscures the name on the stone behind it, and at its feet has been deposited a life-sized though patently lifeless pink hand sticking out from a shirt sleeve, even as the two combined appear to emerge zombielike from the turf. In any other place this would provoke shrieks or chuckles, as "sick" pranks usually do. Oddly enough, in this context the joke doesn't seem "sick" or bad taste but defiant, as if the deceased were in on it too. It is as though laughing with rather than at the dead's irrevocable state—a hopeless "buriedness"—were a relief to everyone concerned, not least those who had most reason to weep when they came to this spot. After all, were the "undead" not invented as a cautionary fable warning us that there are fates worse than death—that eternal wandering is more terrible than returning to dust? And is the skeleton with the sardonic grin not part of that warning? "Instead of being safe where you are here below," that ruin of a face seems to say, "the horrifying trick of destiny would be for you to subsist as naked, homeless, and soulless as I am." In short, specters of the dead function homeopathically to ward off more gruesome realities. In one of Braun's most striking pictures, a gay trio of their number appears as a silhouetted ghost and two skeletons dancing in front of a tomb. Nothing in the presentation approaches the gleeful blasphemy of the Monty Python troupe doing a chorus-line kick from crosses on Golgotha in *The Life of Brian*, but one can almost hear them singing the Python anthem, "Always look on the bright side of death, just before you draw your terminal breath." While the authors of Braun's ensemble would almost certainly be offended by the irreligiousness of the tune, they might nevertheless go home humming it if they heard it rise above their display.

While Halloween therapeutically affords survivors the opportunity to bypass loss by mocking fear, they must first openly acknowledge both before each in turn can be sublimated by gallows humor. Other holidays make no greater demand than cheerful denial, as uncanny as such cheerfulness invariably is under the circumstances, and as irrational as such denial must be. That said, the particular forms it takes have their charms. Take national pride, for example. The old red-white-and-blue that initially brought Braun to New York's netherworld predominates, and its absence from many plots is more than made up for by its Baroque profusion on the most patriotic ones. Those unfamiliar with hyphenated loyalties in the United States, however, may easily confuse it with the single-starred Puerto Rican flag, or fail to take full account of the simultaneous appearance of the Italian tricolor, or miss the declaration inherent in green shamrocks and St. Patrick's Day leprechauns. Indeed, depending on the calendar, a walk in the cemetery can resemble nothing so much as a parade down Fifth Avenue—though most of the flag-waving crowd is conspicuously missing. Another hint at the civic-mindedness of the dead shows up in Braun's photo of a grave featuring a bold sign saying "Vote Tuesday September 12th Democratic Primary." Anyone who follows politics in America will appreciate that this is a gesture not done entirely in jest, nor only to admonish passersby to do their duty; party bosses and big-city machines have long known that a key percentage of the electorate lies beneath the sod, and if "your guys" don't vote the graveyards, "the other guys" will.

More poignant evidence that life after death consists of the ritual overriding of death's claims by the living is to be found in birthday greetings, best wishes for a happy new year, and plainspoken though often gaudy labels that announce the relationship of the person who left this tribute to the person in whose memory he or she brought it: Grandma, Grand Papa, Mother, Mom, Father, Dad, Papito, Husband, Wife, Daughter, Brother, and so on. Then there are the continuity-preserving offerings. Most of them are dimestore equivalents of the kinds of earthly tools, treasures, or talismans with which Egyptian mummies were laid to rest: a baseball, baseball hats, a football jersey (sports equipment is popular), a balloon in the shape of an electric drill, or cartoon deities such as an inflatable SpongeBob or Spiderman. The least of these in material terms turn out to be the most personal and most affecting: a car child-safety seat, the gray upholstery of which merges with the gray of the tombstone to form a kind of ready-made niche evoking the absent child; a plastic doll in a frilly dress, its permanently closed eyes making it resemble the dead babies shown in commemorative pictures from the era when mortality among children was high; a low-lying fence enclosure made of iron above which hover, on iron stems, several separate lumps of rough concrete and pebbles molded in amorphous shapes, as if they were chunks of pavement in flower, though they more likely issue from folk traditions like that of the African-American bottle tree; and, finally, among the humblest, a scattering of objects including a small white cross, a rose, two lengths of sun-bleached driftwood, a broken casting rod with a yellow fly, and in the foreground a stone shard crudely inscribed "Stan the Man."

Whether manufactured or homemade, all the decorations are a means for transforming almost certainly ambivalent, private emotions into publicly digestible, community-reinforcing ones, but their rotation allows for some of those latent or unruly feelings to show. Halloween whistling—even snickering—through the graveyard alternates with pious sorrow at other times of year, stone emblems proclaiming "He has risen" are briefly paired with or exchanged for ephemeral but aggressively cute bunny rabbits produced by the Easter industry, and the shadow of a kitsch Orpheus wanders a meticulously planned and maintained underworld, forever hopeful that he can bring his Big Apple Eurydice back. Braun, of course, is no such phantom, nor does he snobbishly look down on the taste or sentiments of the dead and their bereft families. That is among the chief merits of his artfully self-effacing pictures, an indication of his respect for everyone's prerogative to remember, lament, or rejoice in the departed as they see fit, to let go gracefully or cling with vulgar passion. Neither have I introduced the word "kitsch" with scorn, for if, as it has often been defined, kitsch signifies bringing low that which was high, then, as Holbein and Bergman have already reminded us, death does this even more categorically, annihilating the marginal advantage of being well bred by returning each one of us to dust like everyone else. So what harm can come of looking sympathetically on the far slopes of Walt Whitman's democratic vistas? Braun has done it, from the Bronx to Staten Island and from dawn to dusk. Rather than finding them lugubrious, his camera has discovered their anything-but-hidden vitality and has responded in kind.

ROBERT STORR

IS A CURATOR, ARTIST AND CRITIC WHO TEACHES AT YALE UNIVERSITY. AMONG HIS MANY BOOKS IS *MODERN ART DESPITE MODERNISM*.

LORD CARNARVON

Can you see anything?

HOWARD CARTER

Yes, wonderful things.

—The explorer Howard Carter to his patron Lord Carnarvon,
as he looked into the tombs of Tutankhamun in 1922

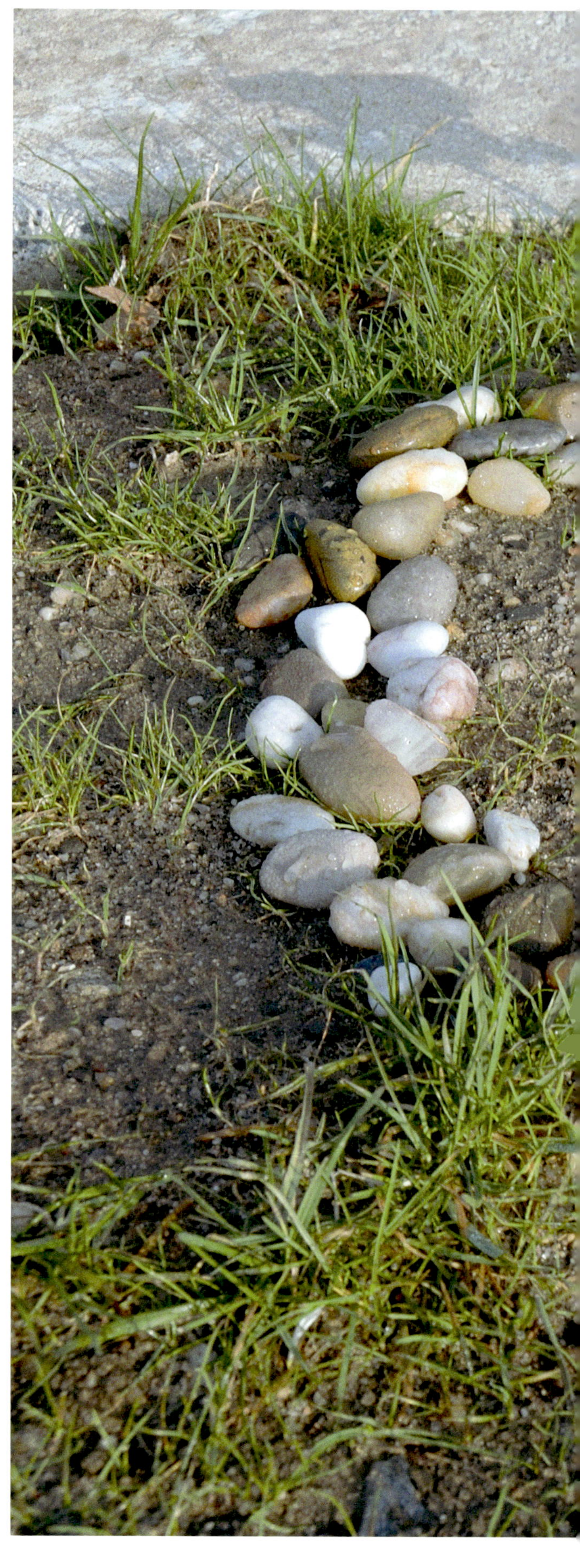

#1

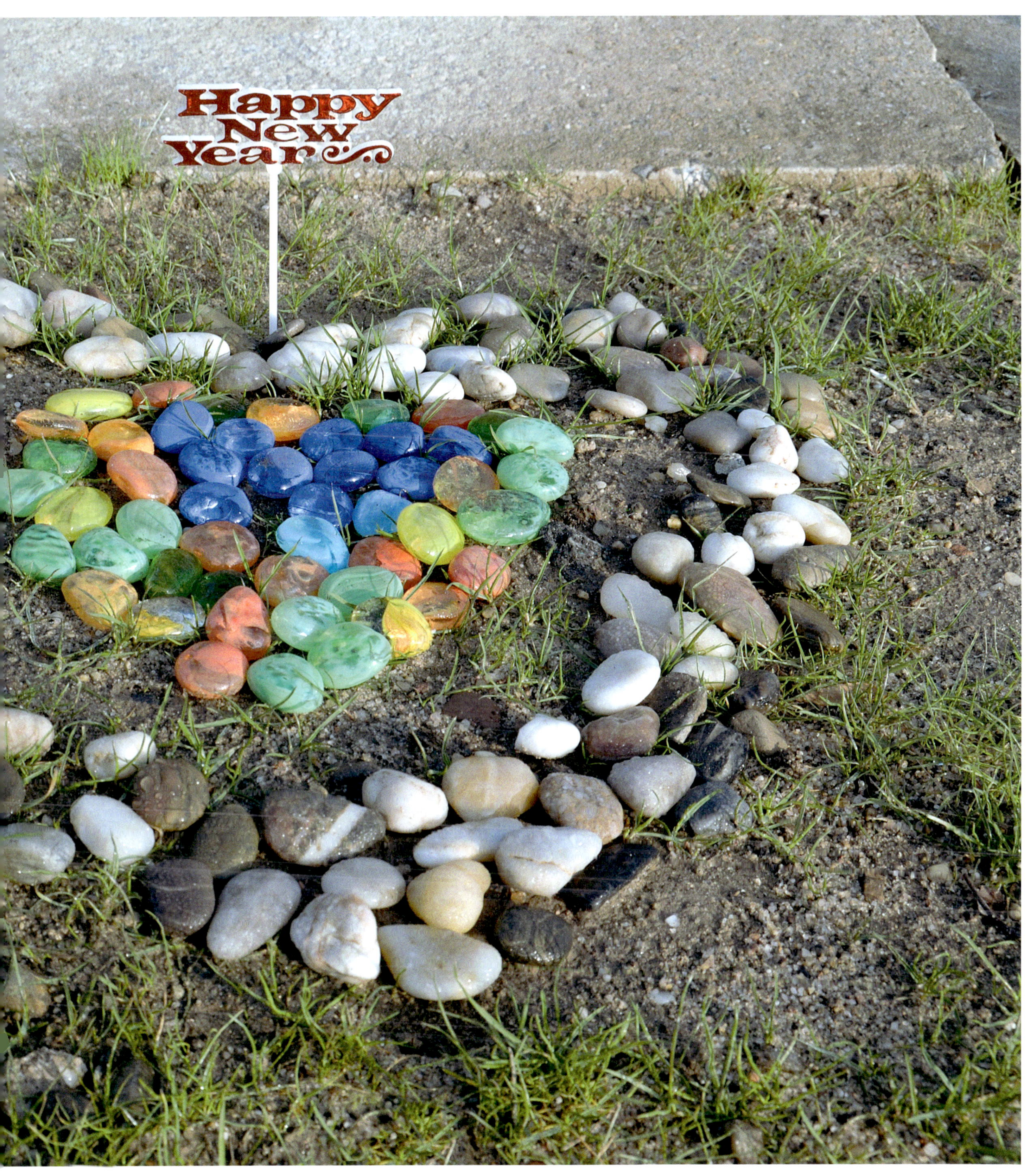
Happy
New
Year

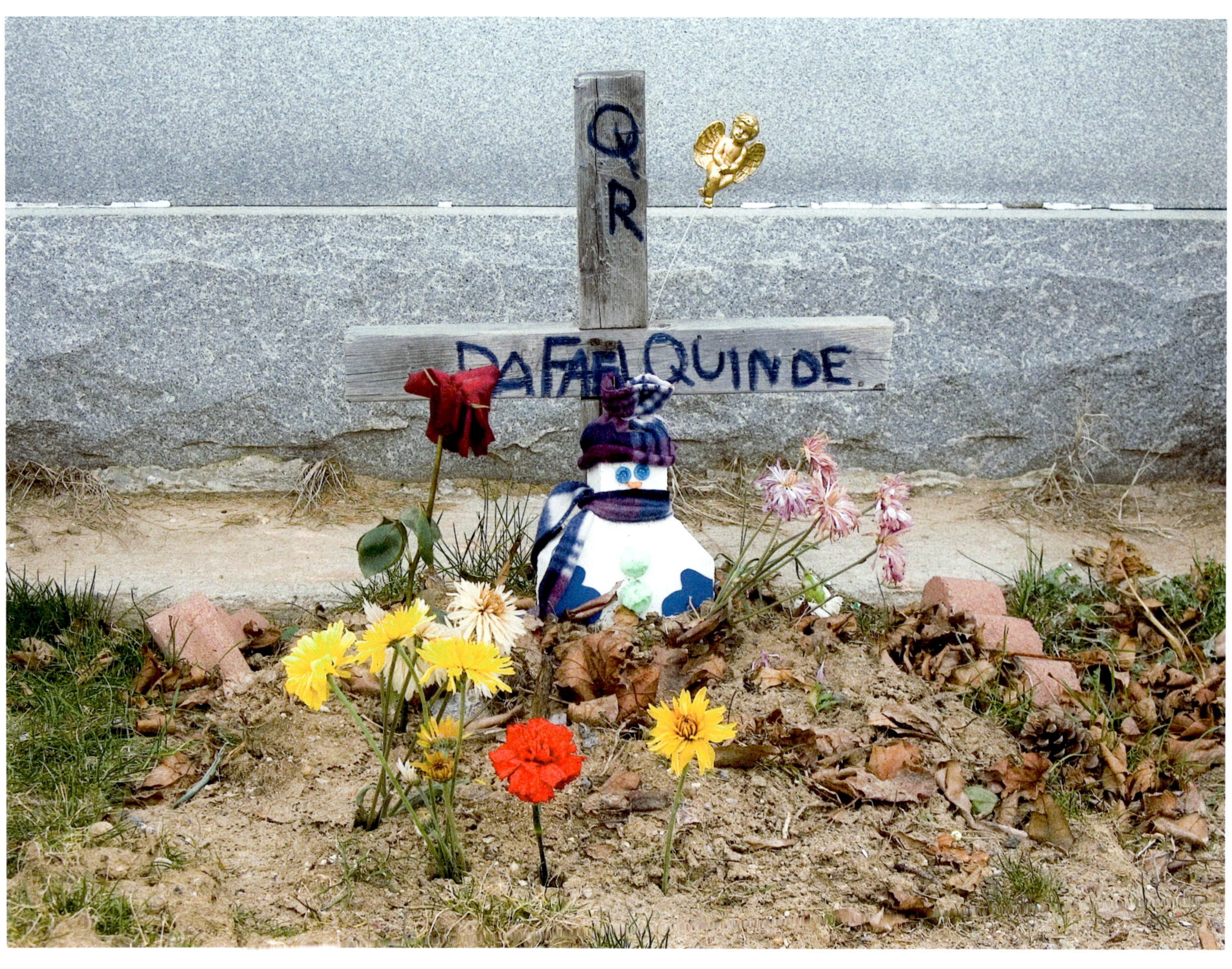

#2

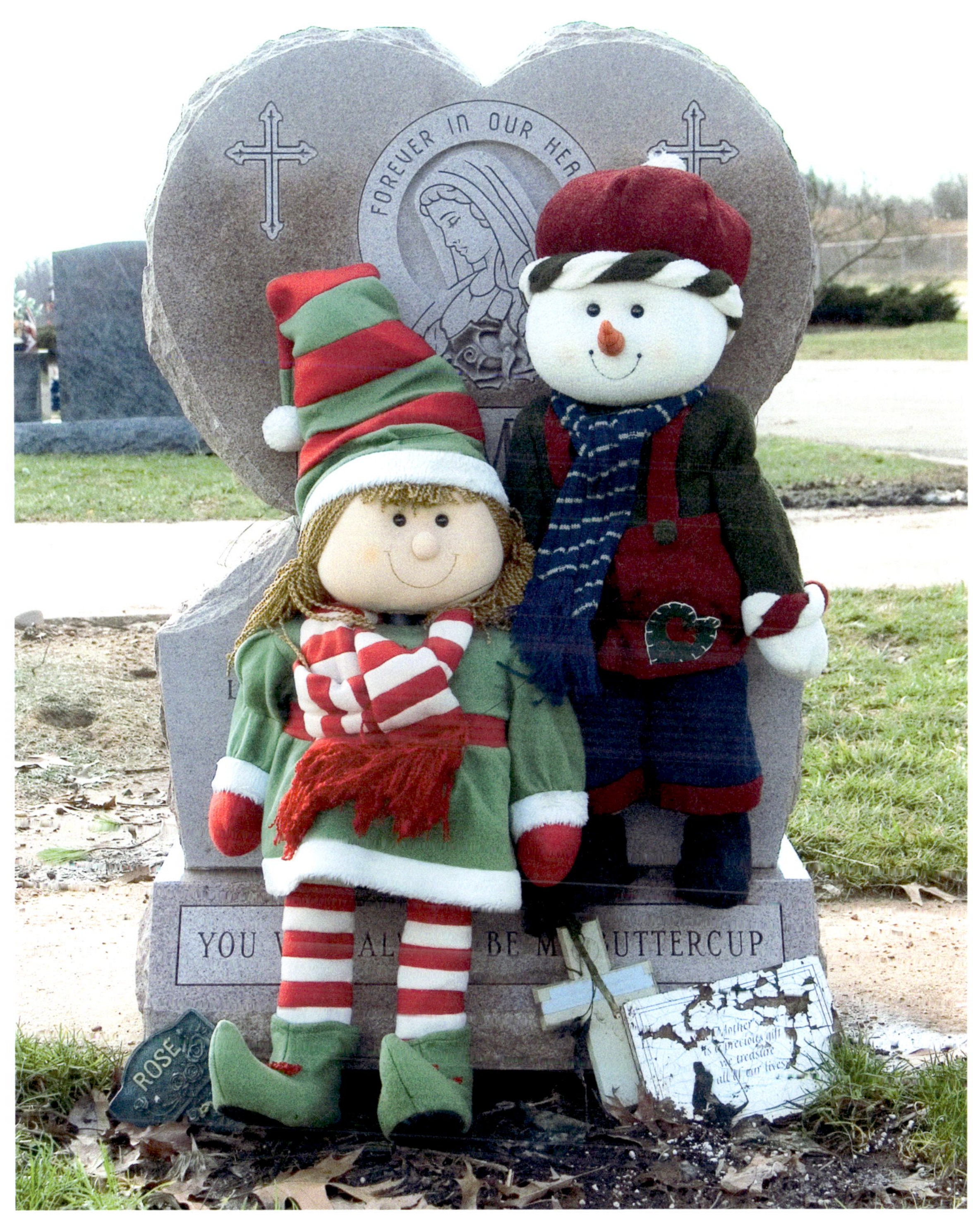
FOREVER IN OUR HEA
YOU
BE
UTTERCUP
ROSE

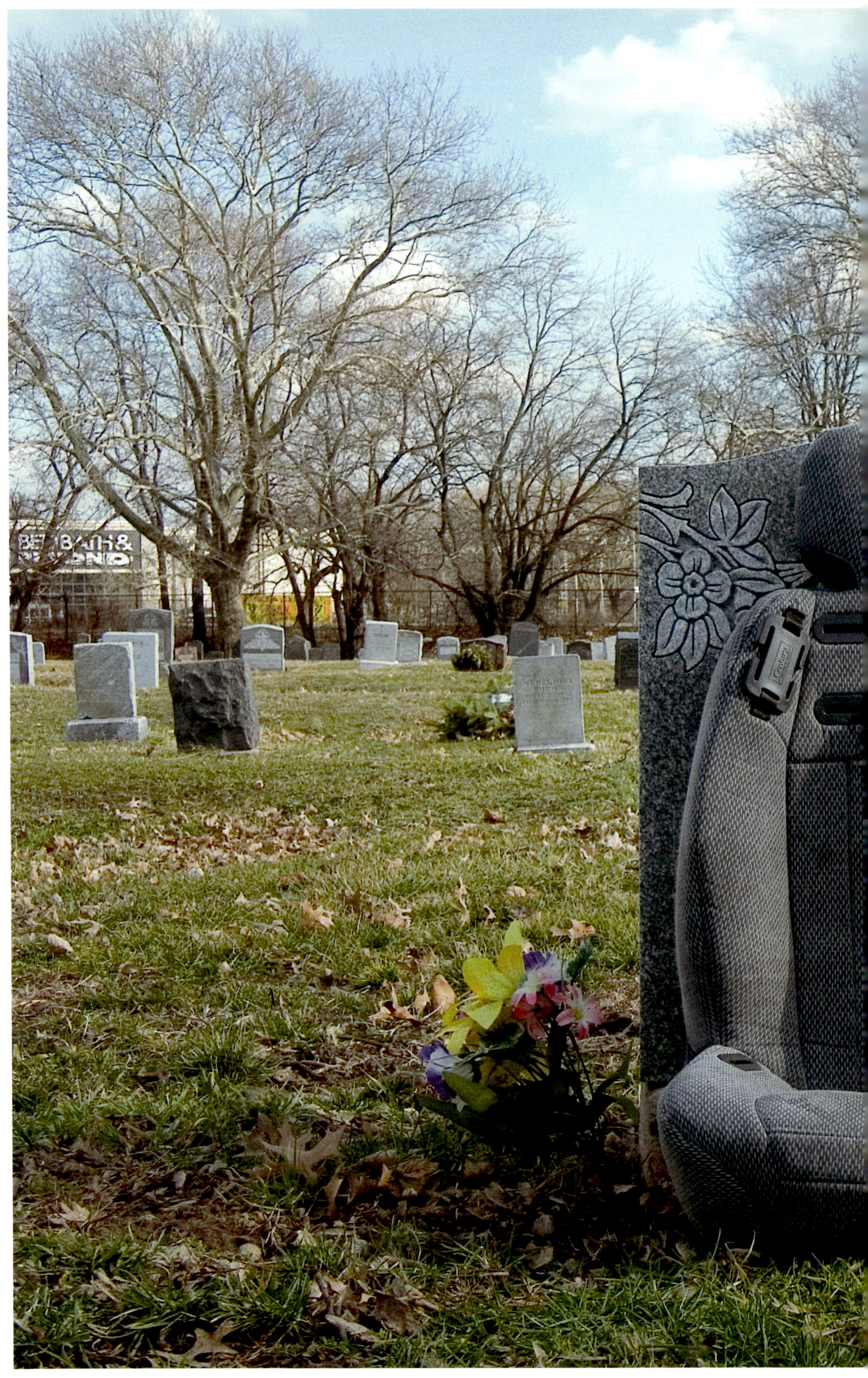

#4

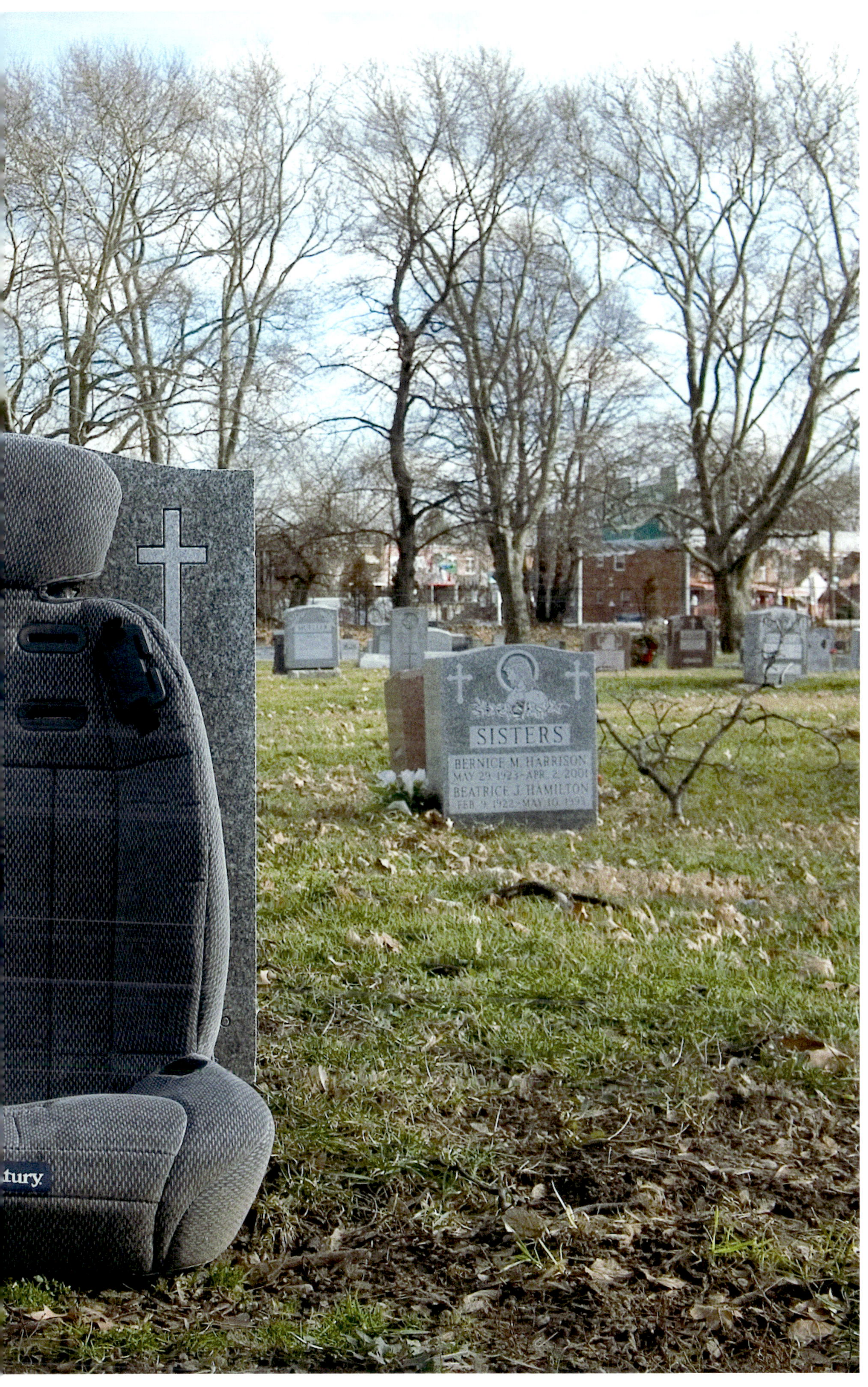
SISTERS
BERNICE M. HARRISON
BEATRICE J. HAMILTON

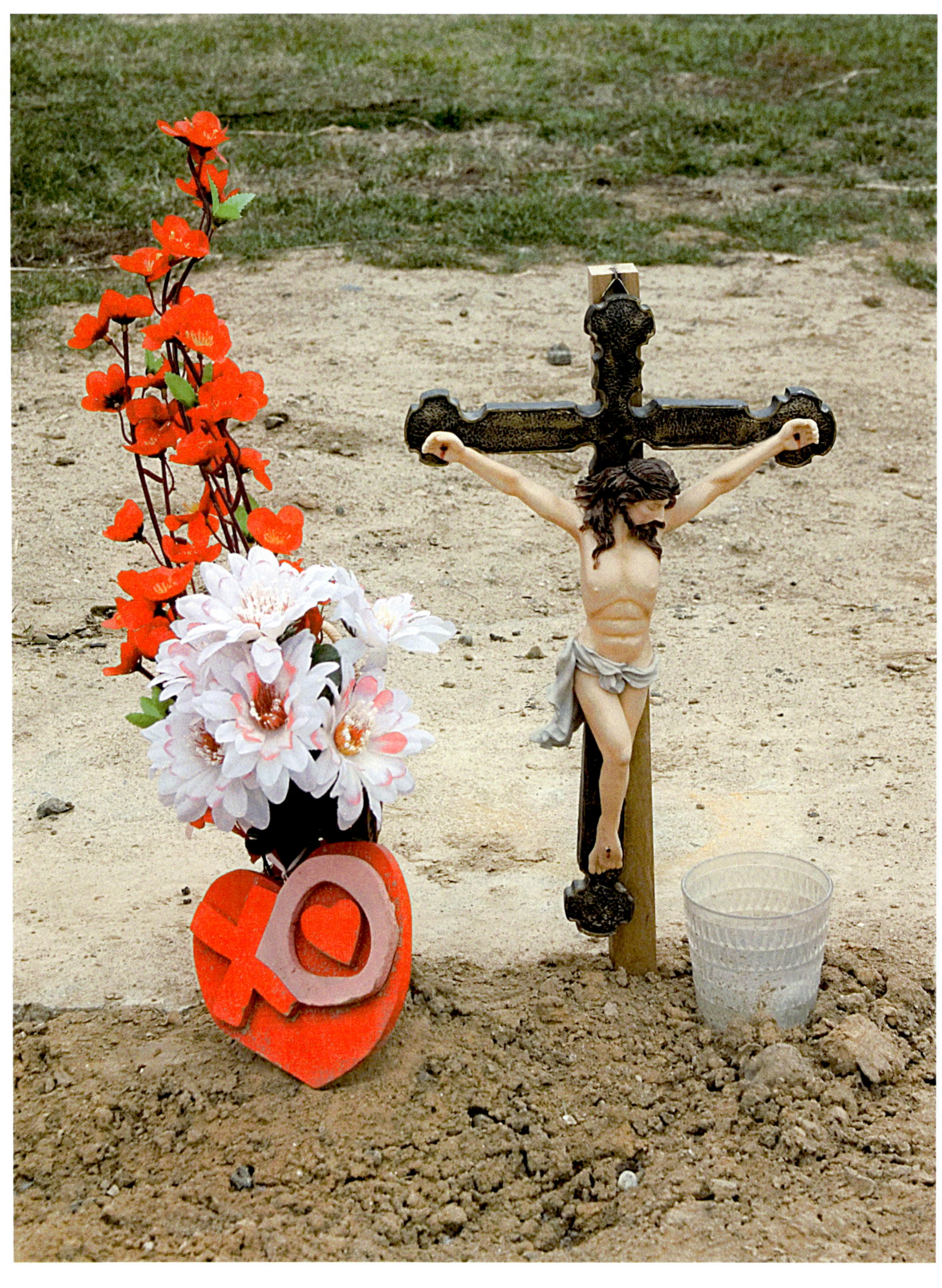

#5

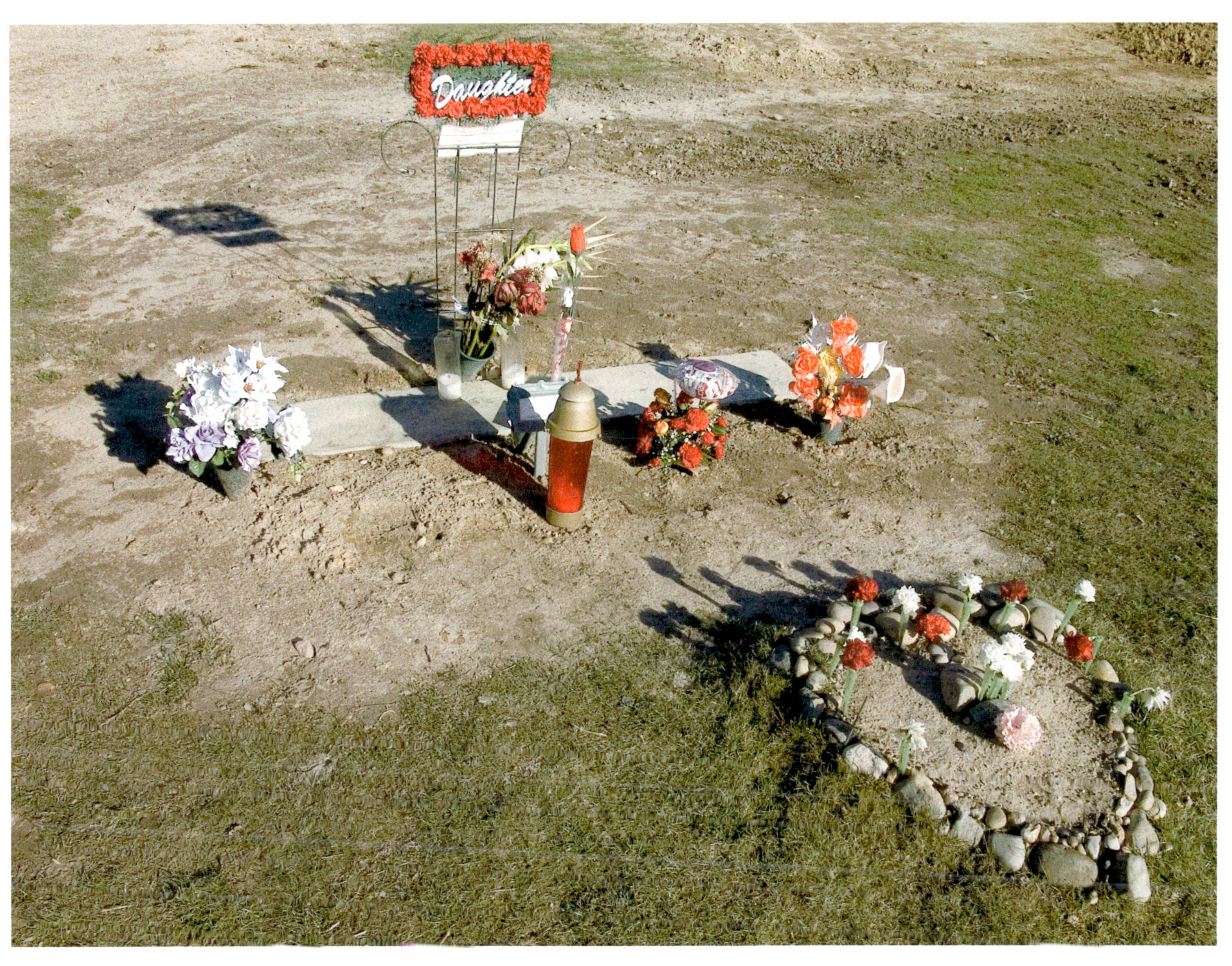
Daughter

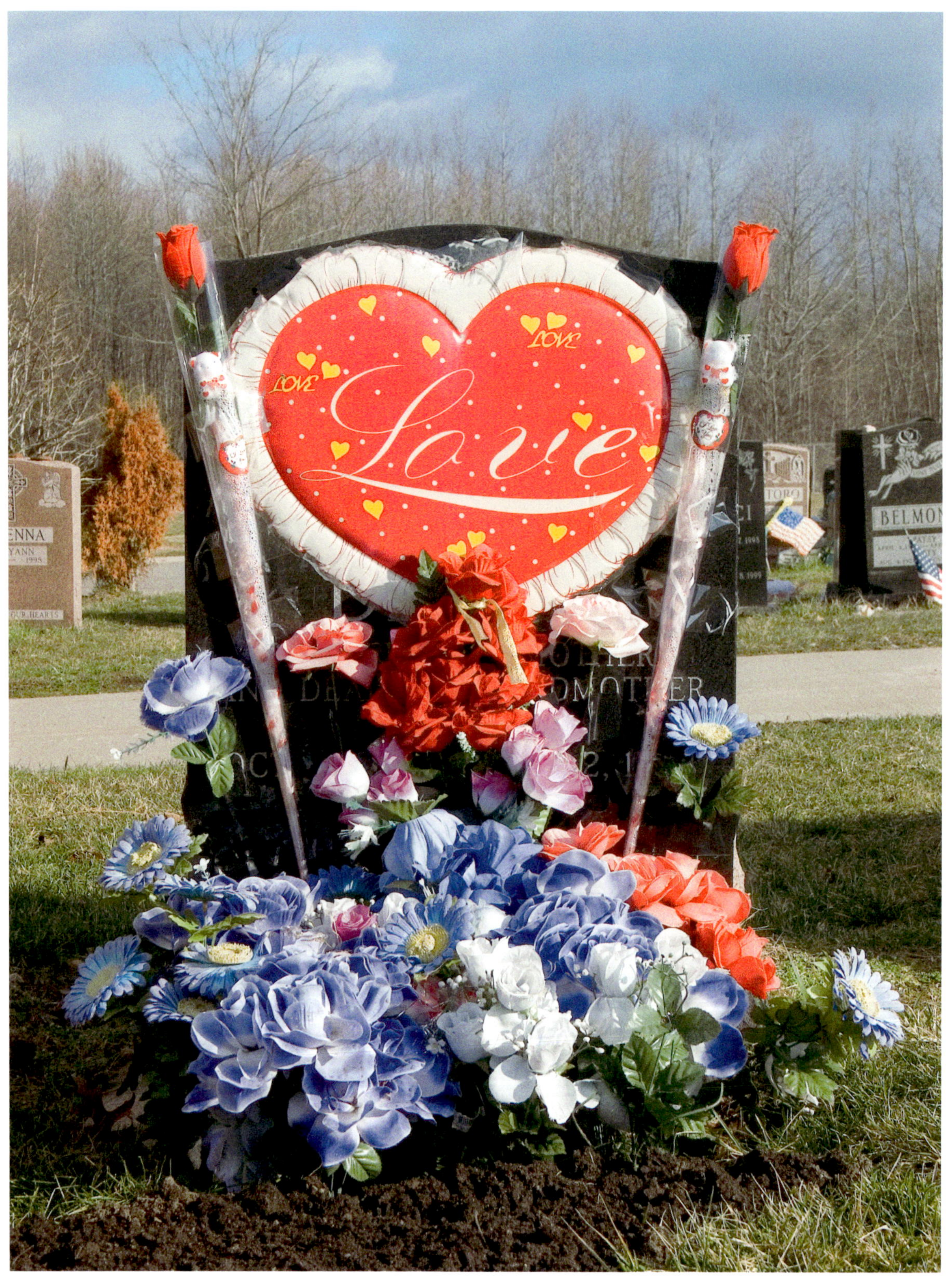

#7A

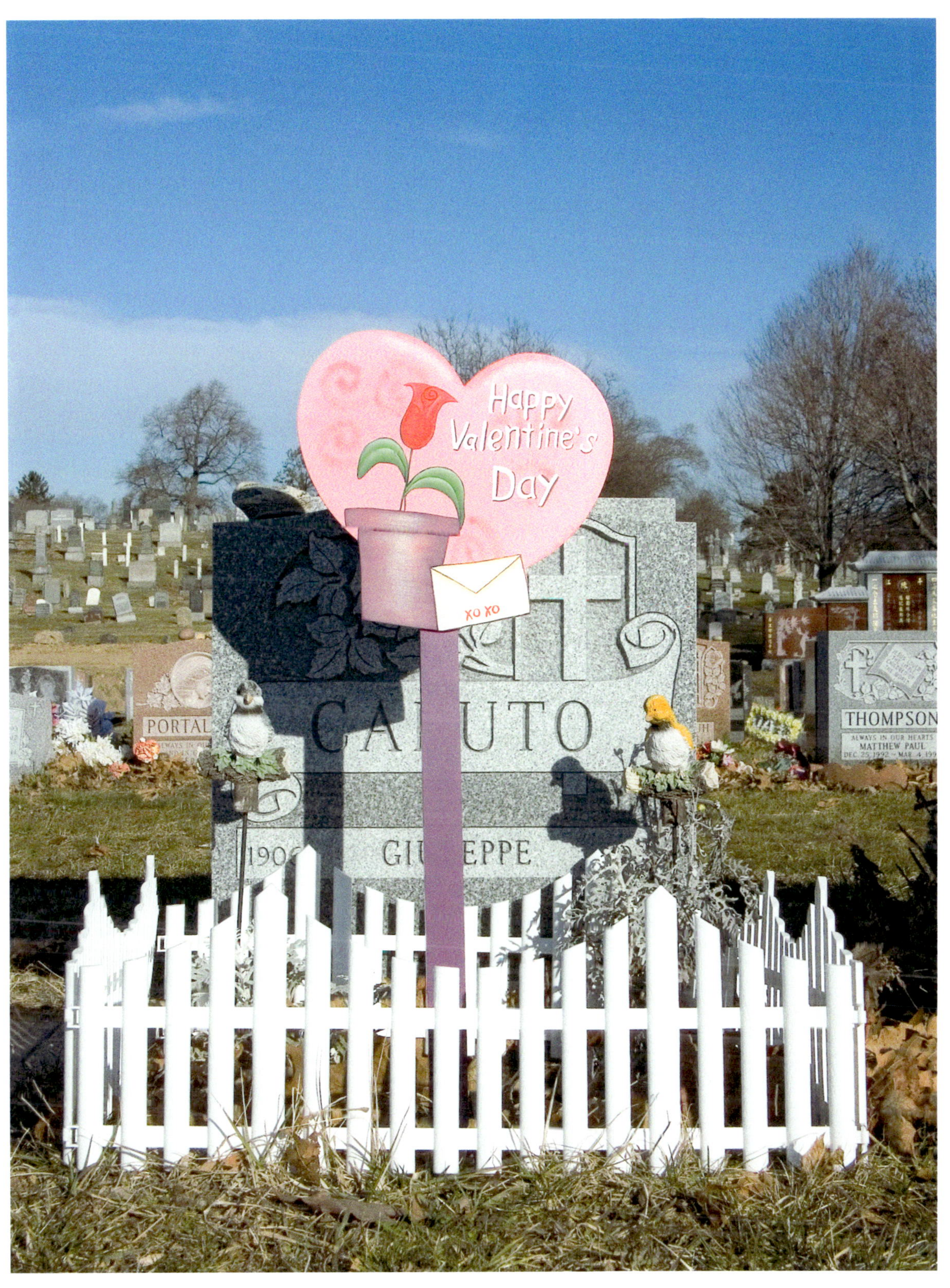
Happy Valentine's Day
XO XO
PORTAL
THOMPSON
ALWAYS IN OUR HEARTS
MATTHEW PAUL

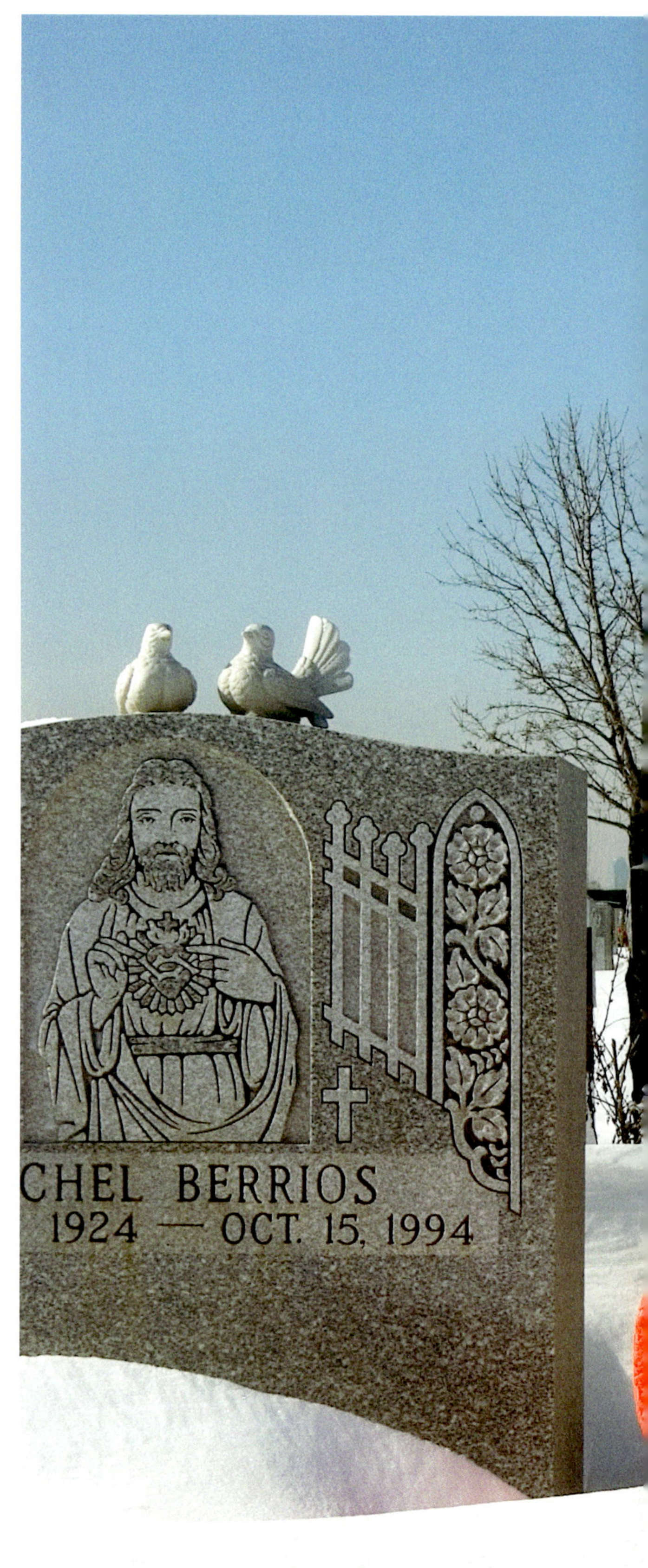
CHEL BERRIOS
1924 — OCT. 15, 1994

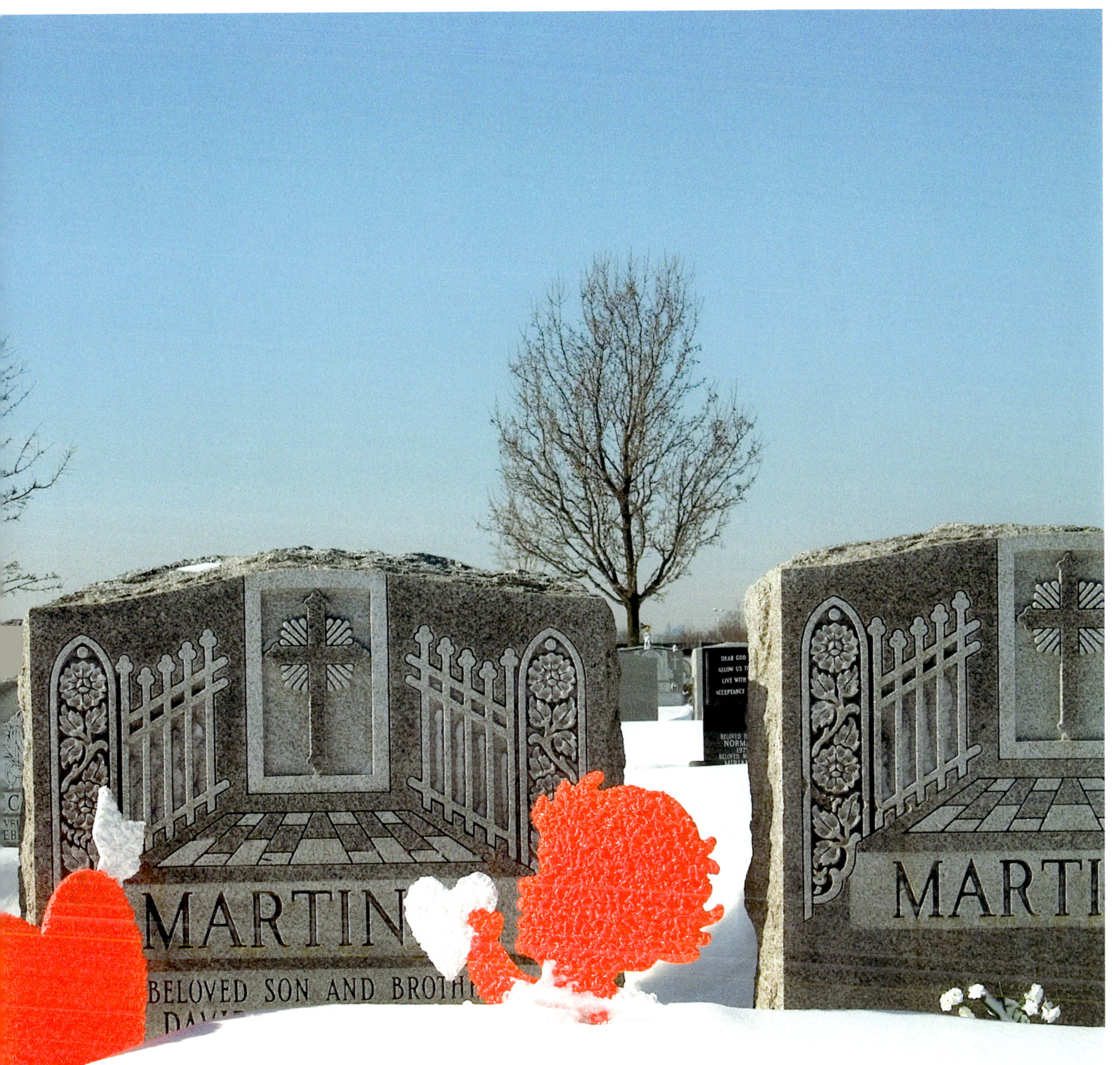

MARTIN
BELOVED SON AND BROTH
DEAR GOD
LIVE WITH
ACCEPTANCE
MARTI

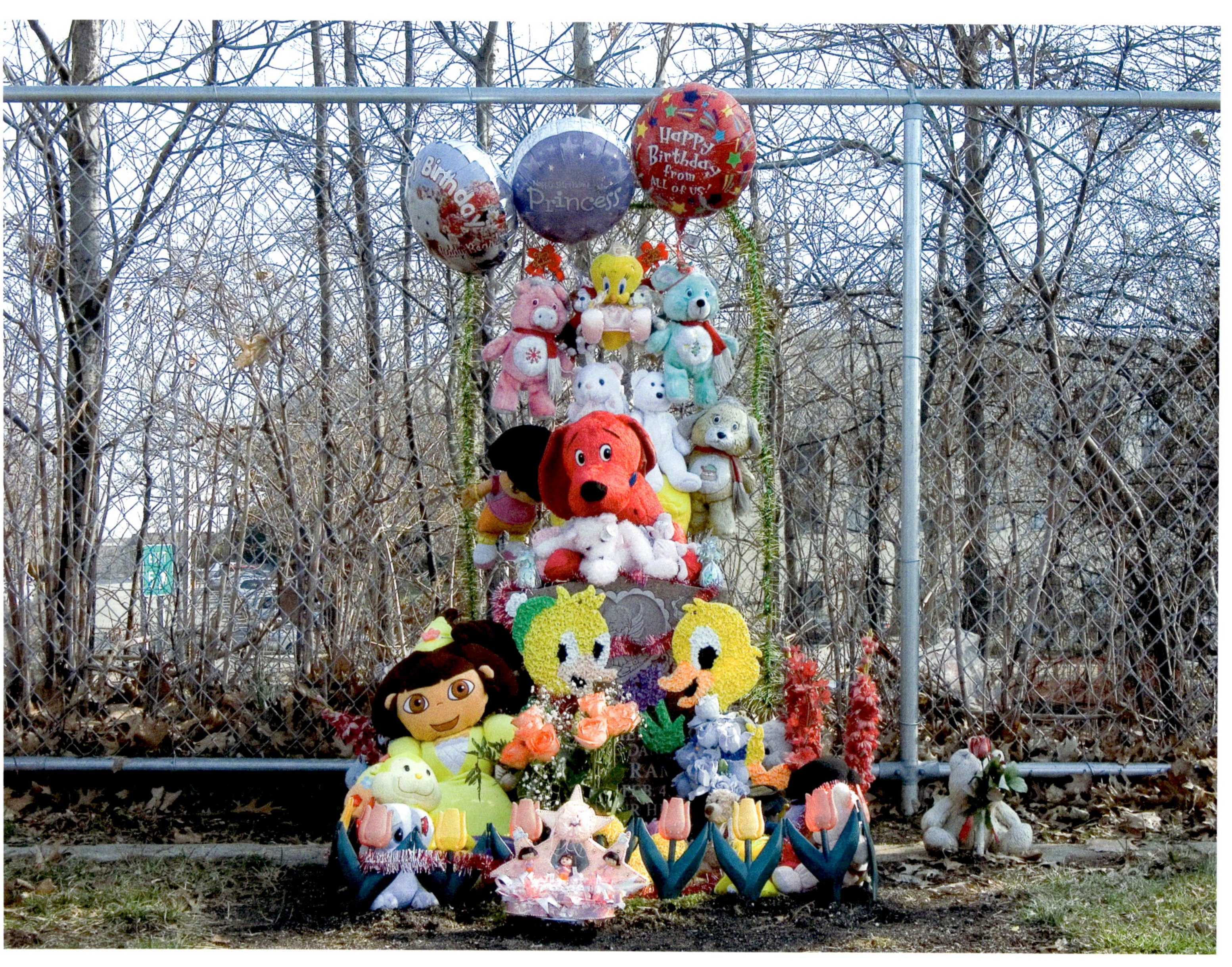

#10

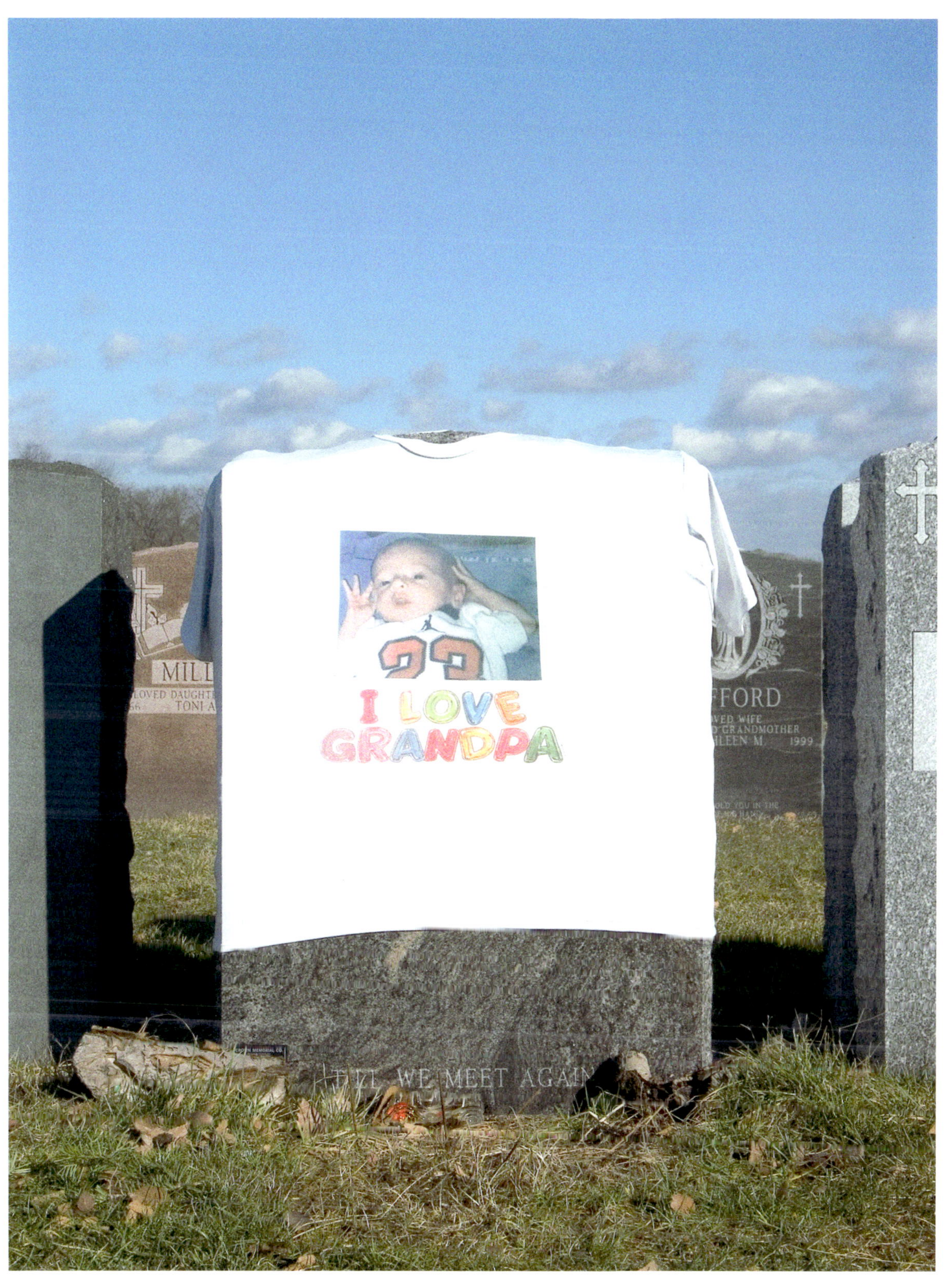
I LOVE
GRANDPA

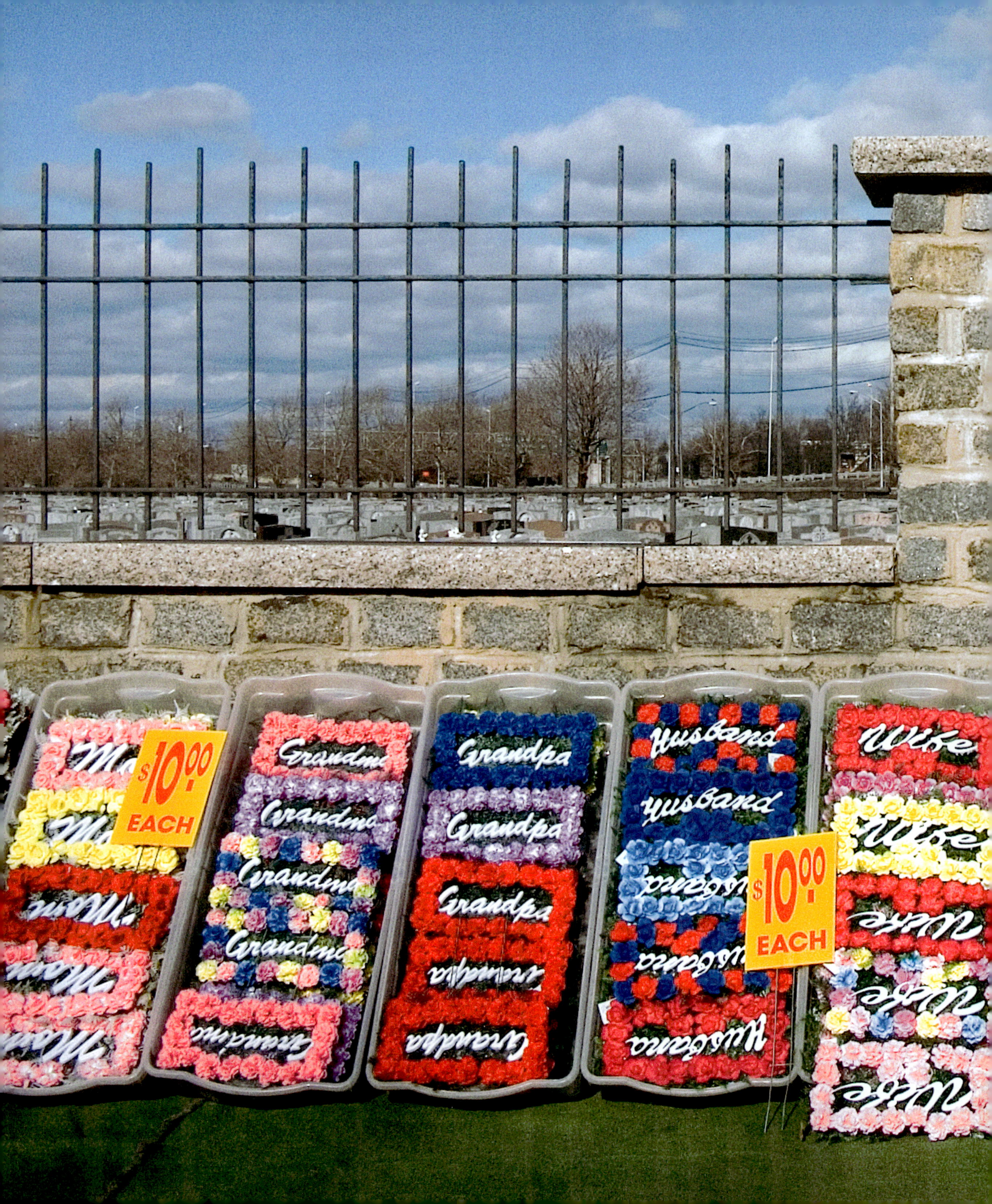

$10.00 EACH
Grandpa
Grandpa
Grandpa
Husband
Husband
$10.00 EACH
Wife
Wife

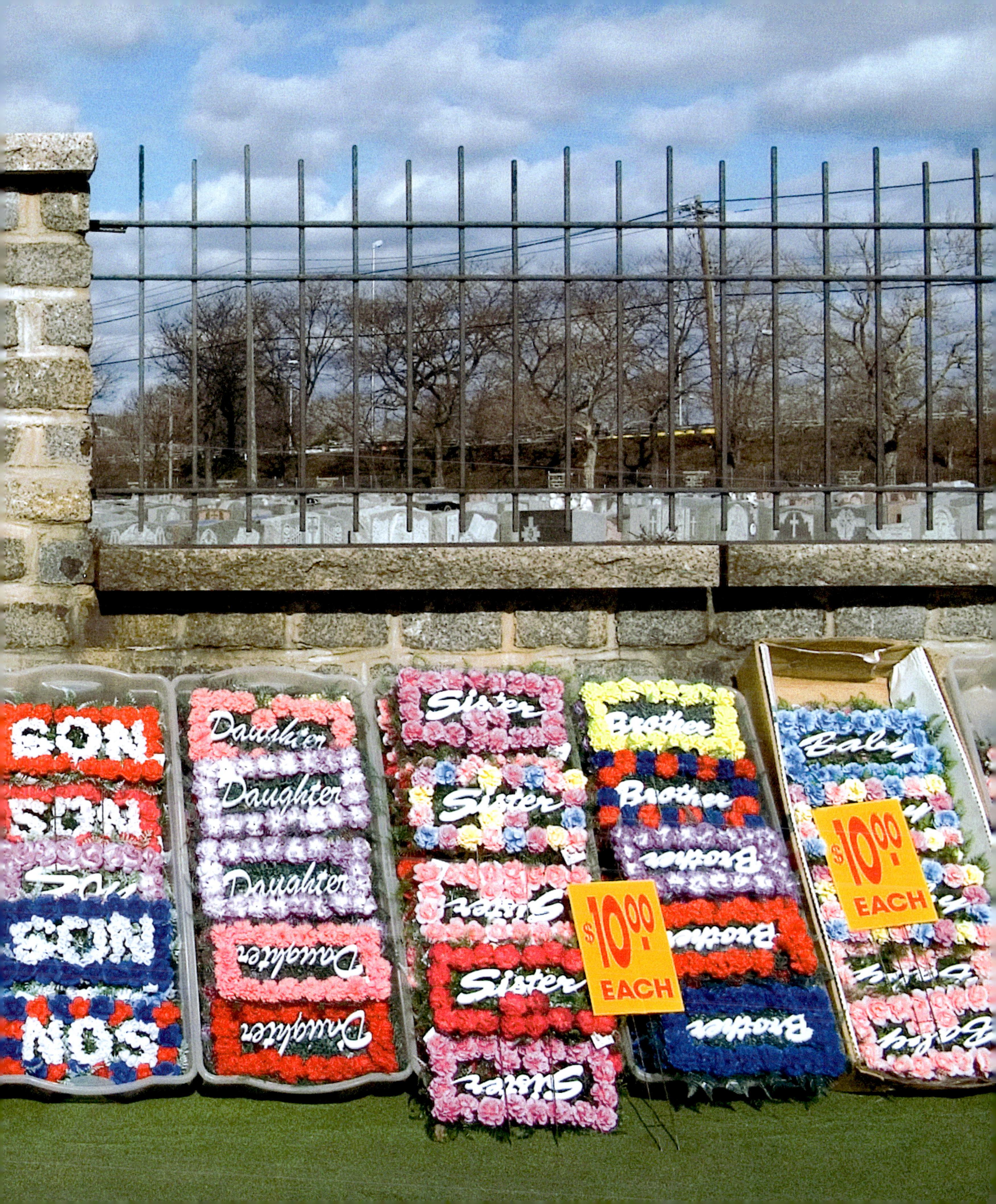

SON
Daughter
Daughter
Daughter
Sister
Sister
Sister
Brother
Brother
Baby
$10.00 EACH
$10.00 EACH

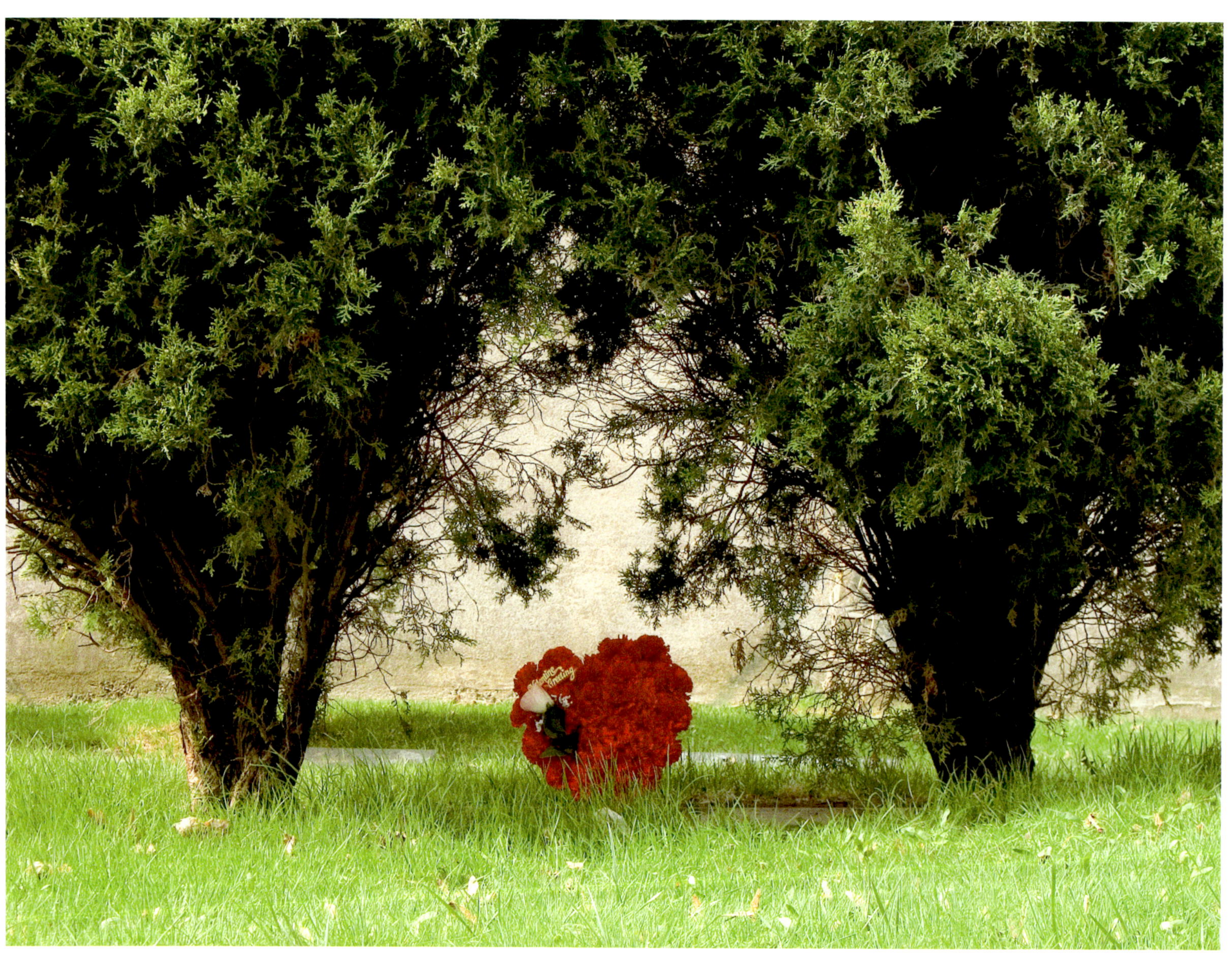

#12

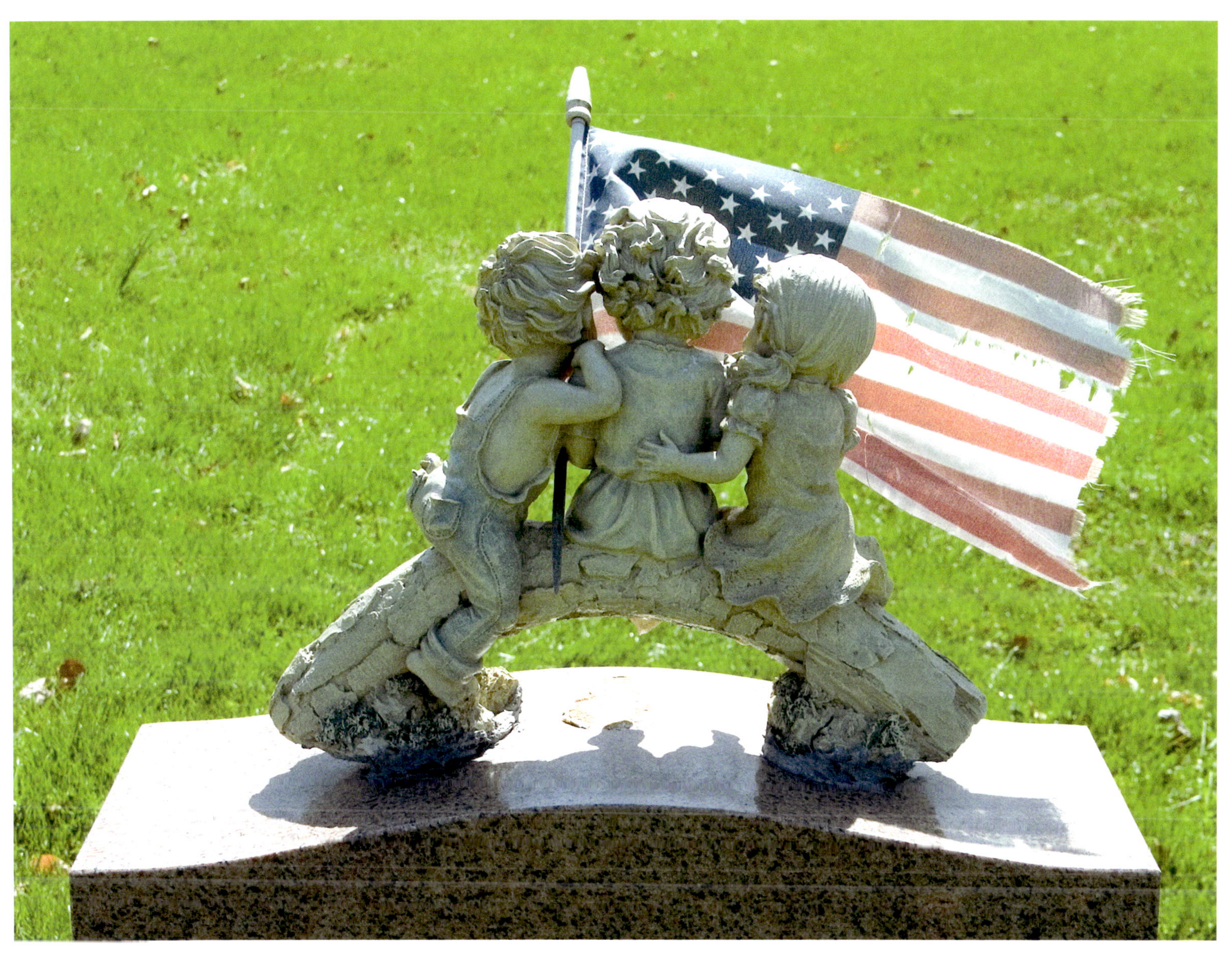

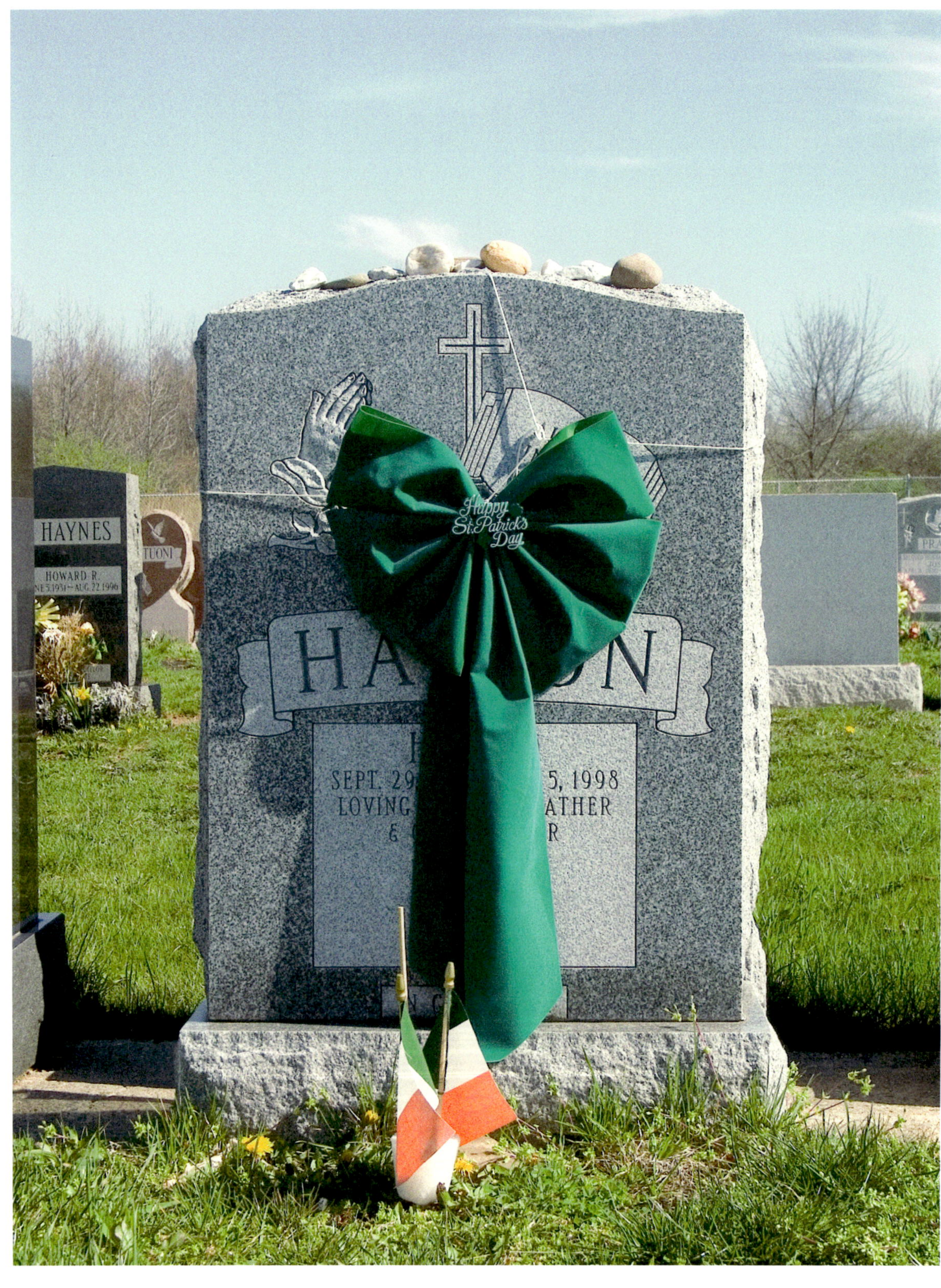

#14

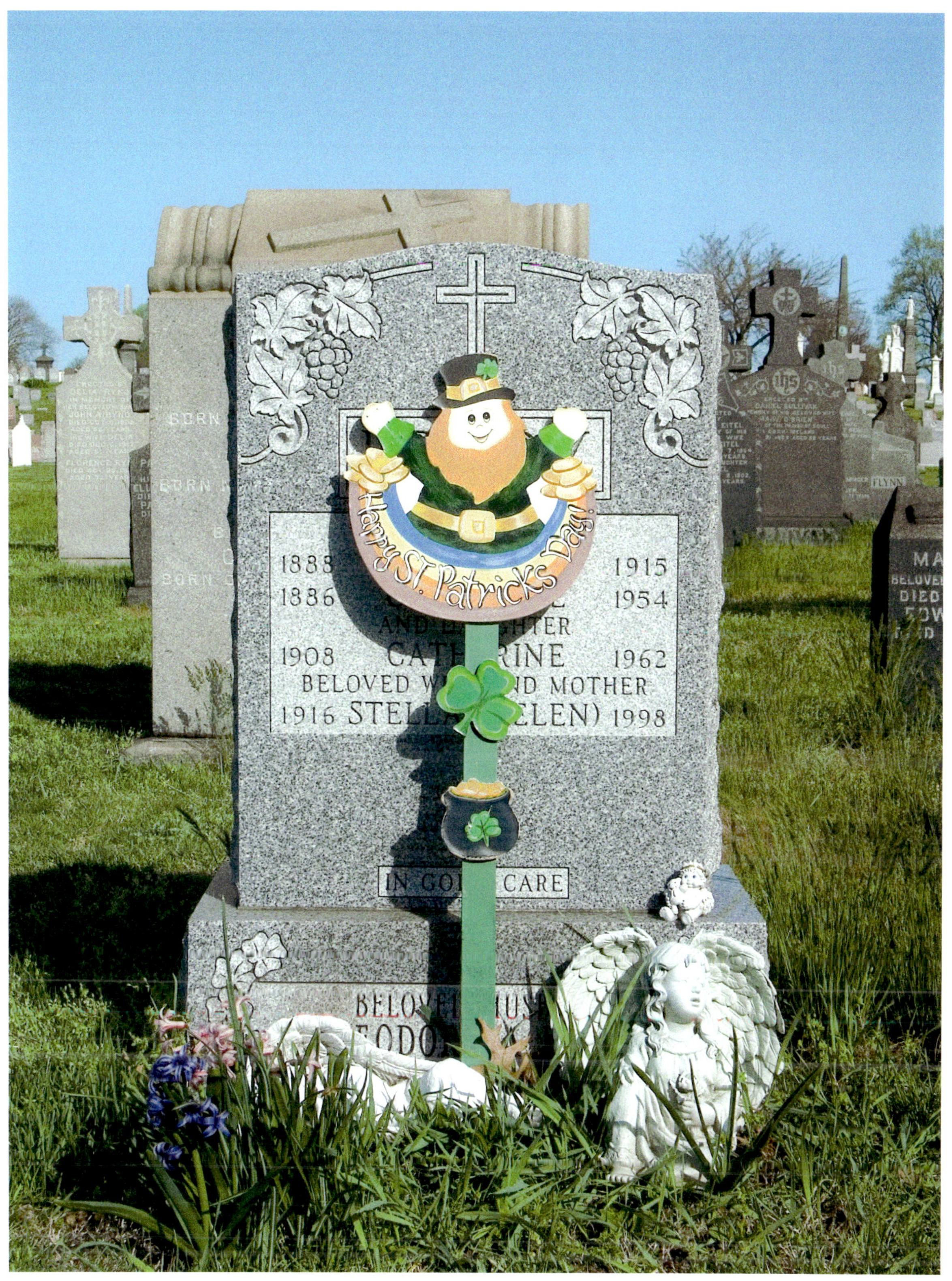
Happy St. Patricks Day!
1888 1915
1886 1954
1908 1962
BELOVED
MOTHER
1916 1998
CARE
FLYNN

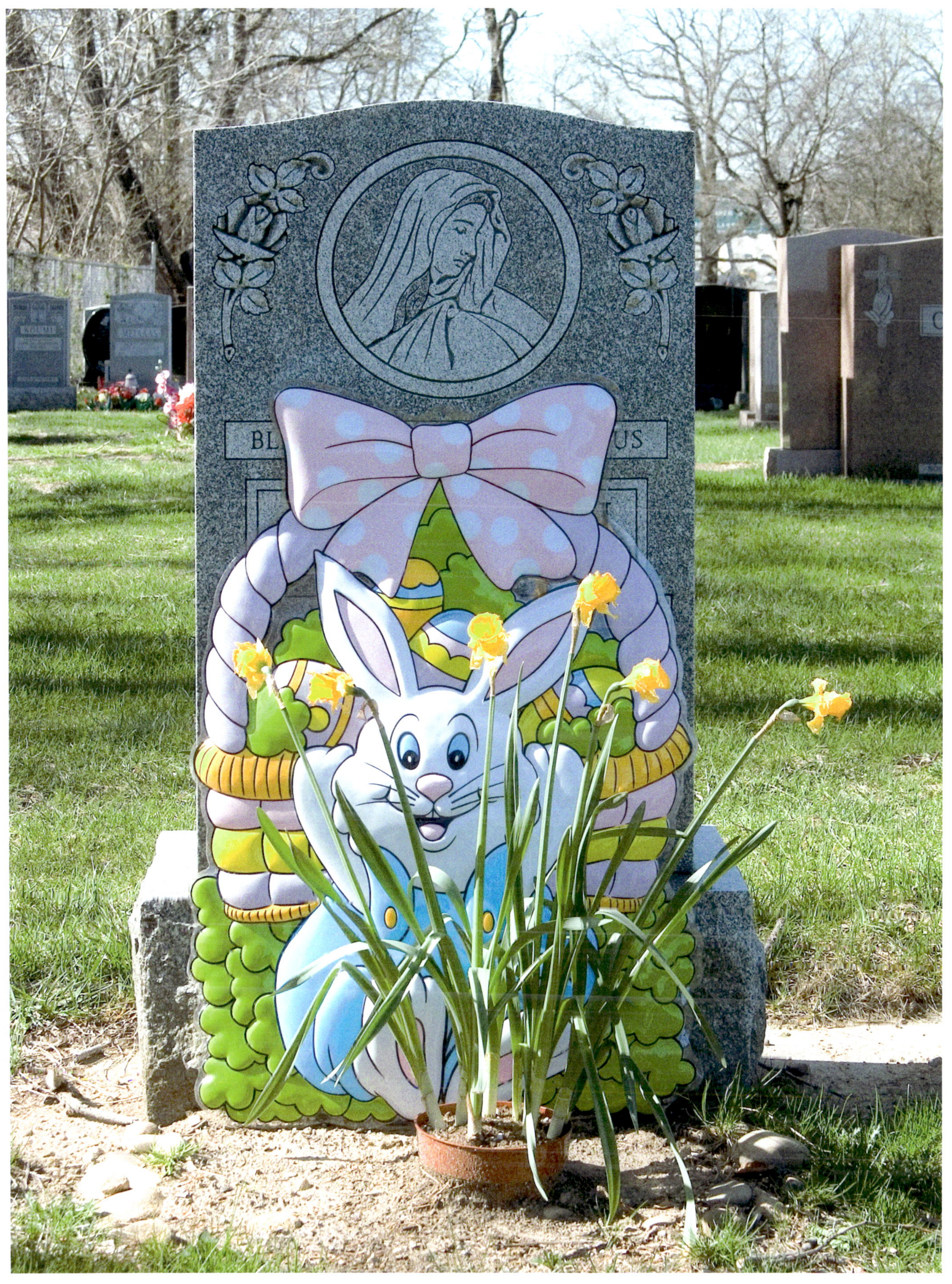

#16

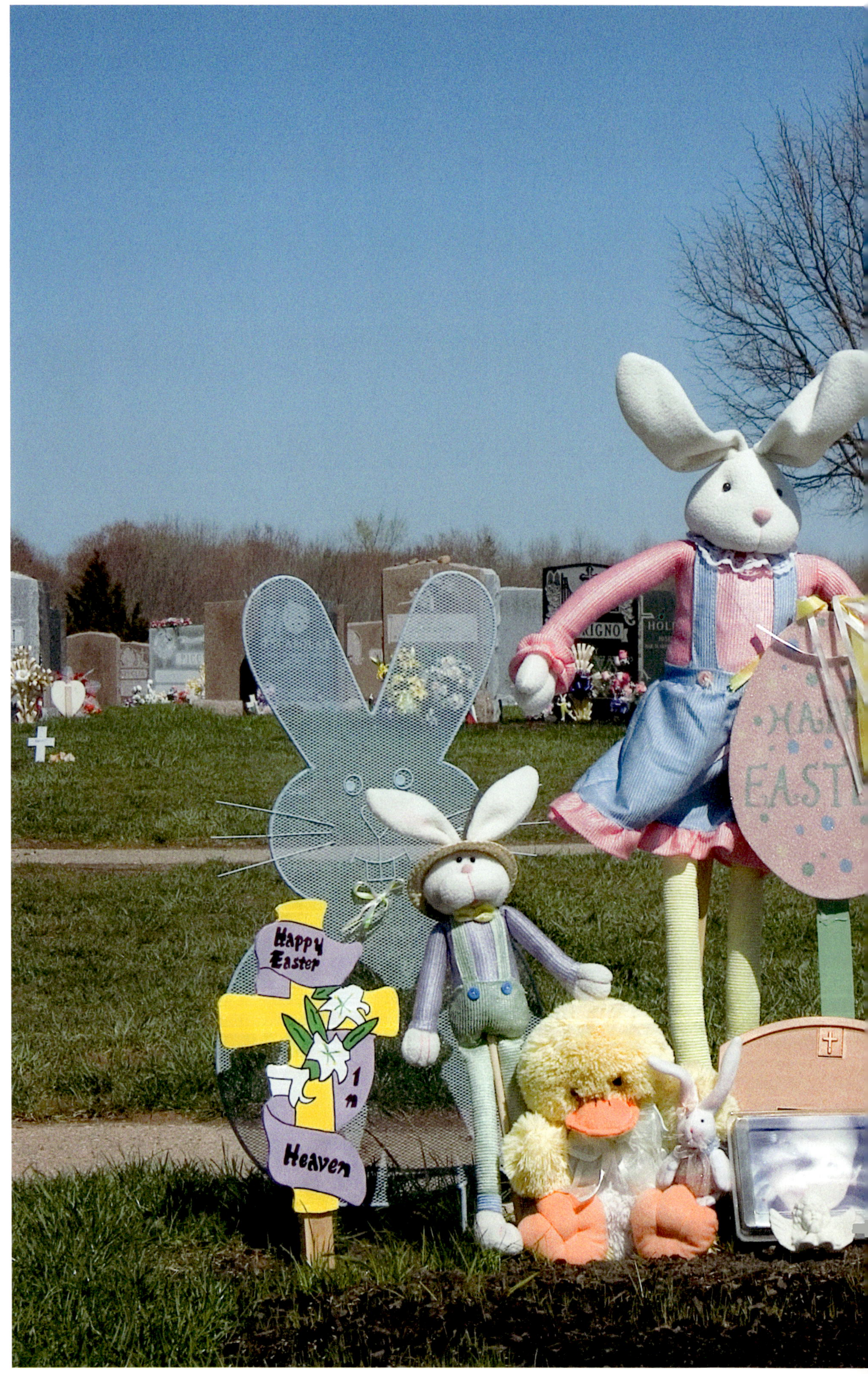

#17A

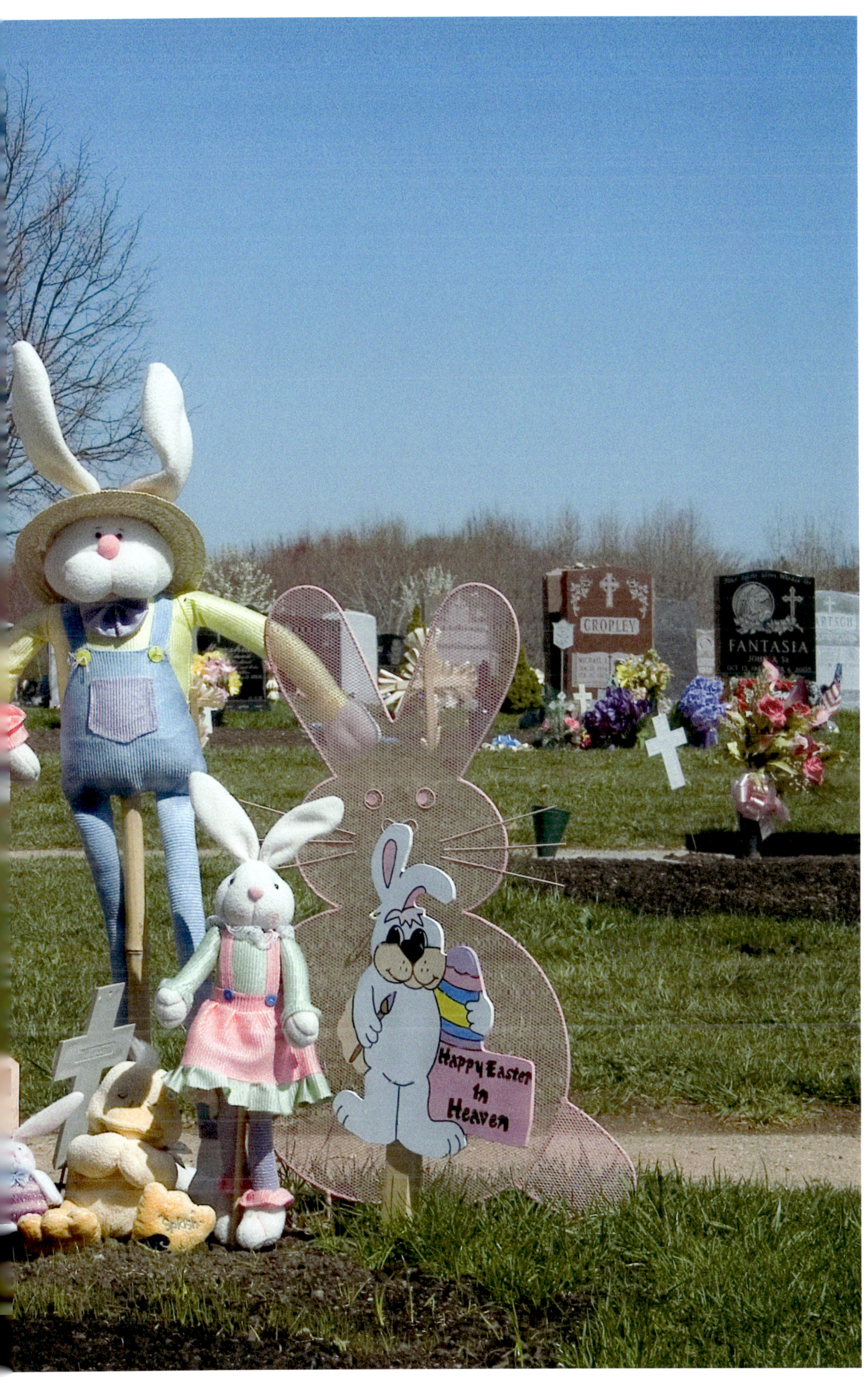
CROPLEY
FANTASIA
Happy Easter
In
Heaven

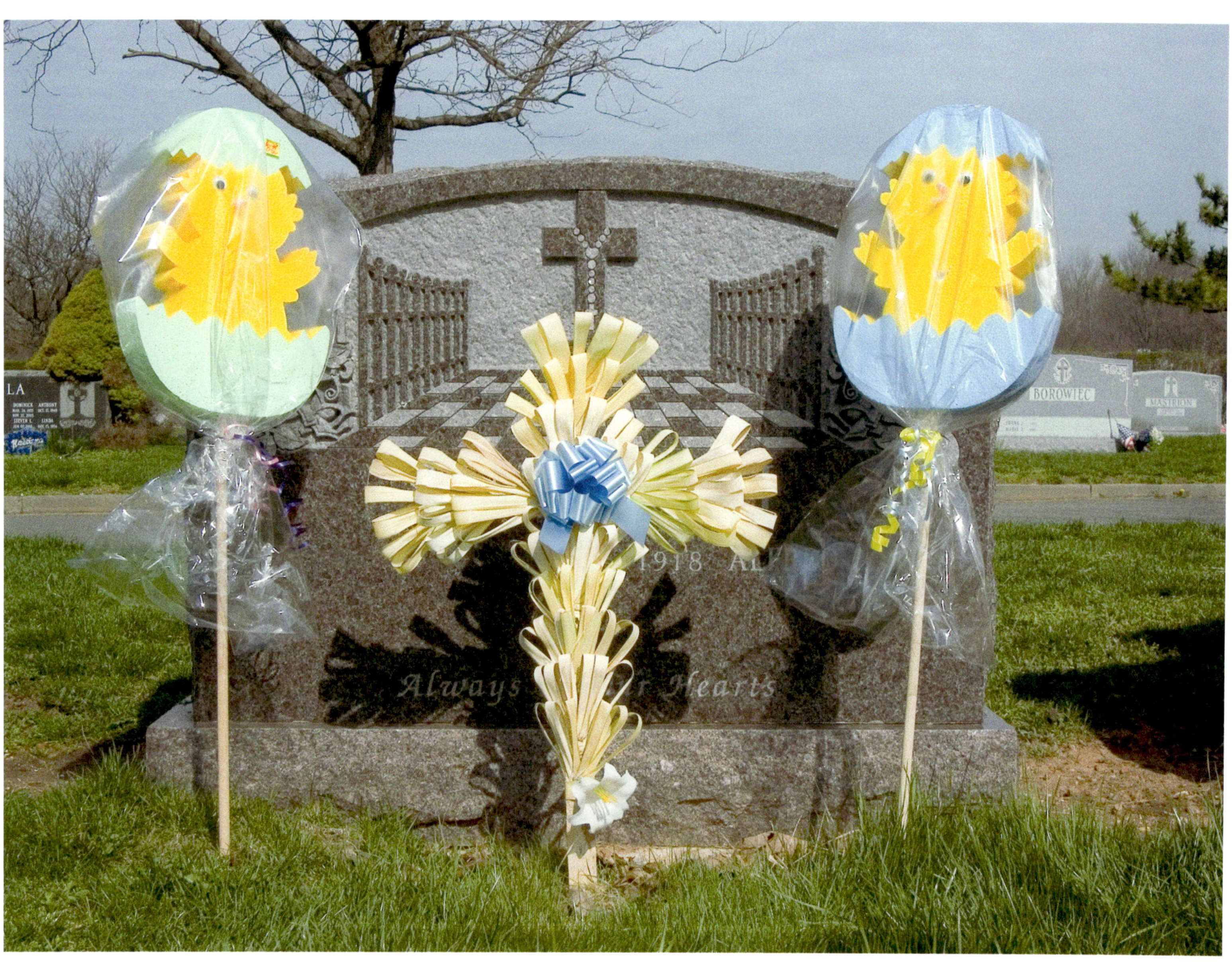

#18

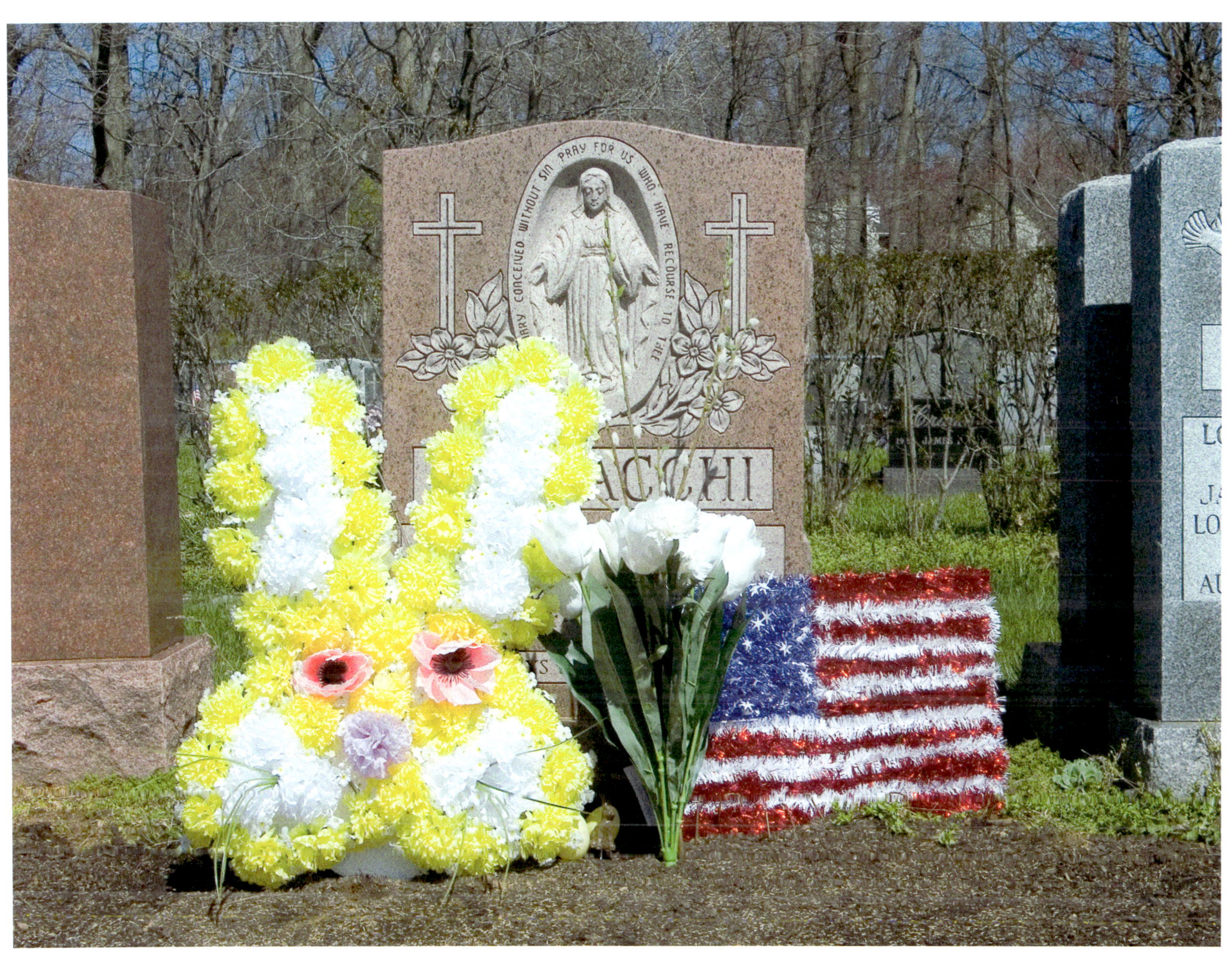
ARY CONCEIVED WITHOUT SIN PRAY FOR US WHO HAVE RECOURSE TO THEE
ACCHI

#19

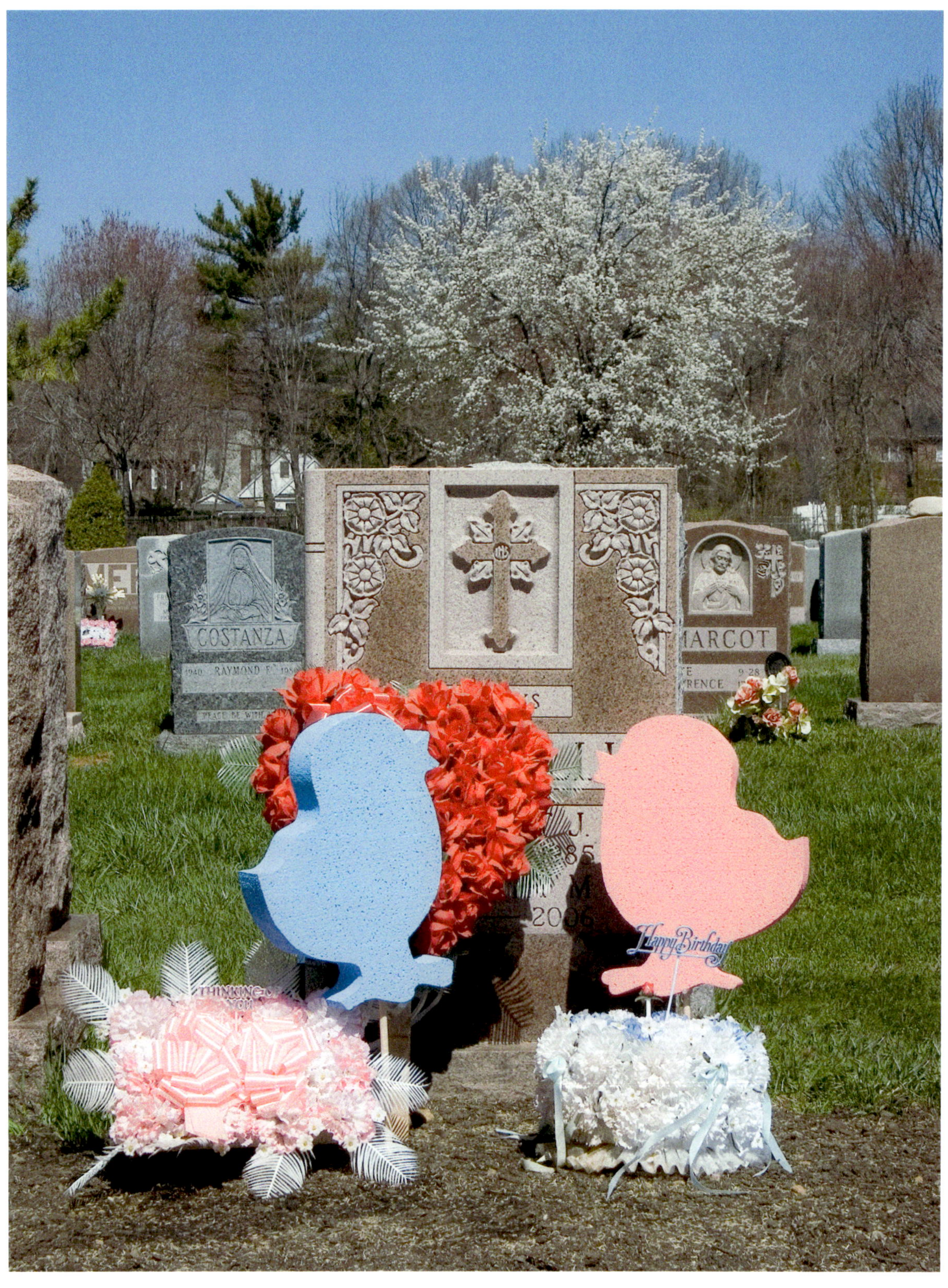

#20

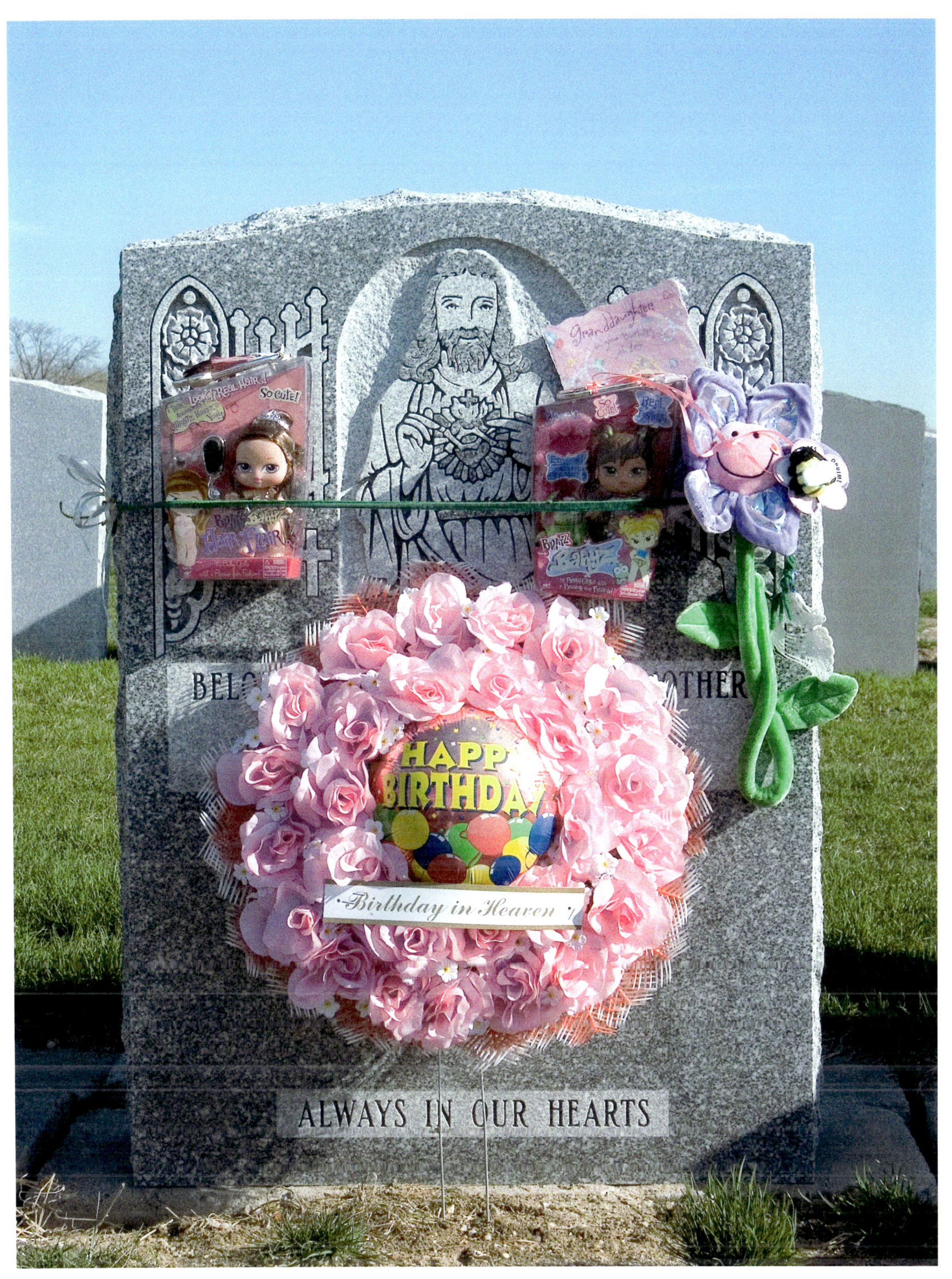

#21

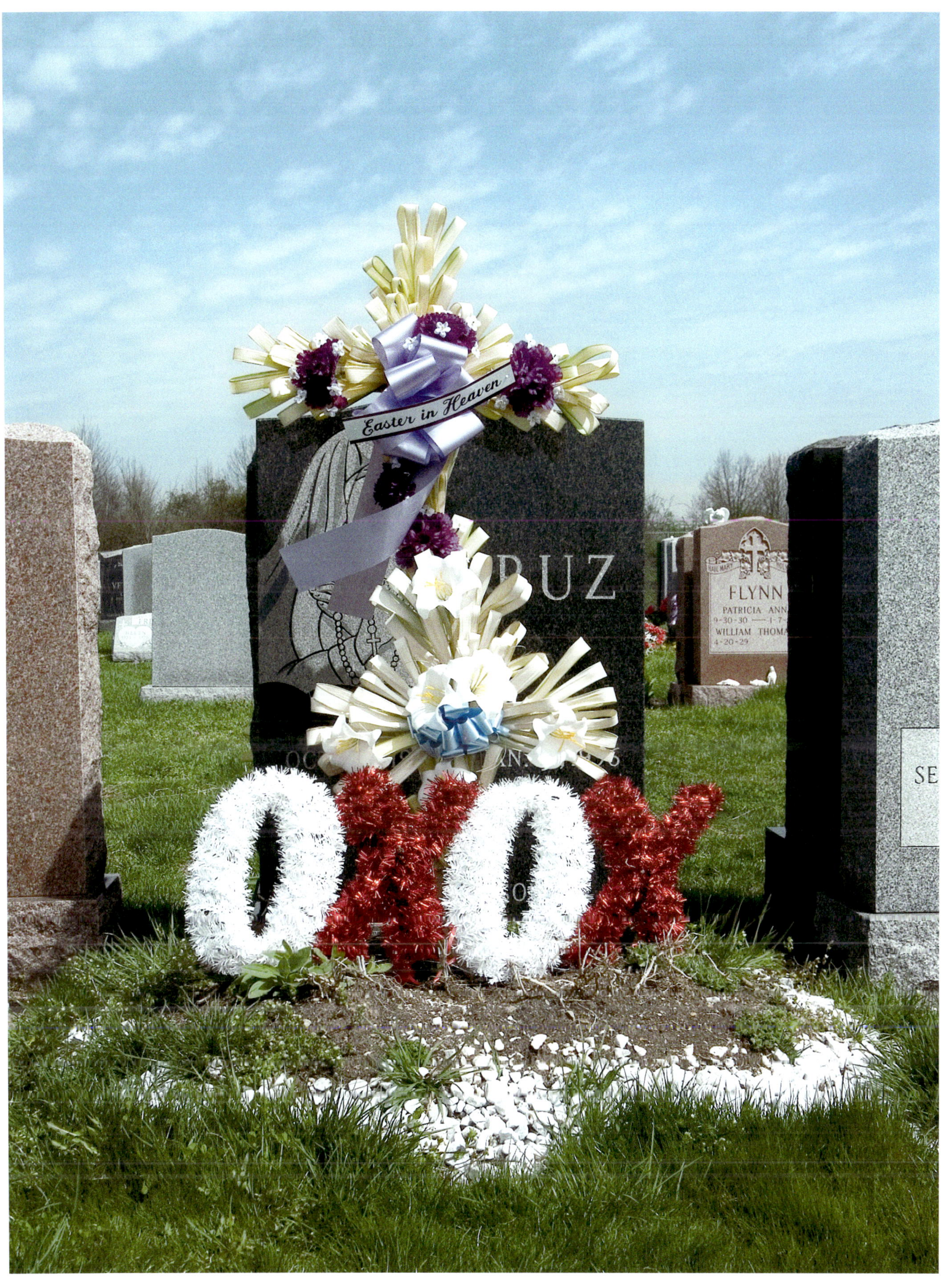

#22

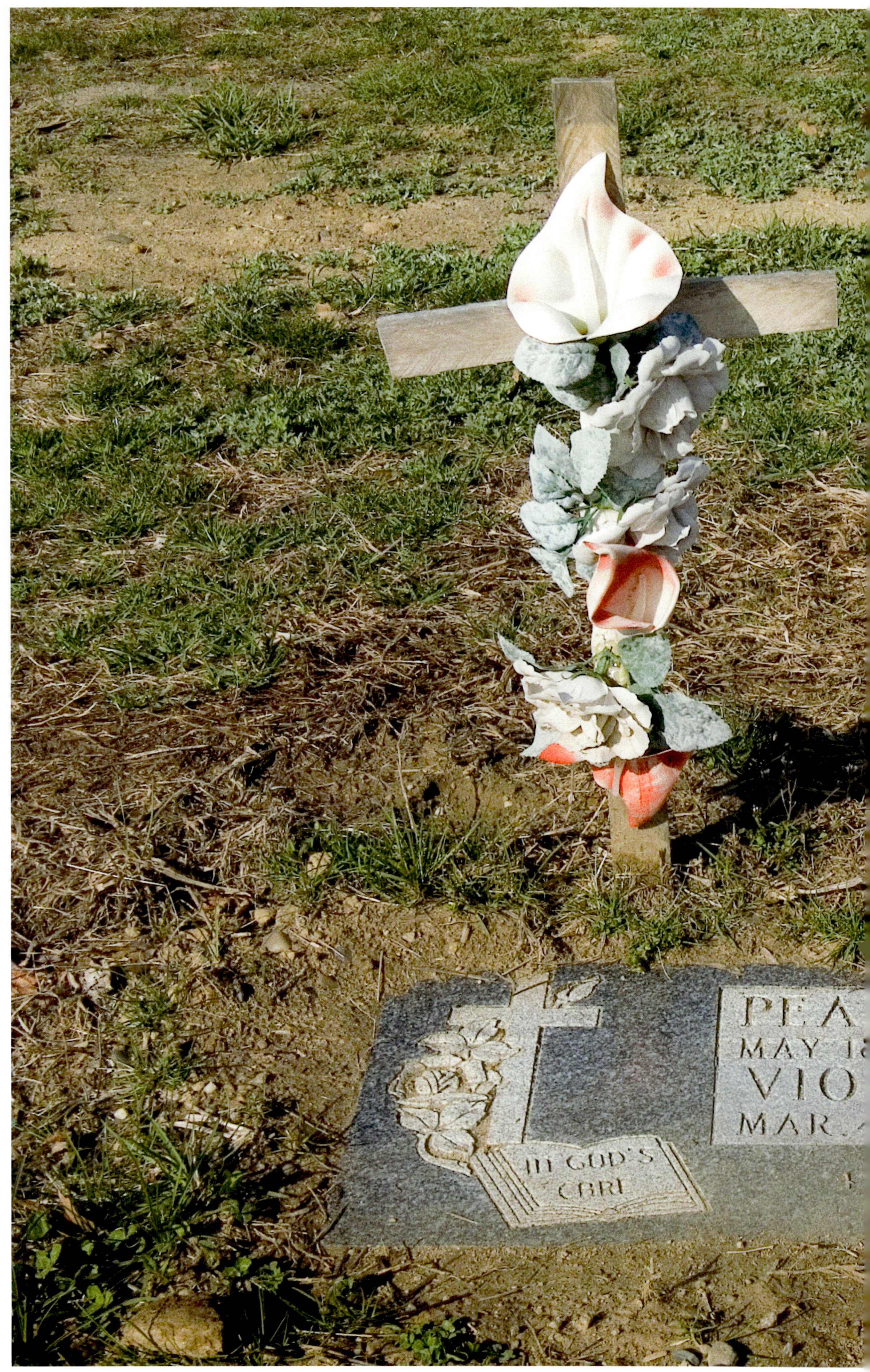

#23

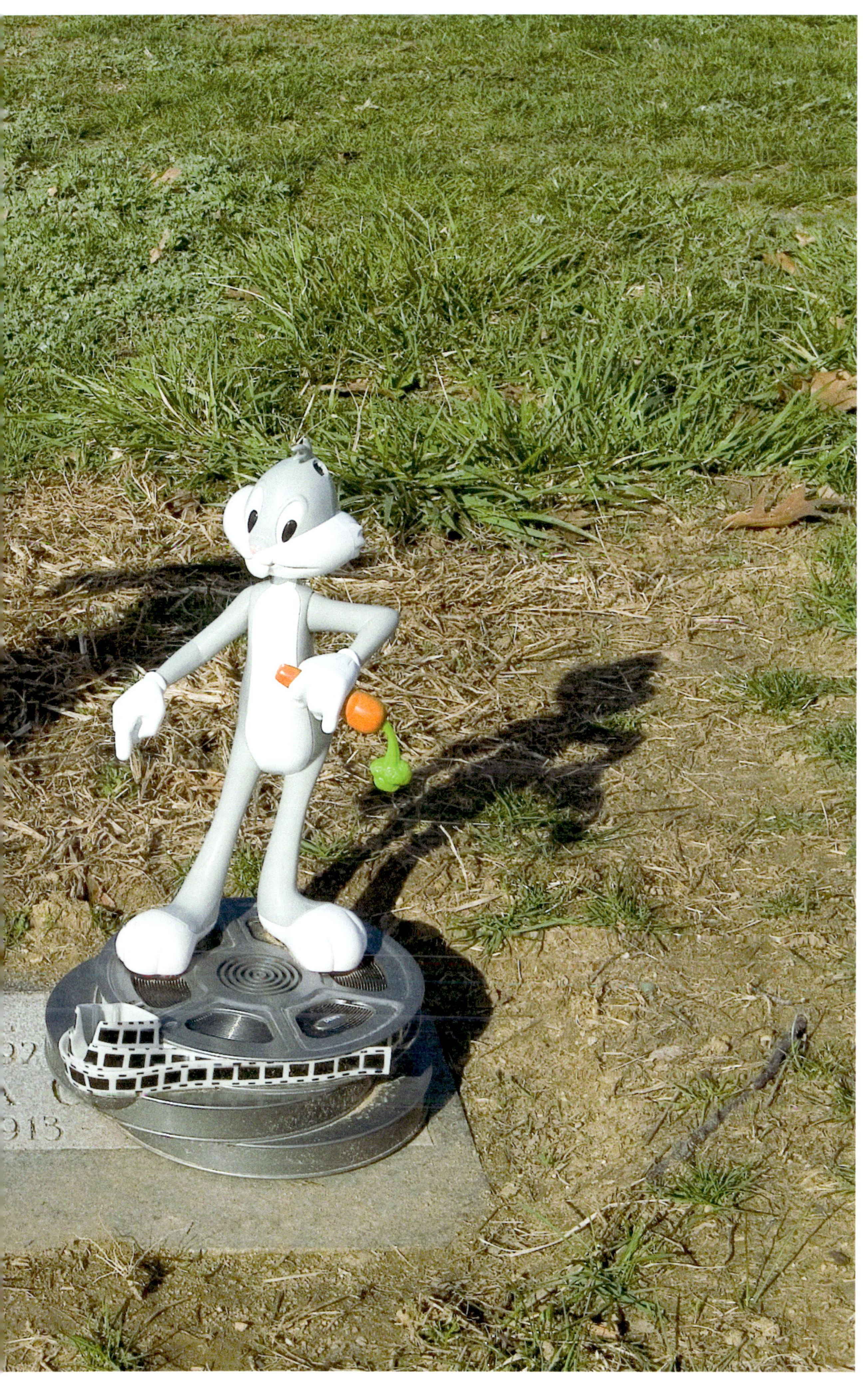

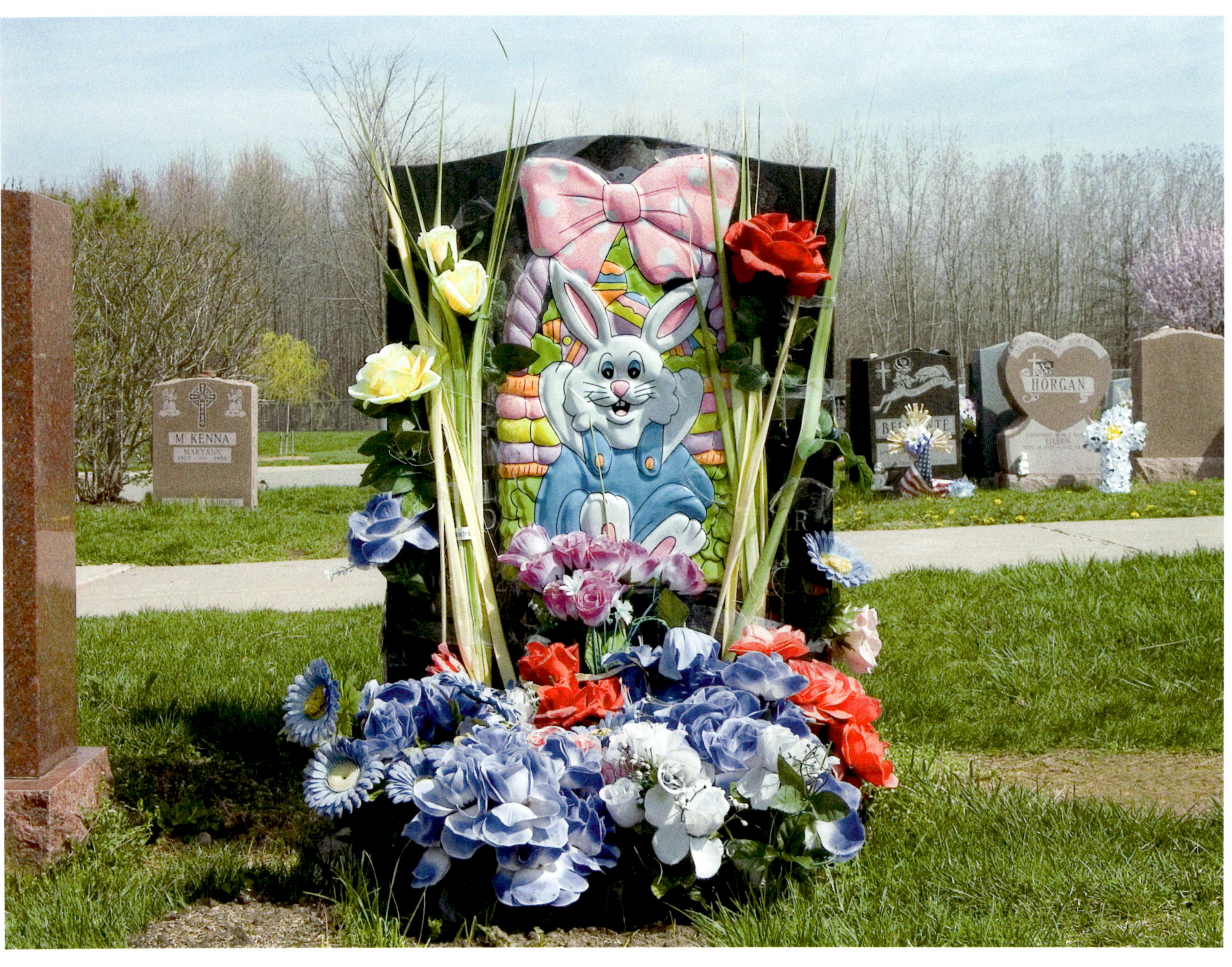

#7B

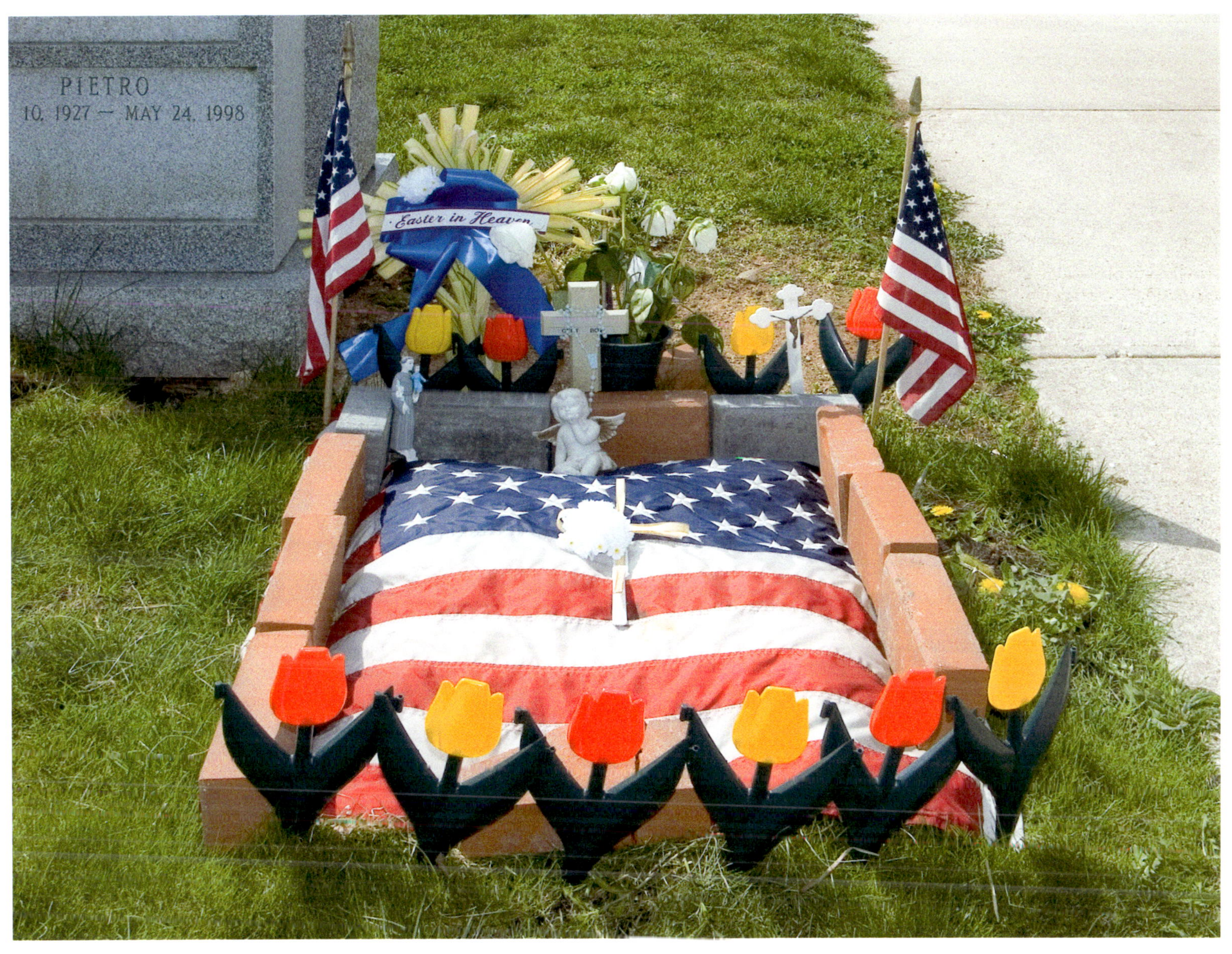

#24

CLINE
RAPP
CONCETTA
1884 — 1961
BELOVED MOTHER
AND GRANDMOTHER
BELOVED WIFE
AND DEAR MOTHER
LAURA G DE MENDEZ
DE QUIROS
FEBRUARY 27 1958
ANTONIO MENDEZ
DE QUIROS
THOMAS J. DURKES
KATHERINE DURKES

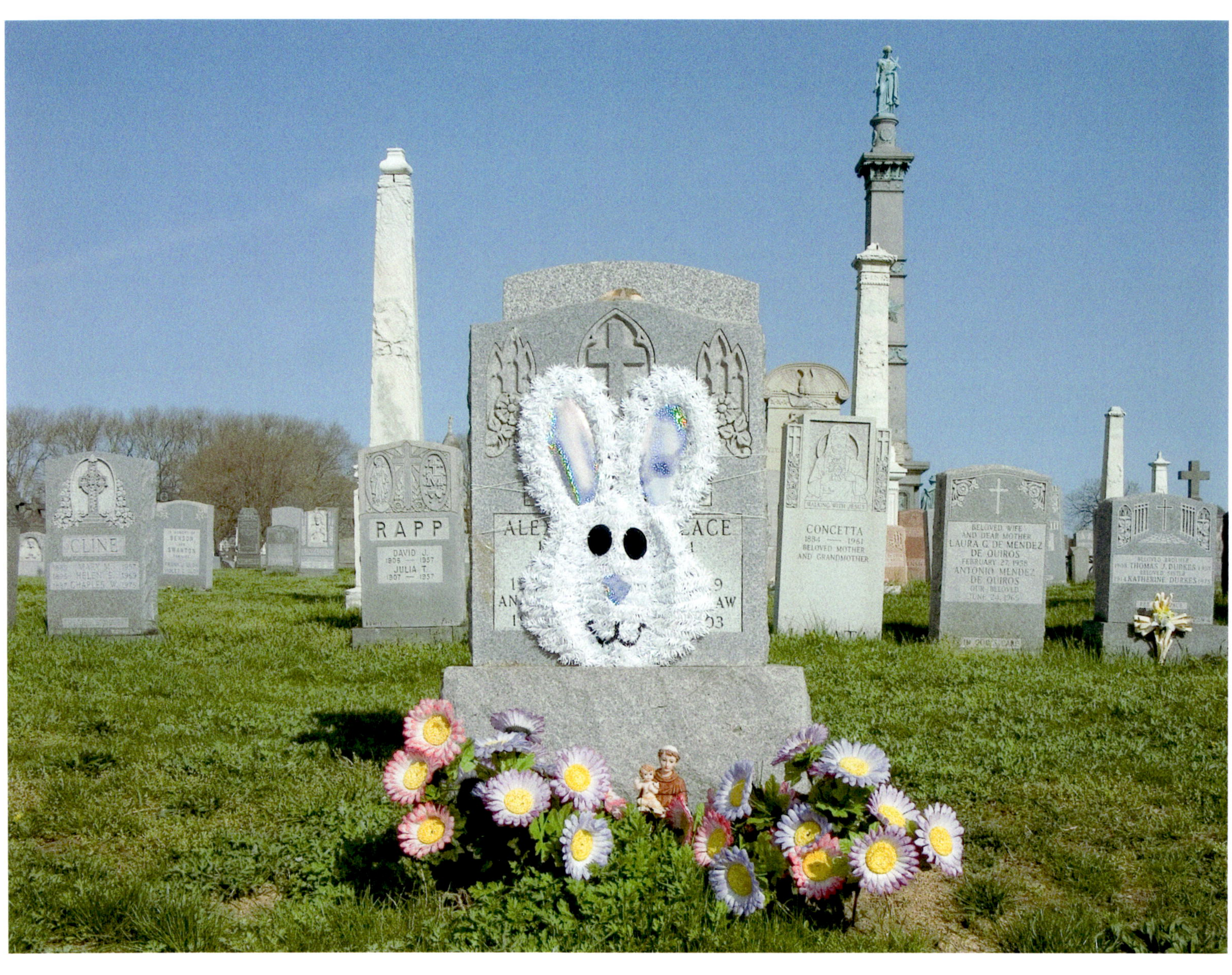

#25

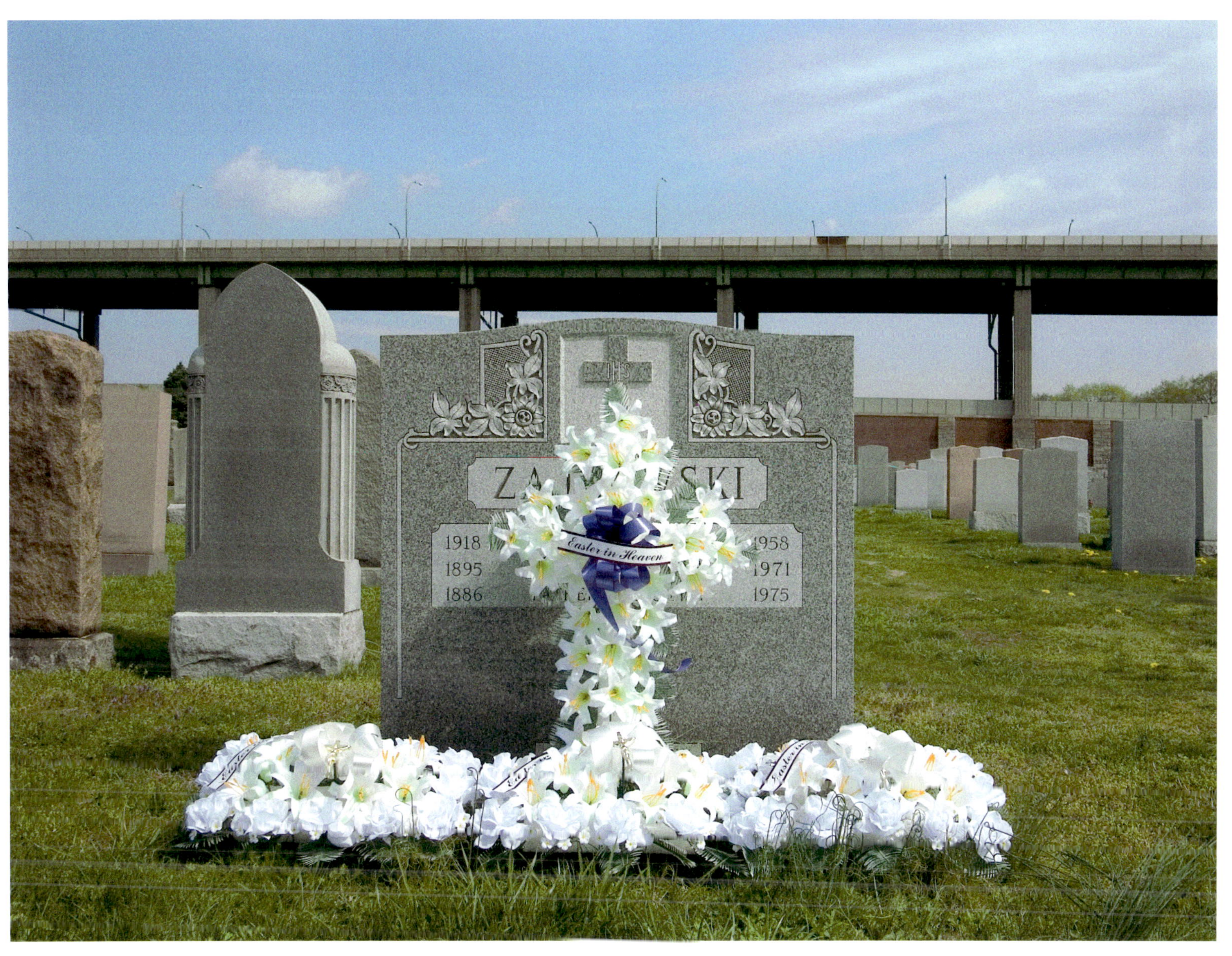

#26

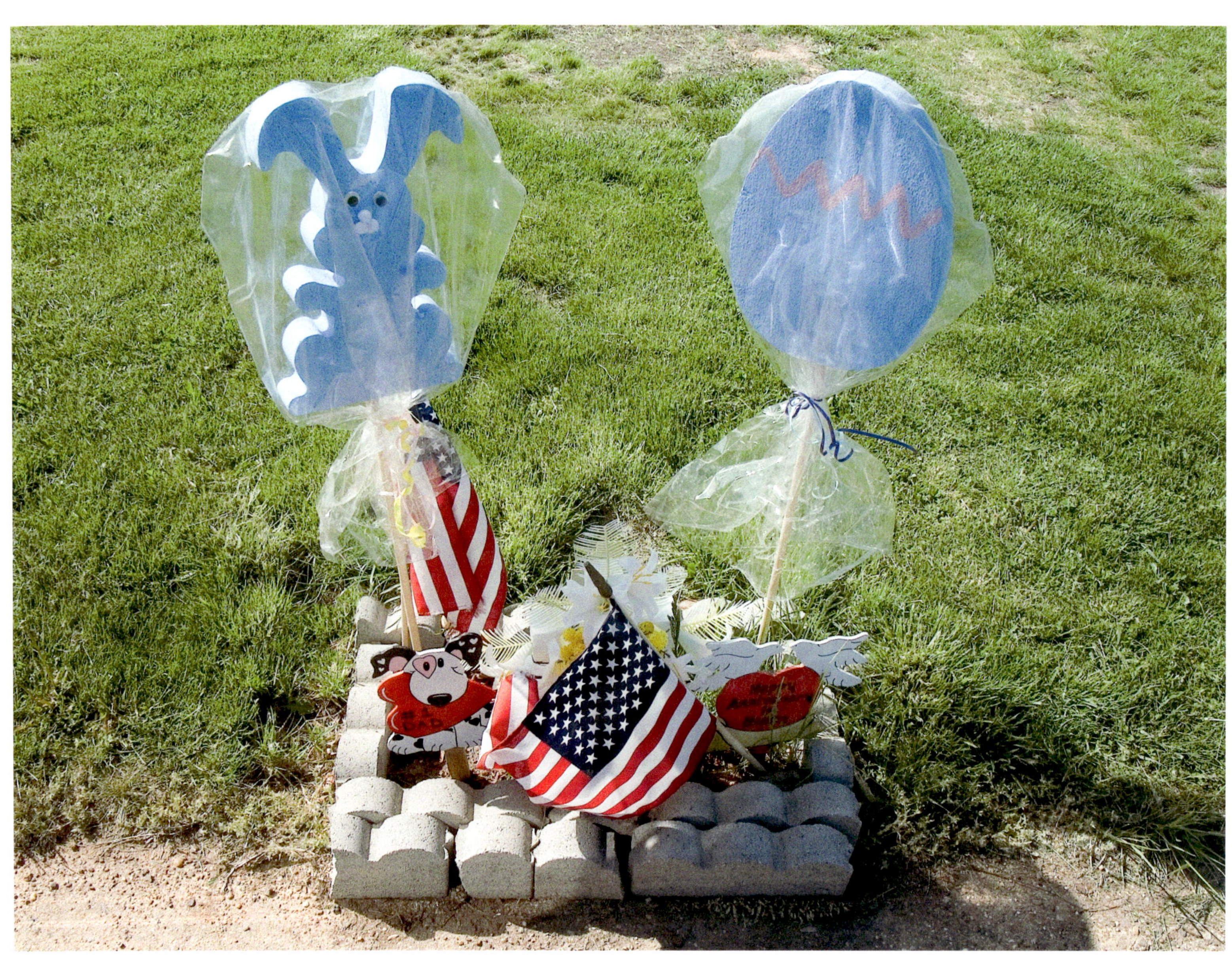

#27

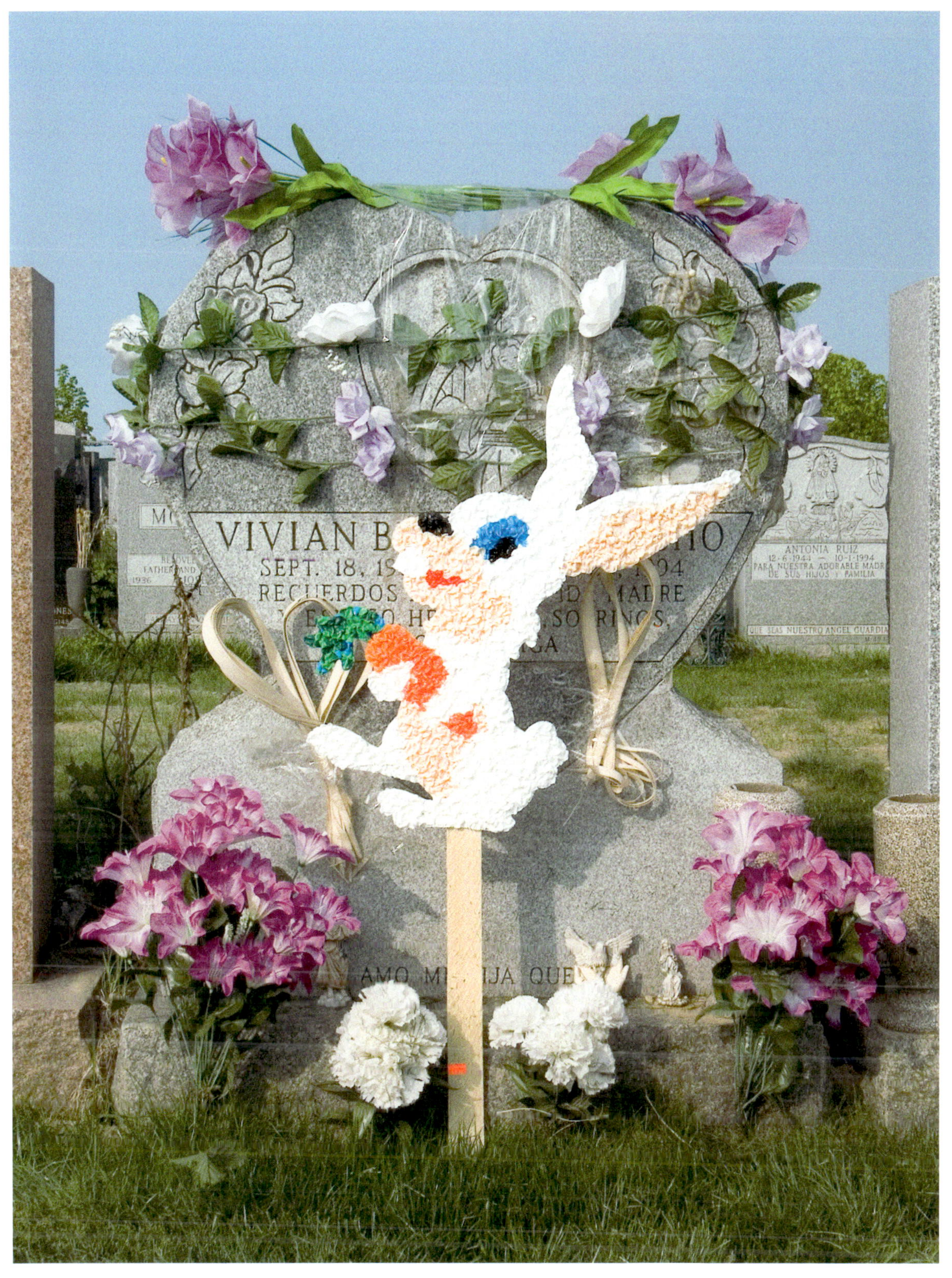
VIVIAN B
SEPT. 18, 19
RECUERDOS
ANTONIA RUIZ
12-6-1944 — 10-1-1994

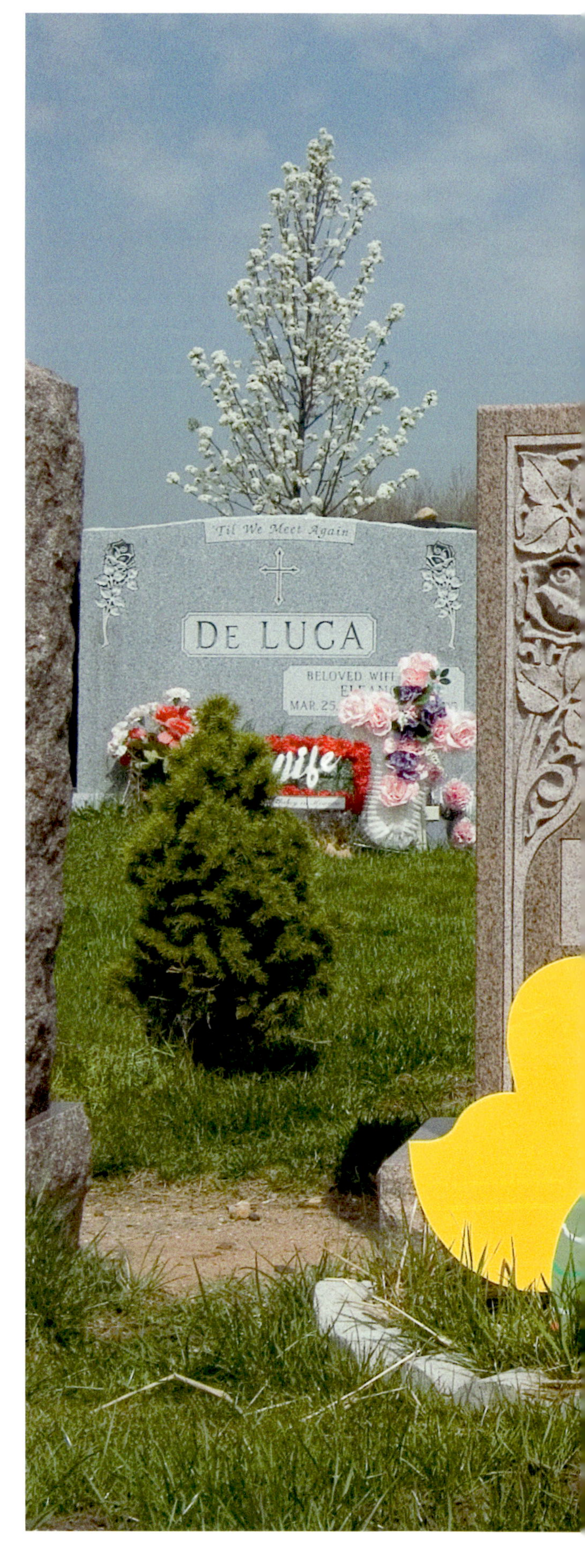

#29

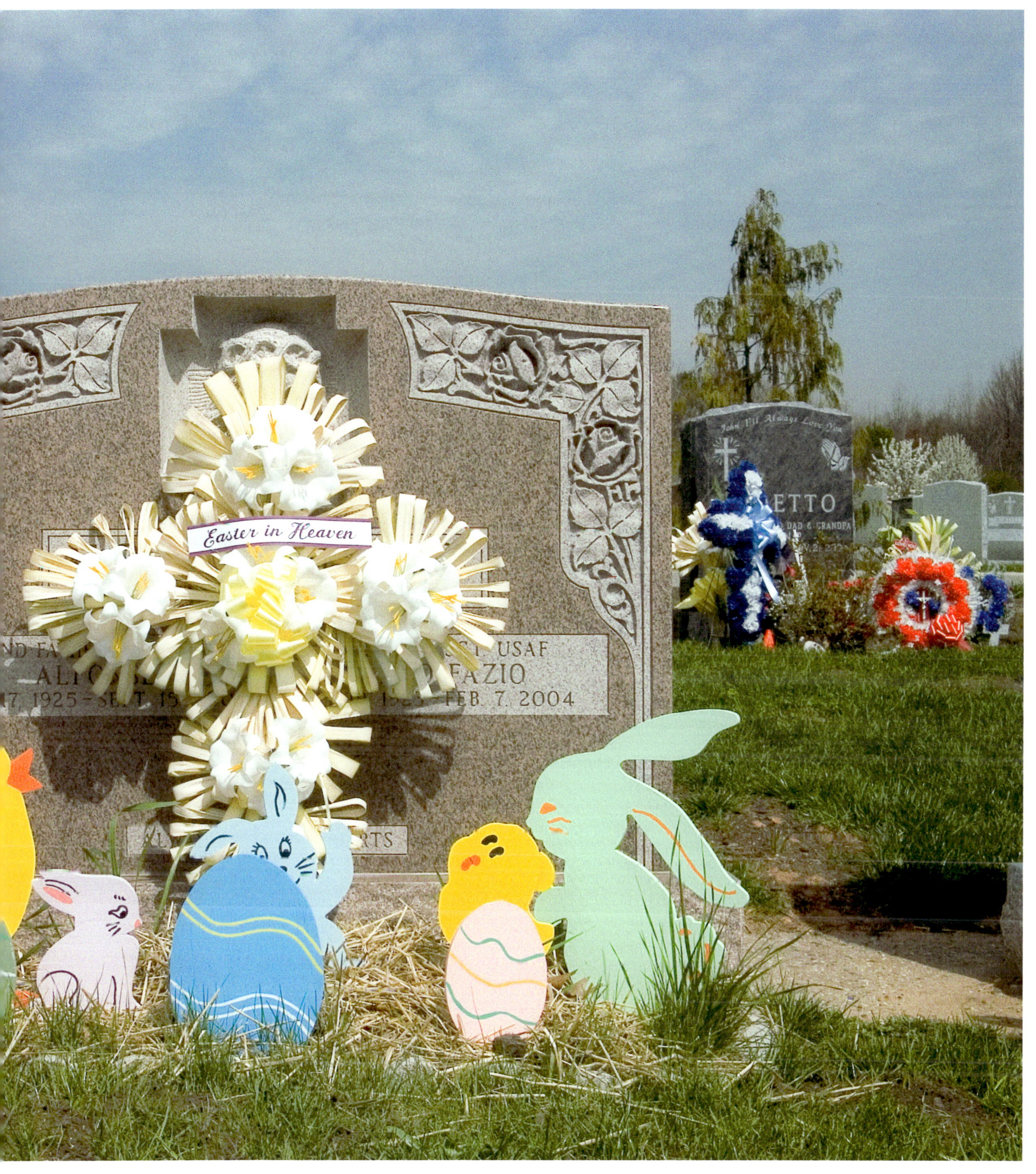
Easter in Heaven
USAF
FAZIO
FEB. 7, 2004
ETTO
John I'll Always Love You
DAD & GRANDPA

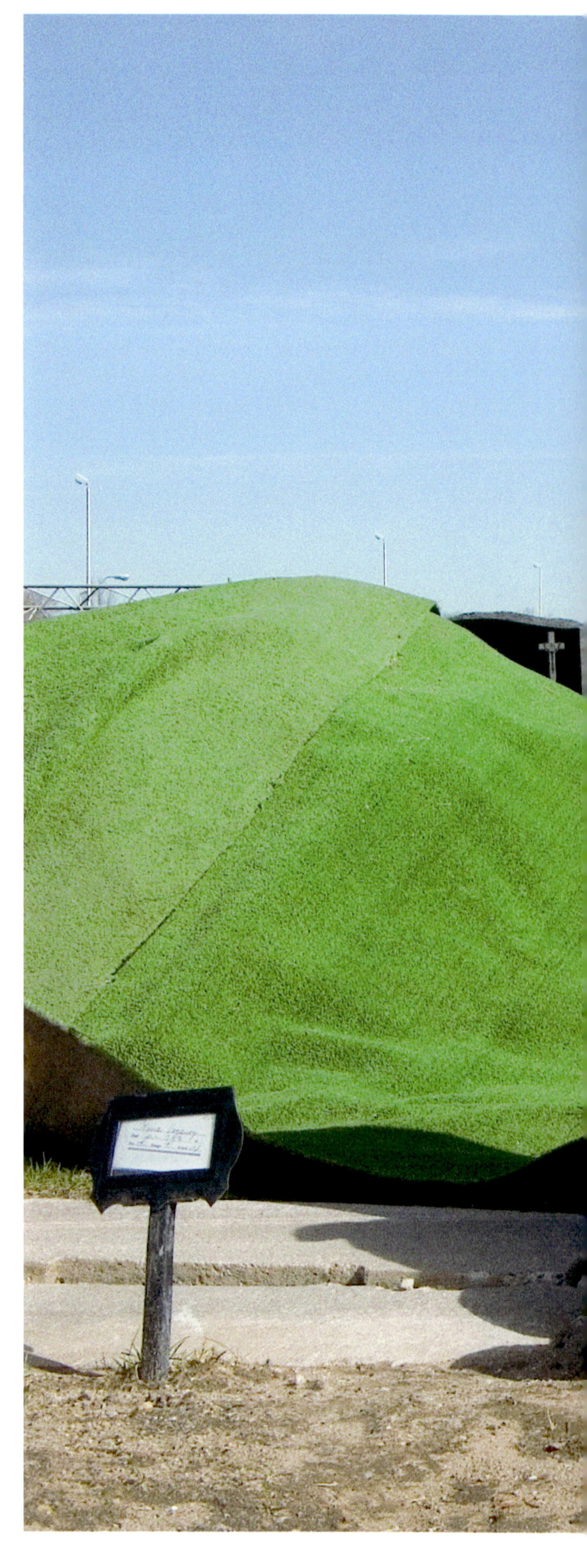

#30

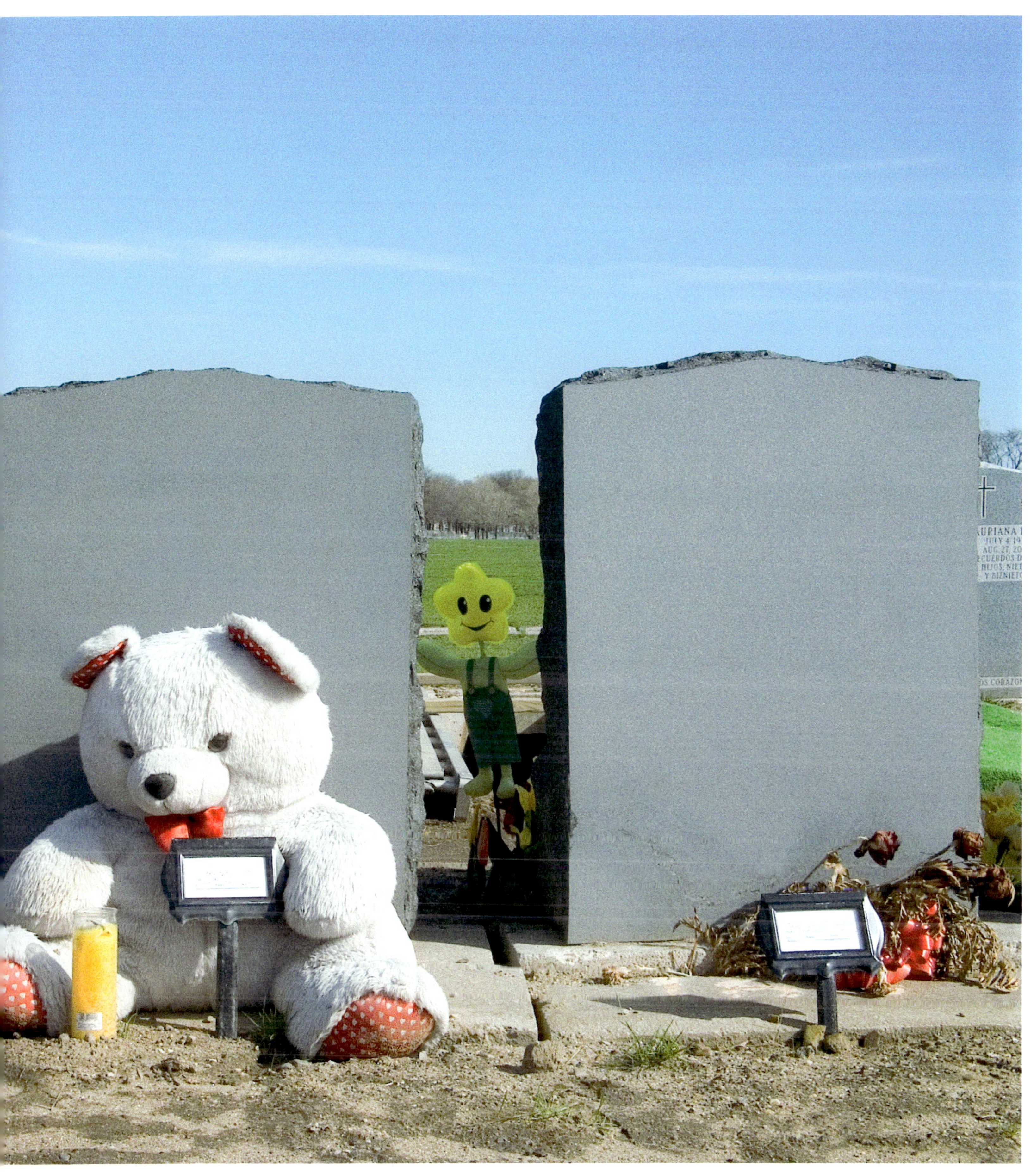

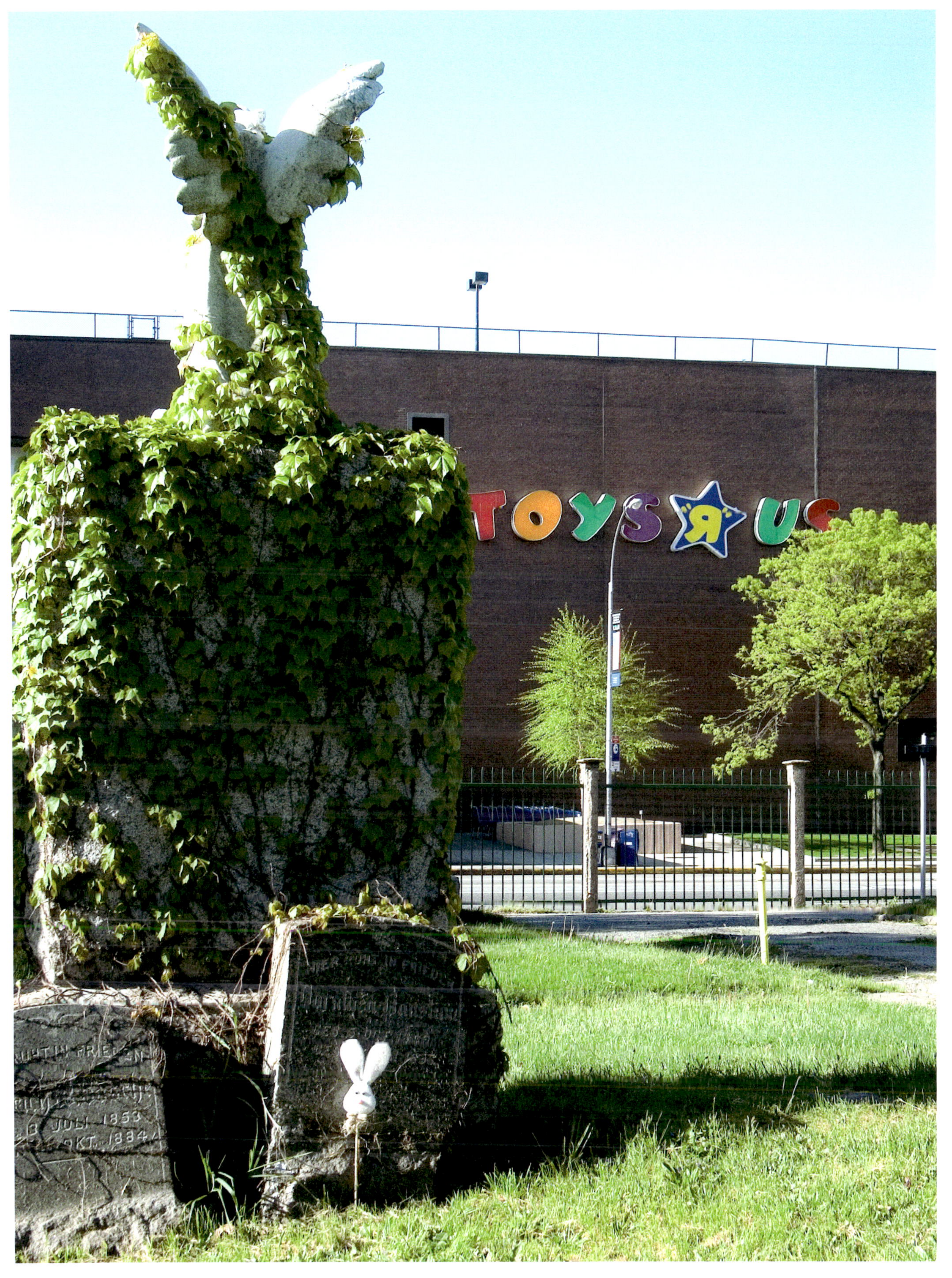

#31

VALDIVIELSO
FRANSICO
1894 — 1980
VINCENTA
1895 —
REST IN PEACE
DALY
THOMAS
1917 — 1980
HOY

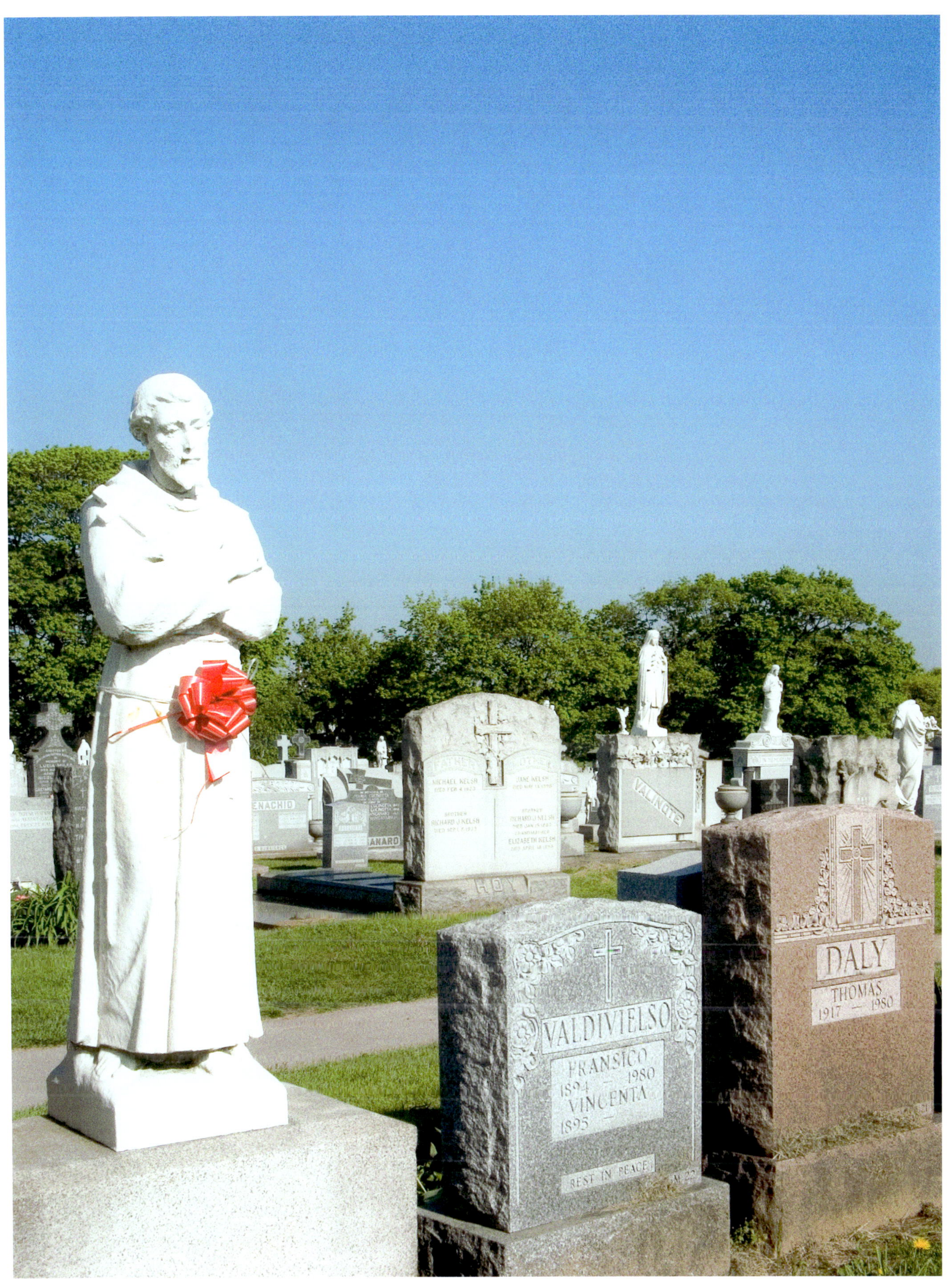

#32A

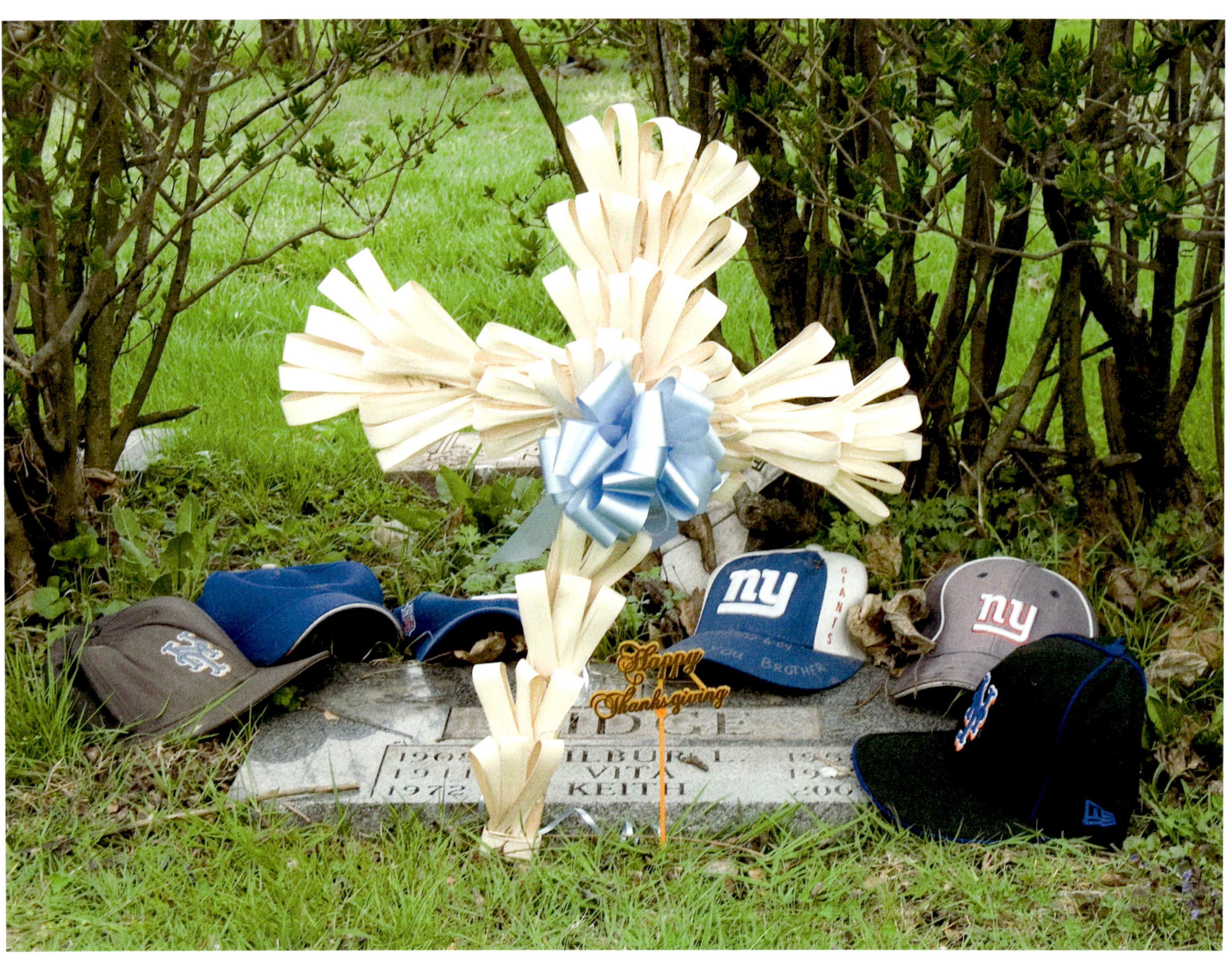

#33

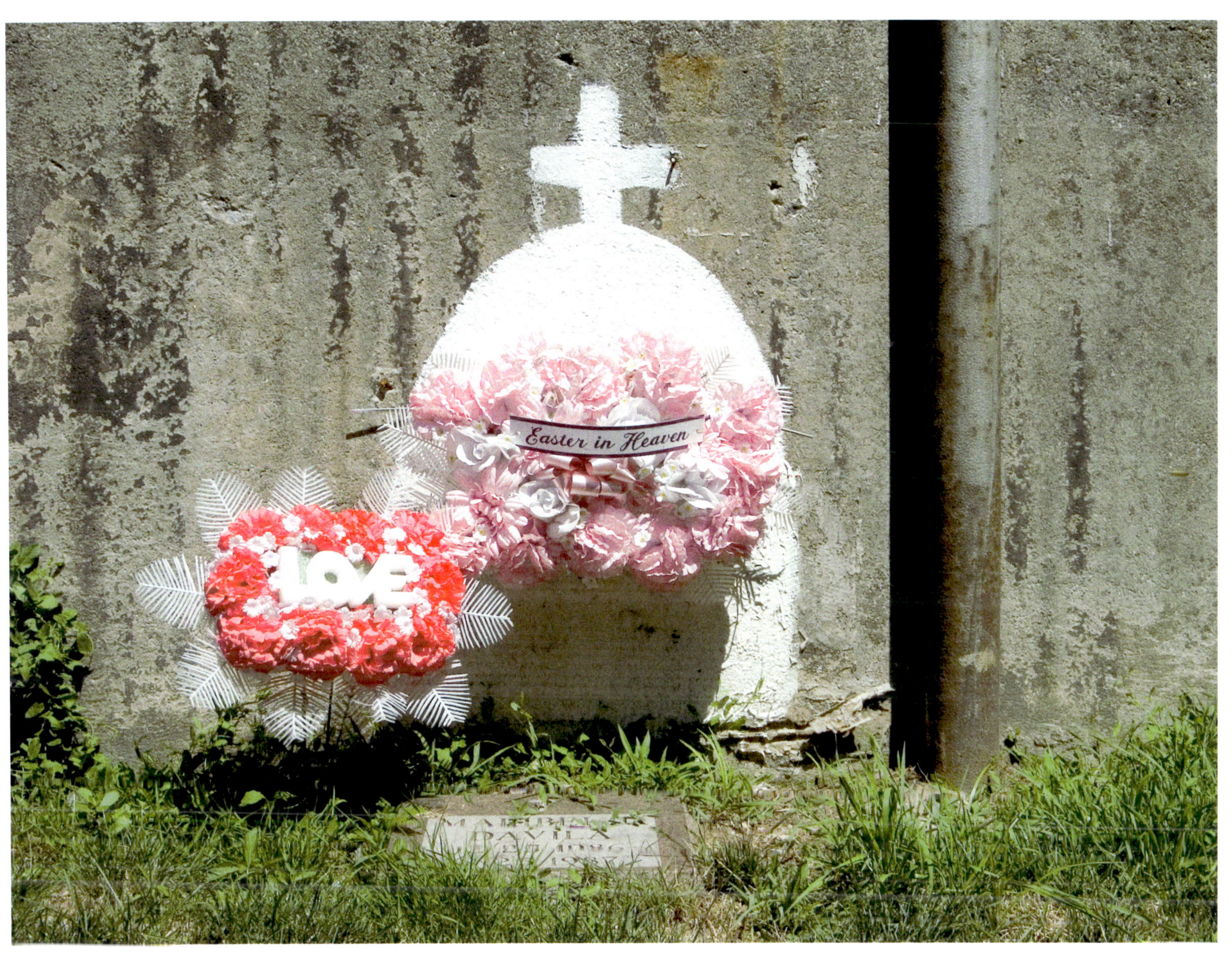

#34

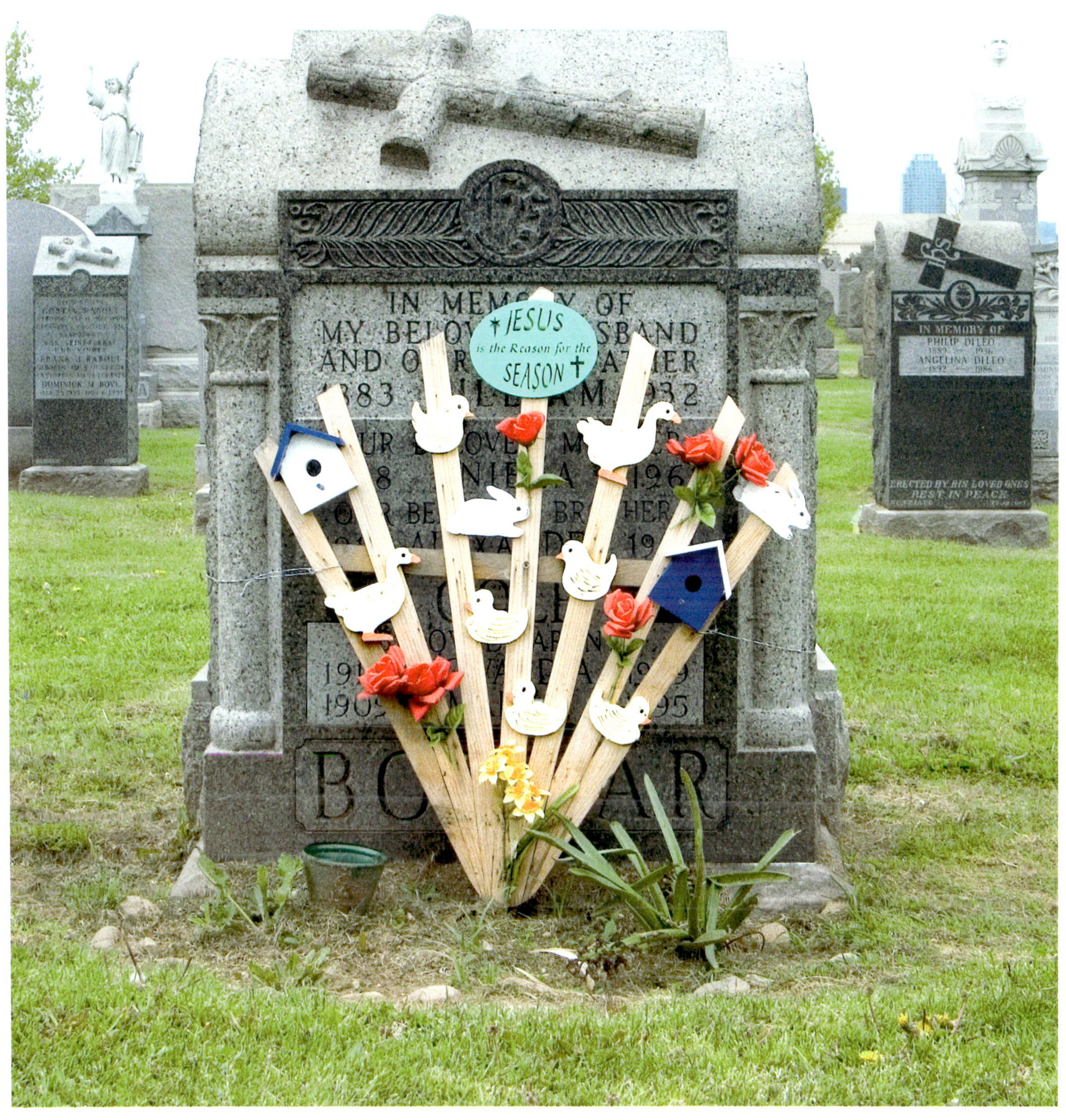
JESUS
is the Reason for the
SEASON
IN MEMORY OF
PHILIP DILEO
ANGELINA DILEO
ERECTED BY HIS LOVED ONES
REST IN PEACE

#35

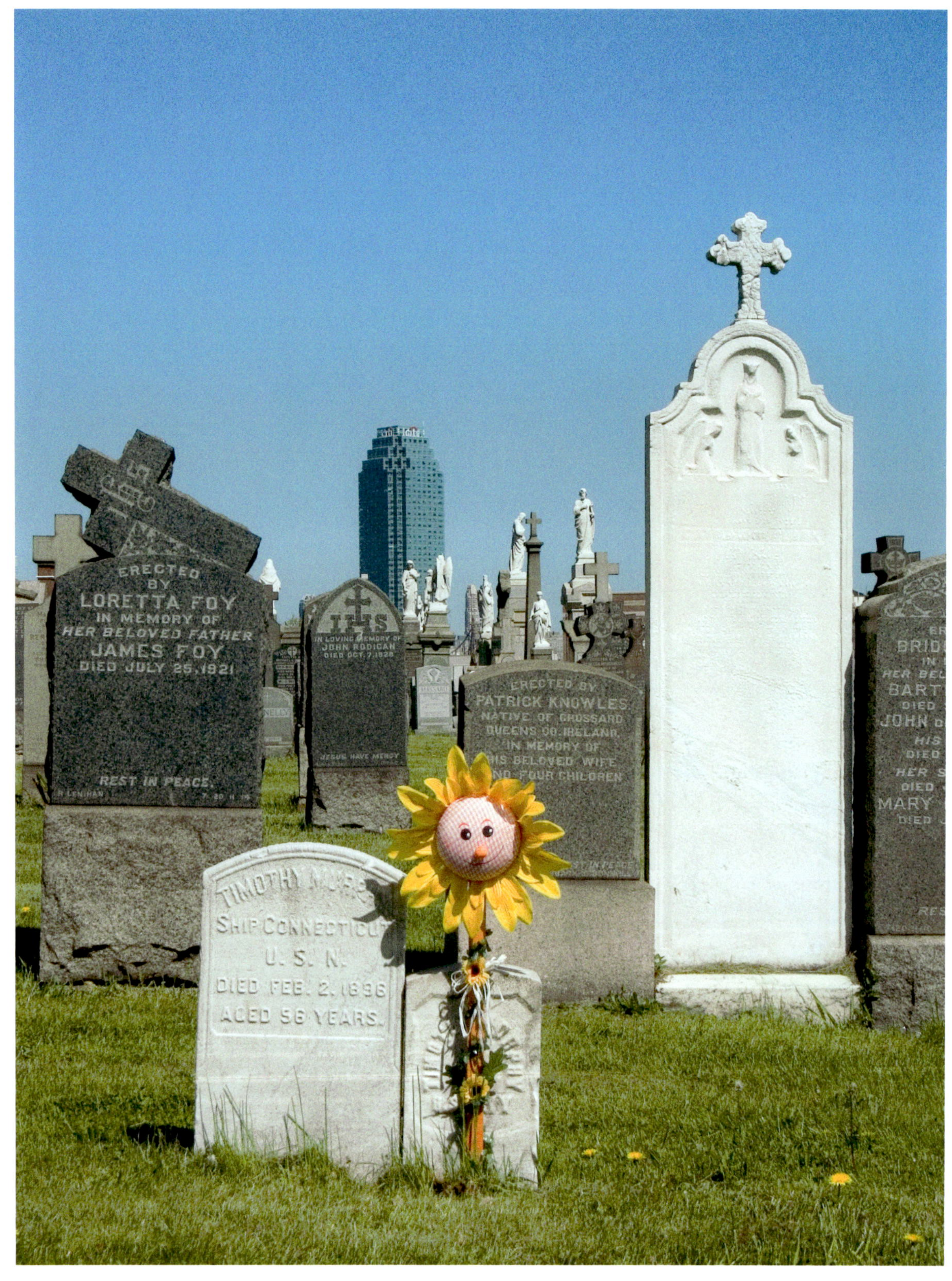
ERECTED
BY
LORETTA FOY
IN MEMORY OF
HER BELOVED FATHER
JAMES FOY
DIED JULY 25, 1921
REST IN PEACE.
IHS
JESUS HAVE MERCY
ERECTED BY
PATRICK KNOWLES
IN MEMORY OF
U. S. N.
DIED FEB. 2, 1896
AGED 56 YEARS.

#36

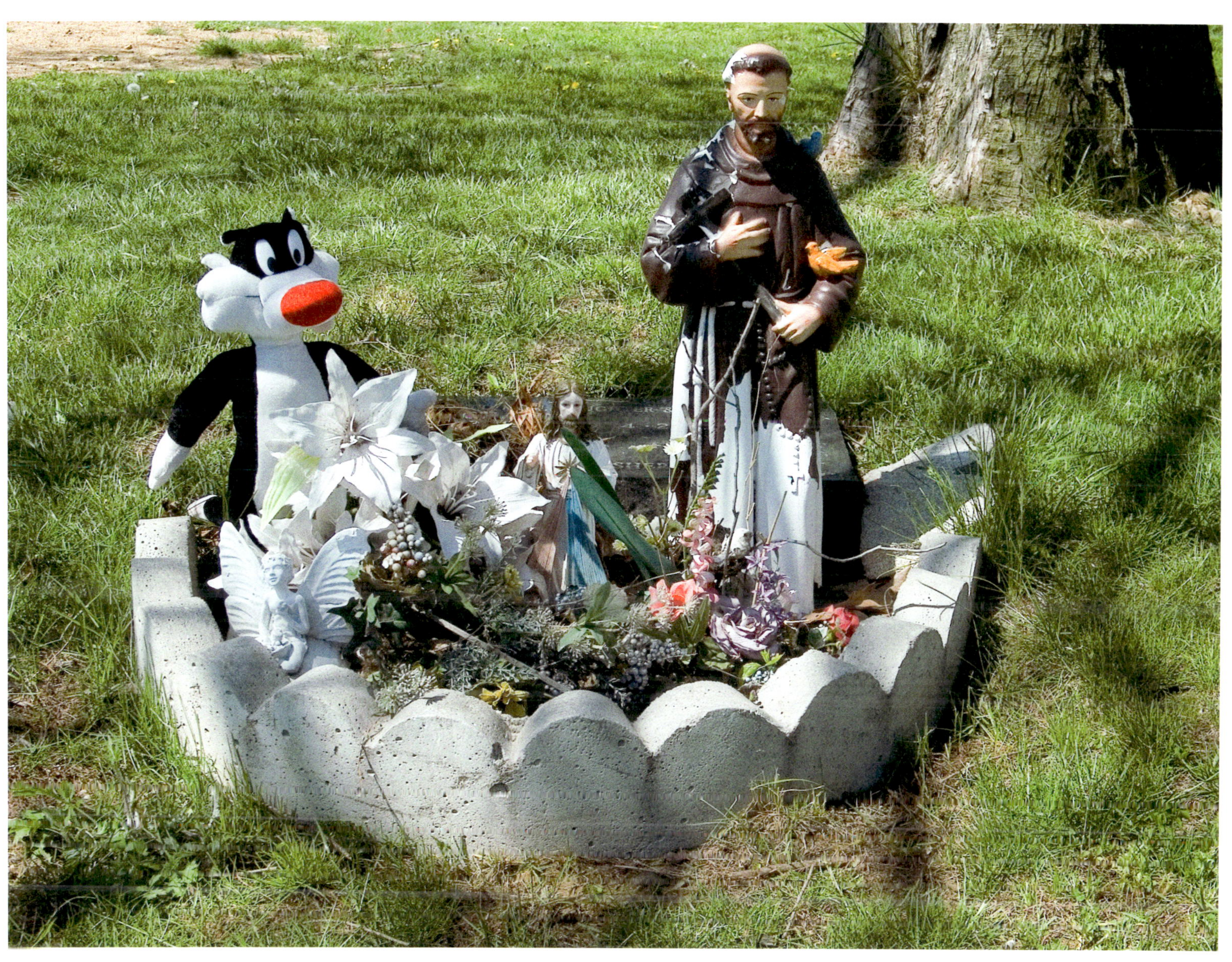

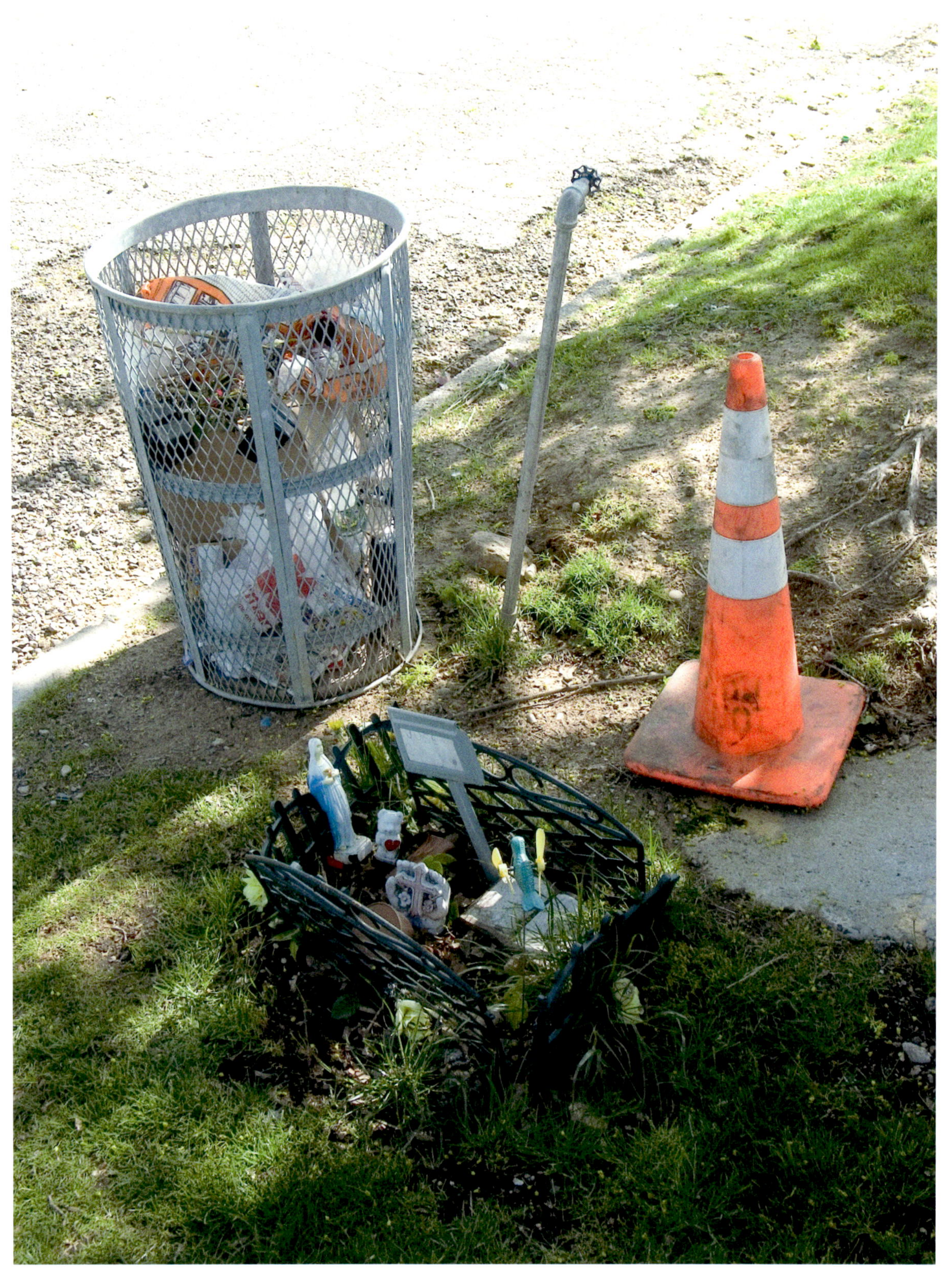

#38

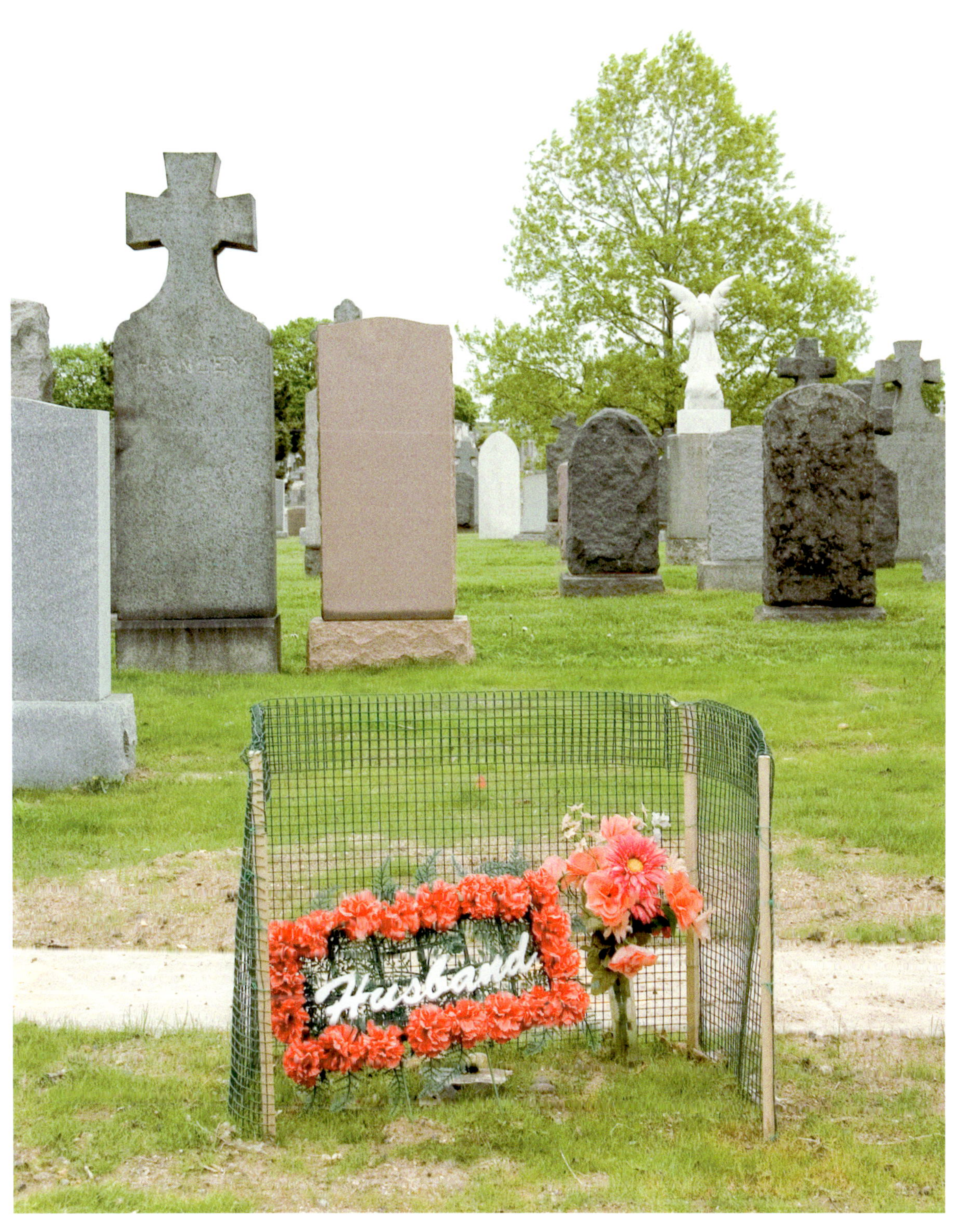
Husband

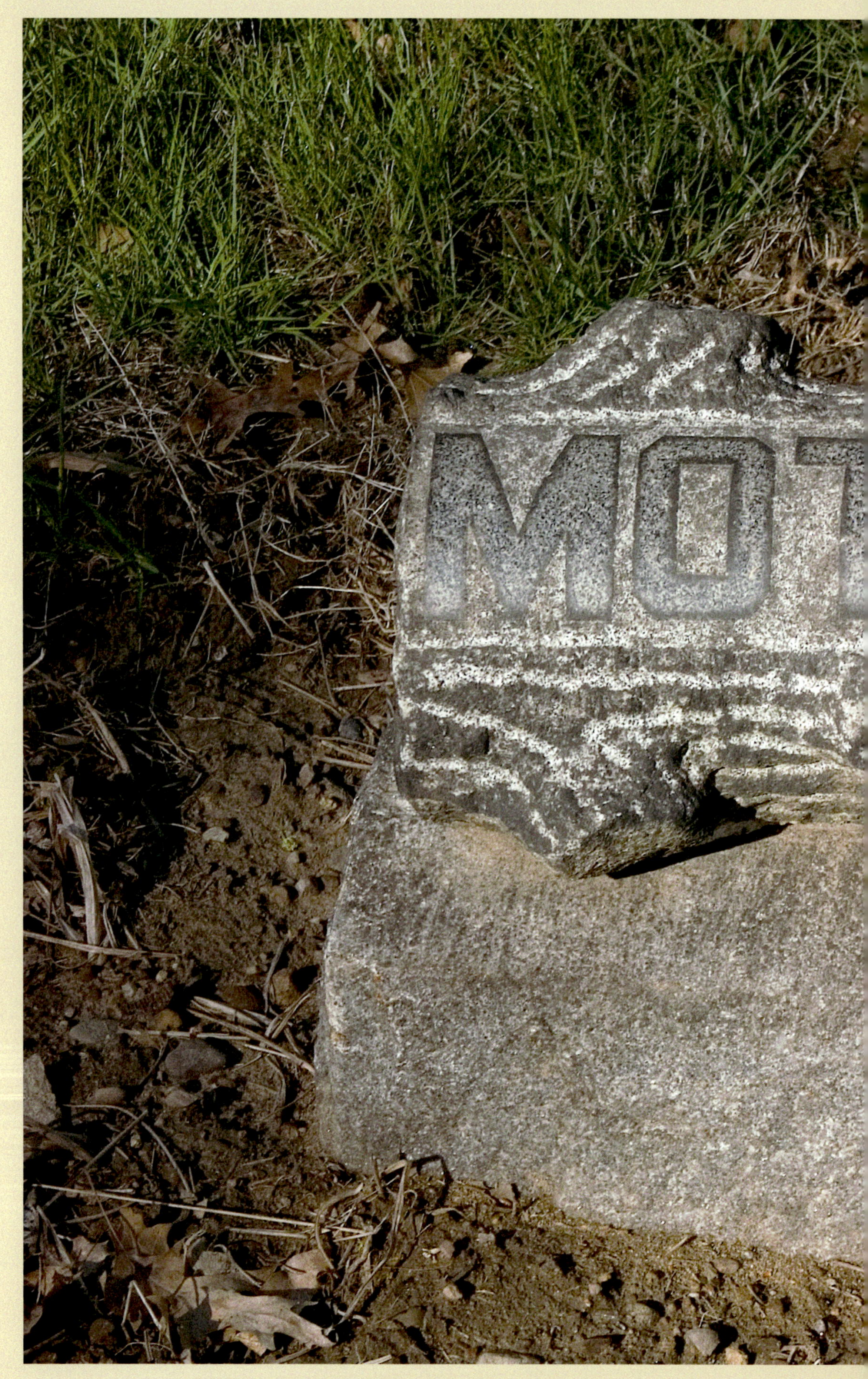

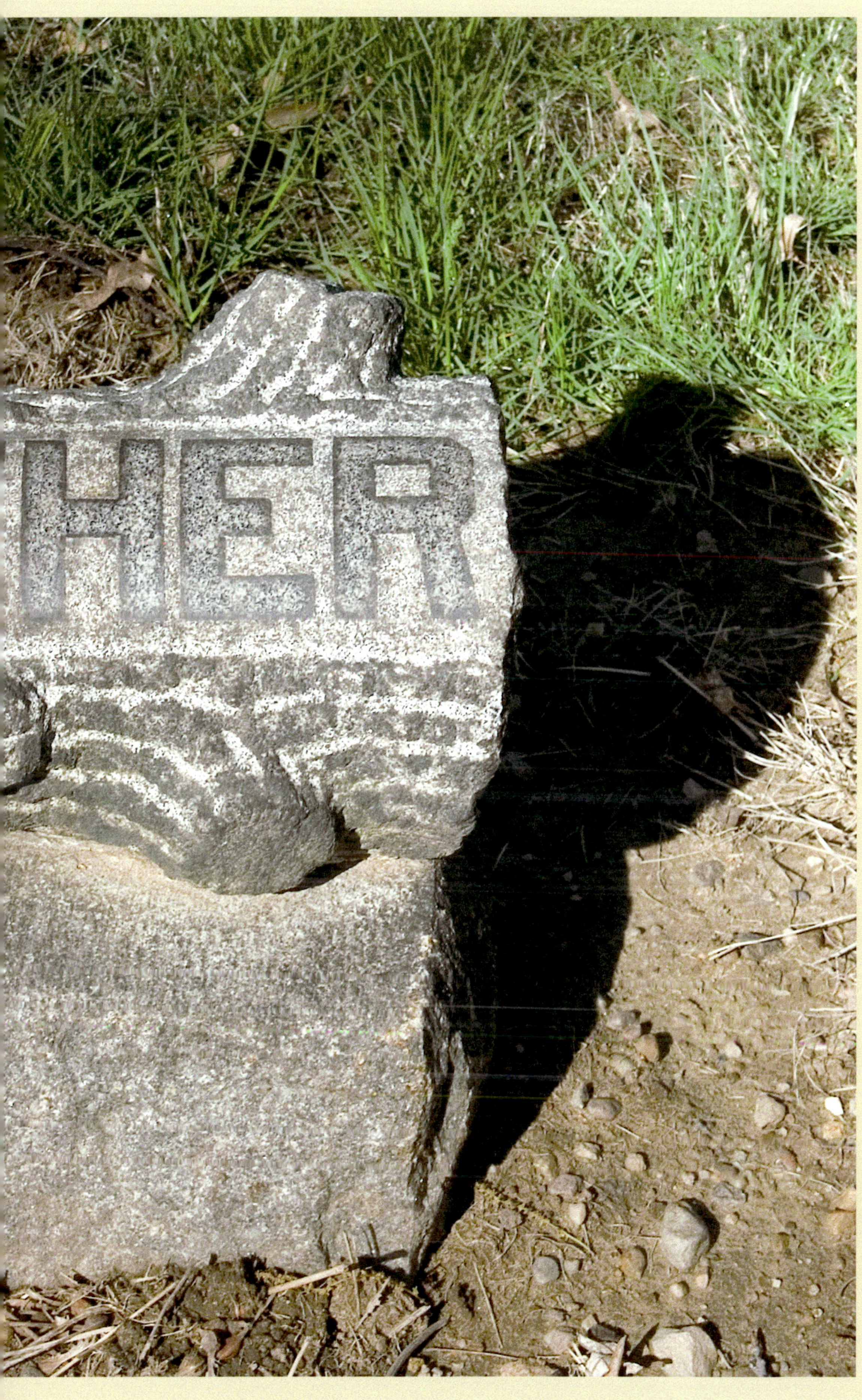
HER

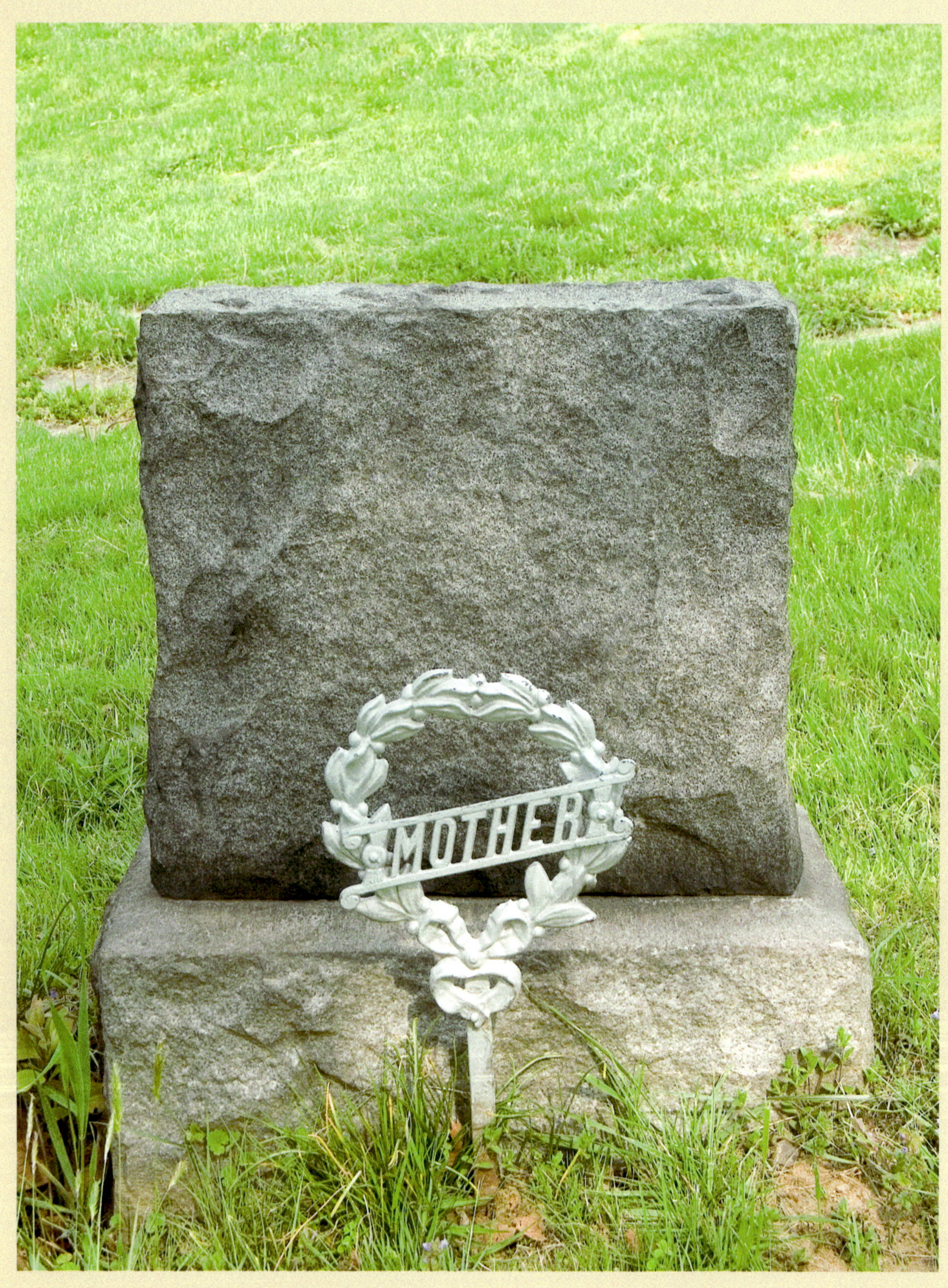
MOTHER

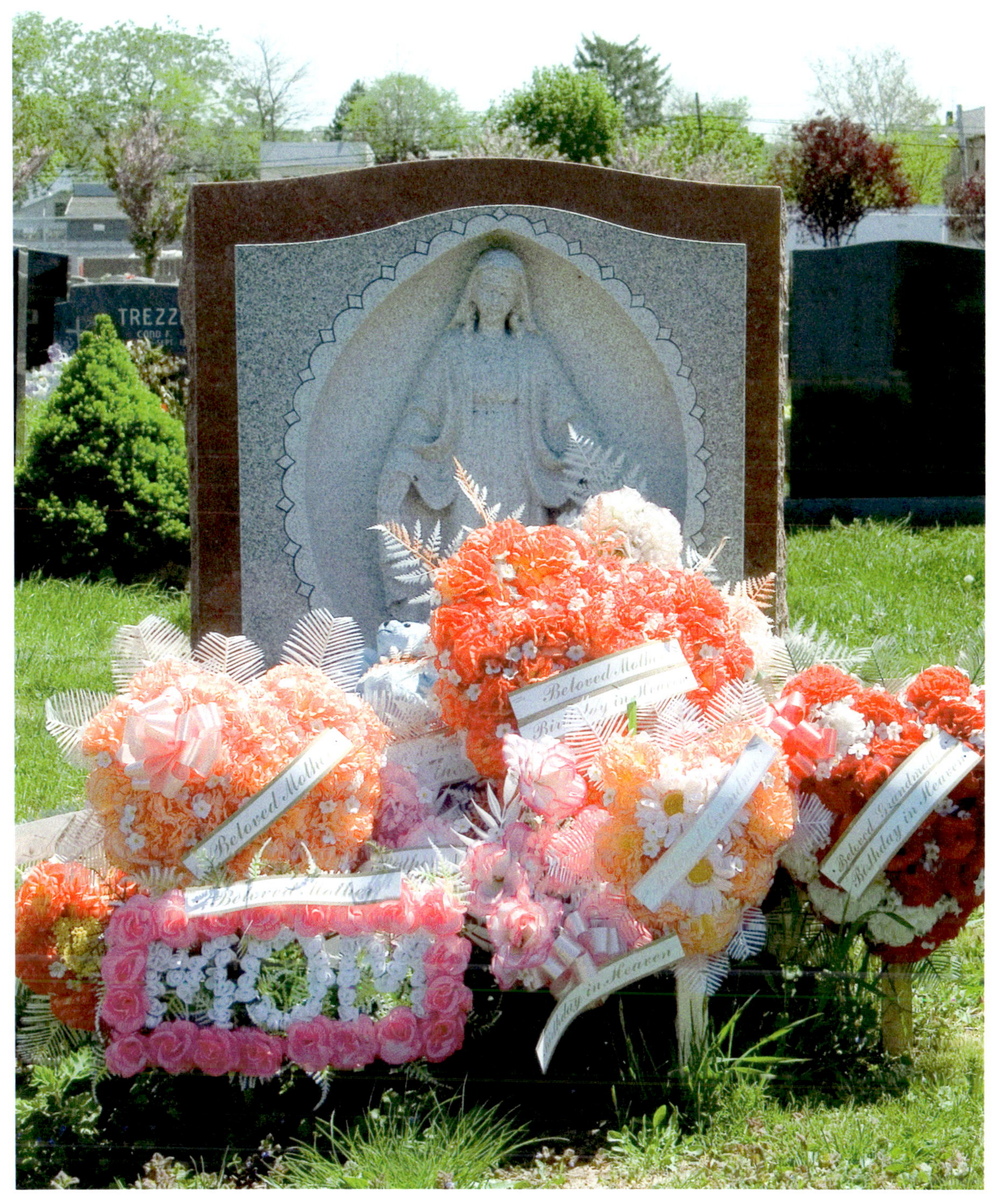
Beloved Mother
MOM
Birthday in Heaven

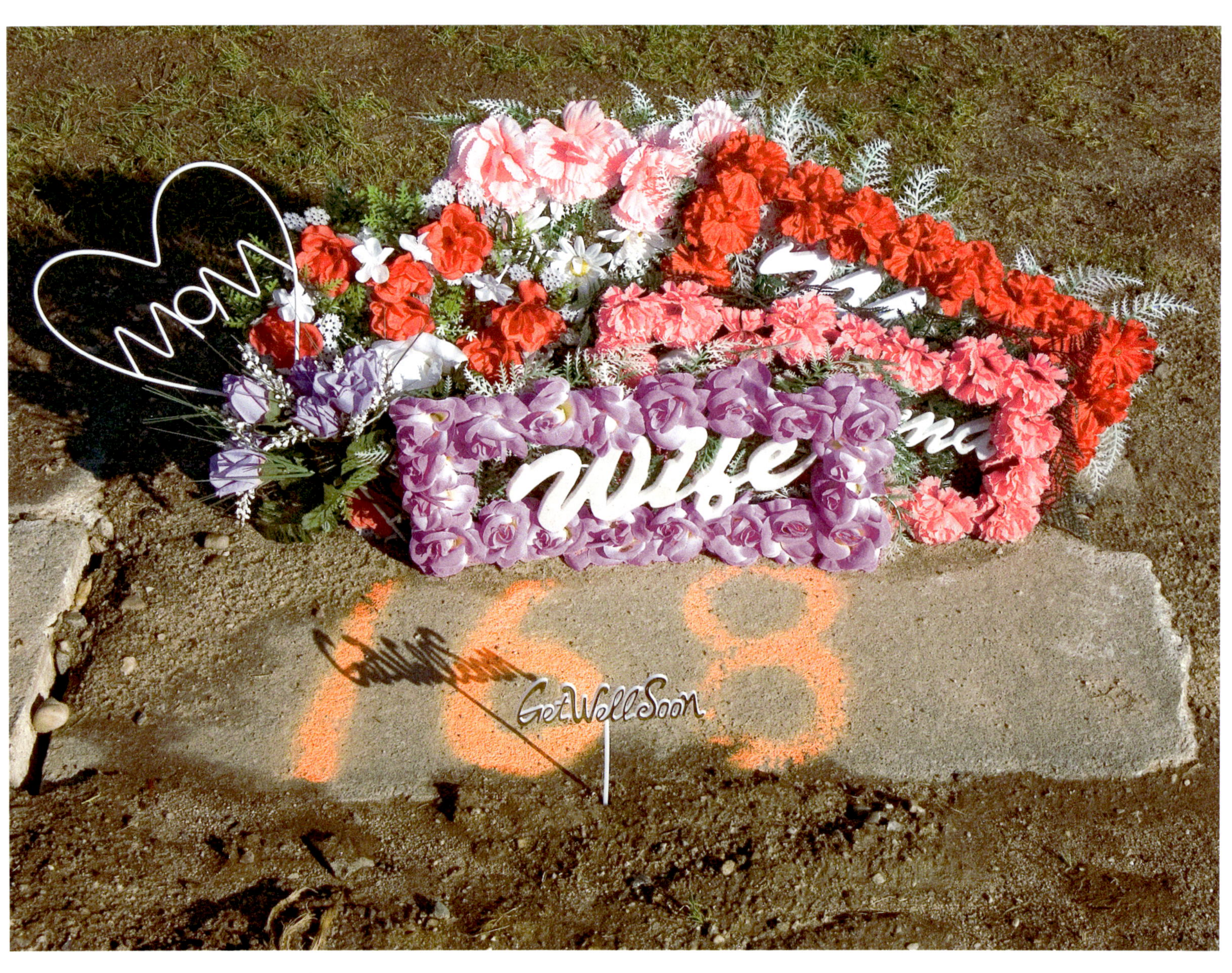

#41

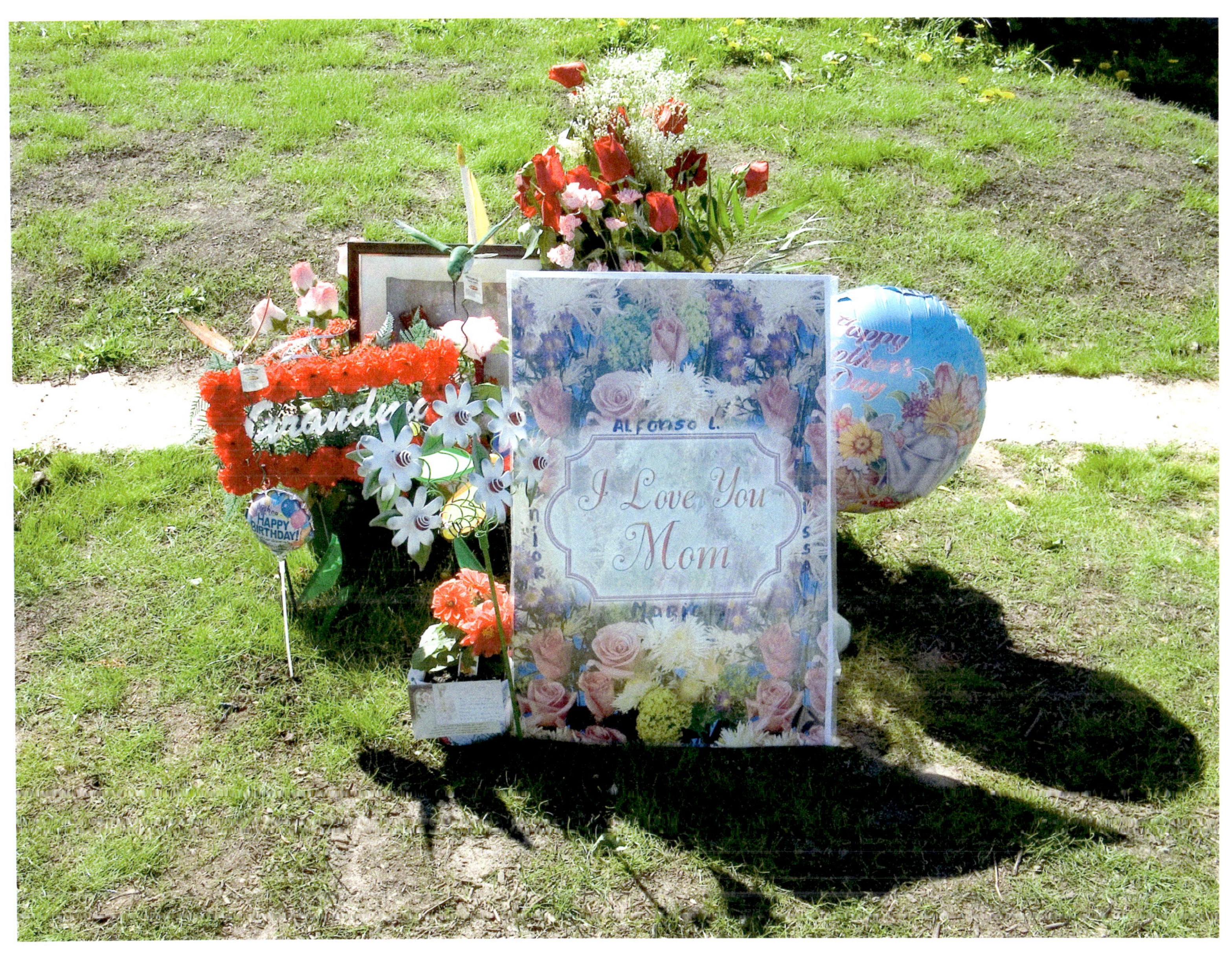

#42

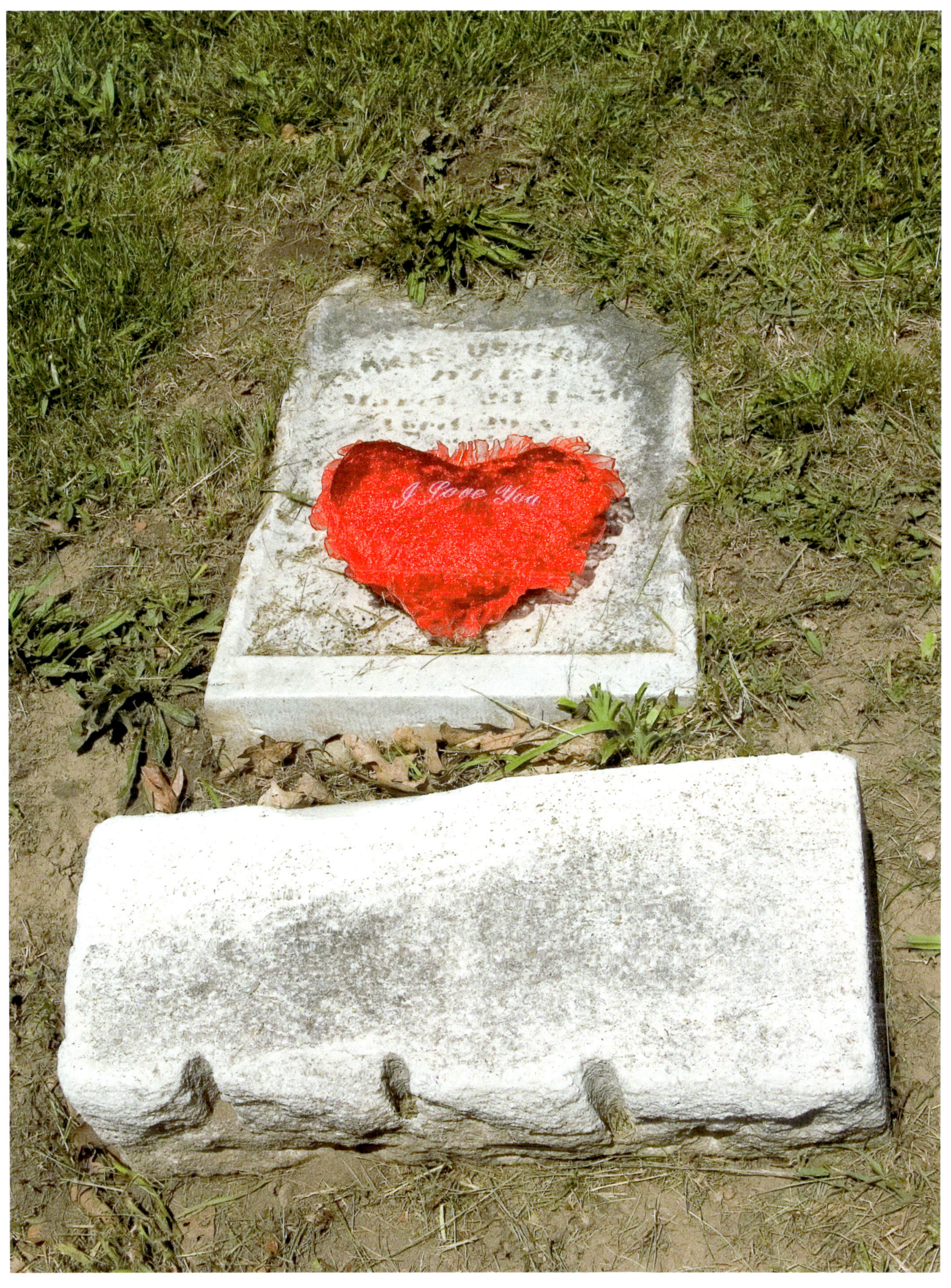

#43

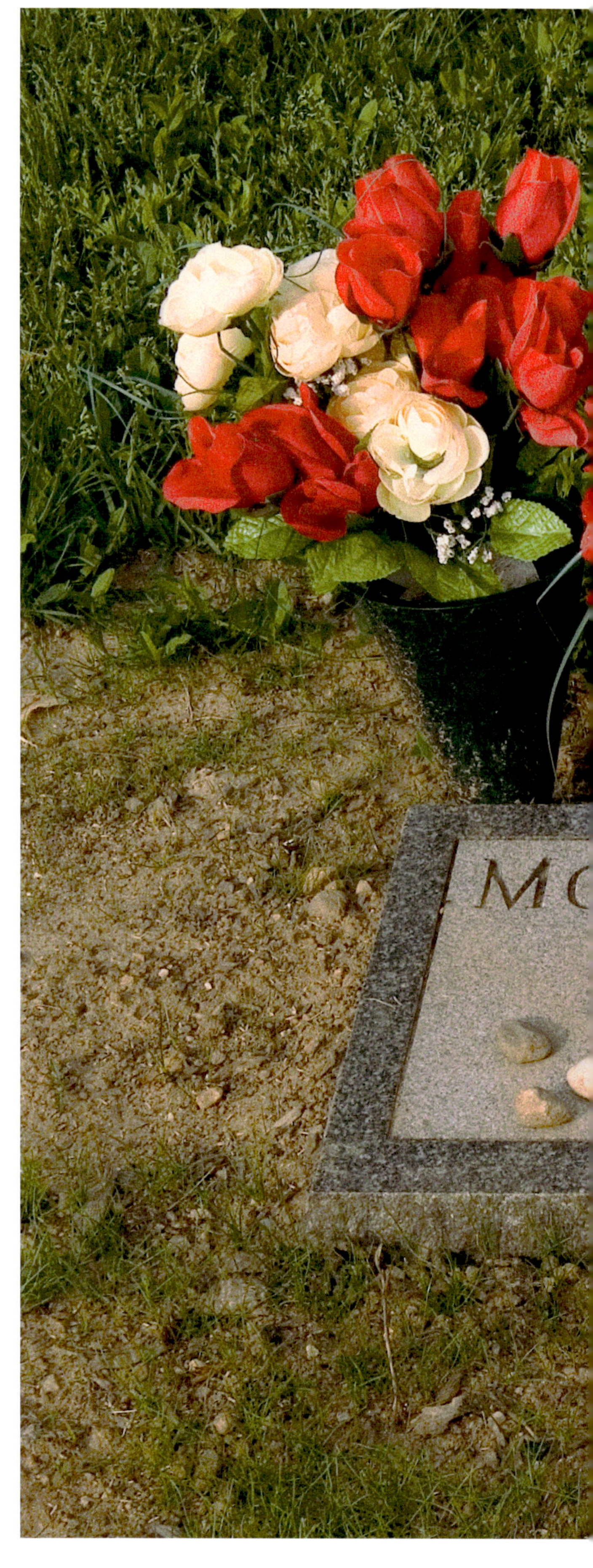

#44

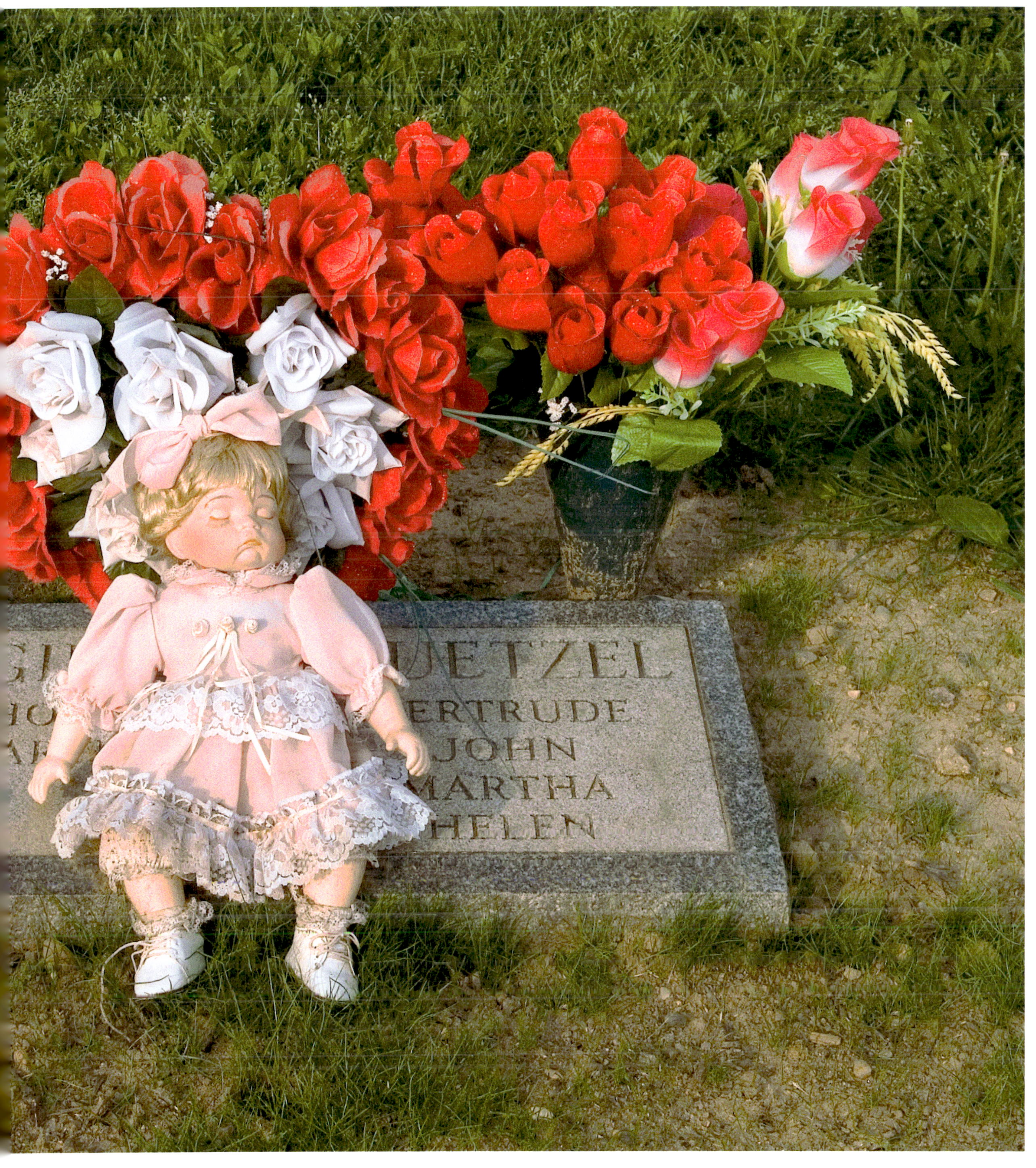
UETZEL
ERTRUDE
JOHN
MARTHA
HELEN

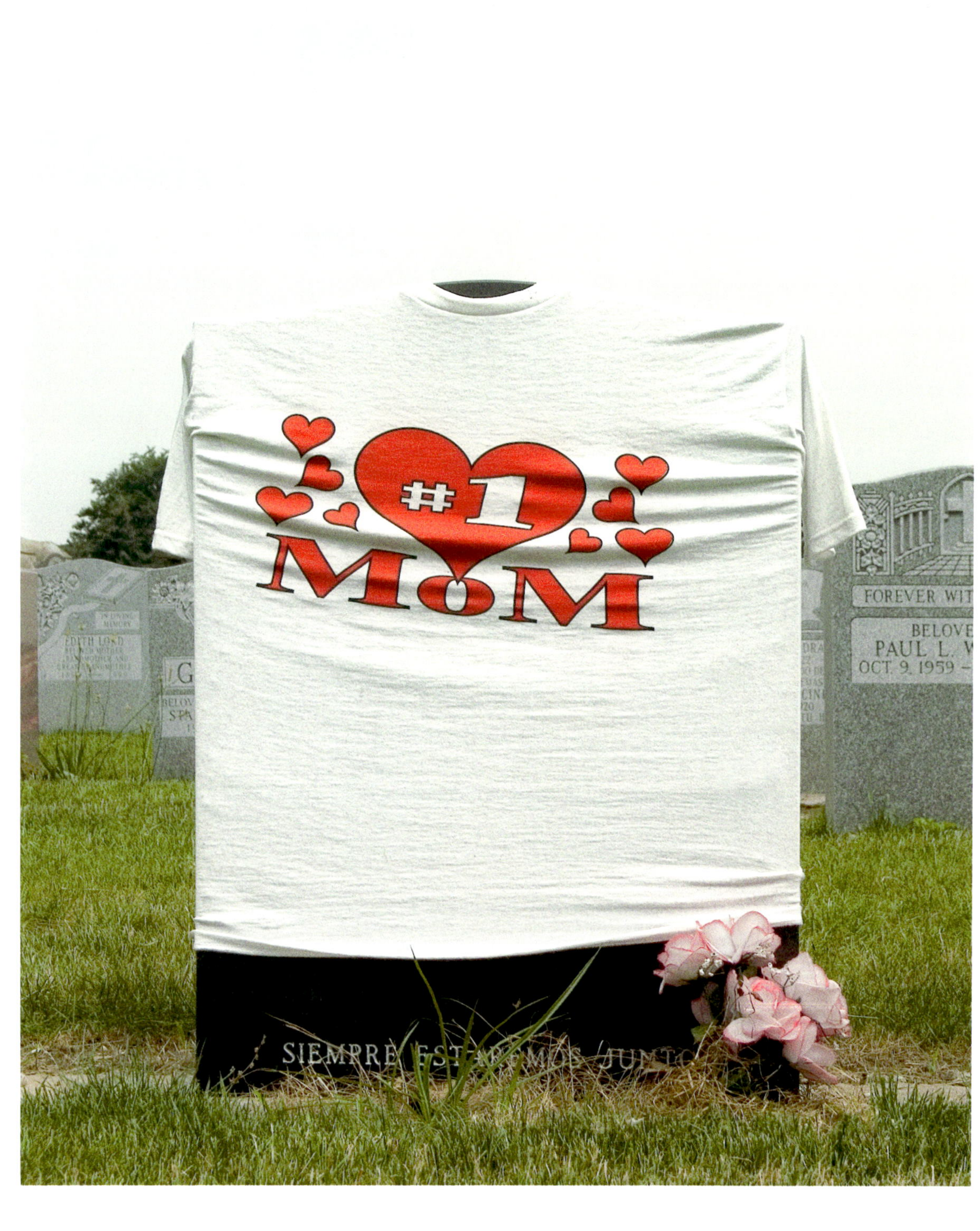

#45

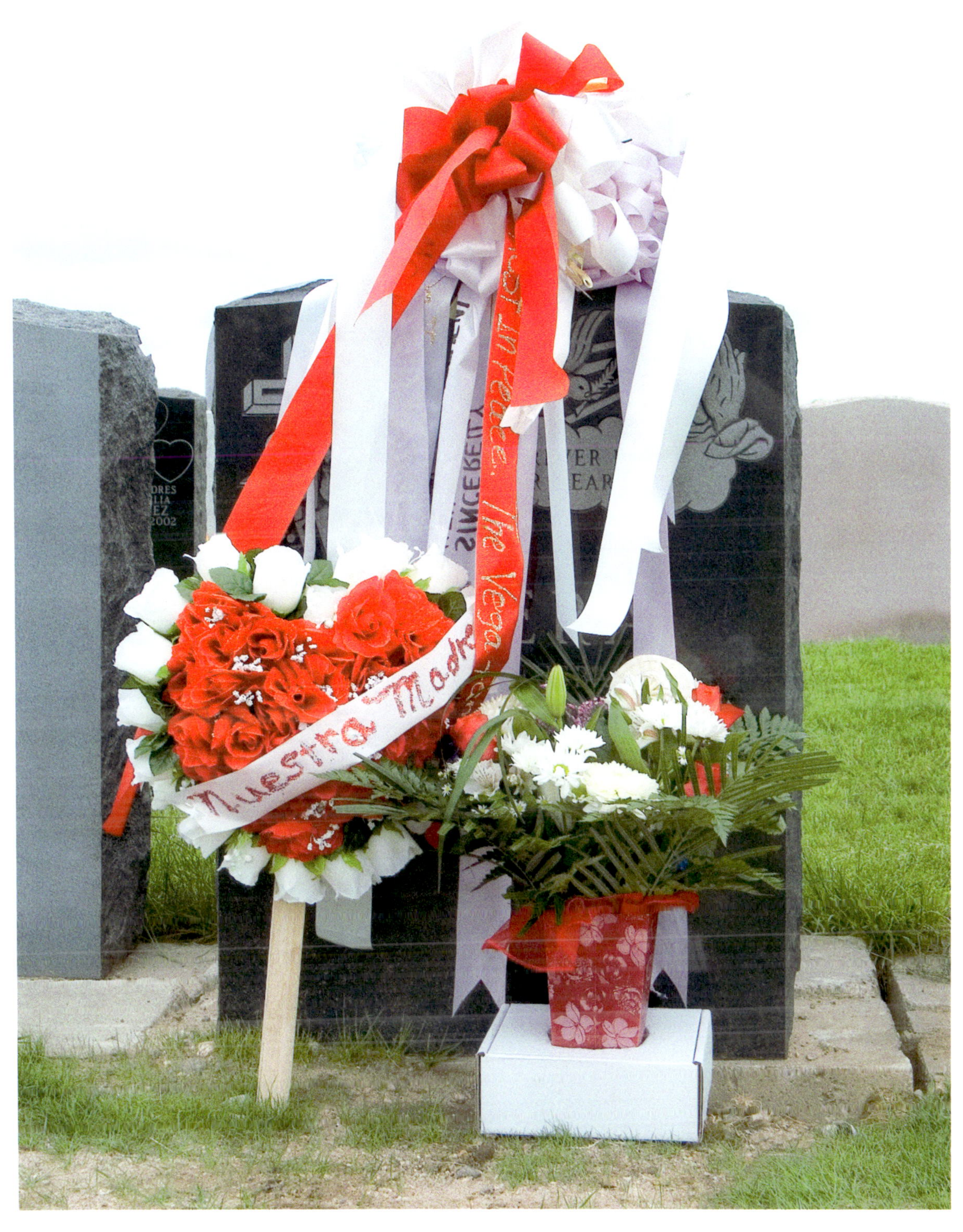

#46

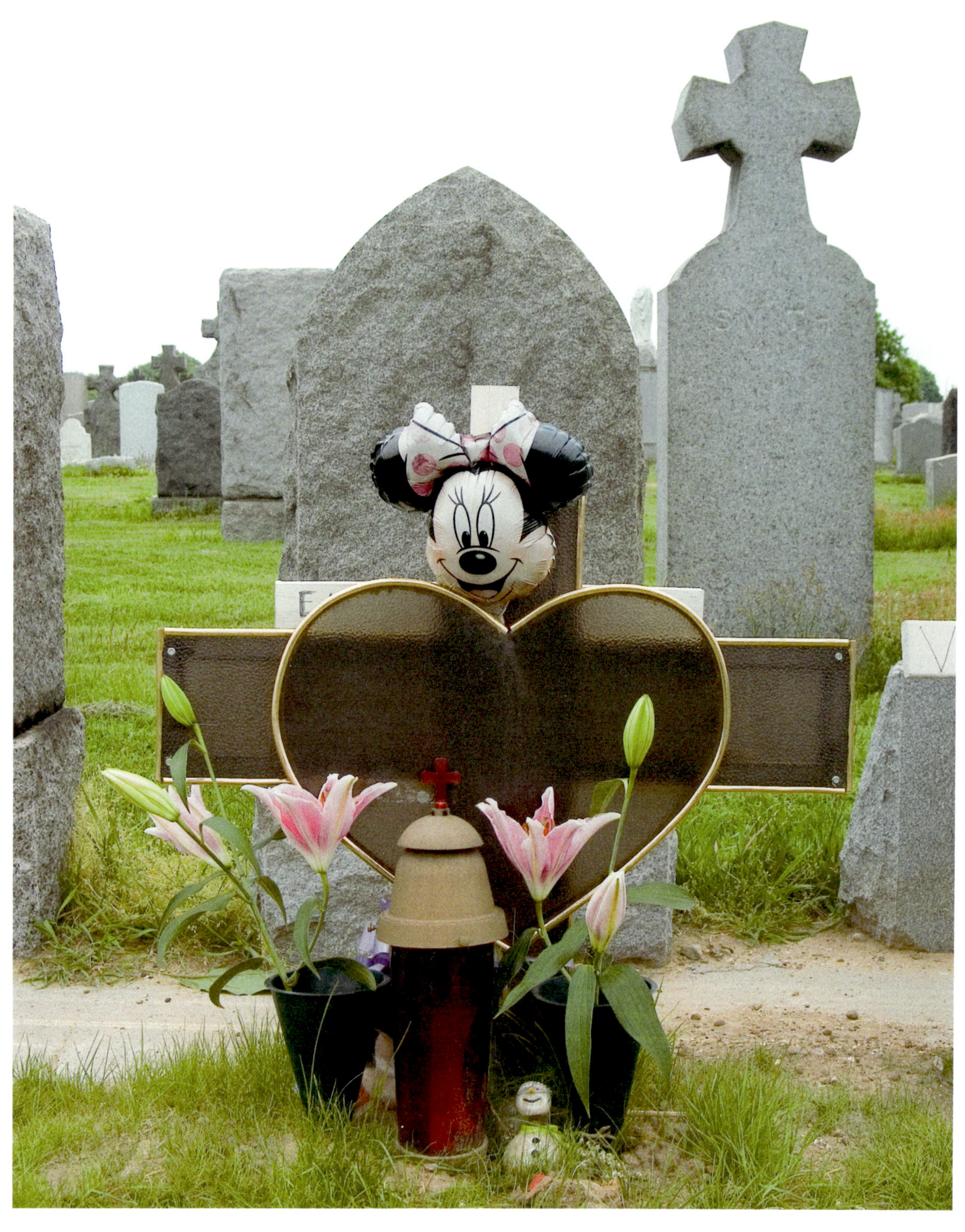

#47

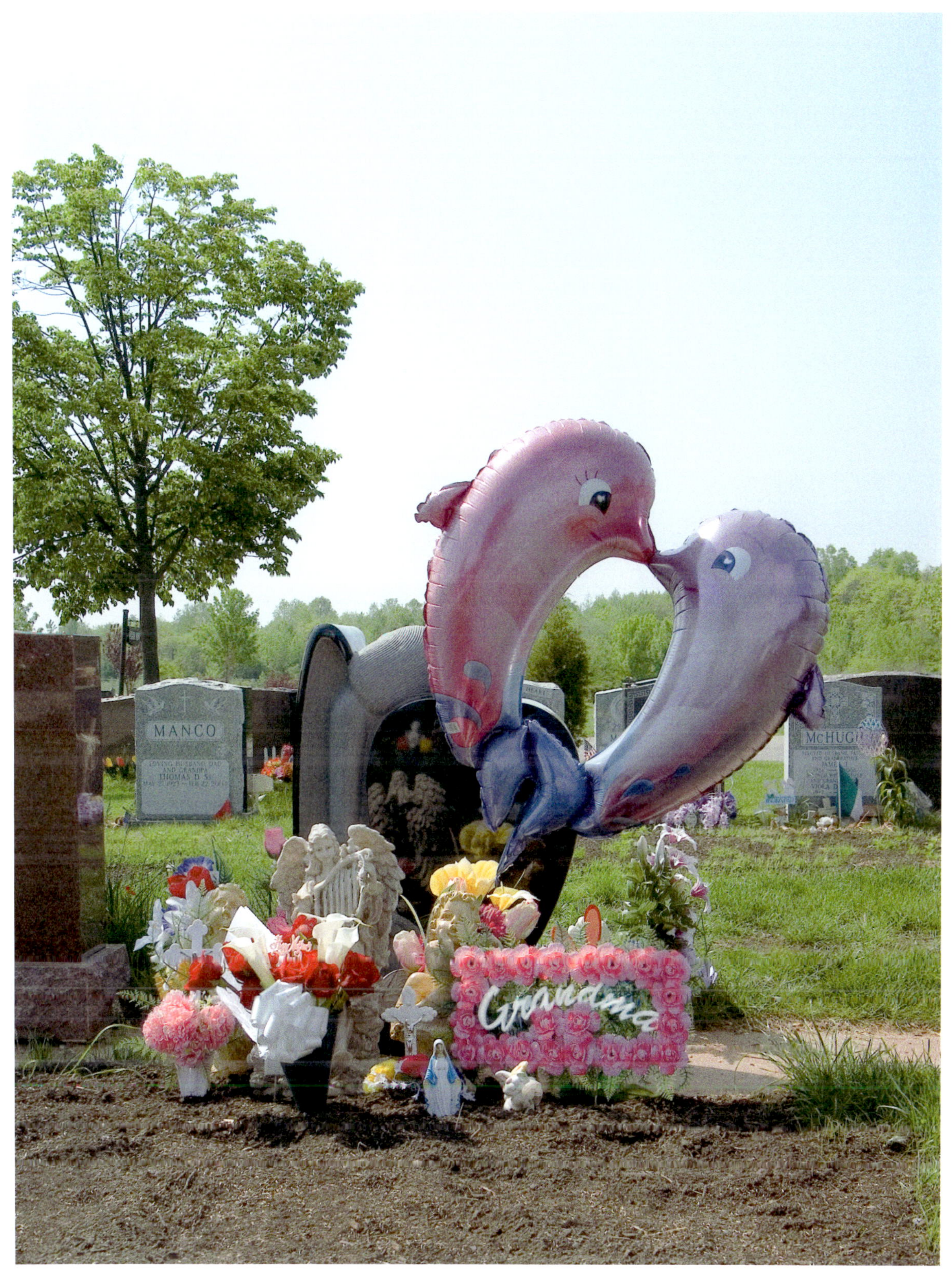
MANCO
Grandma

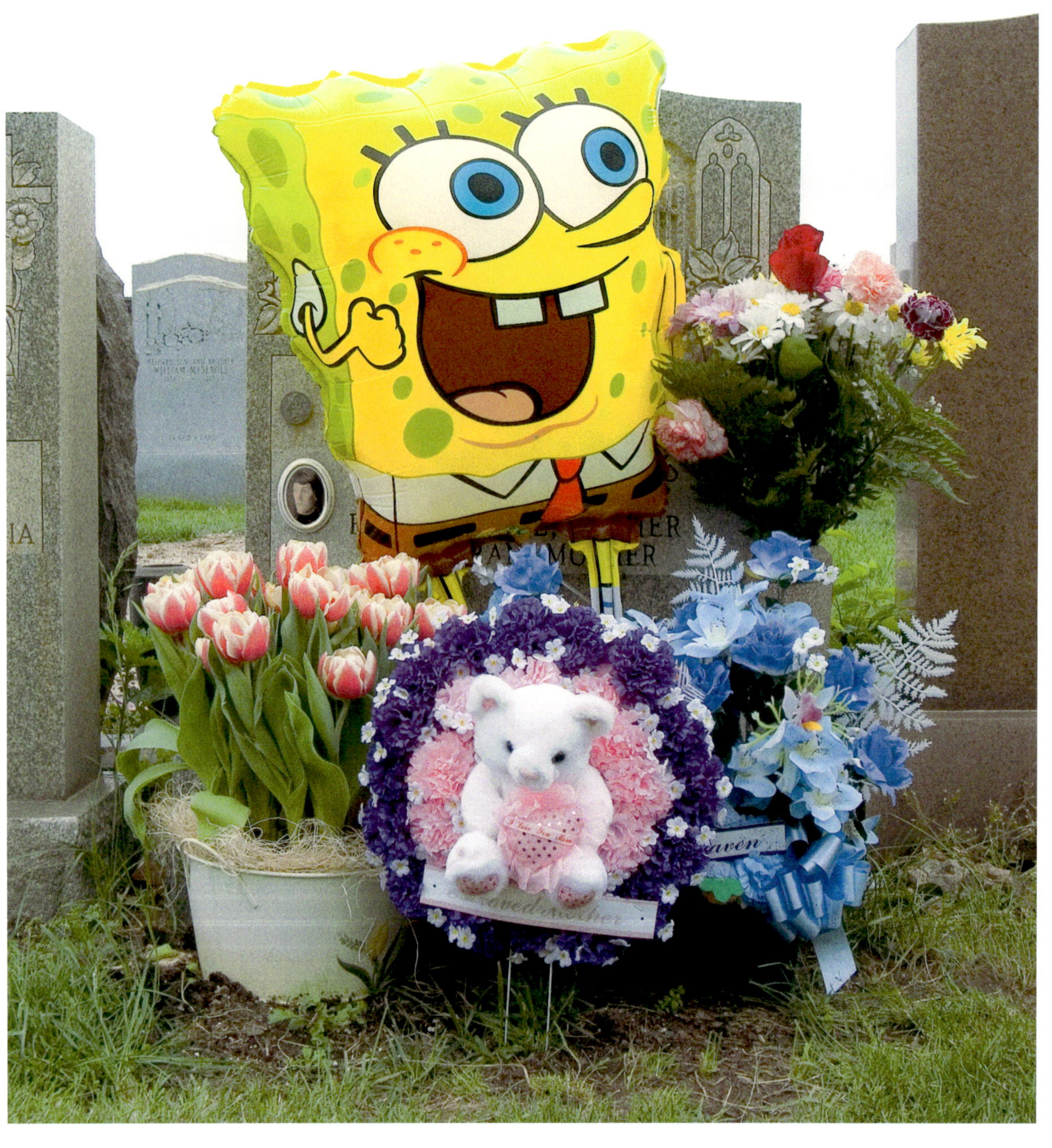

#49

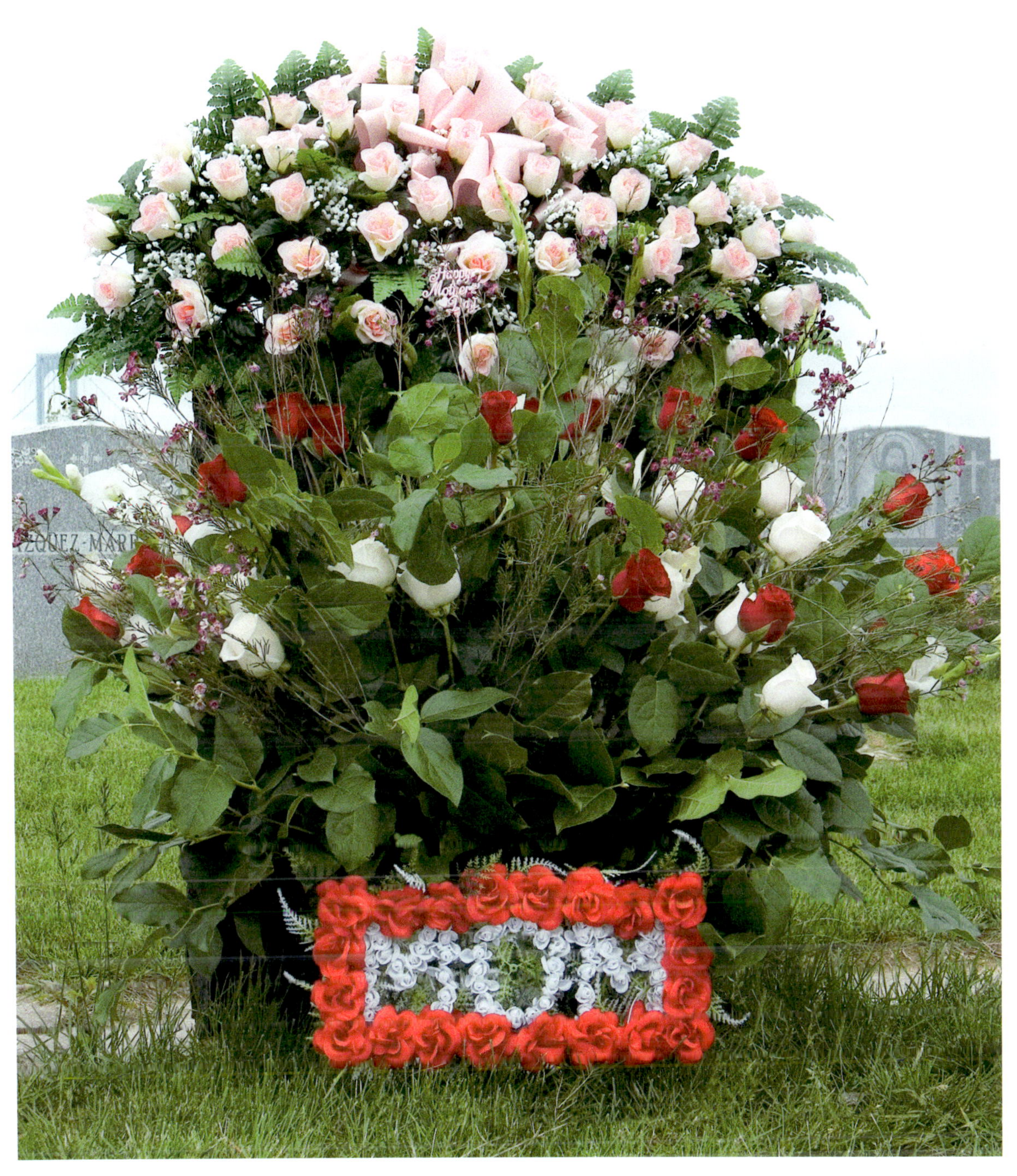

#50

LOVING
IEMORY
) OUR BELC
FATHER
AFAEL BONIL
19·16–2·8·94
OM YOUR BELOVE
OTHER CHILD
COTT LEE OI
19·66–12·1
AMON ANDR
25·47–10·2
LOVED SON, BR
UR HEARTS
I love you
I love you mom
Happy
Happy Mother's
Coors Light

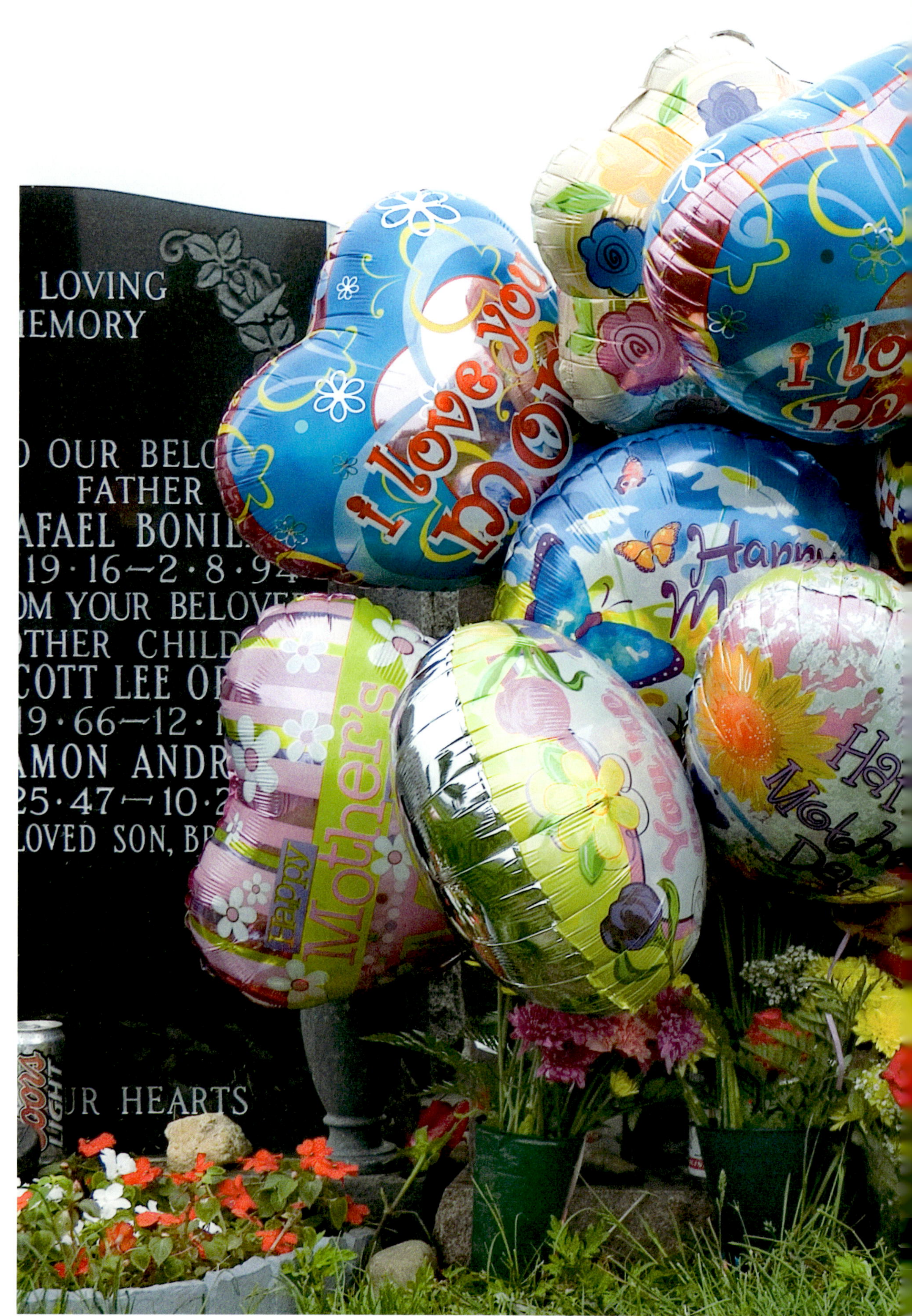

#51

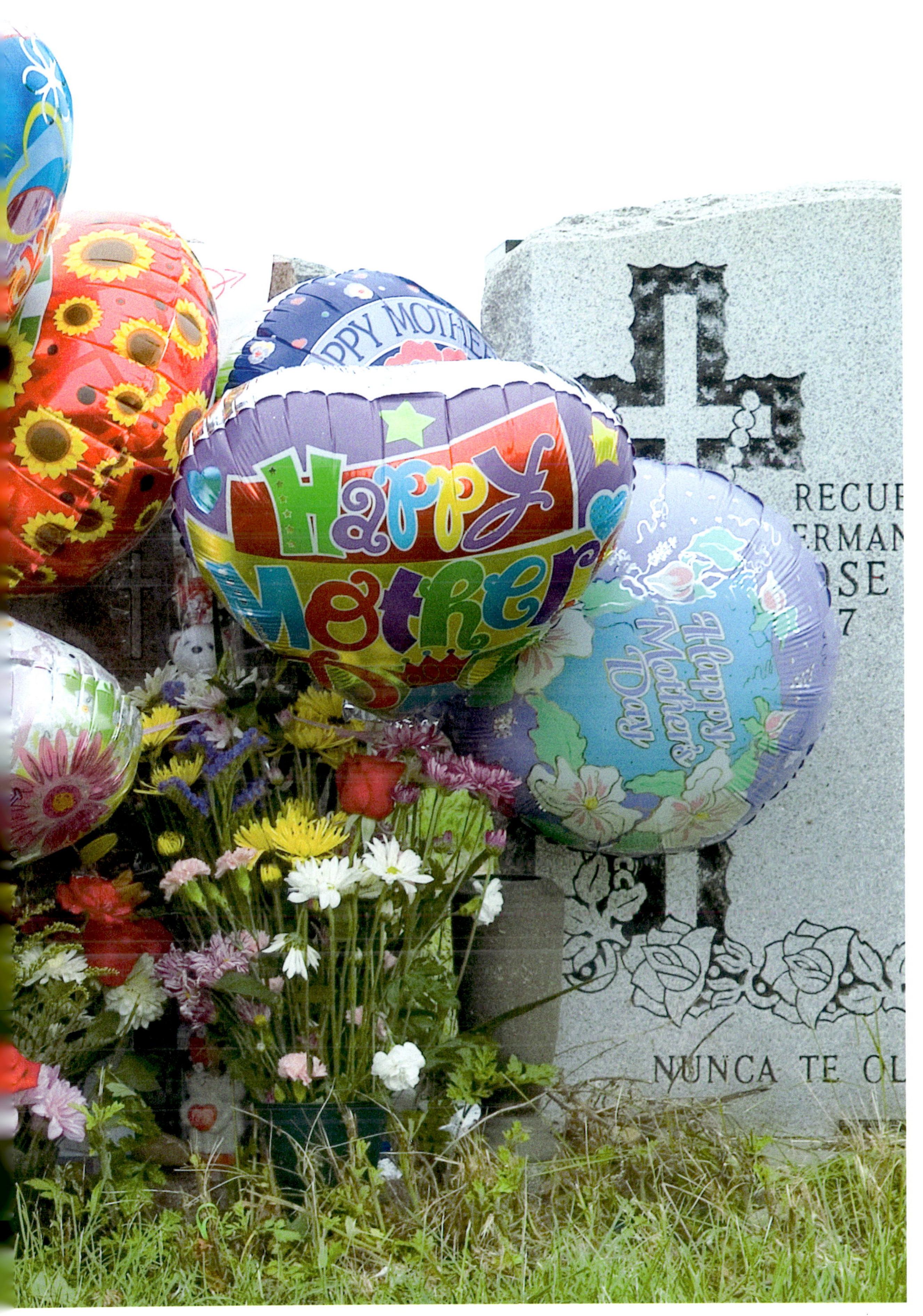
Happy Mother's
Happy Mother's Day
RECUE
ERMAN
OSE
NUNCA TE OL

Happy Mother's Day
ROA
ND BROTHER
OR 1990
E YOU
LUZ
8-12-1929 —
RECUERD
ESPOSO Y
ROBERT
7-7-1968 —
BELOVED F
& BRO
NUNCA TE C

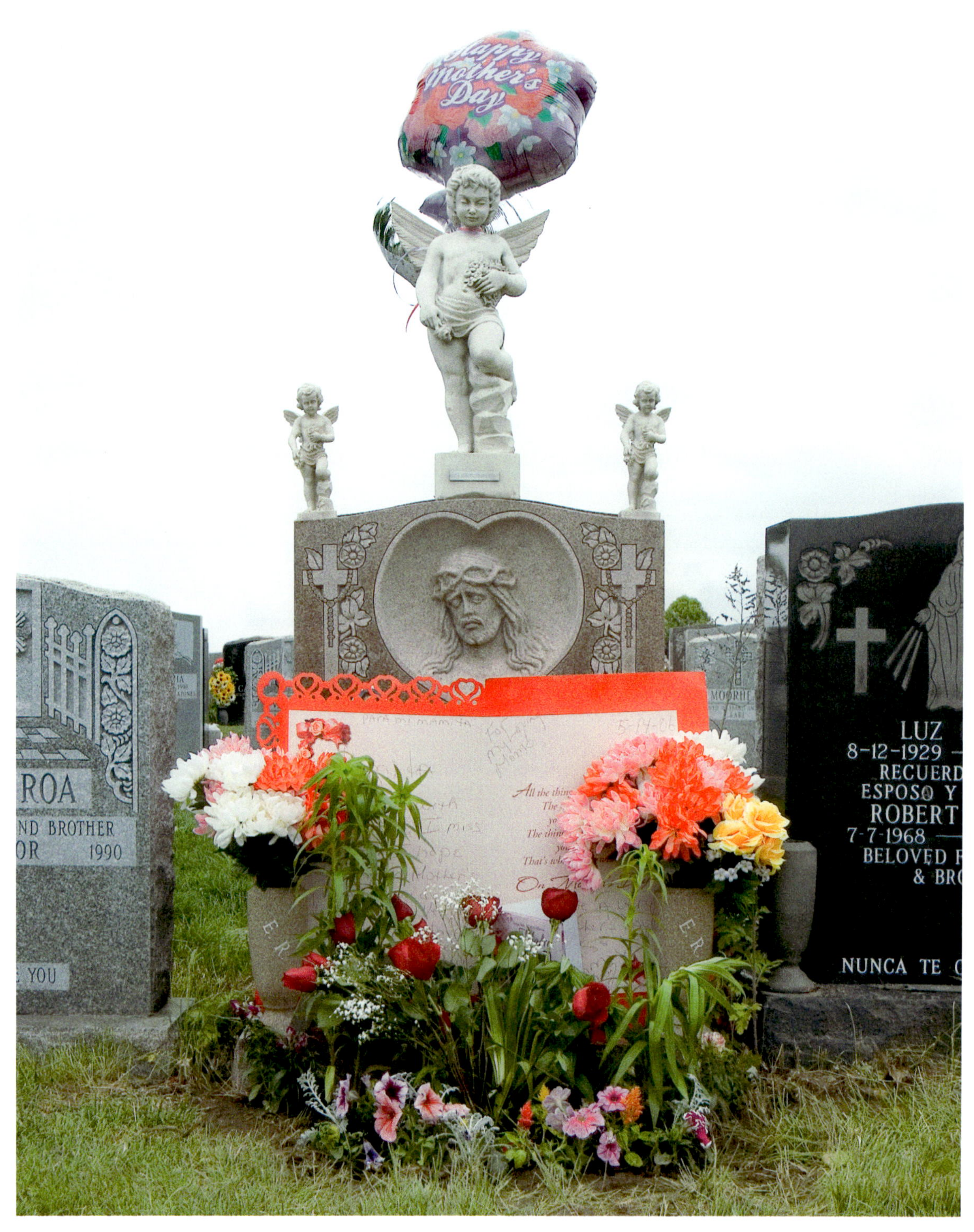

#52

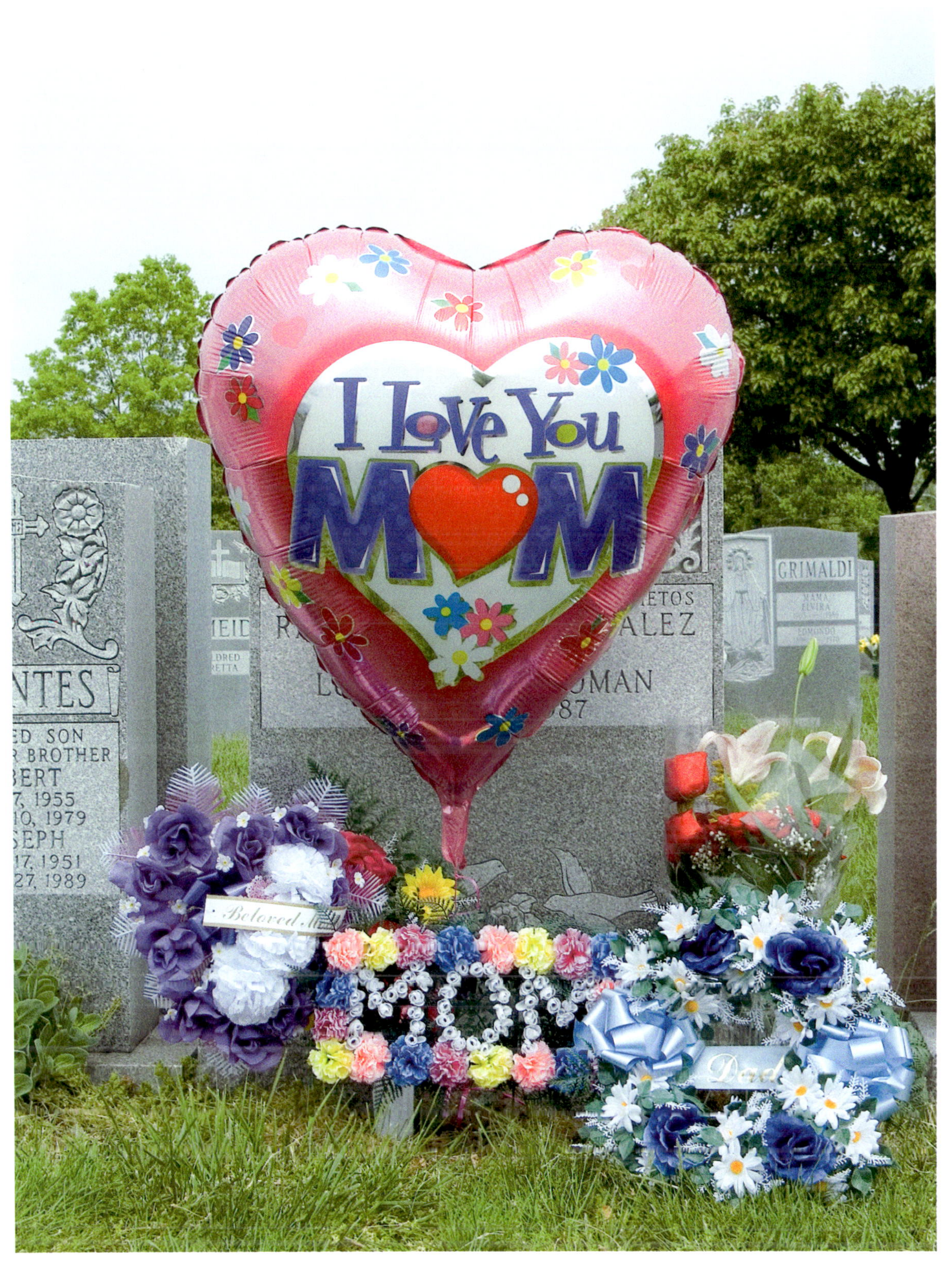
I Love You
GRIMALDI
MOM

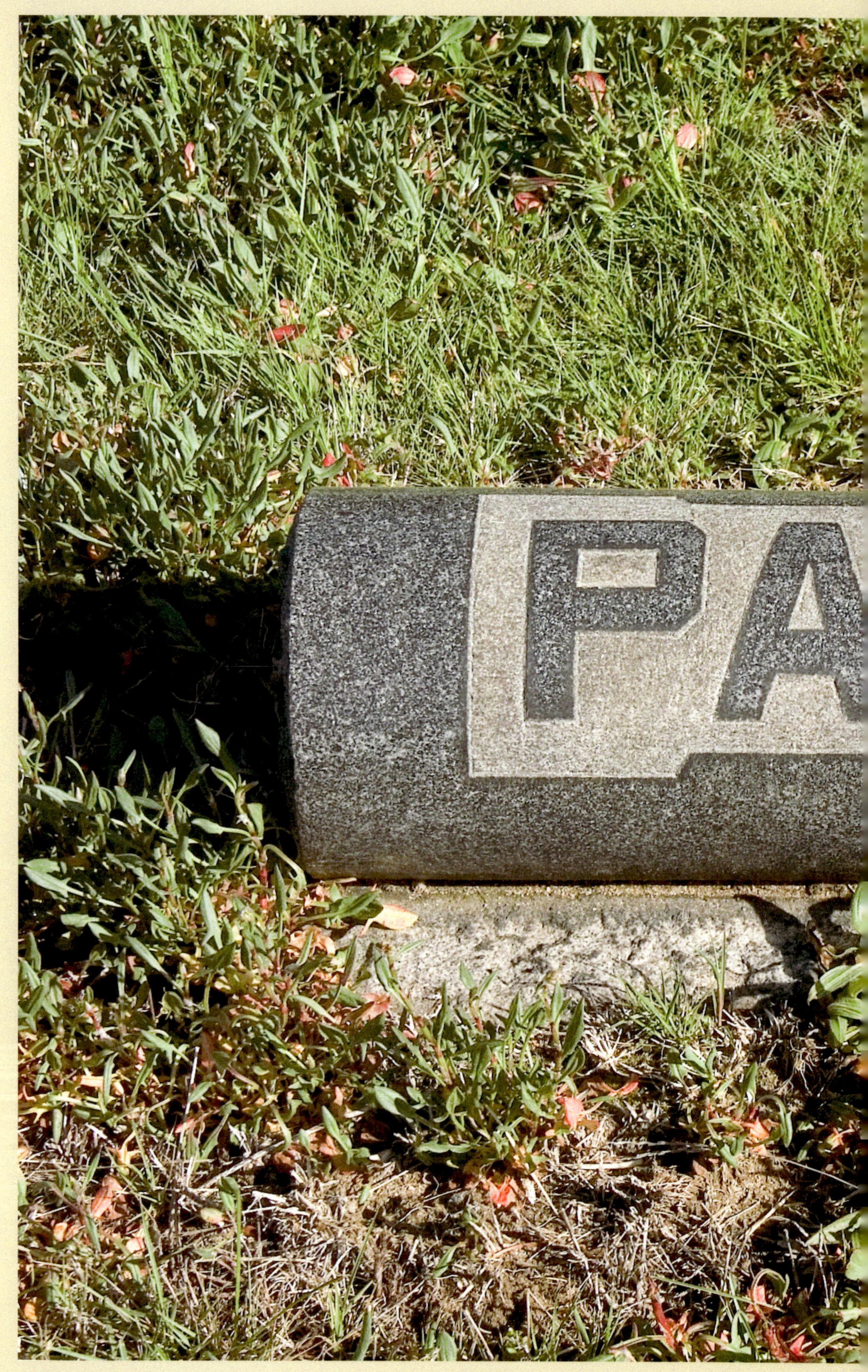
PA

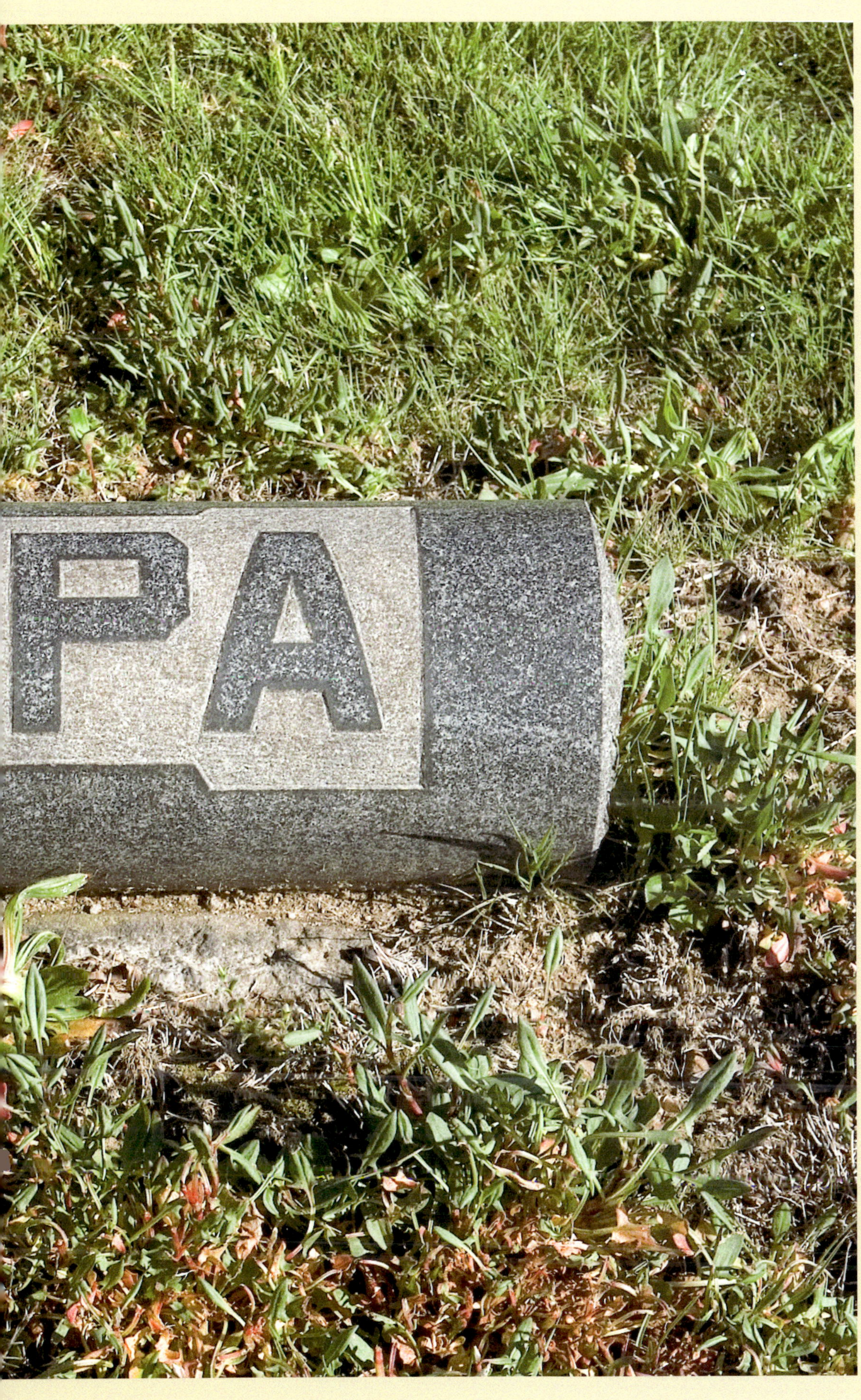
PA

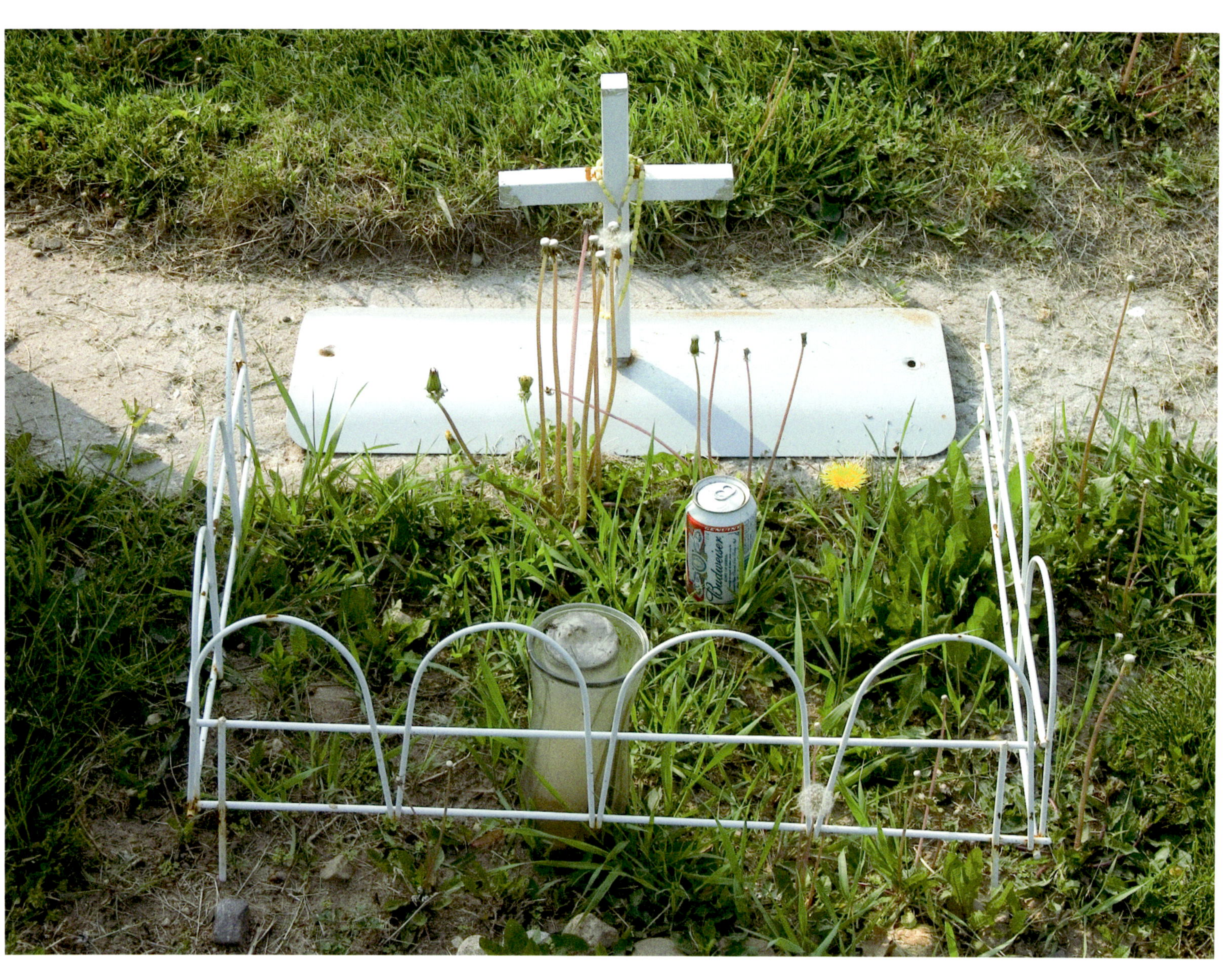

#54

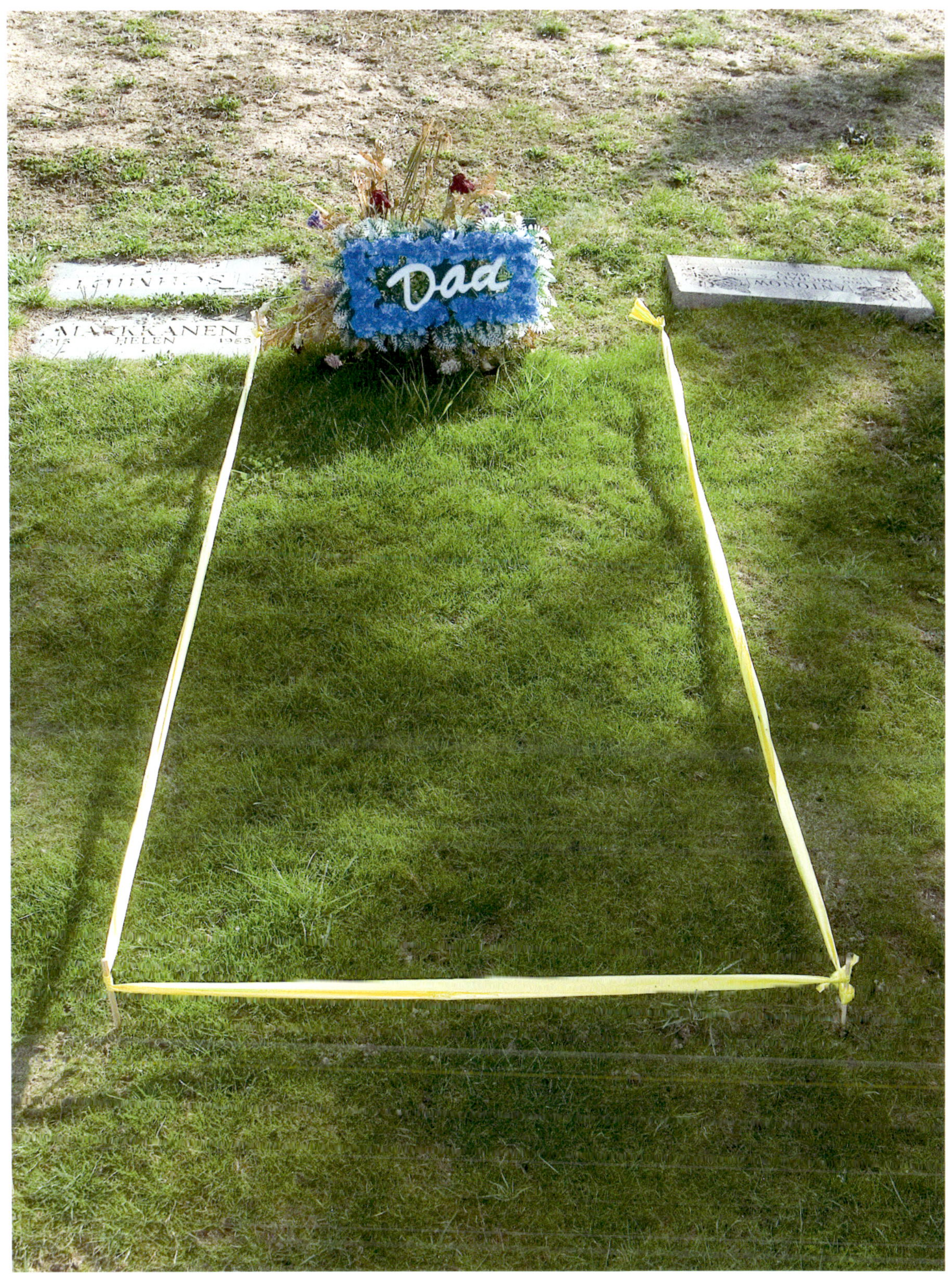

#55

JULIAN J. G. CARUSO
DESTINY C. MORALES
DOMINICK A. TORMO
AMANDA S. ISALES
TIJANI OSUMANU
RAMA ANN OSUMANU
DENNIS J. O'CONNELL
DYLAN J. O'CONNELL
AUGUSTA J. SPENCER
RENNY CUFFY
JOSHUA OLSEN
KAITLYN ESPOSITO
MIGUEL A. MARRERO
ASHLEYONA G. MARRERO
ANGEL A. CRAWFORD
ALEXIS MAWU-ELOM BUBB
LUCY BROGAN
ANGEL GRASSADONIO
FAITH GRASSADONIO
ANGELINA ORTIZ
BABY LOPEZ
ALLISON A. HARKINS
JULIAN

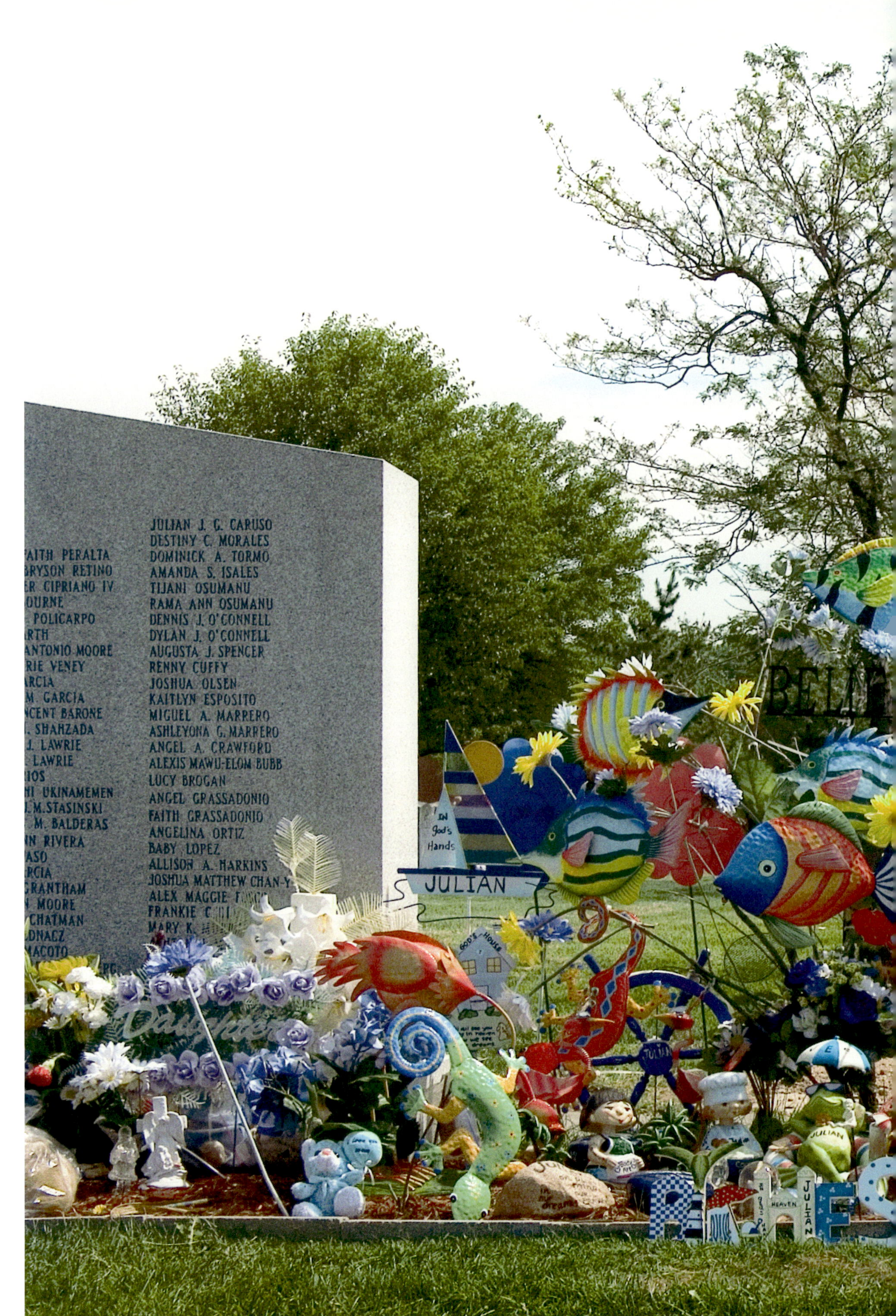

#56A

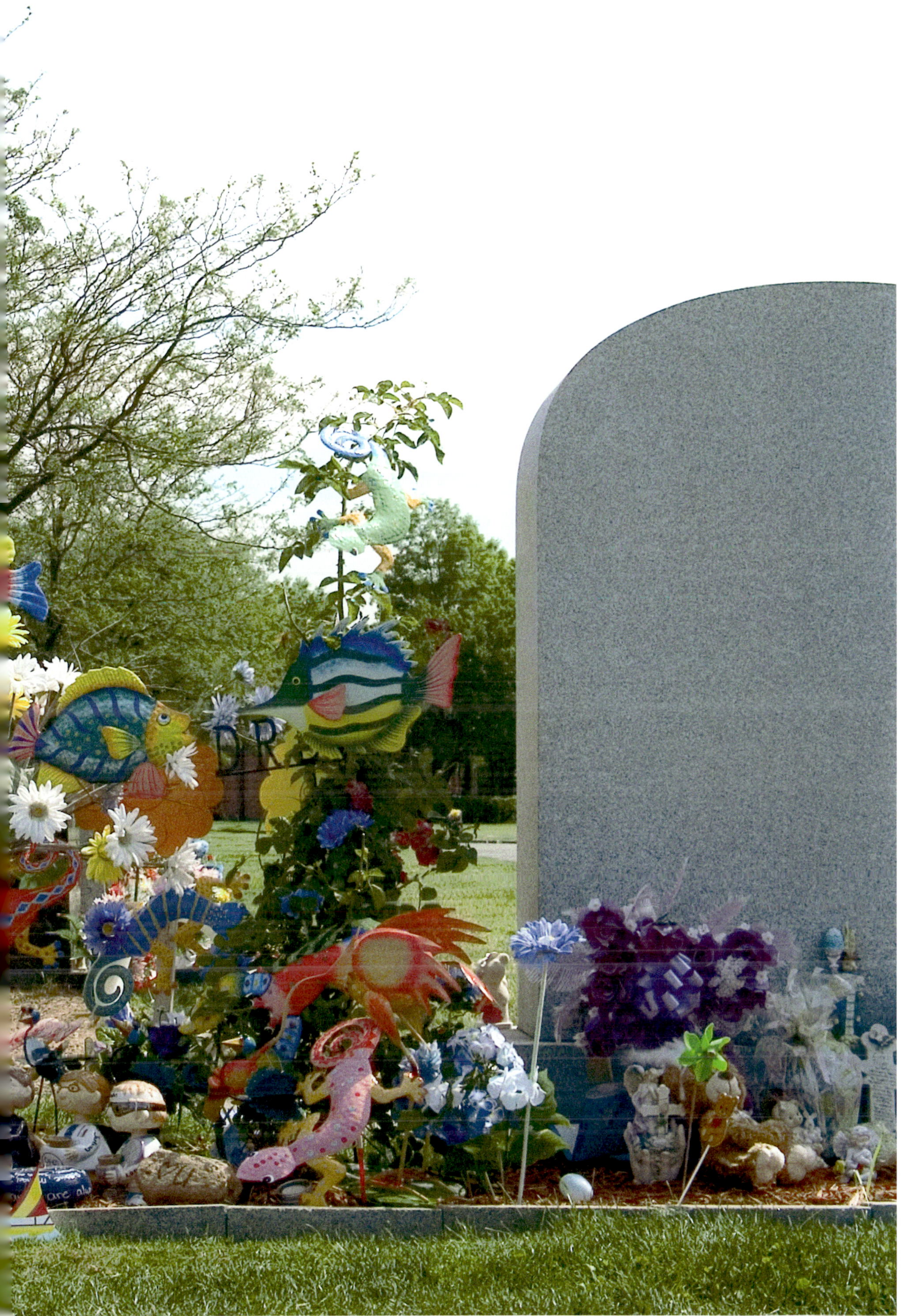

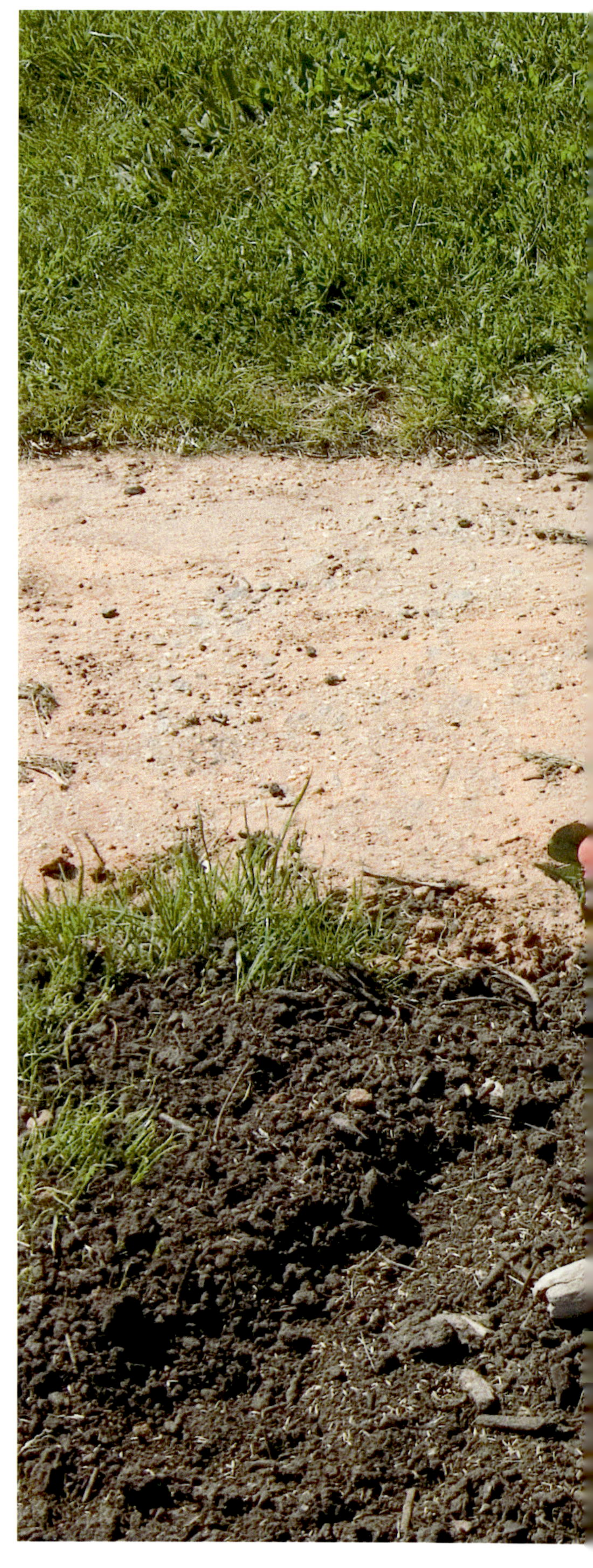

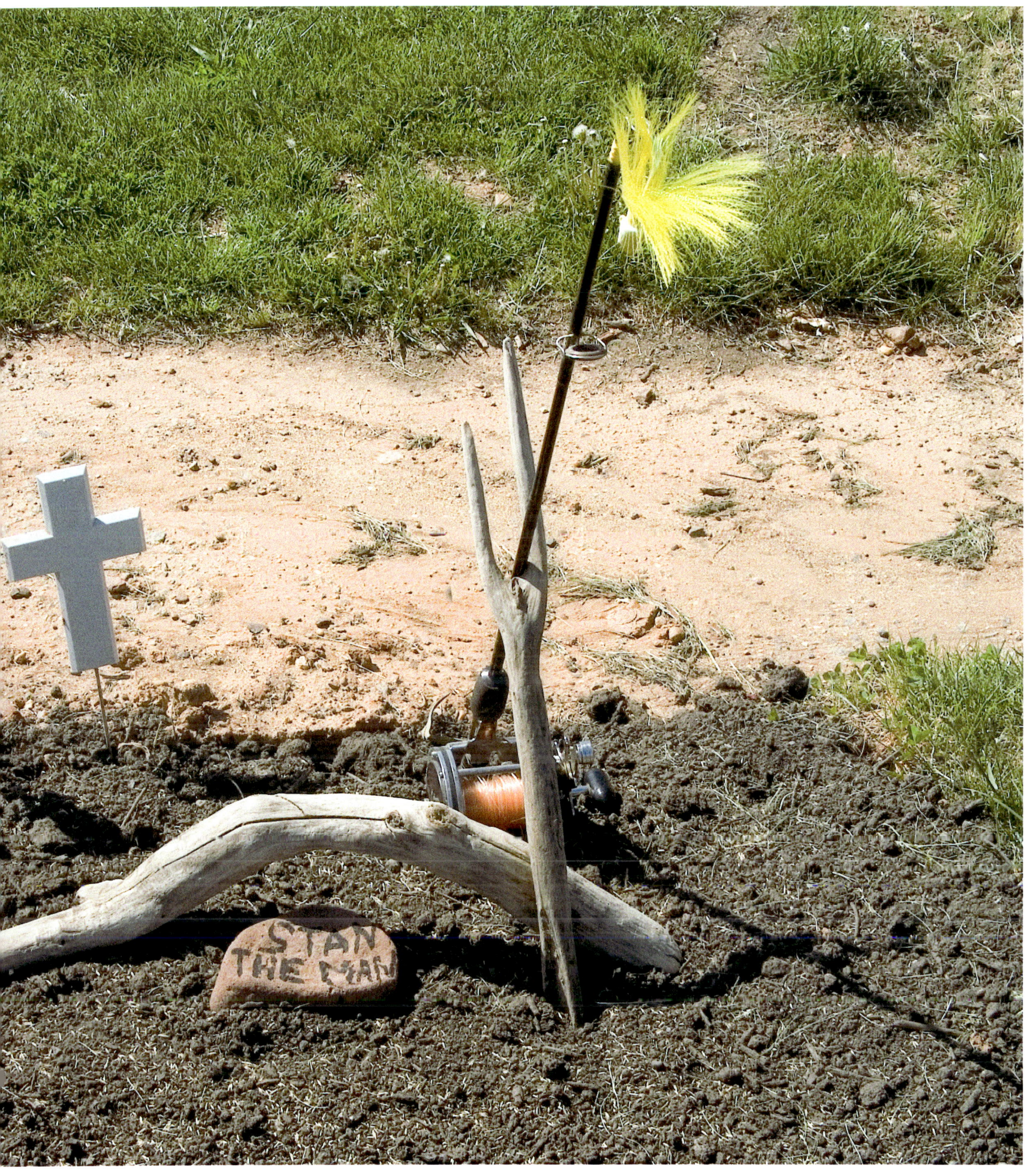
STAN
THE MAN

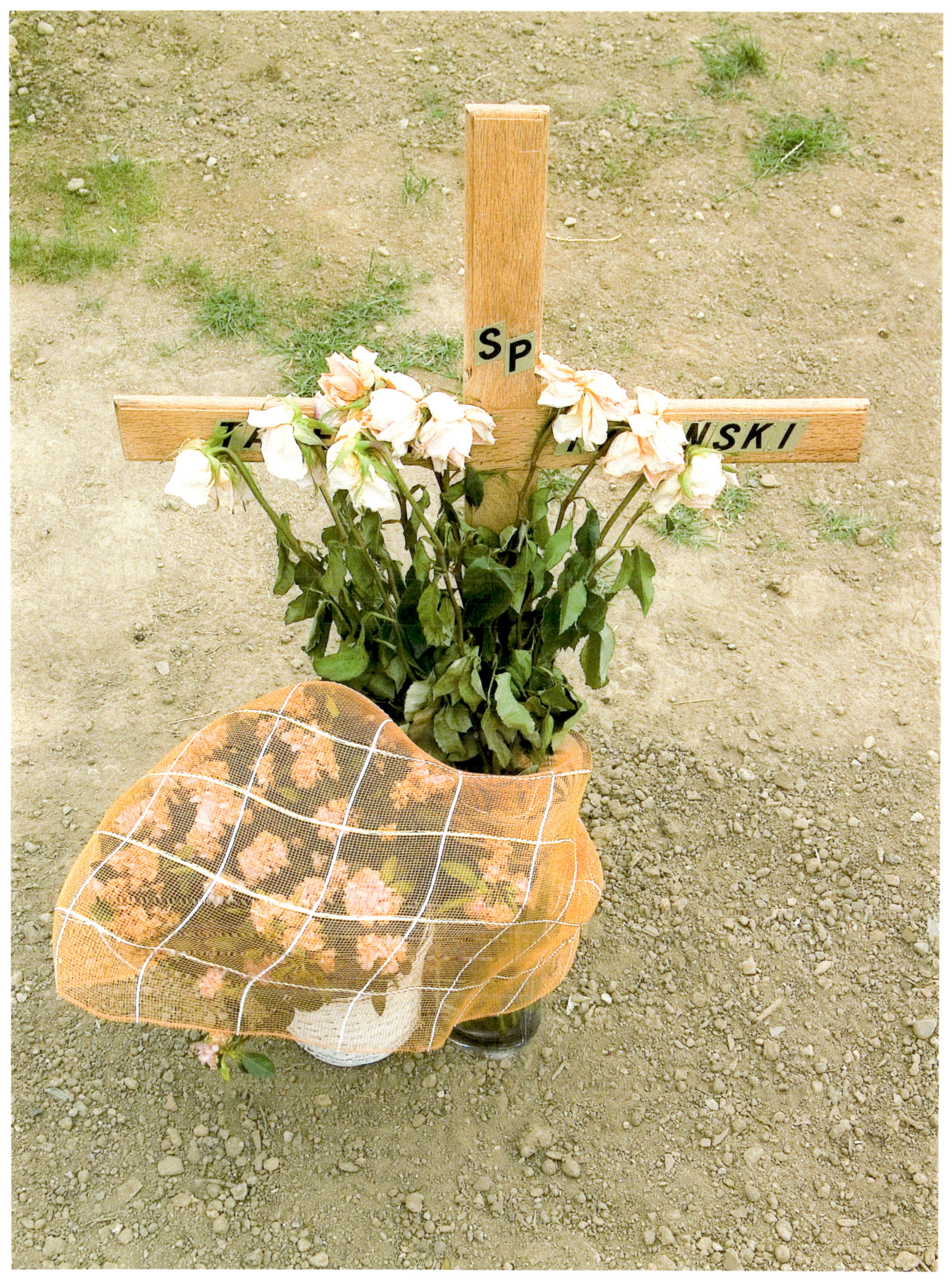
SP

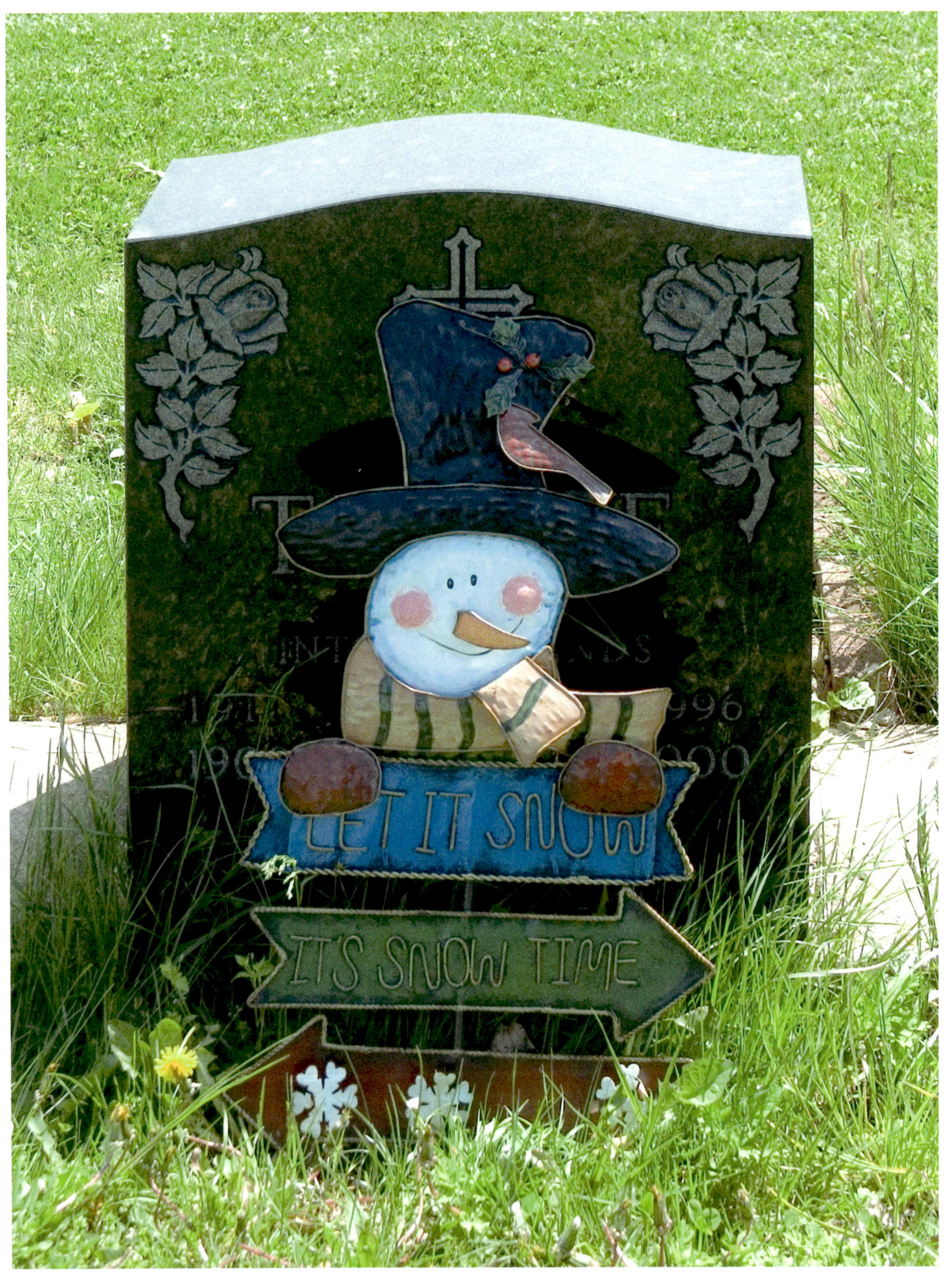

#59

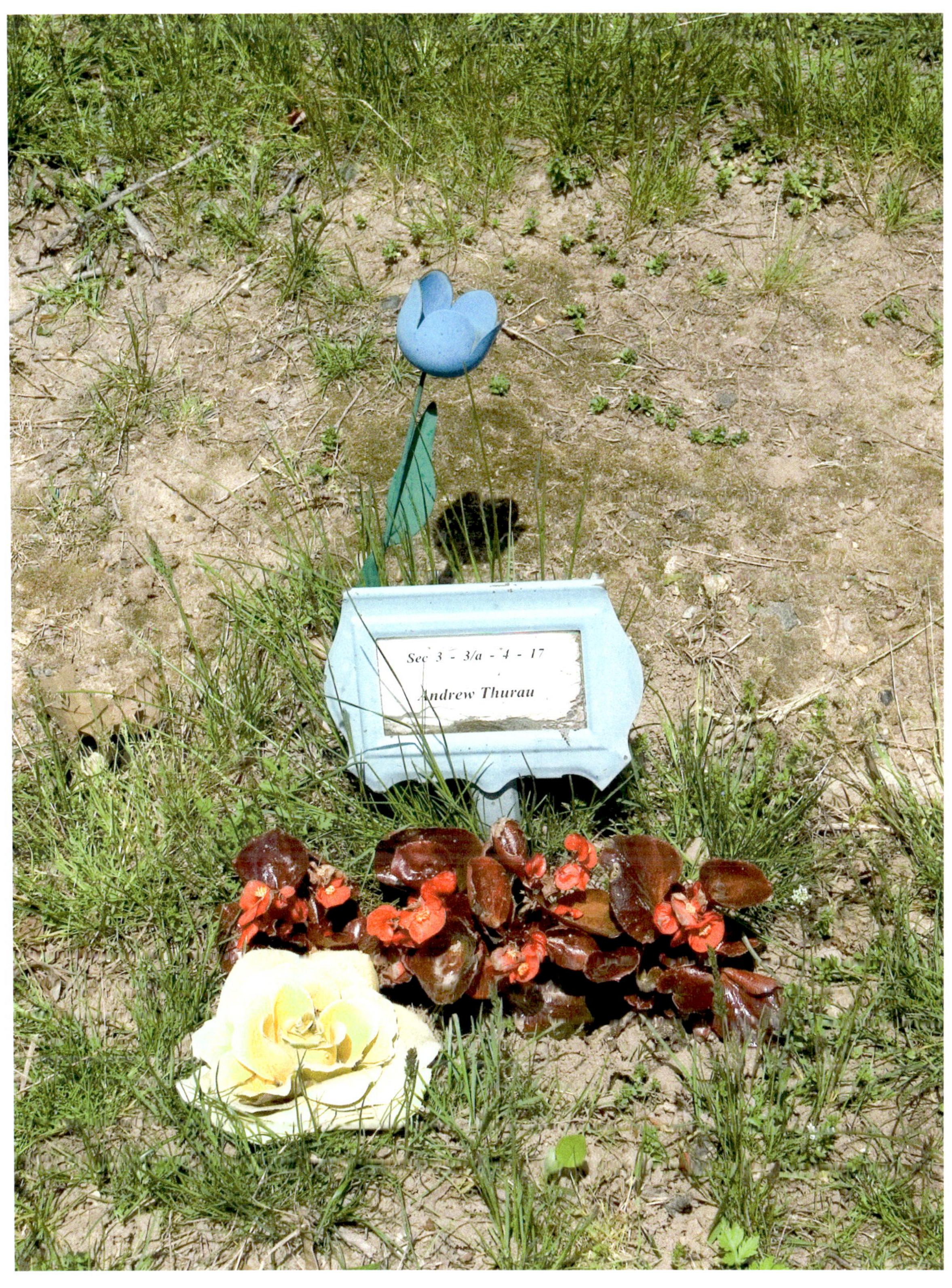

#60

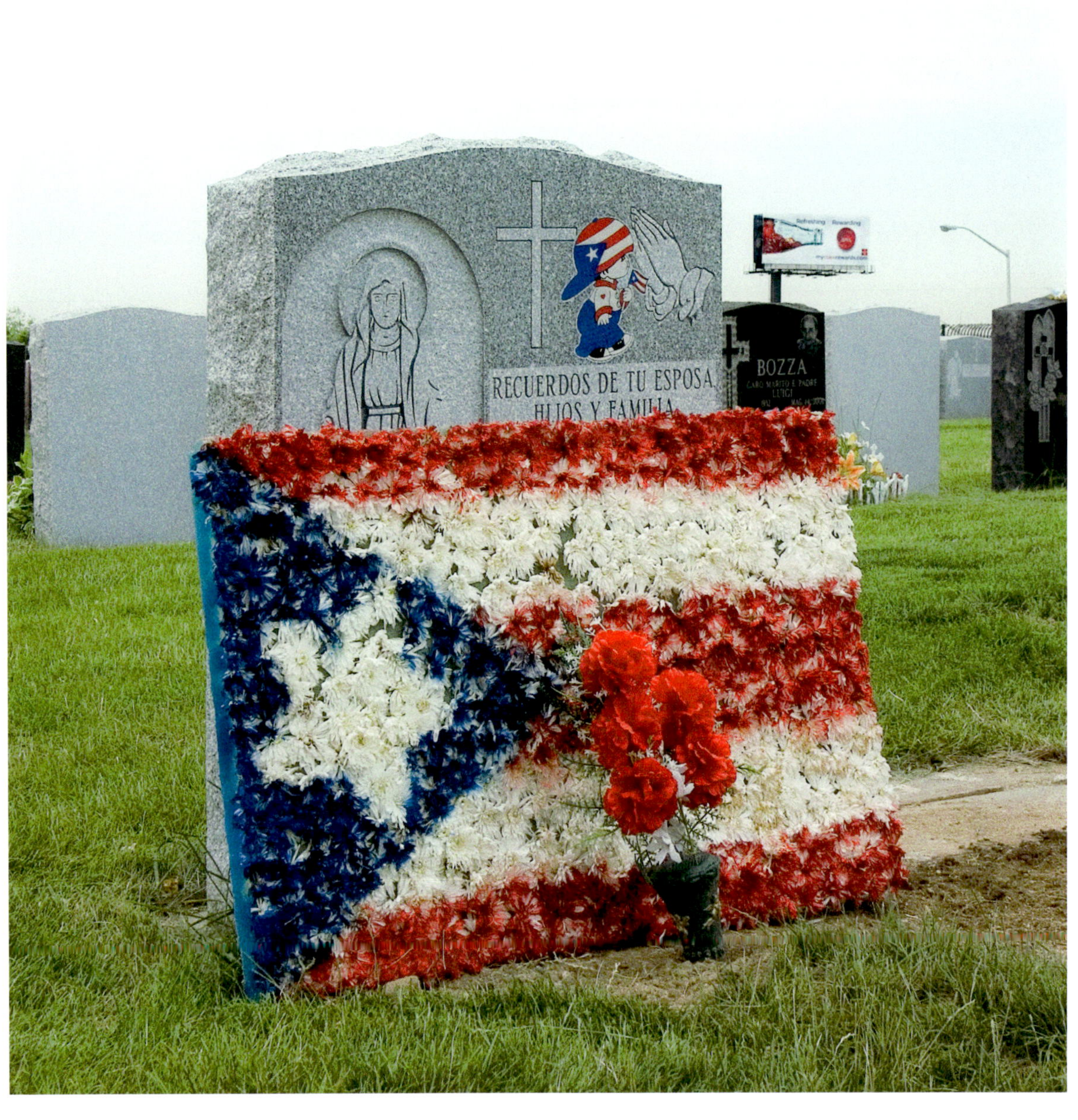

#61

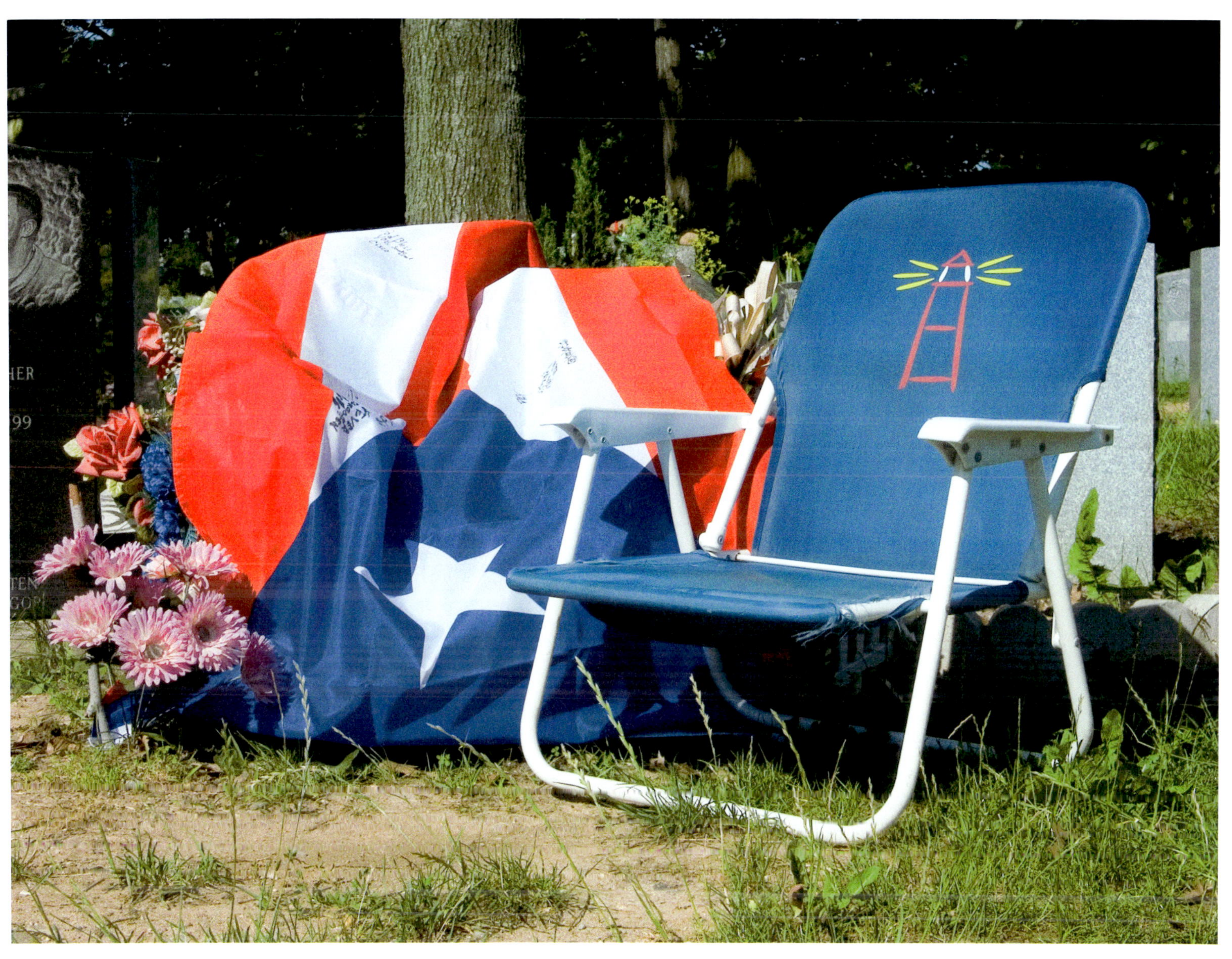

#62

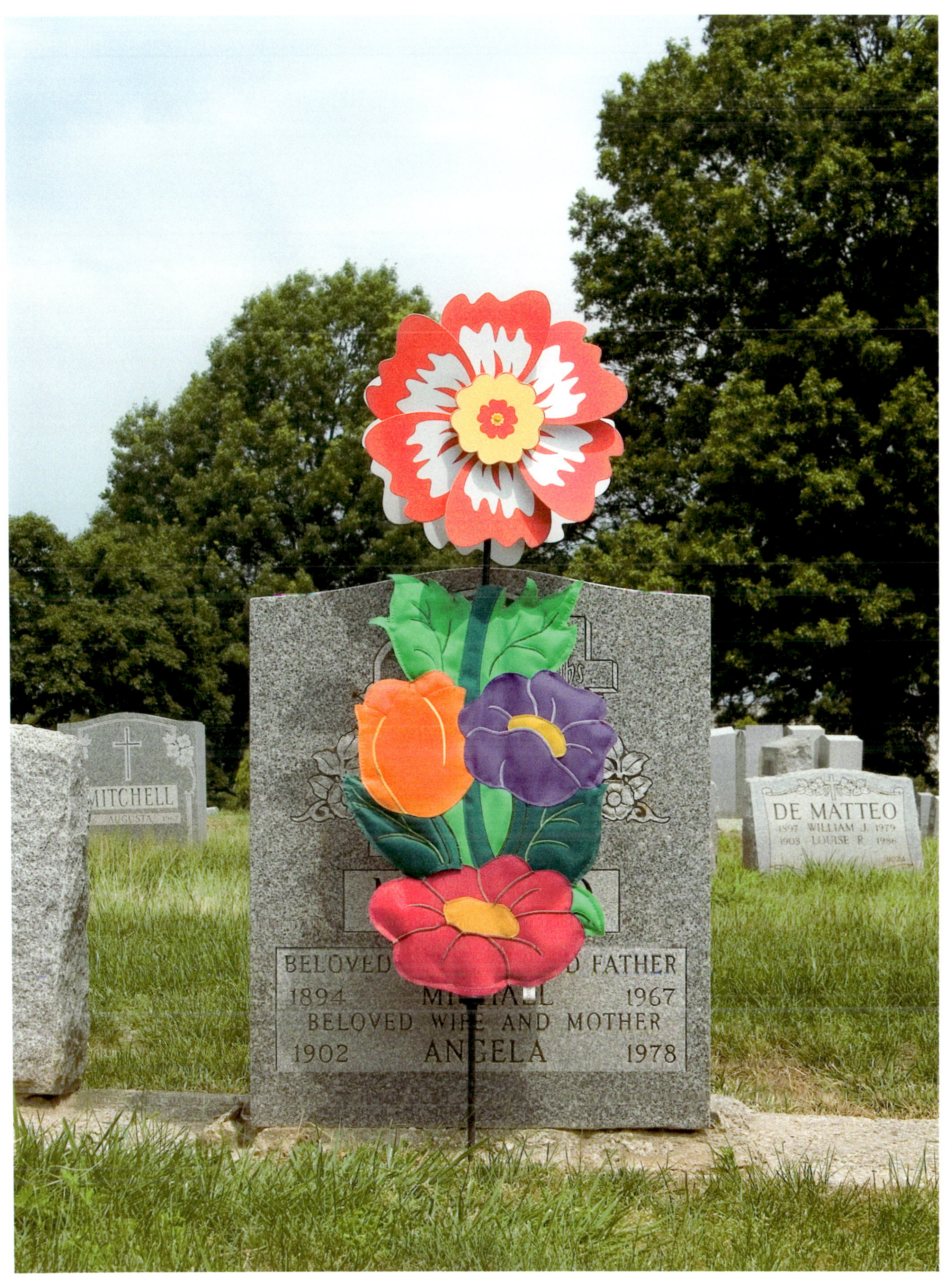
MITCHELL
DE MATTEO
1897 WILLIAM J. 1979
1903 LOUISE R. 1986
BELOVED
D FATHER
1894
1967
AND MOTHER
1902 ANGELA 1978

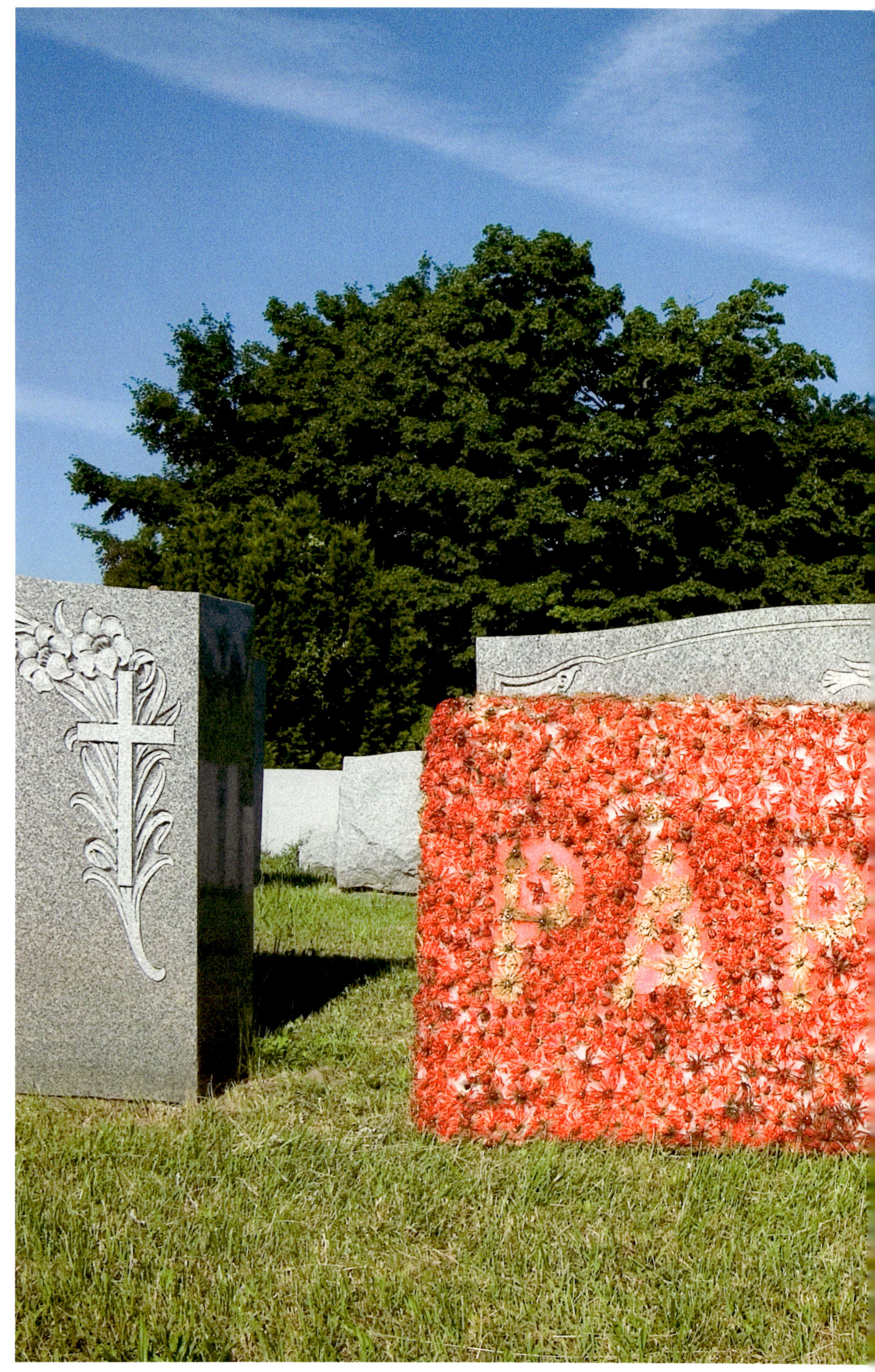

#64

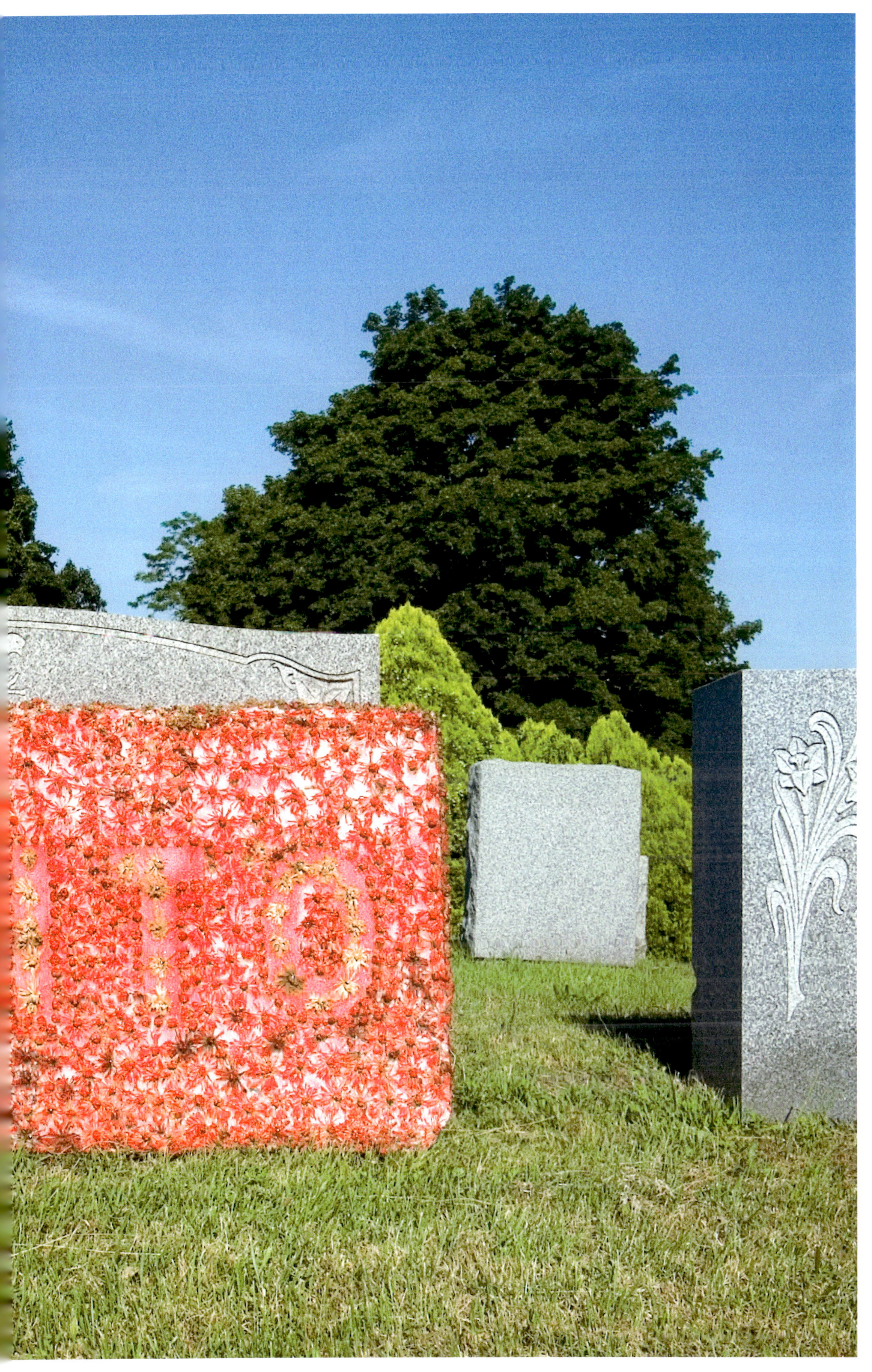

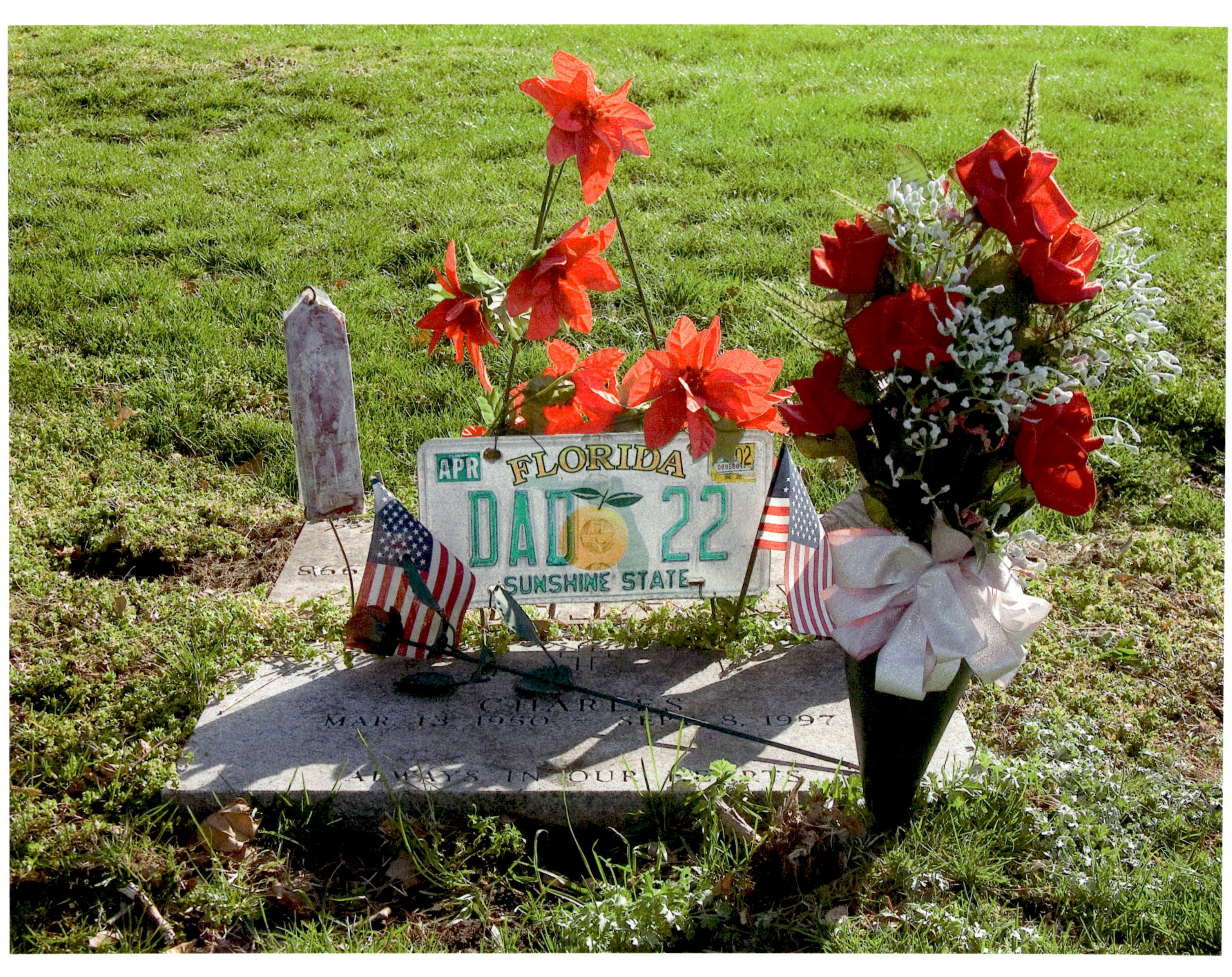

#65

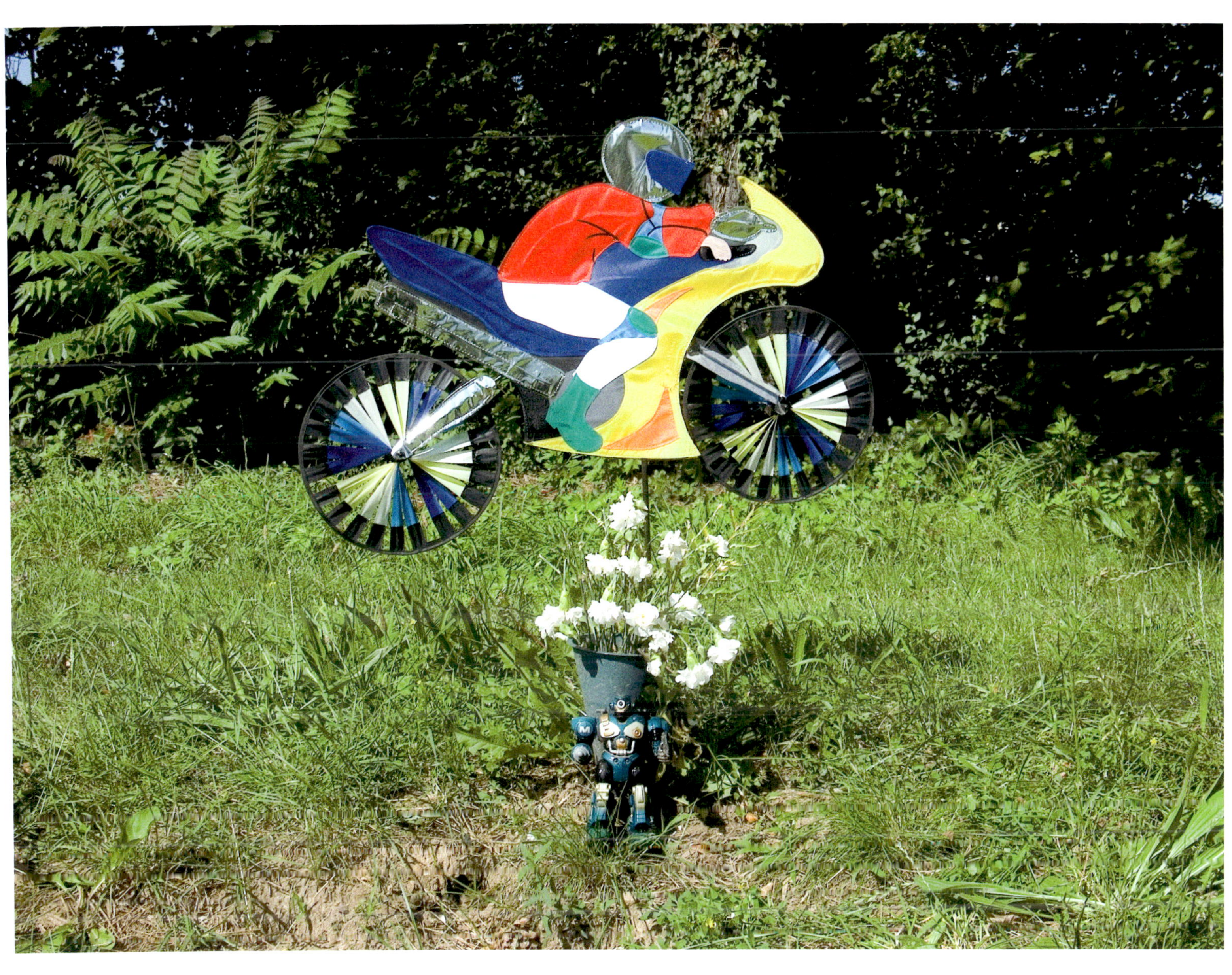

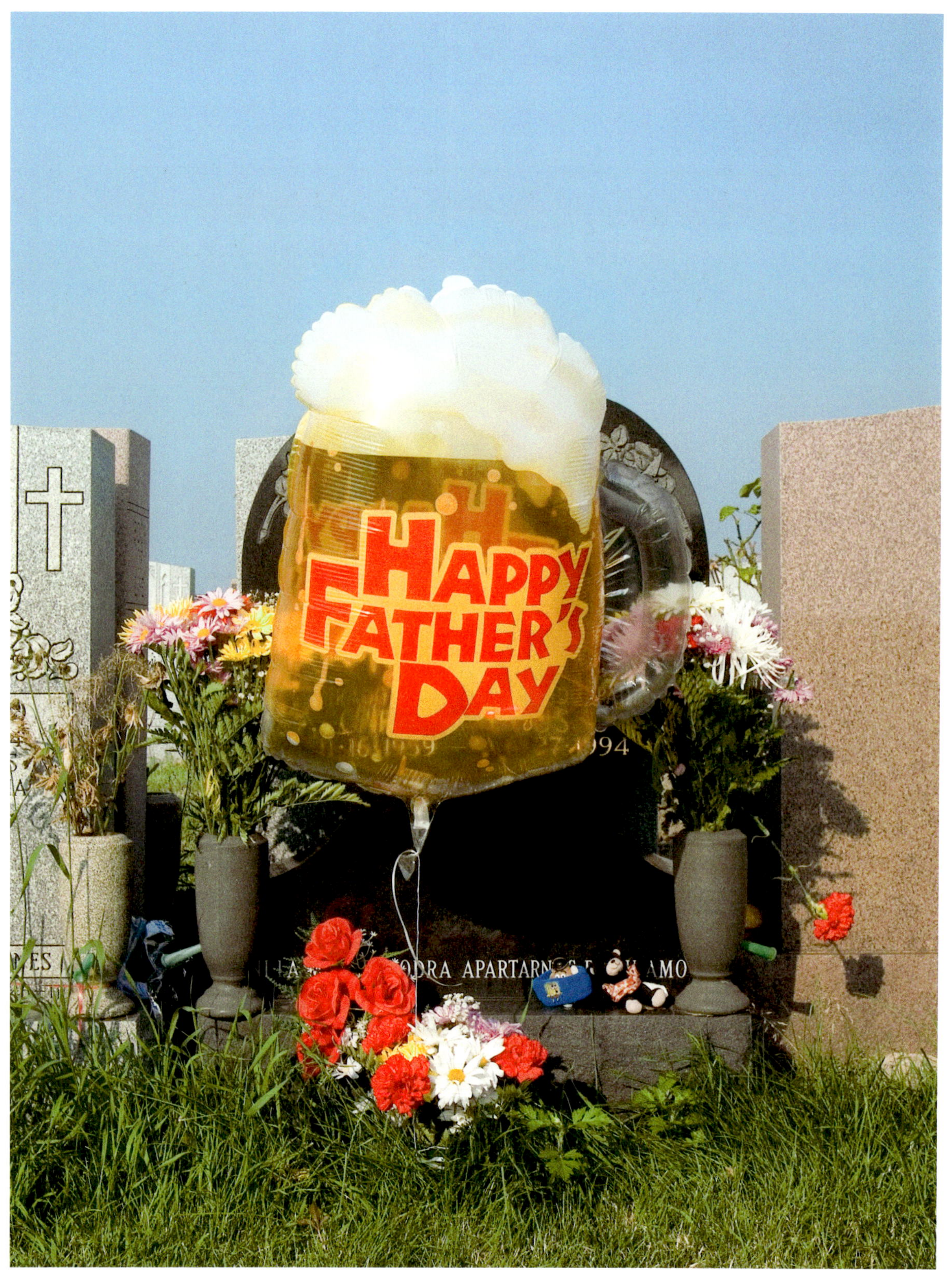

#67

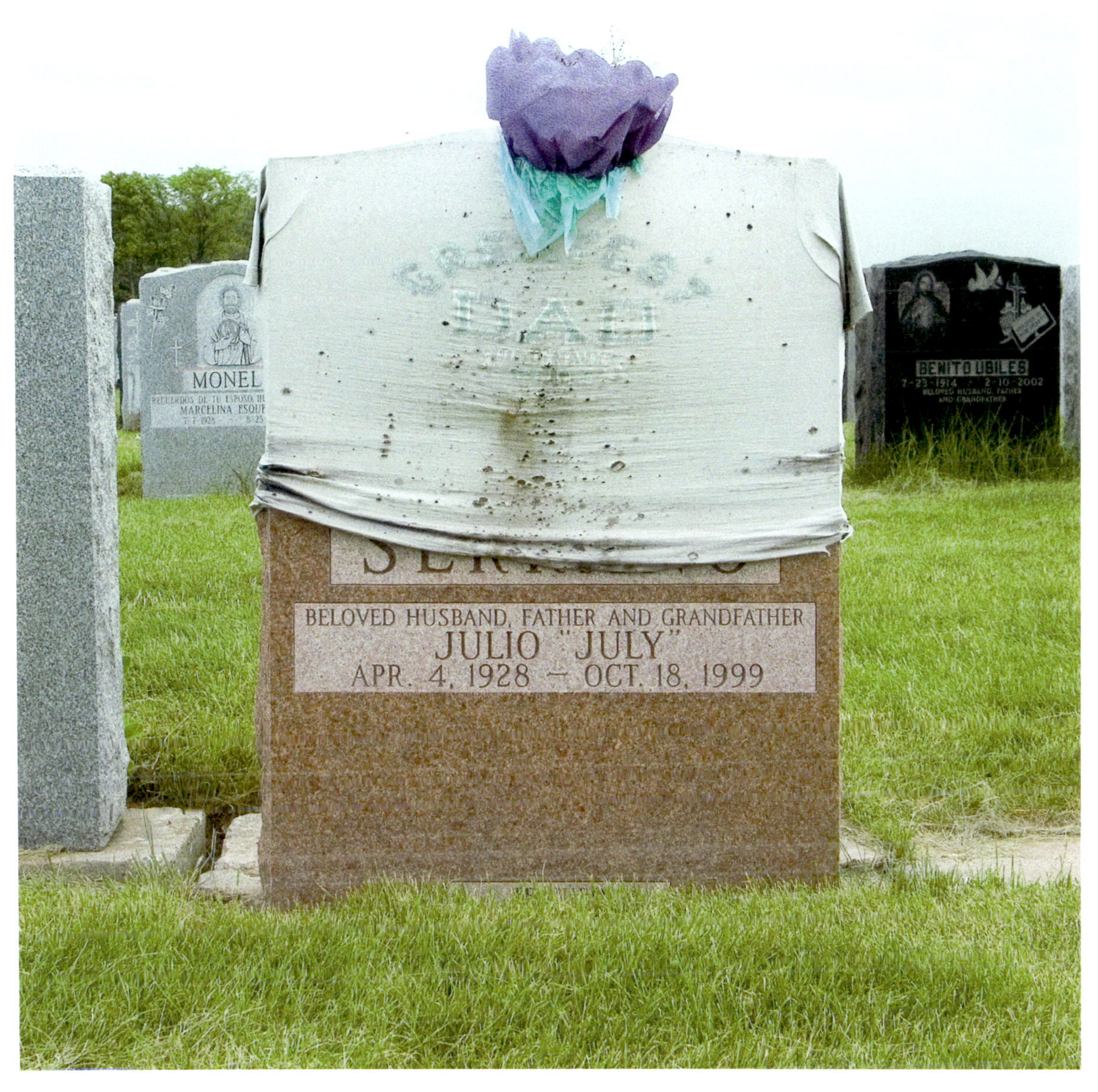
BELOVED HUSBAND, FATHER AND GRANDFATHER
JULIO "JULY"
APR. 4, 1928 – OCT. 18, 1999
BENITO UBILES
7-23-1914 2-10-2002

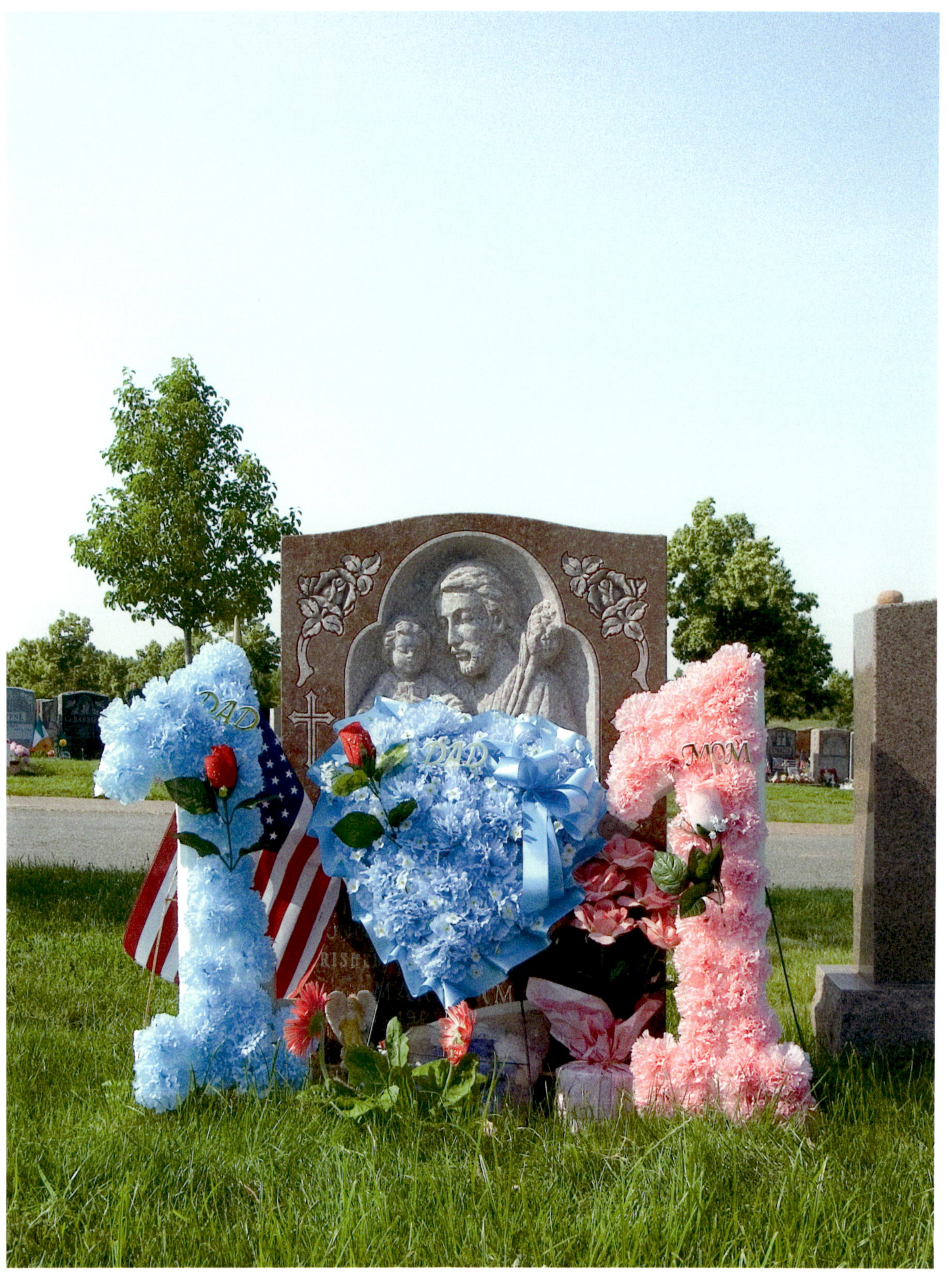

#69

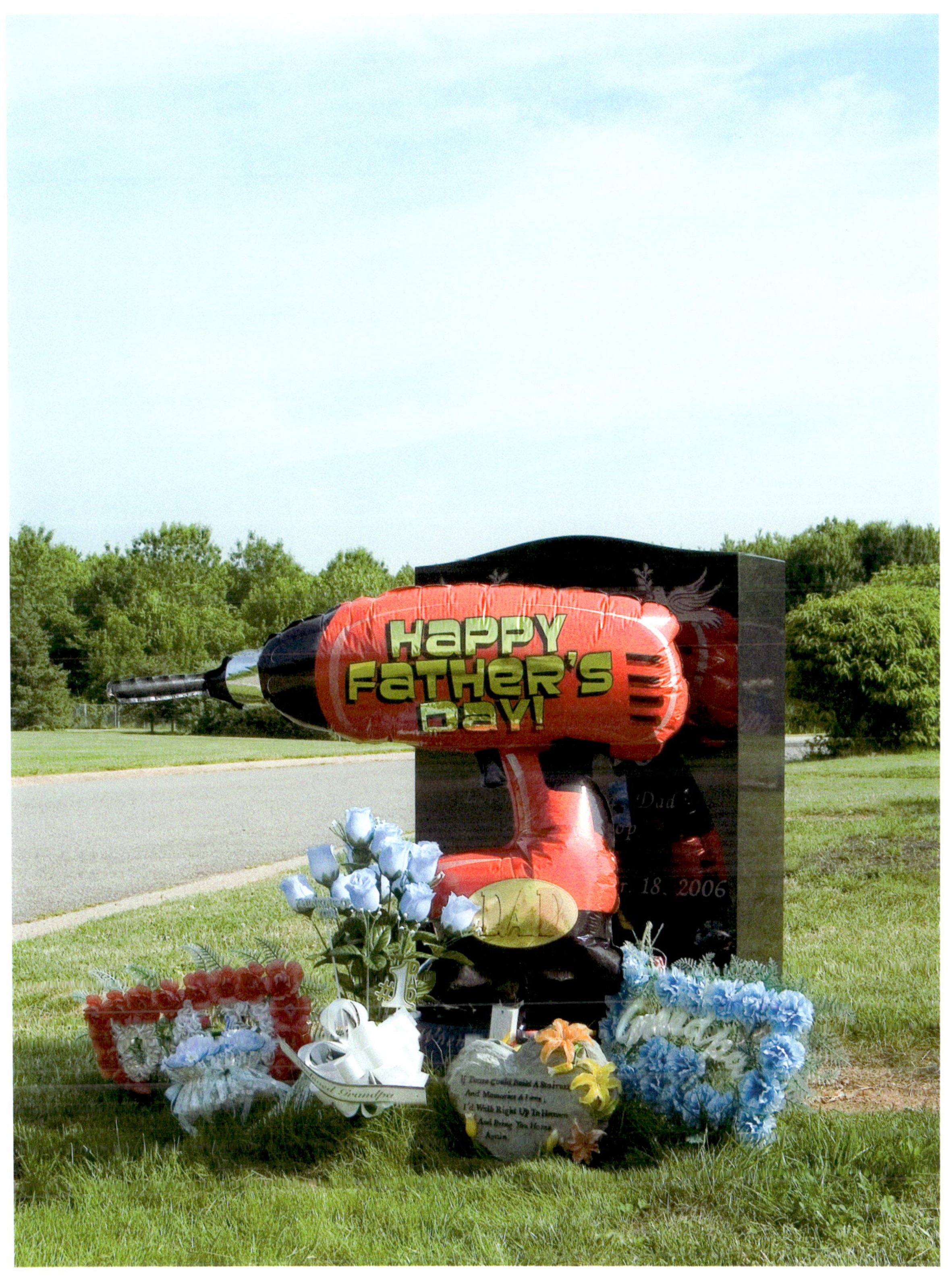

#70

GARTY
SISTER
1905 GENEVIEVE 1911
BROTHER
1907 TIMOTHY F. 1955
TULUMELL
DOMENICA 1960
GIUSEPPE 1960
MANDELINE
IN MEMORIAM
ROSE JULY 6, 1990
A LOVING MOTHER
PETER MAR. 17, 1960
A LOVING FATHER
AUGUST
ROSE
MARGARET
1909 - 1988
WILLIAM
BERTHA
LORA
1930
1980

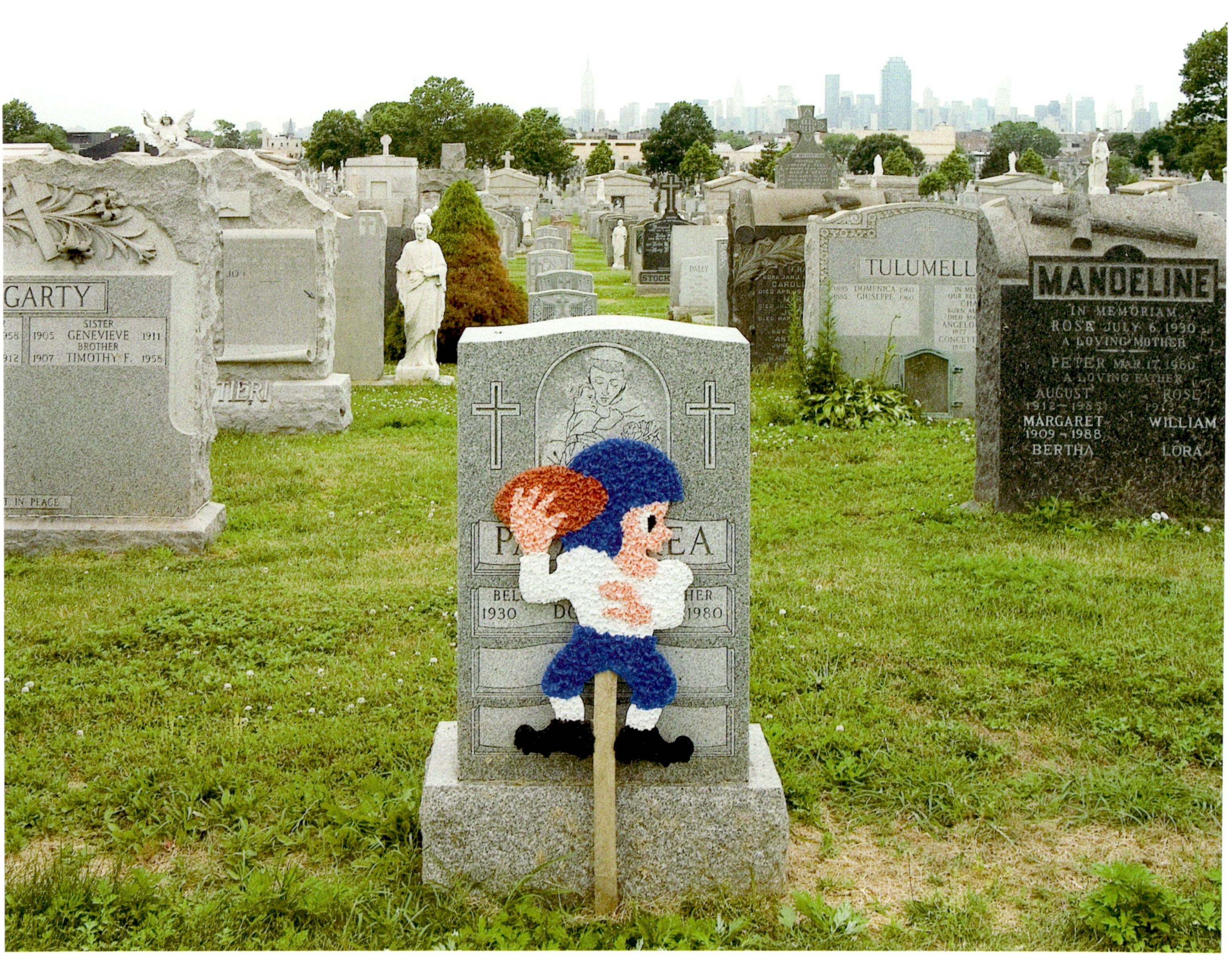

#71

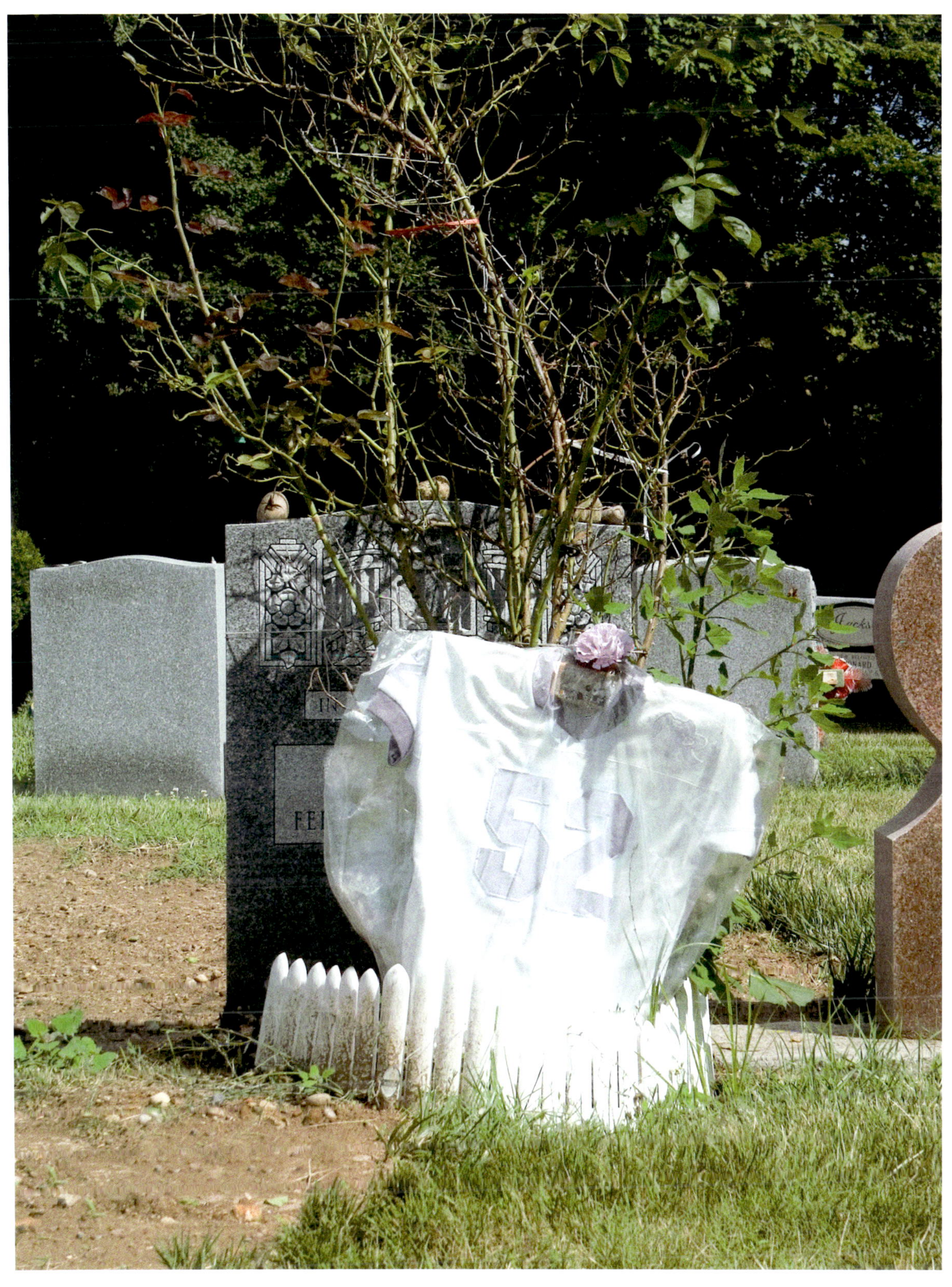

#72

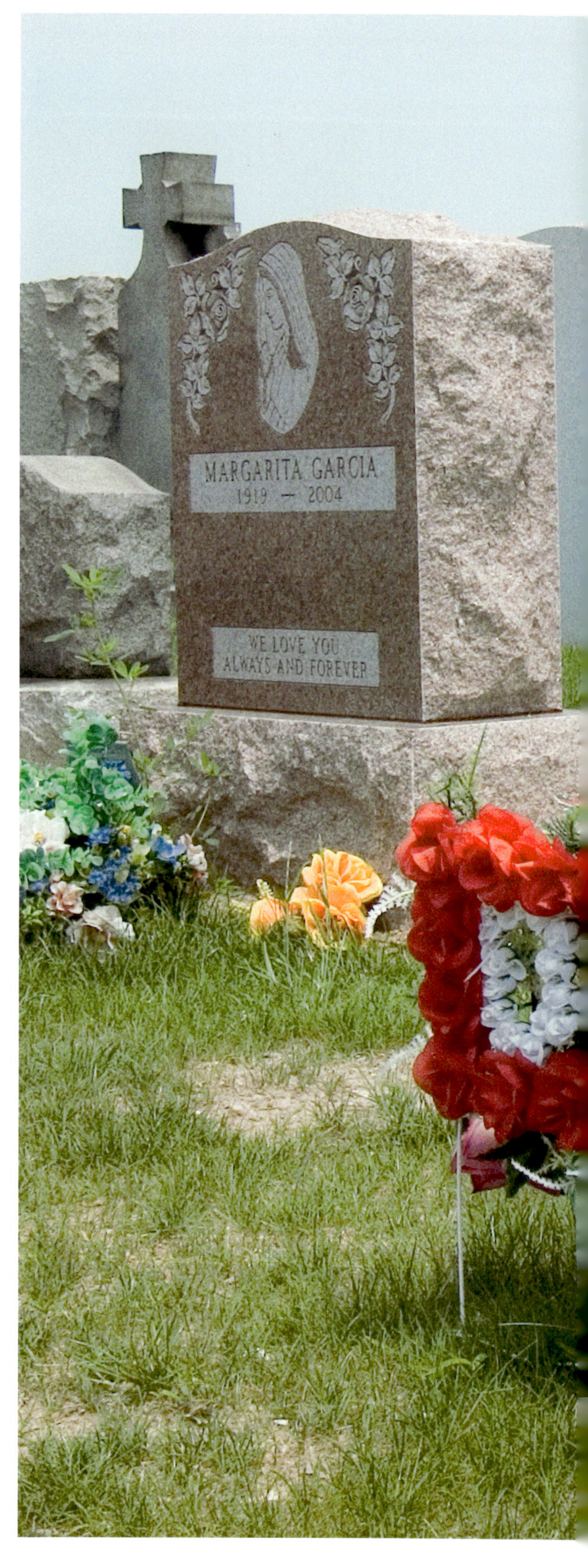

#73

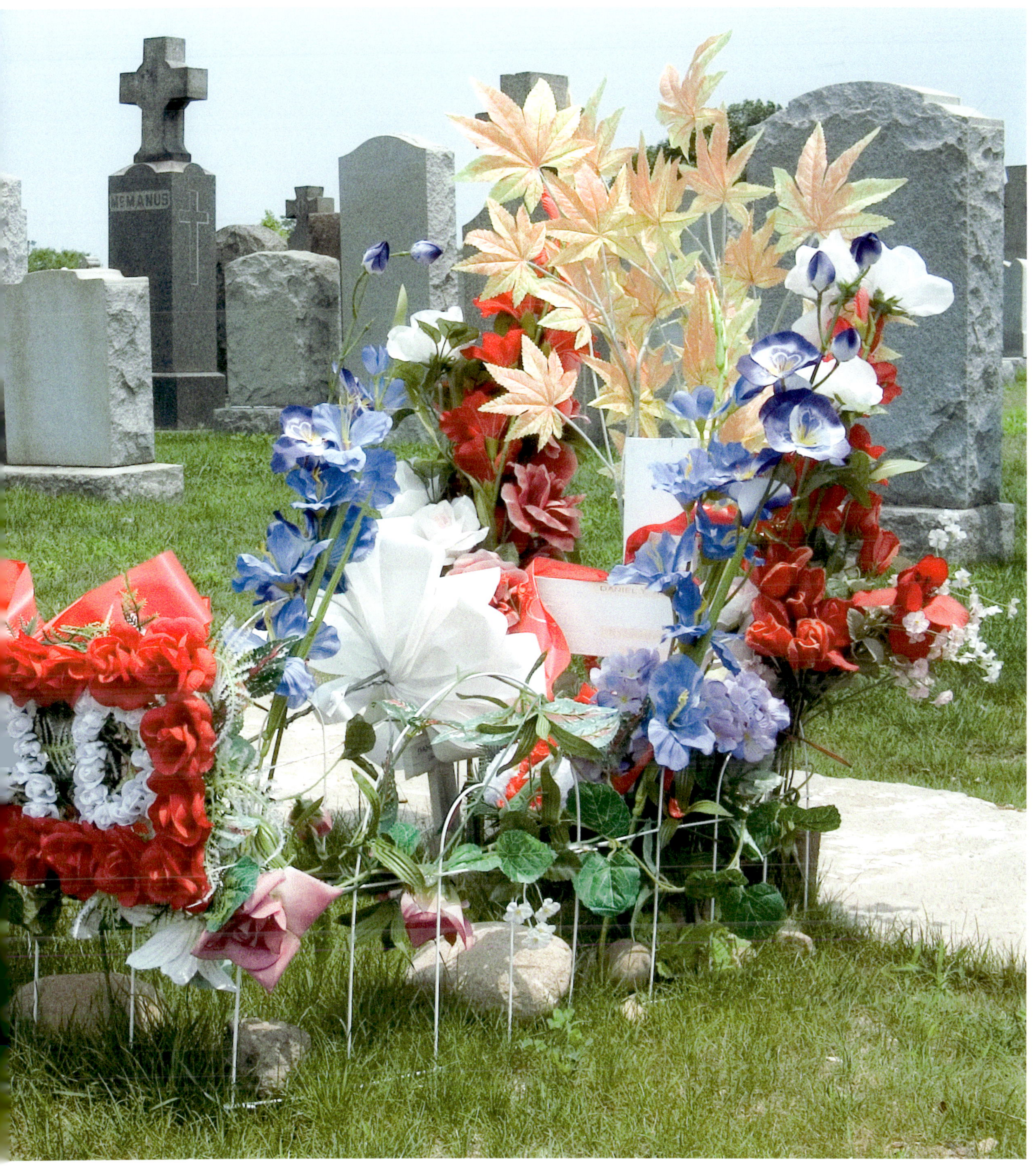
McMANUS

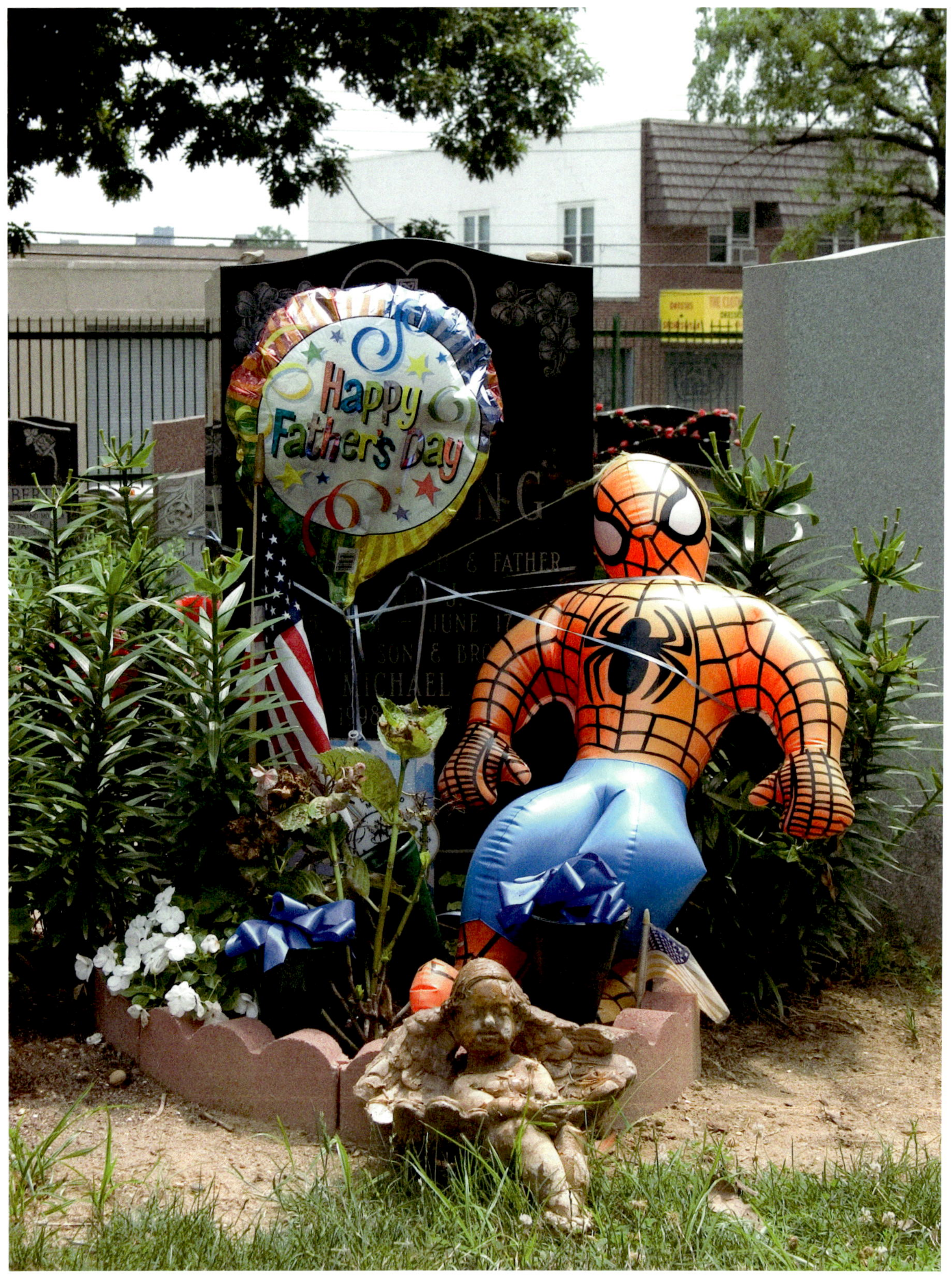

#74

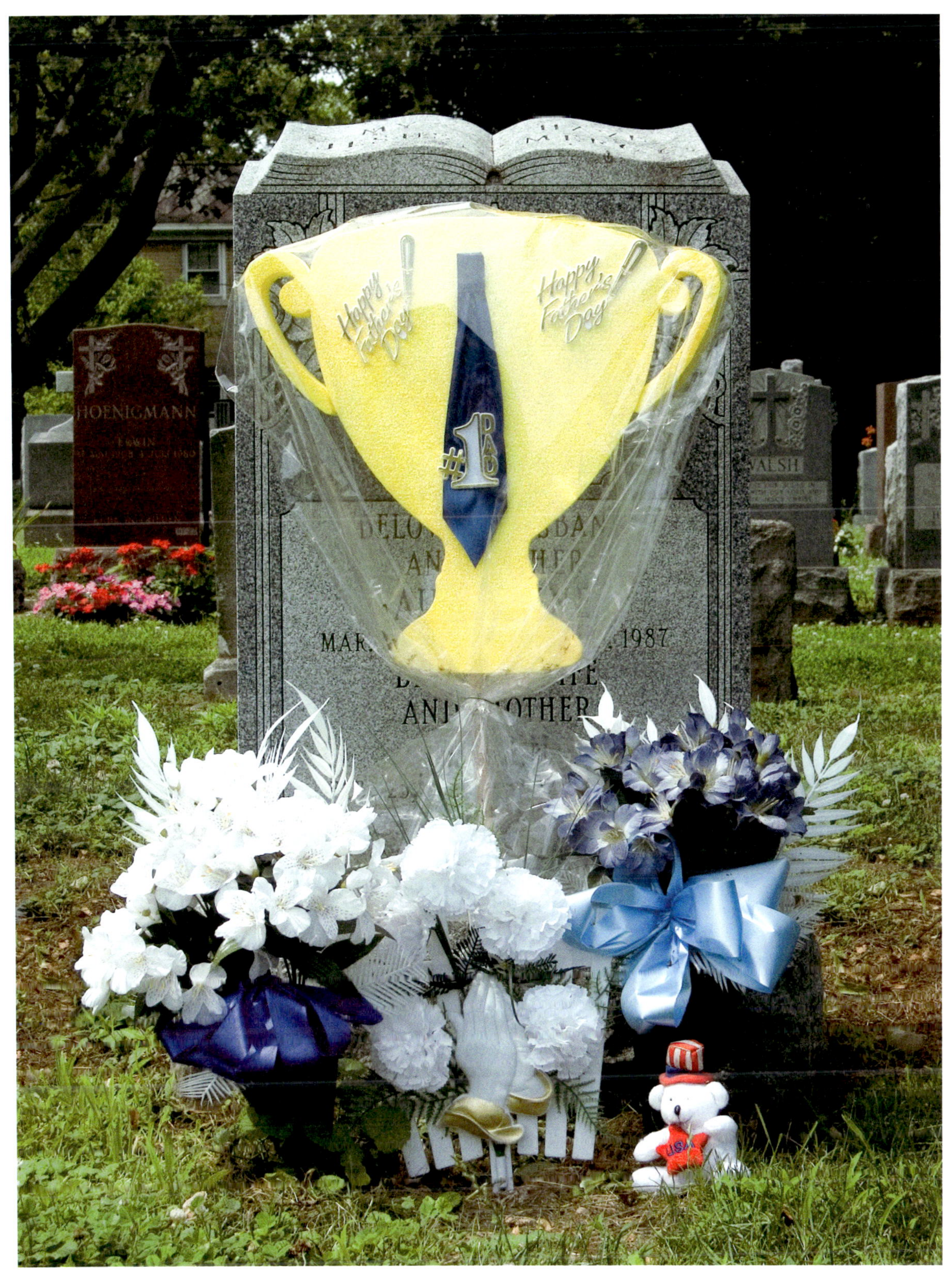
Happy Father's Day!
#1 DAD
Happy Father's Day!
HOENIGMANN

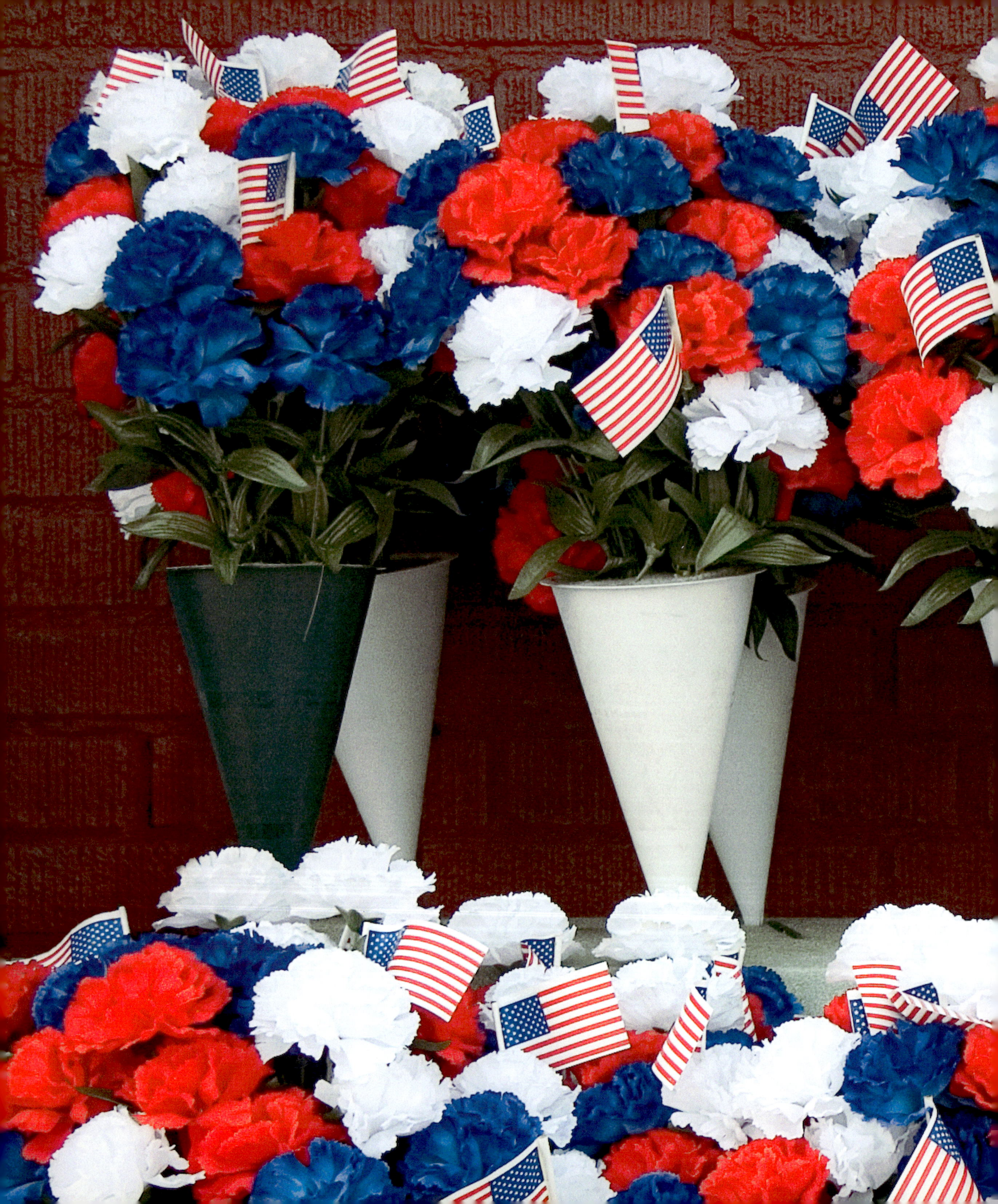

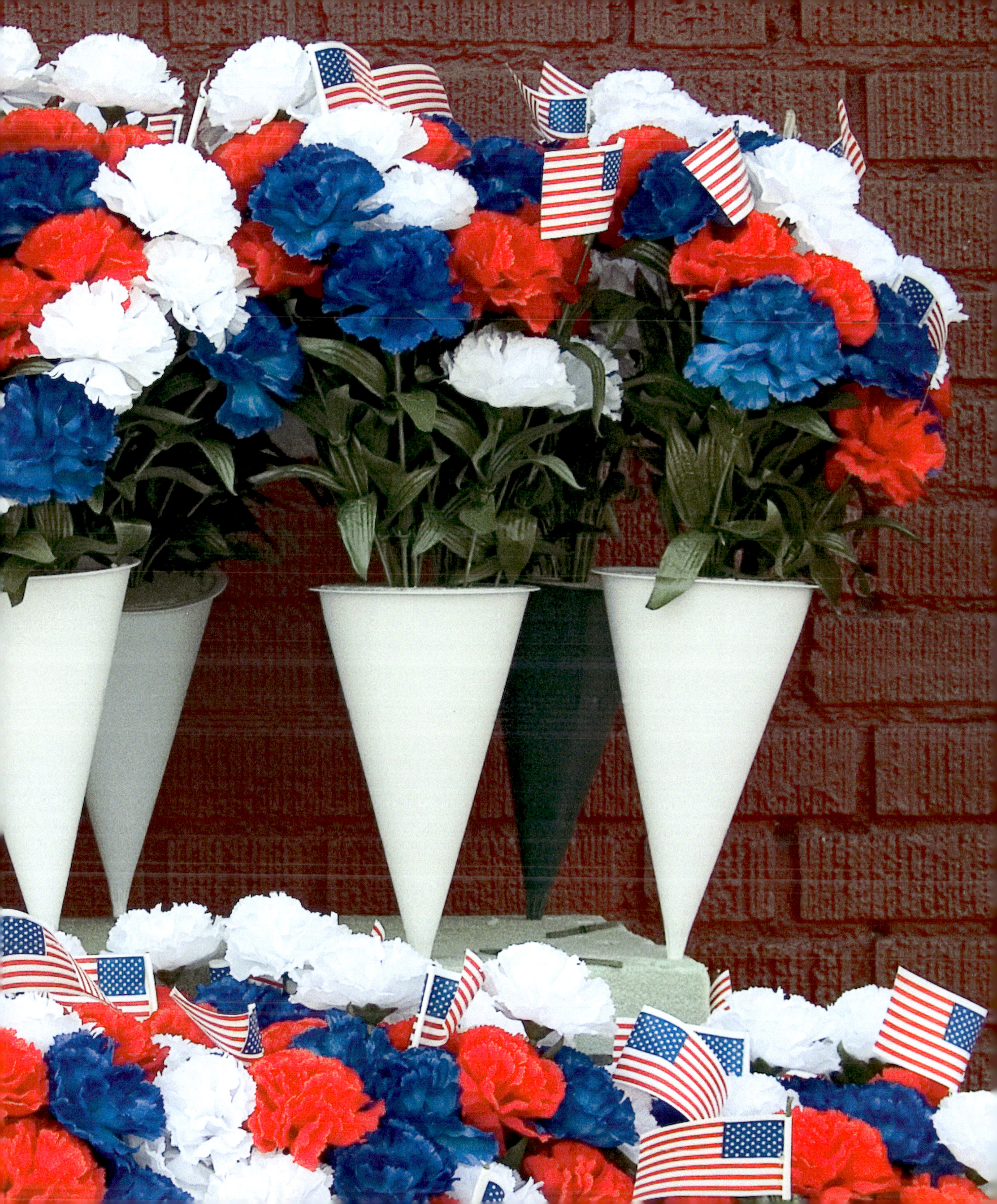

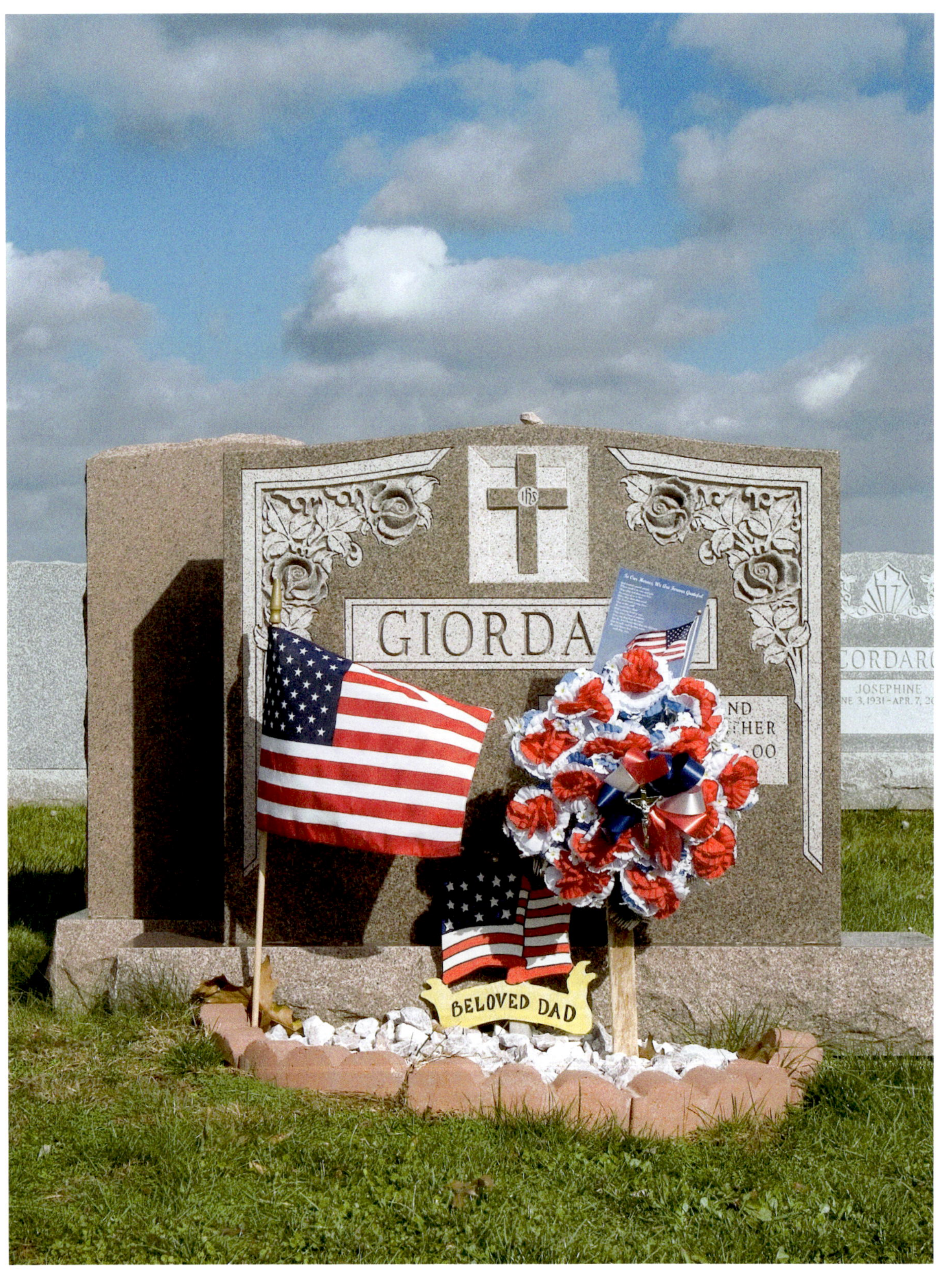

#76

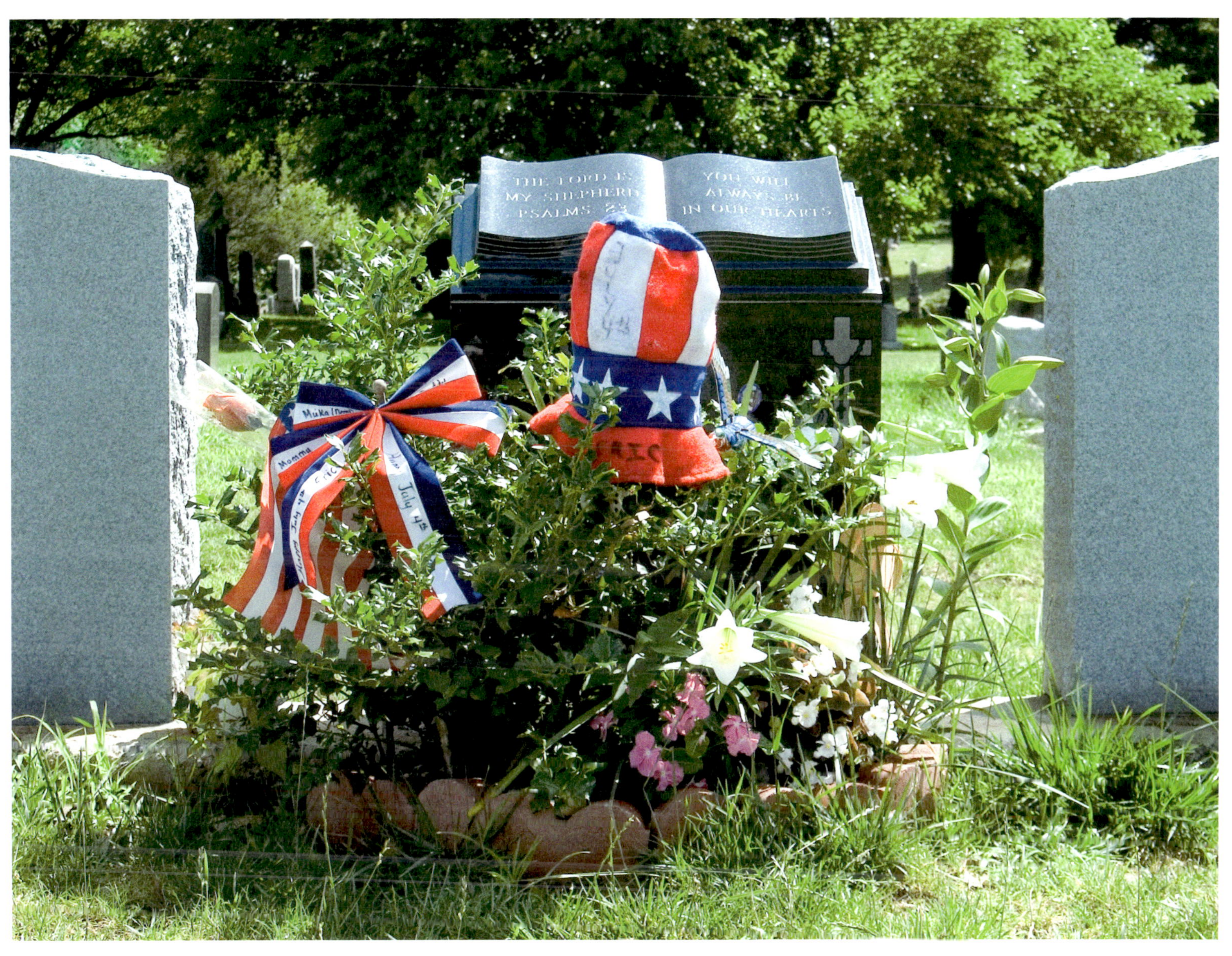
THE LORD IS
MY SHEPHERD
PSALMS 23
YOU WILL
ALWAYS BE
IN OUR HEARTS

#77

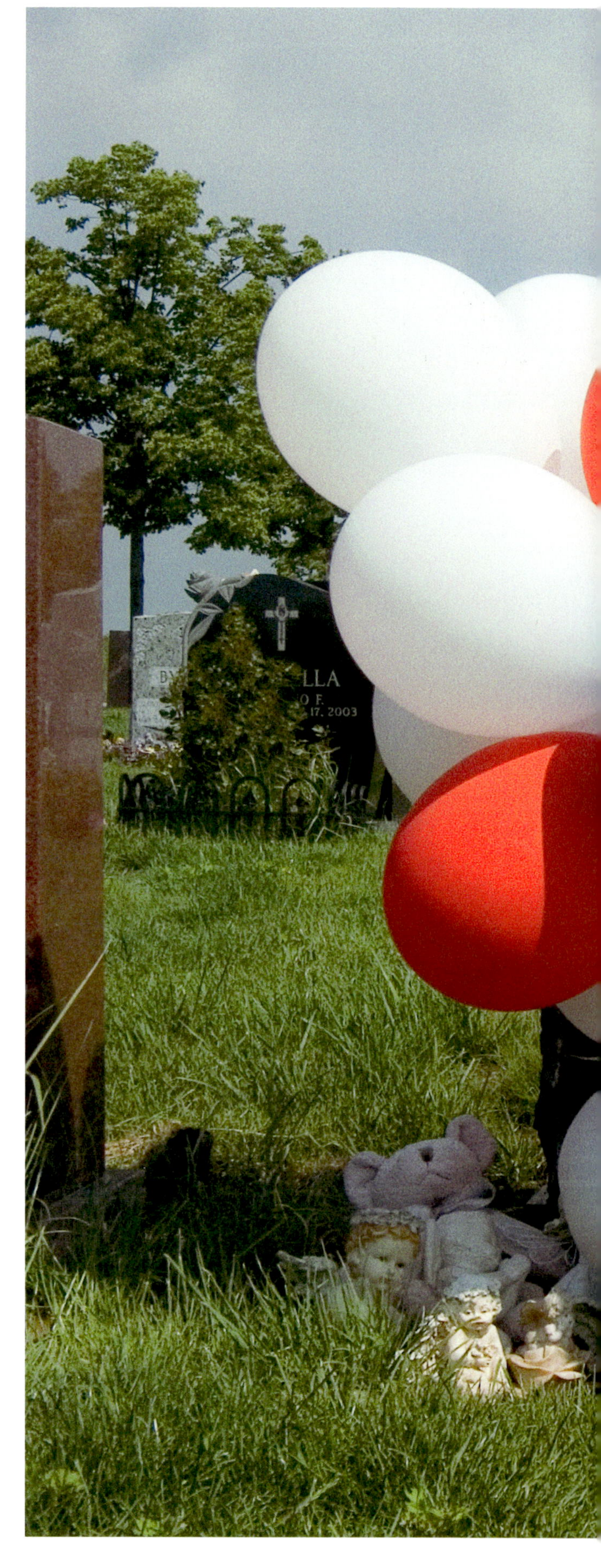

#78

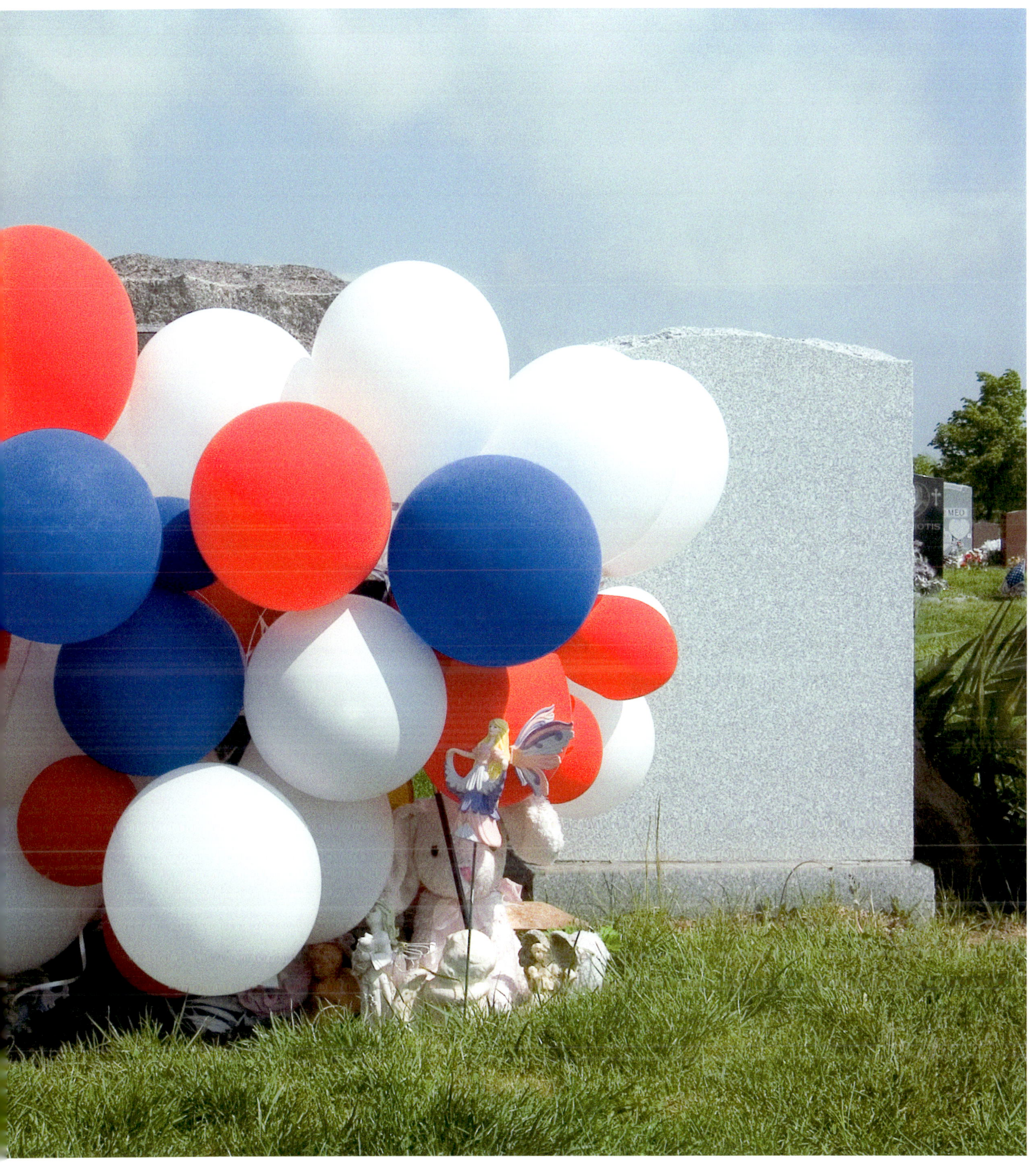

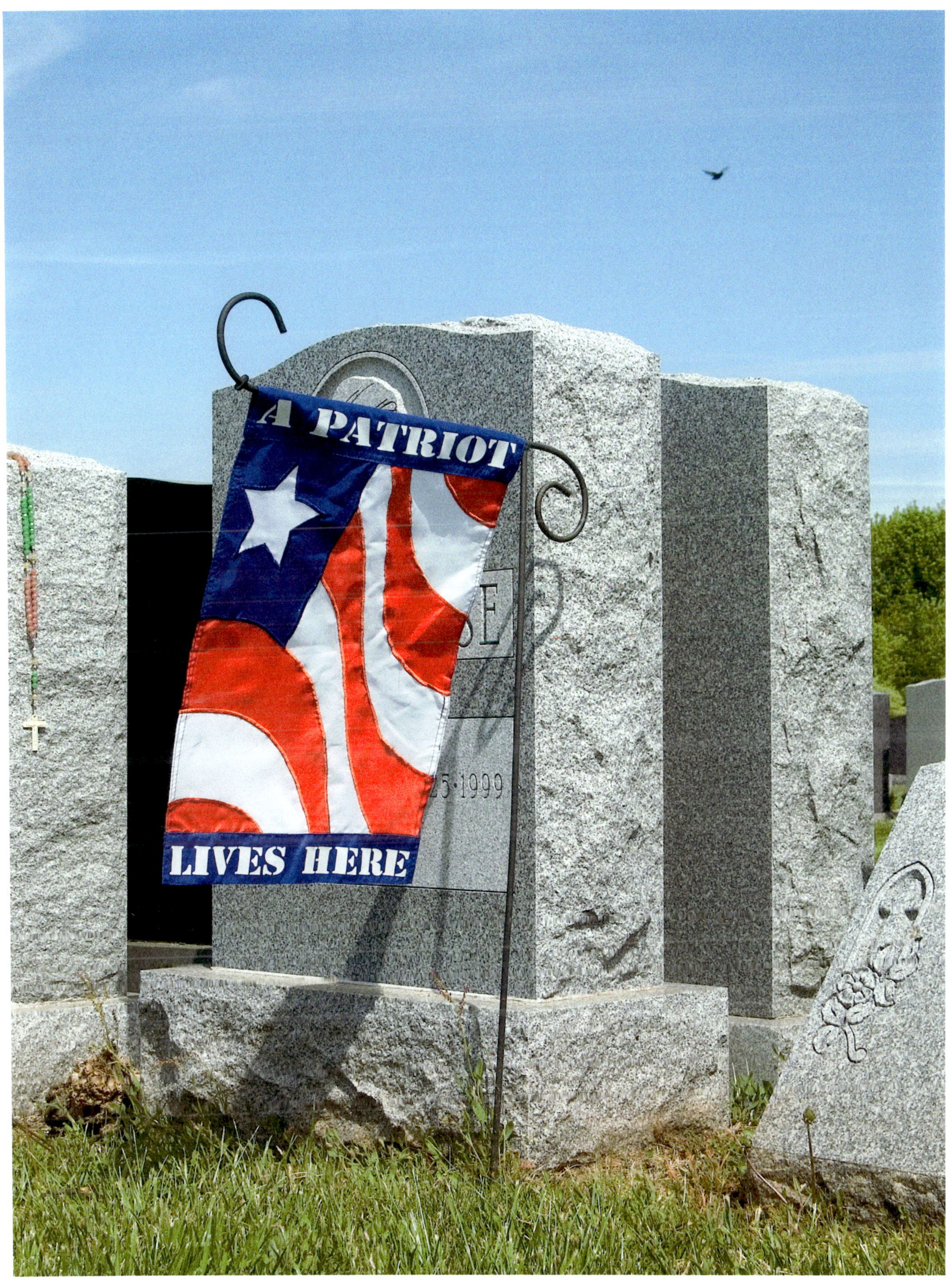
A PATRIOT
LIVES HERE
25·1999

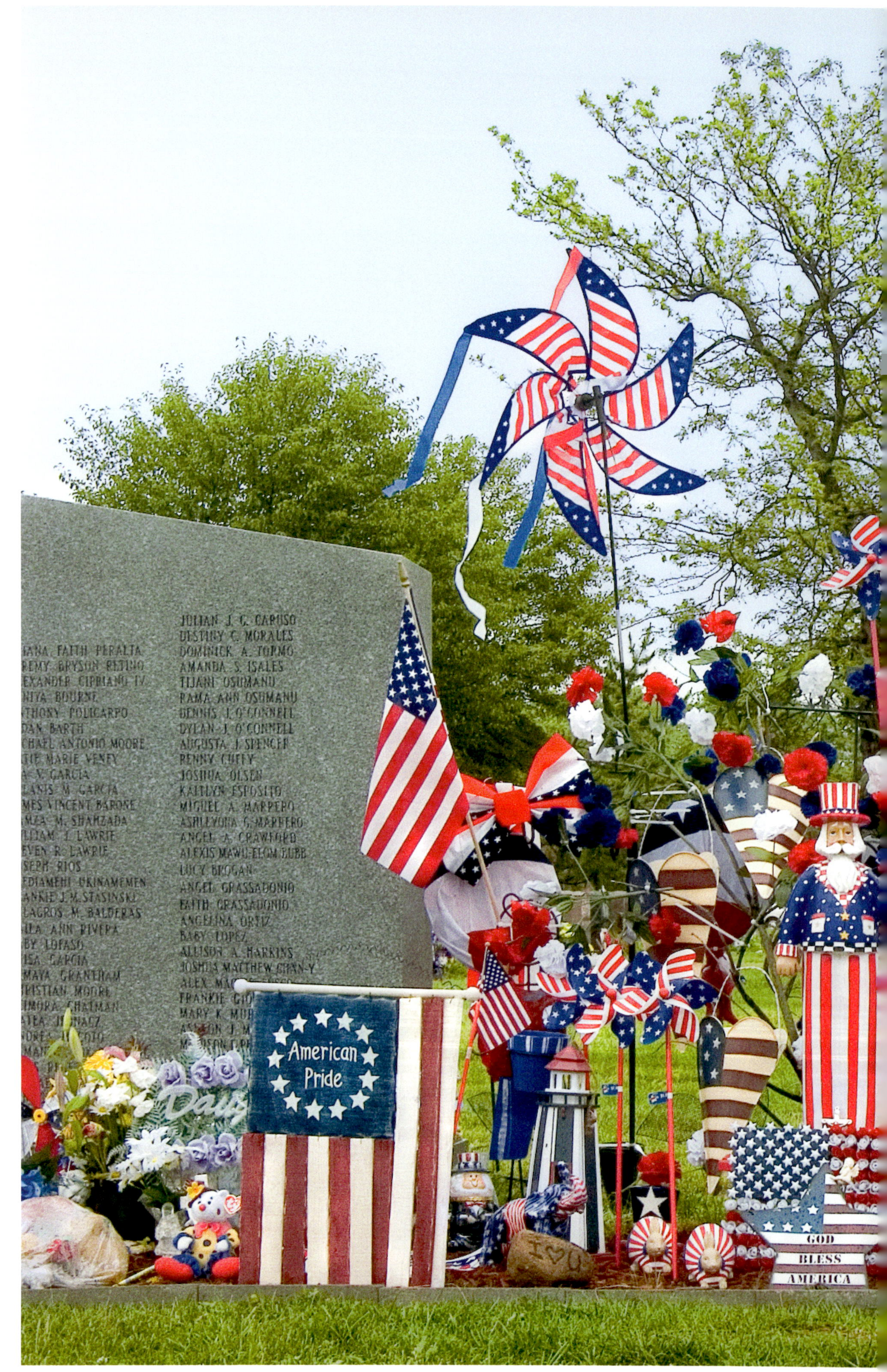

#56B

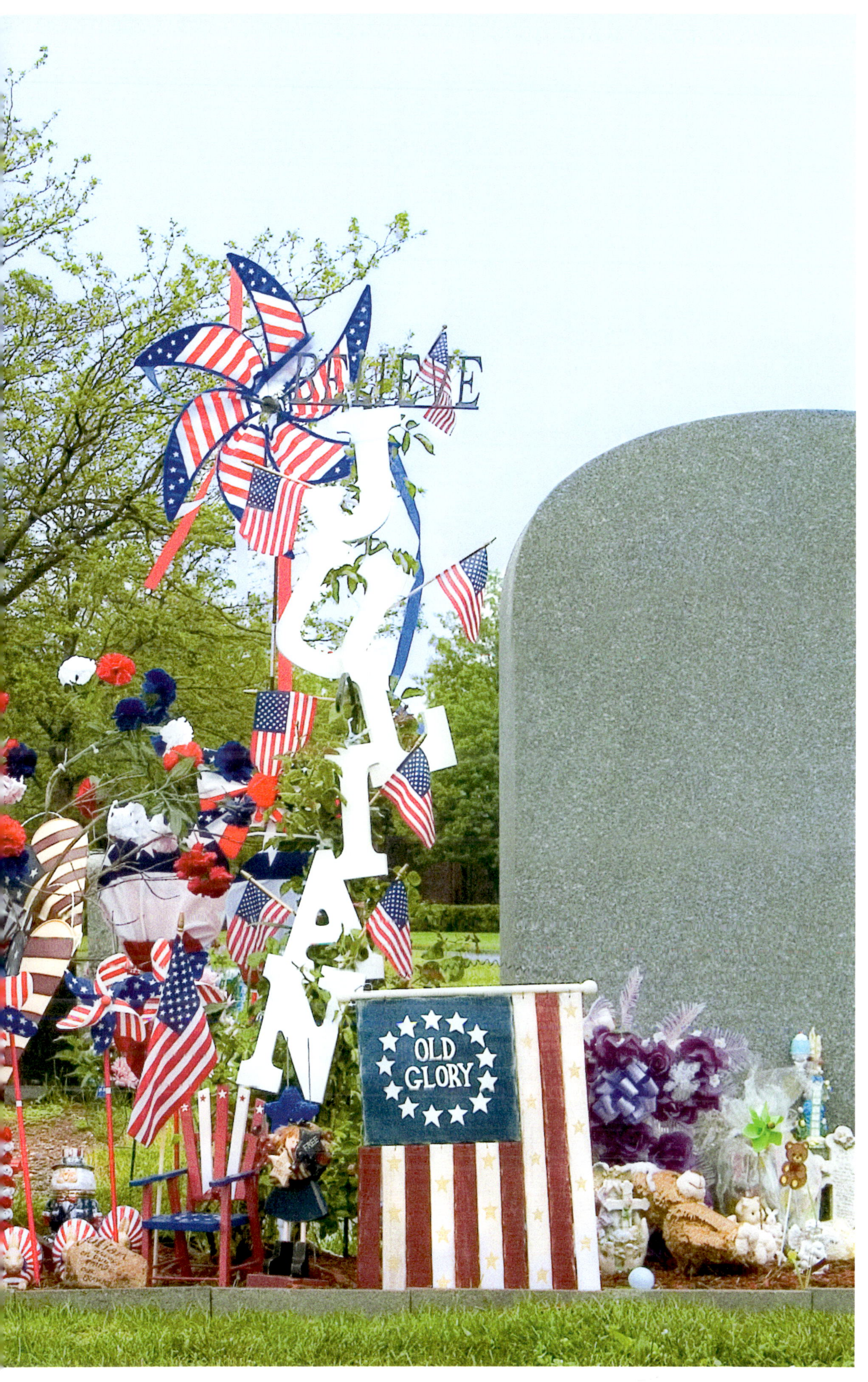
BELIEVE
OLD
GLORY

BELOVED HUSBAND
AND FATHER
WILLIAM H.
1914 — 1960
BELOVED WIFE
AND MOTHER
JANE M.
1916 — 1993

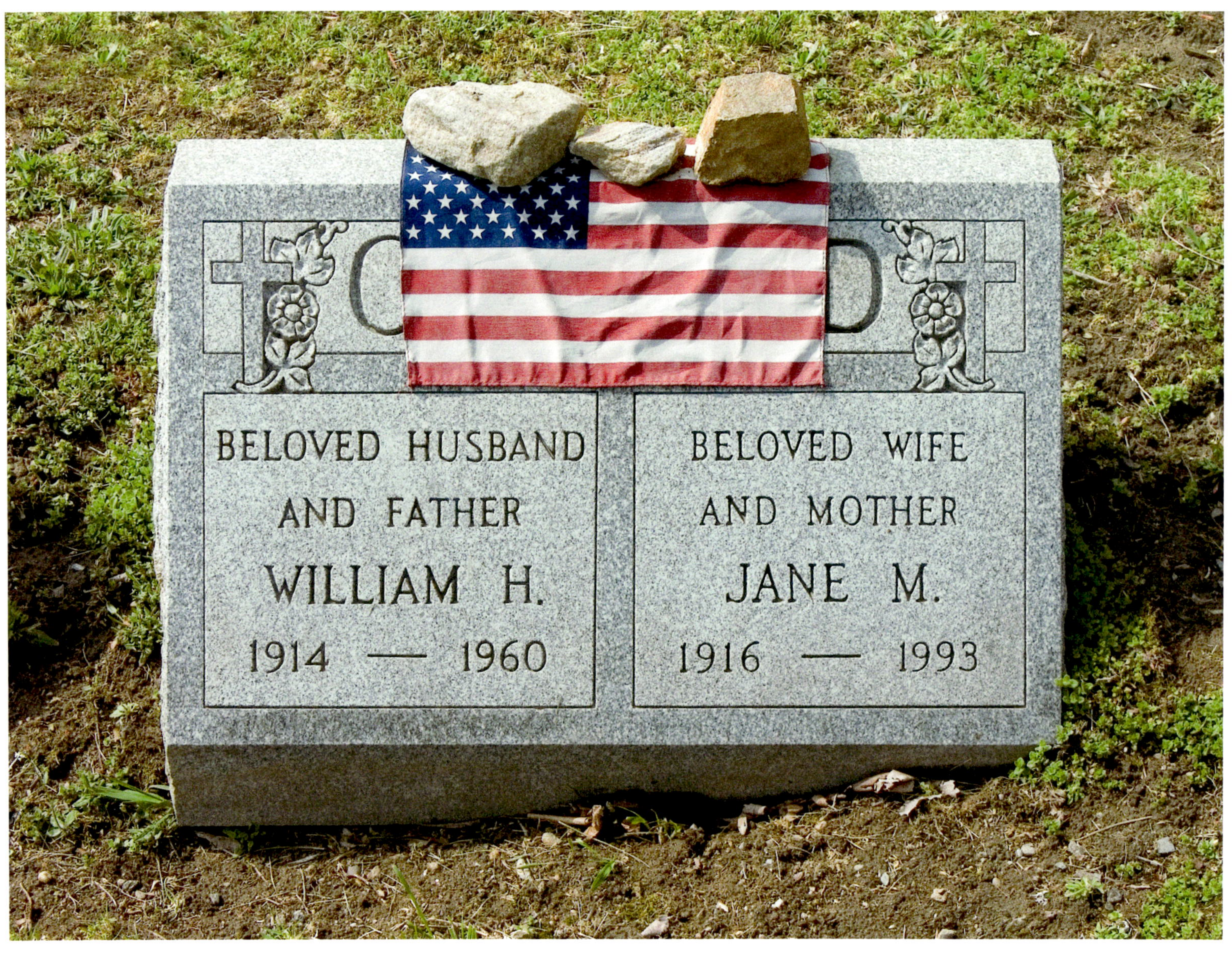

#80

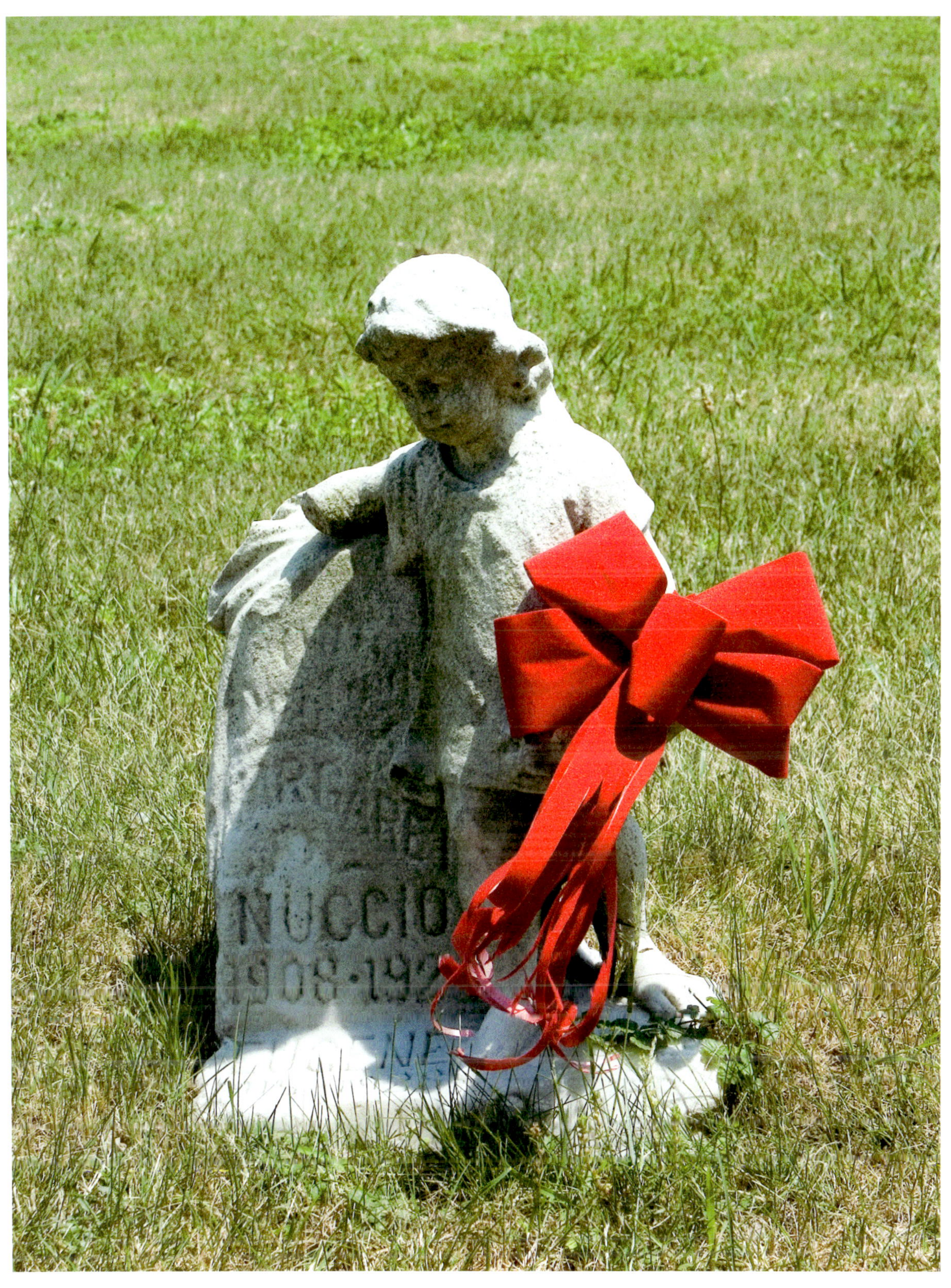
NUCCIO
1908·192

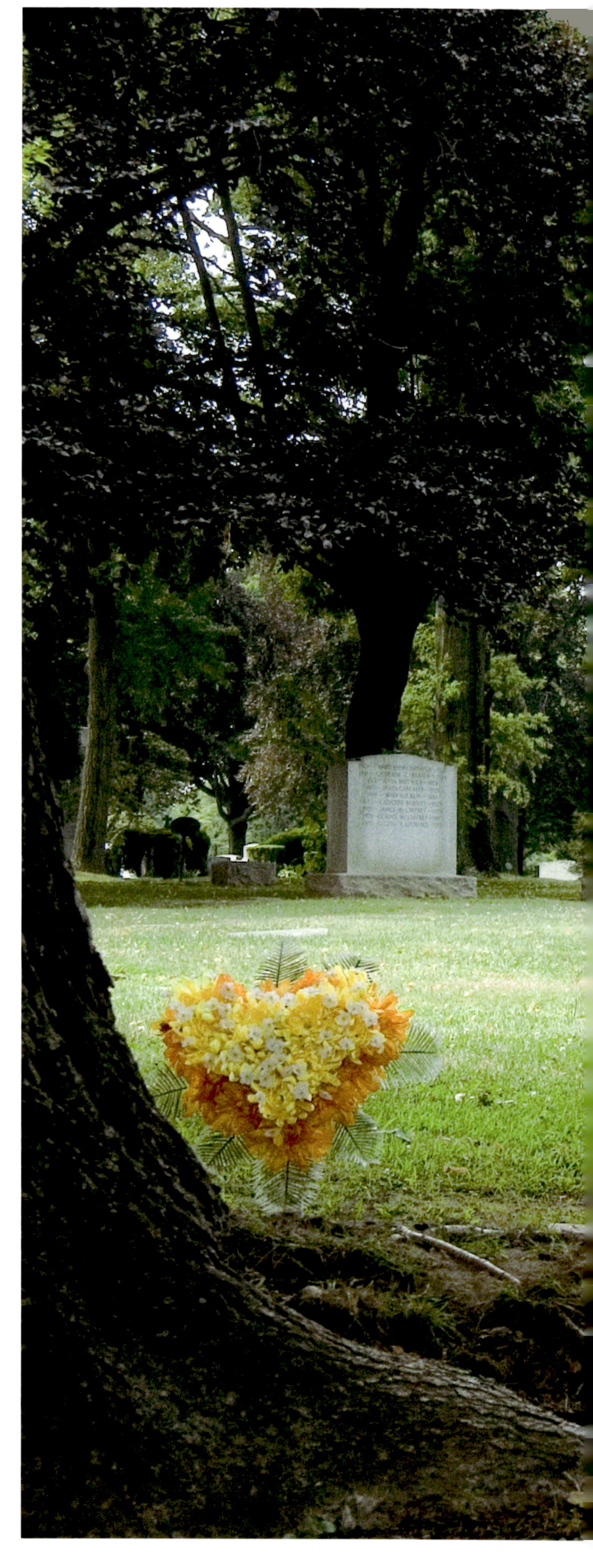

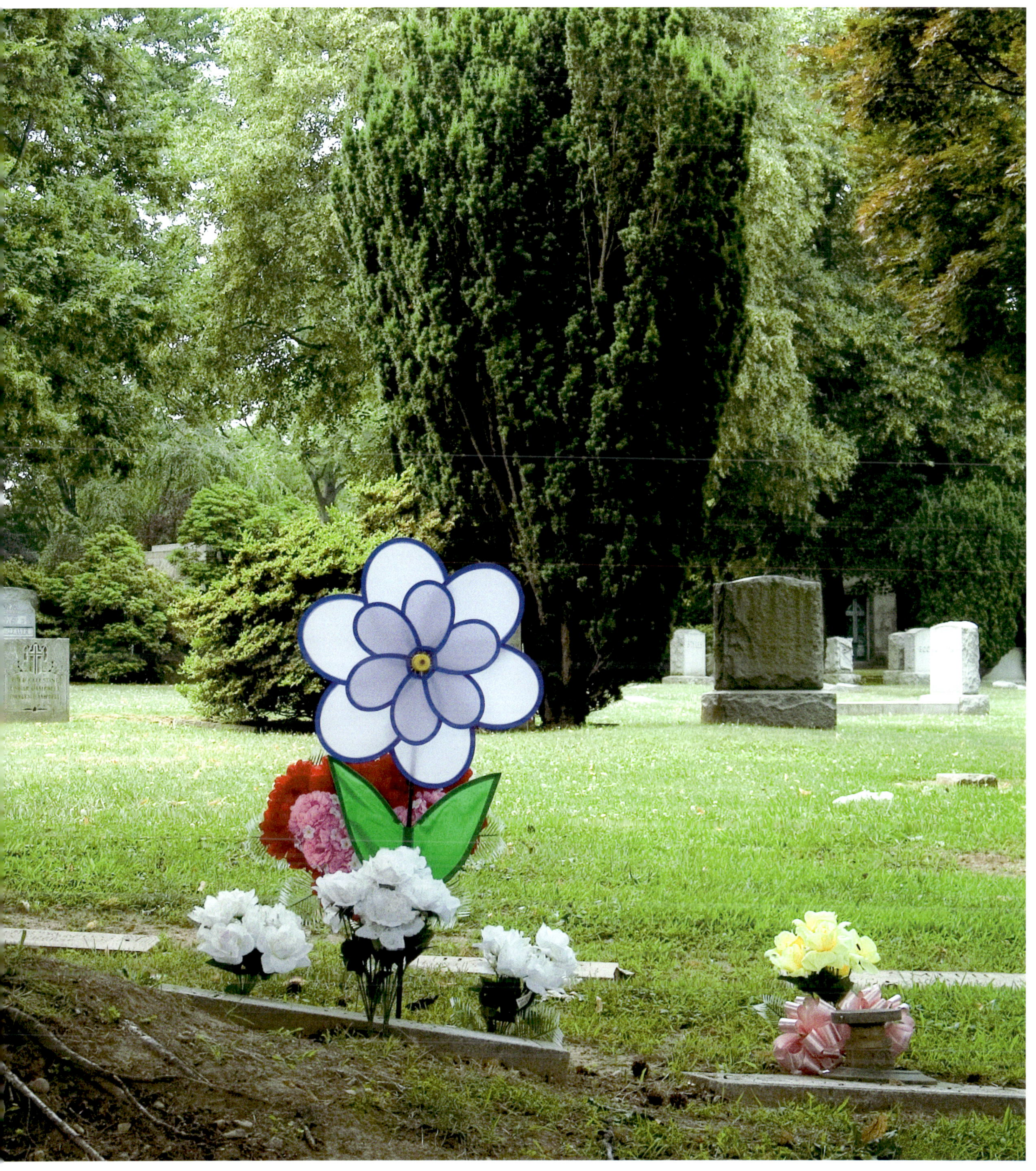

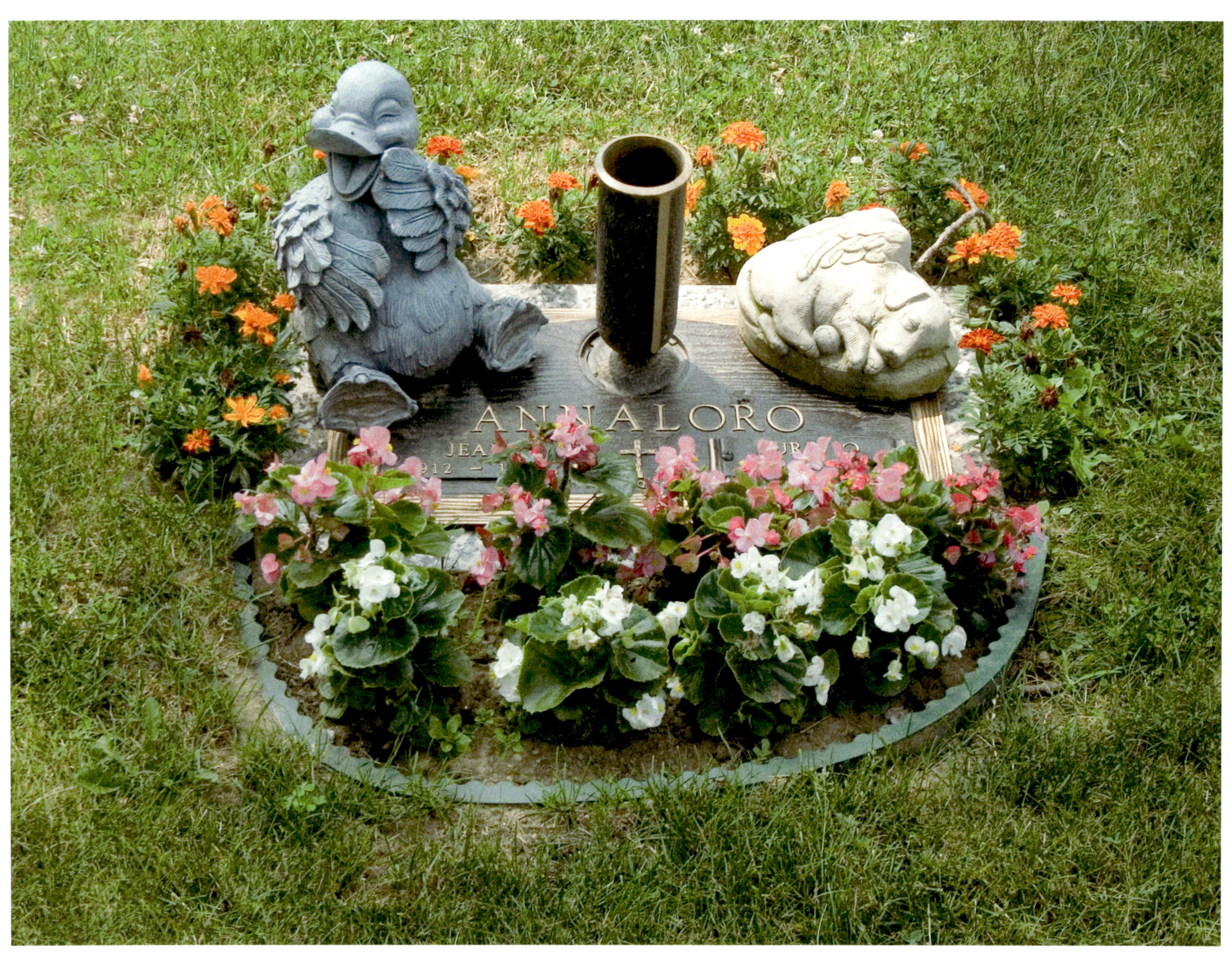

#83

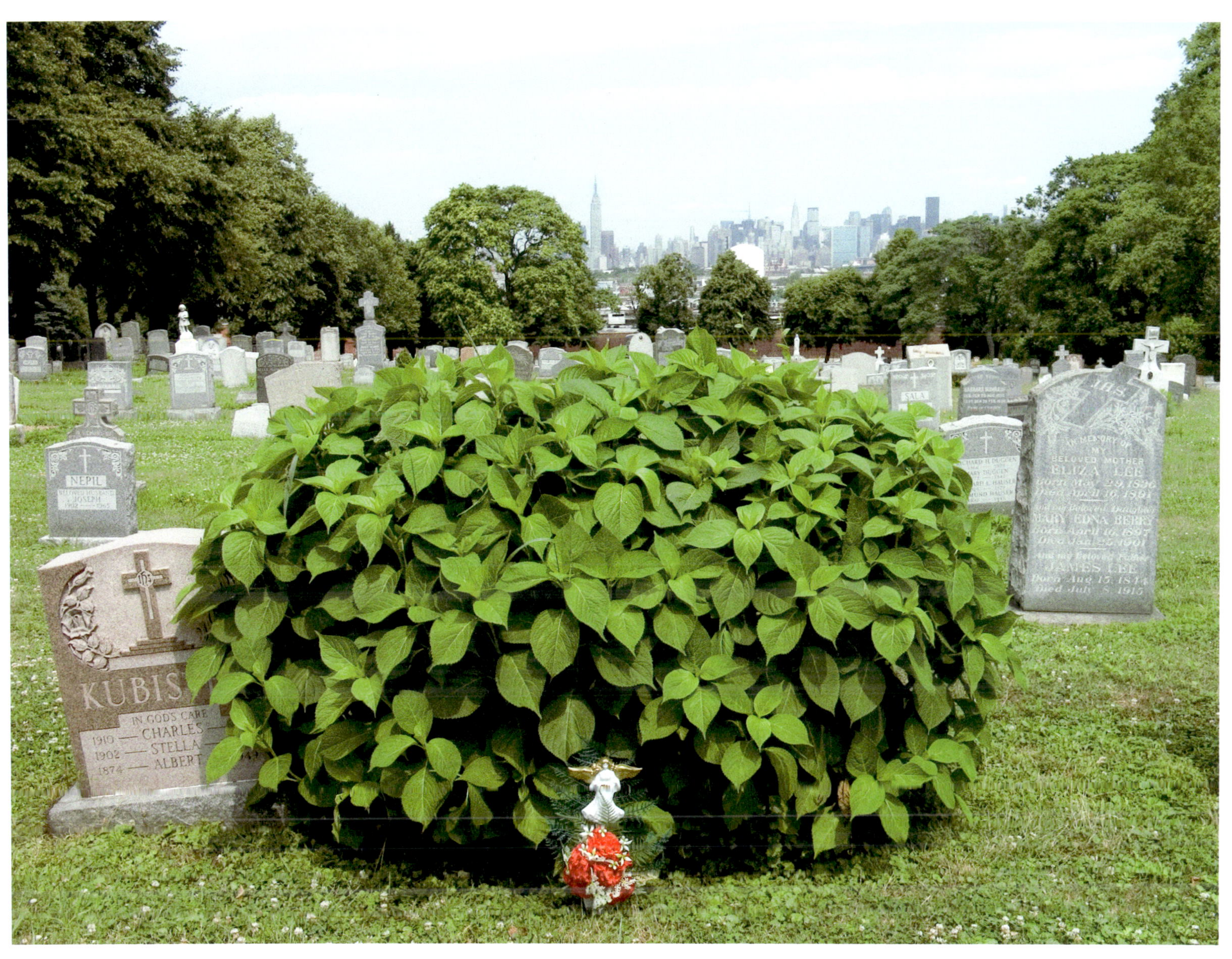
NEPIL
SALA
MY
BELOVED MOTHER
ELIZA LEE
JAMES LEE
Died July 8 1915
KUBIS
IN GOD'S CARE
1910 — CHARLES
1902 — STELLA
1874 — ALBERT

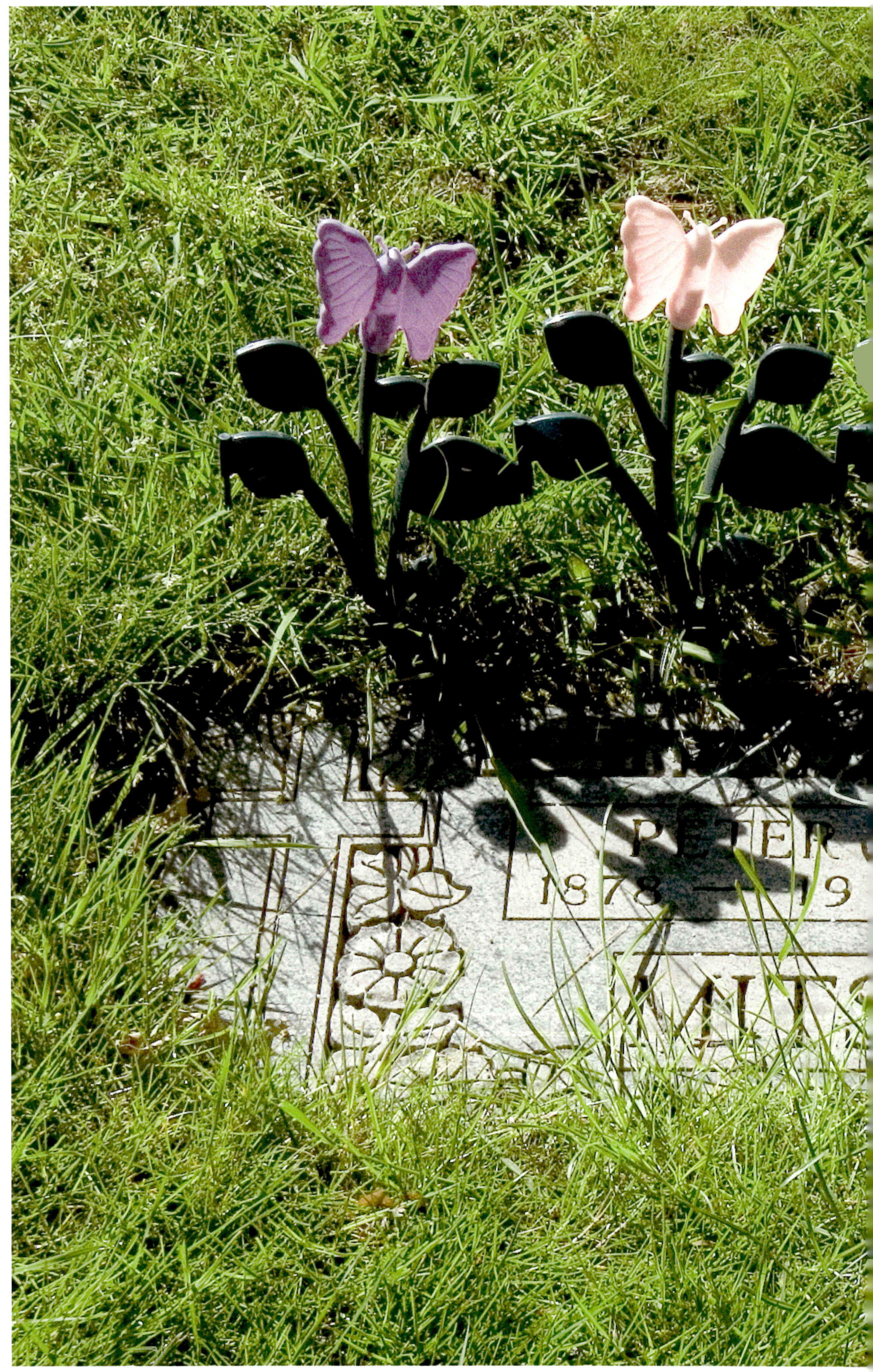

#85

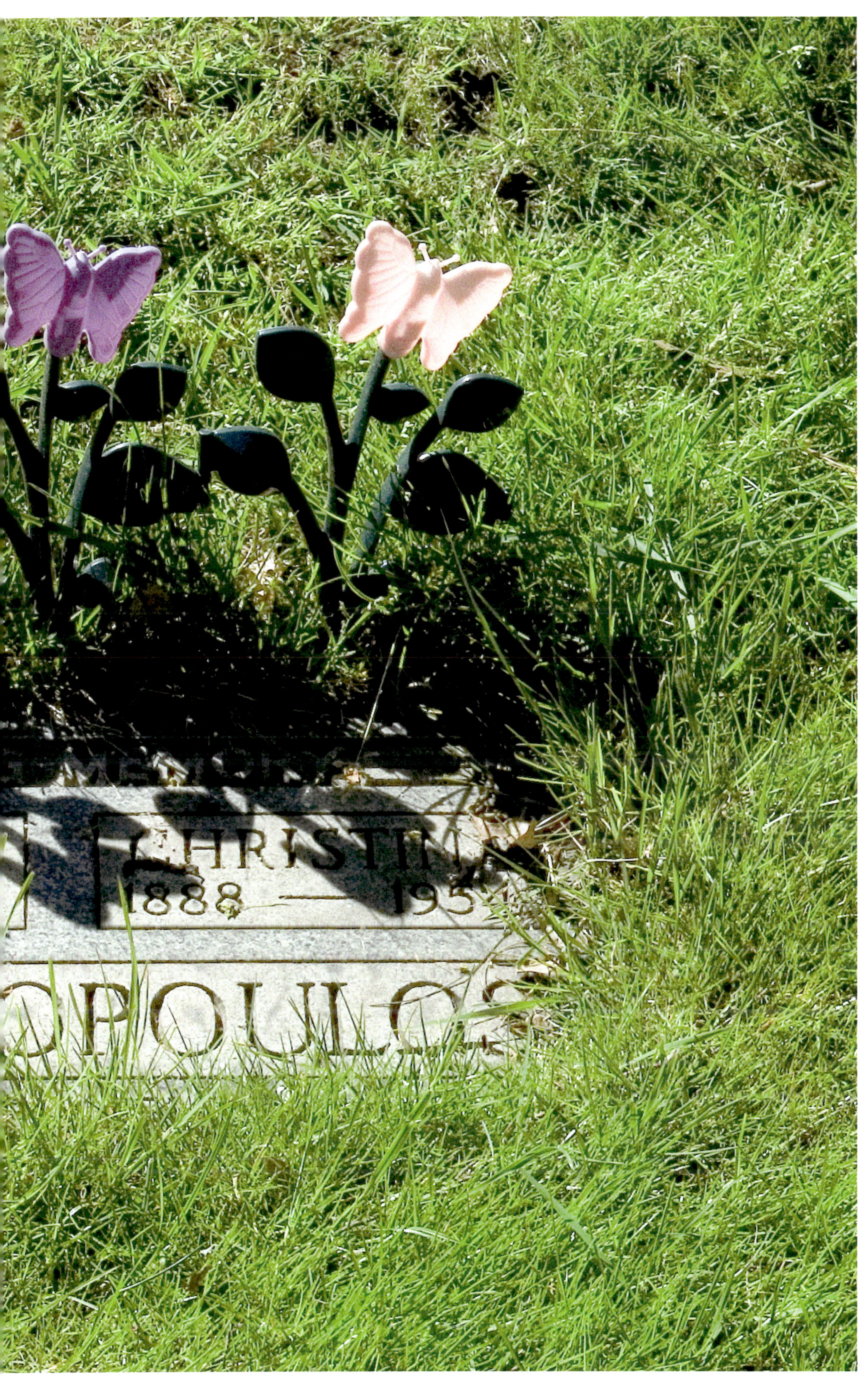
CHRISTIN
1888
OPOULOS

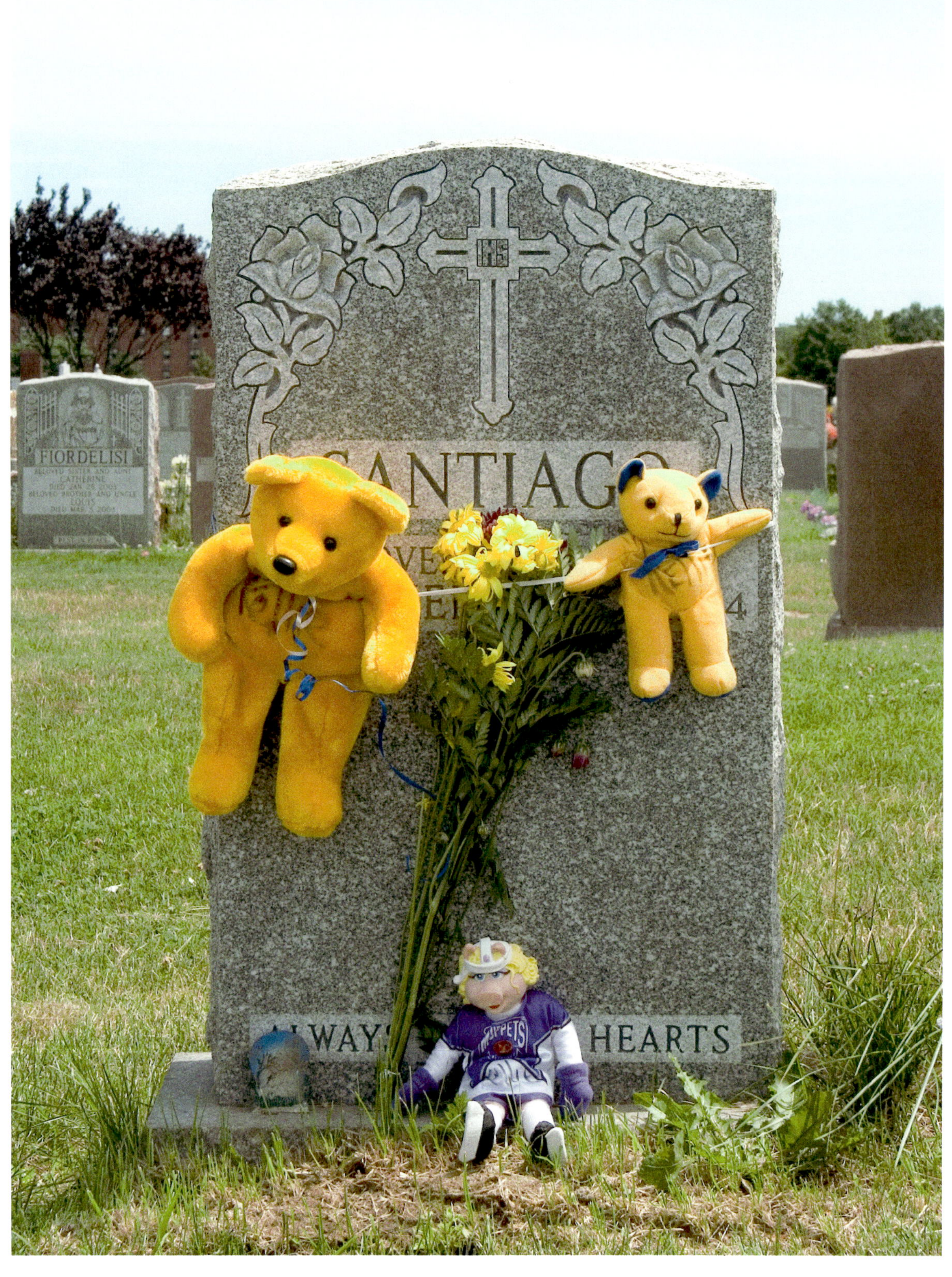

#86

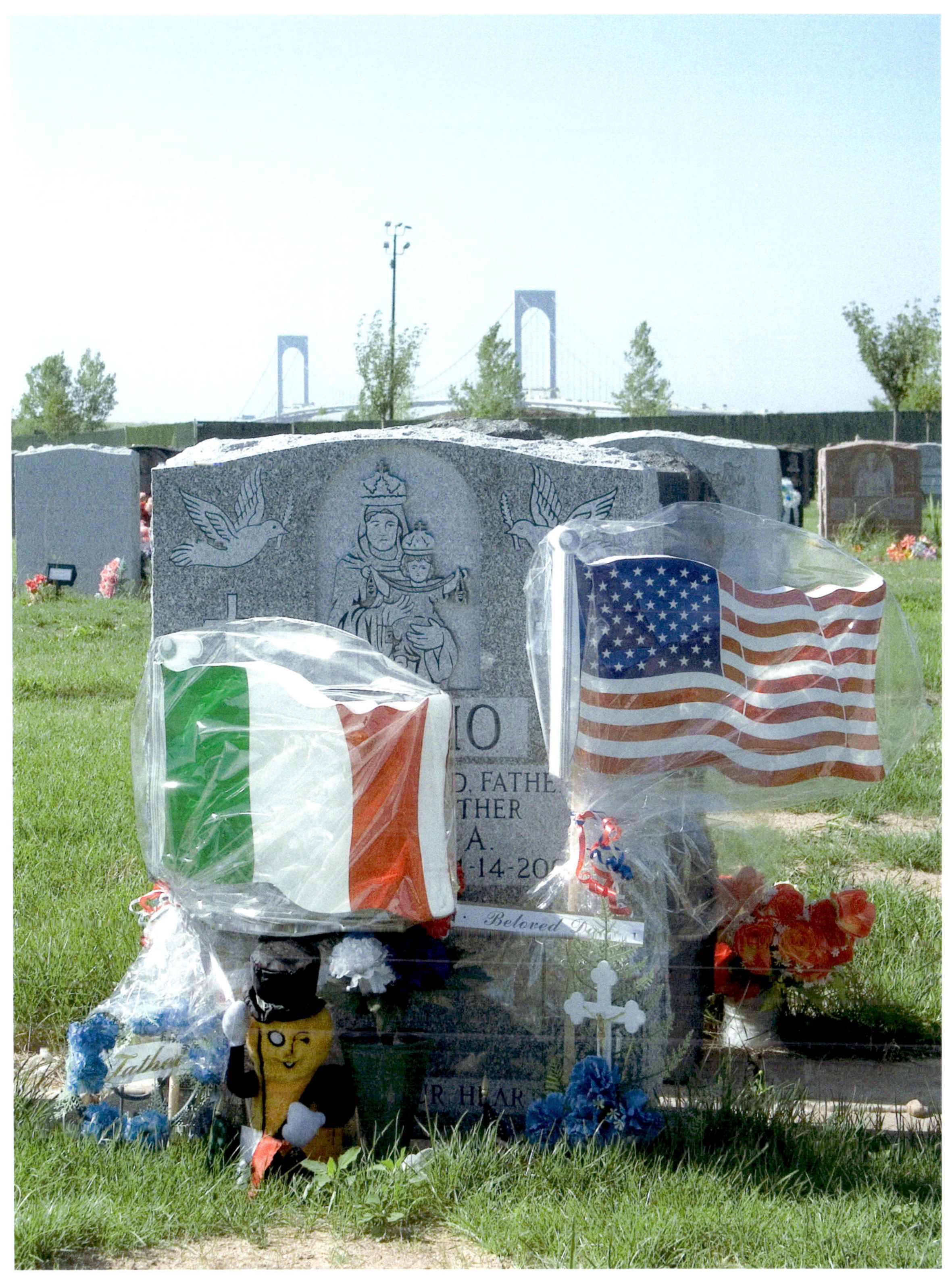
FATHER
Beloved
Father

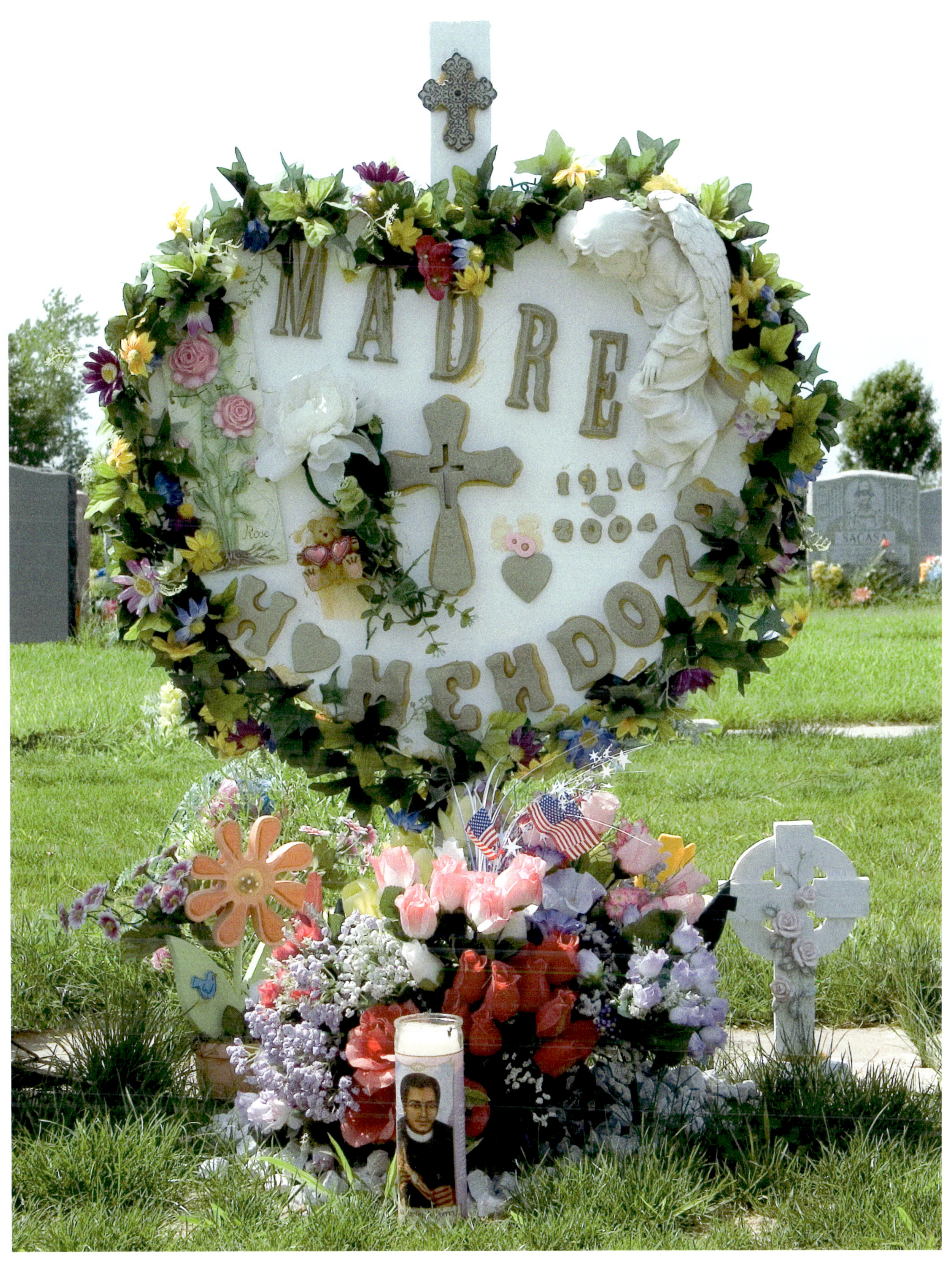

#88

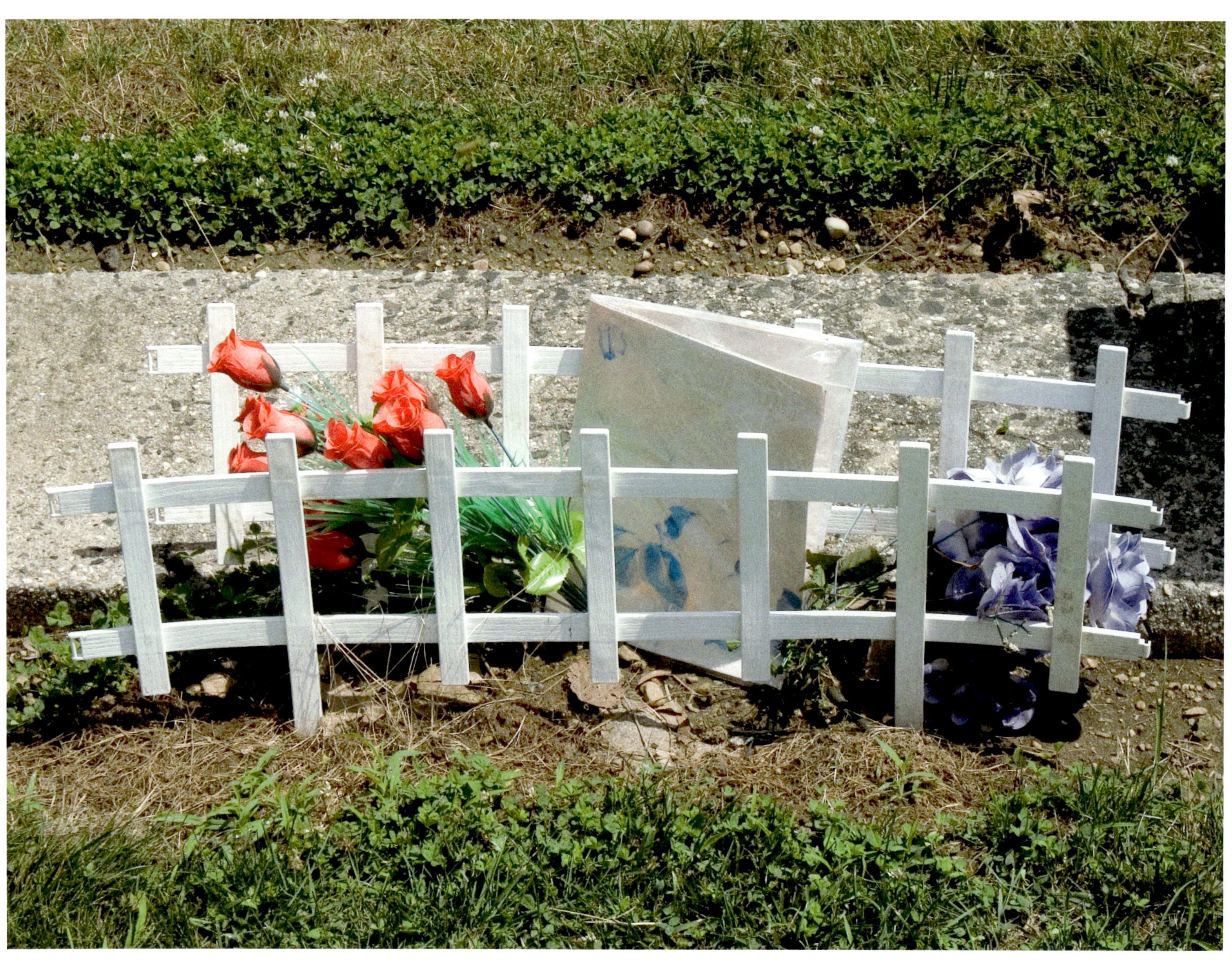

#89

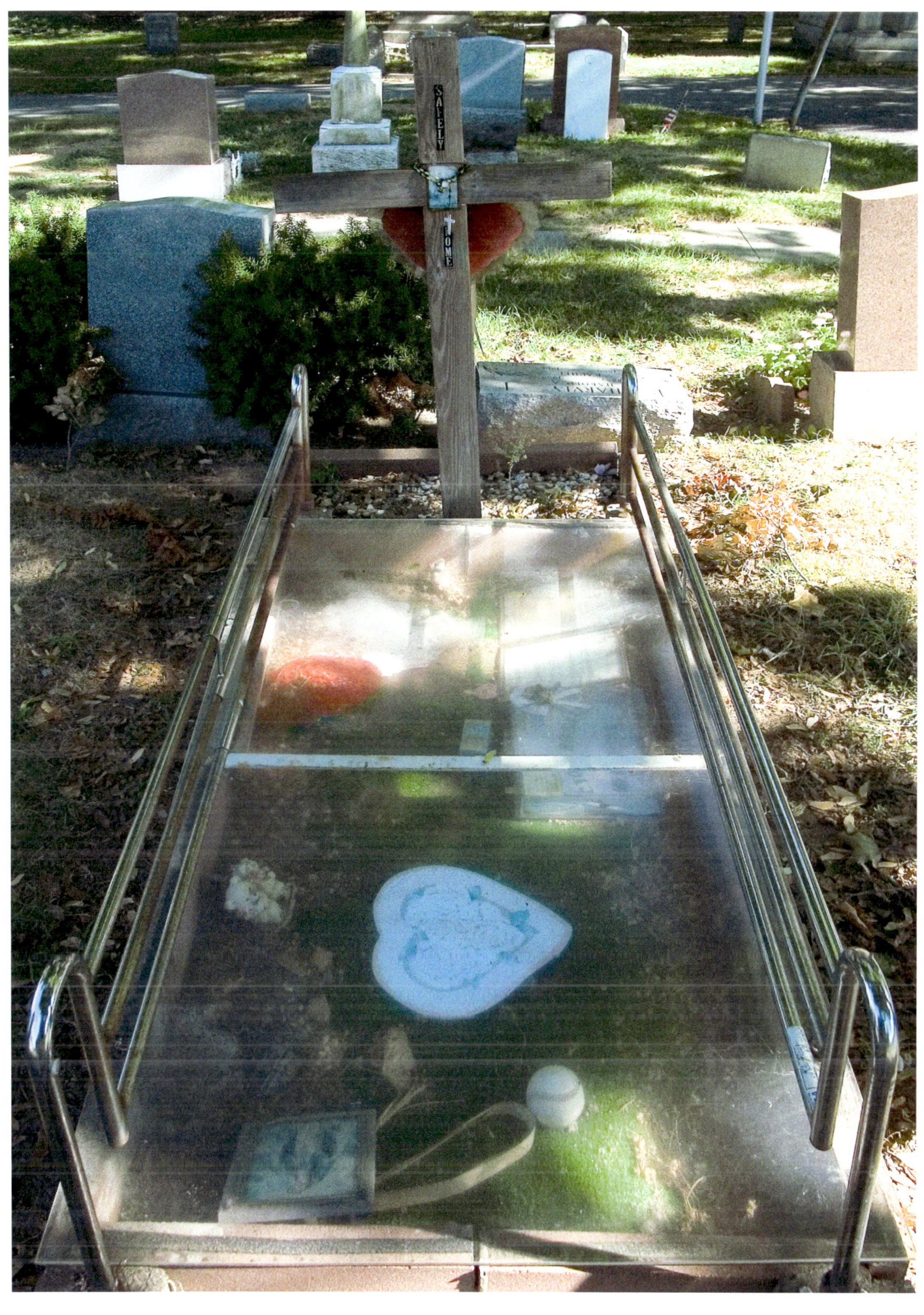
SAFELY

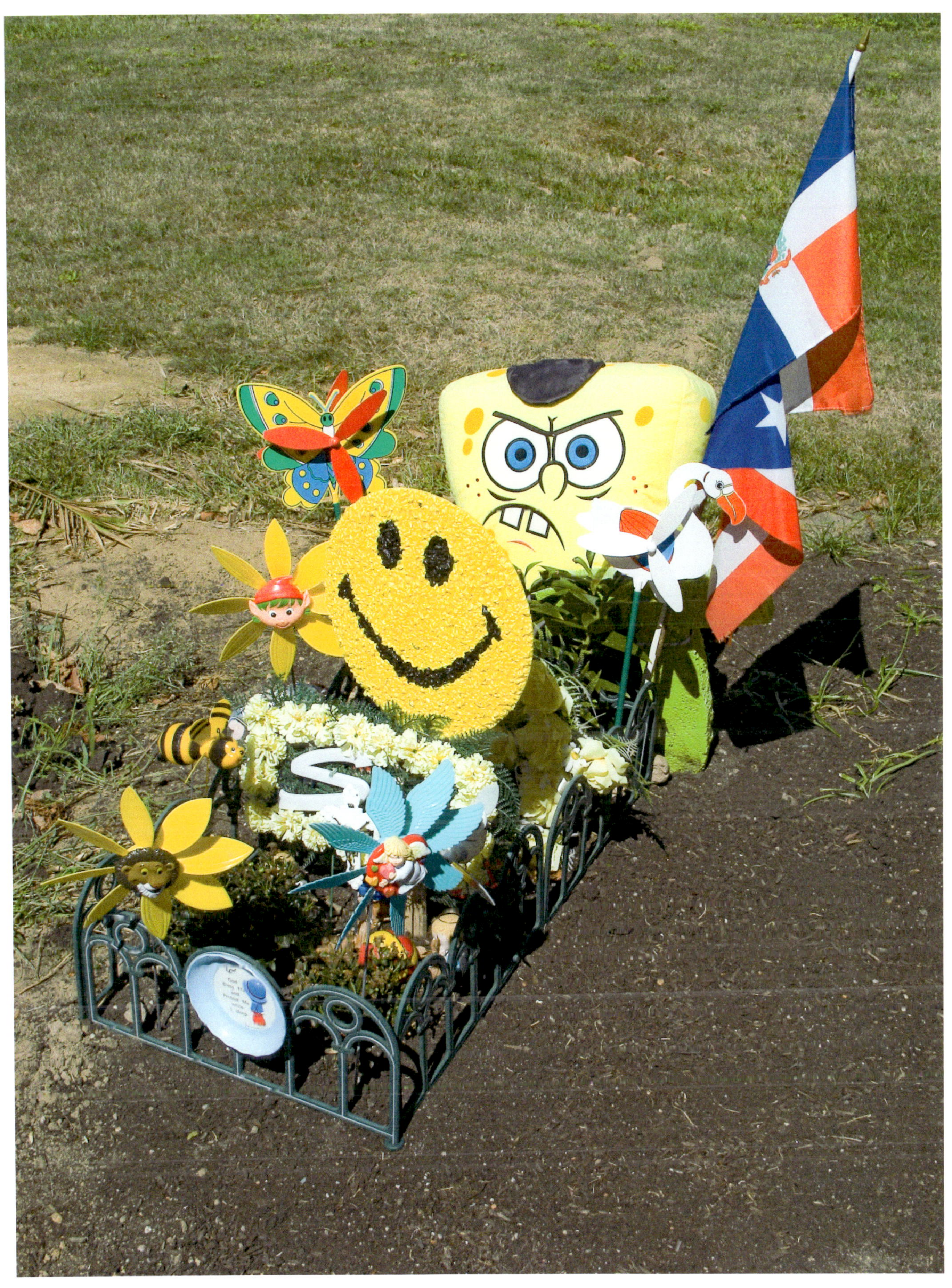

#91

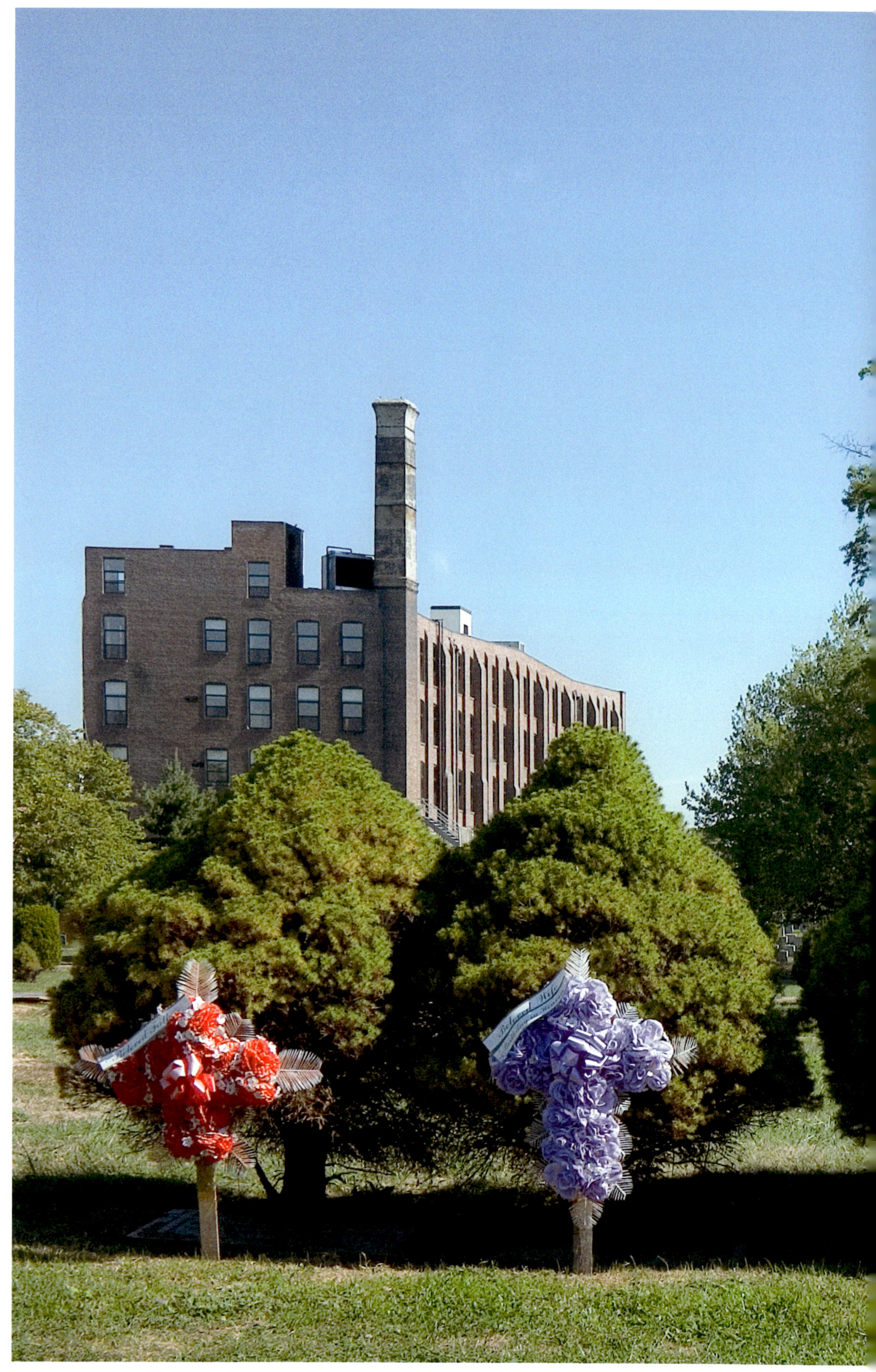

#92

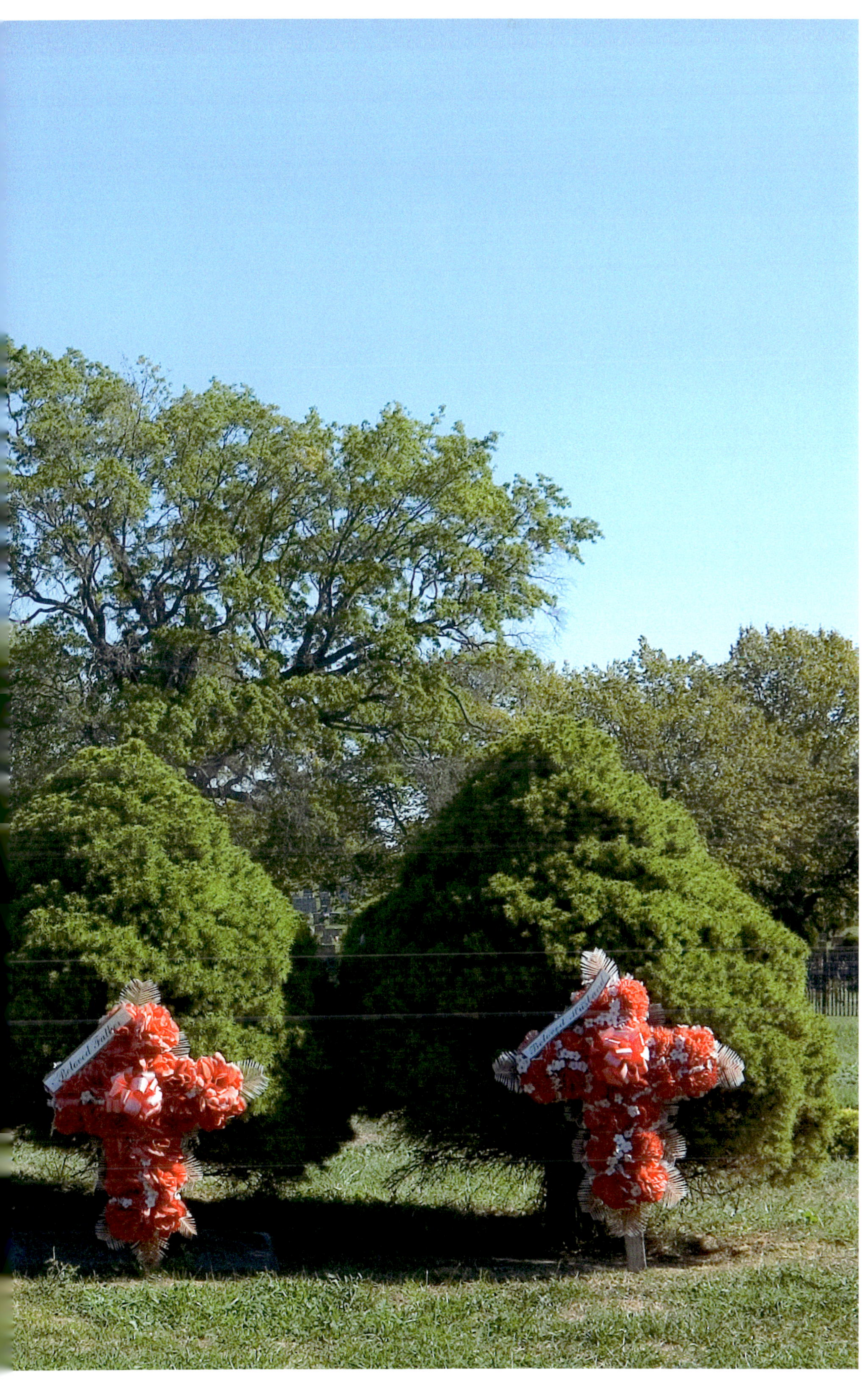
Beloved Father
Beloved Husband

D HUSBAND
GRANDFATHER
S HERRERA
42-JULY 1, 1999
ARE
R HEARTS
WE MISS YOU

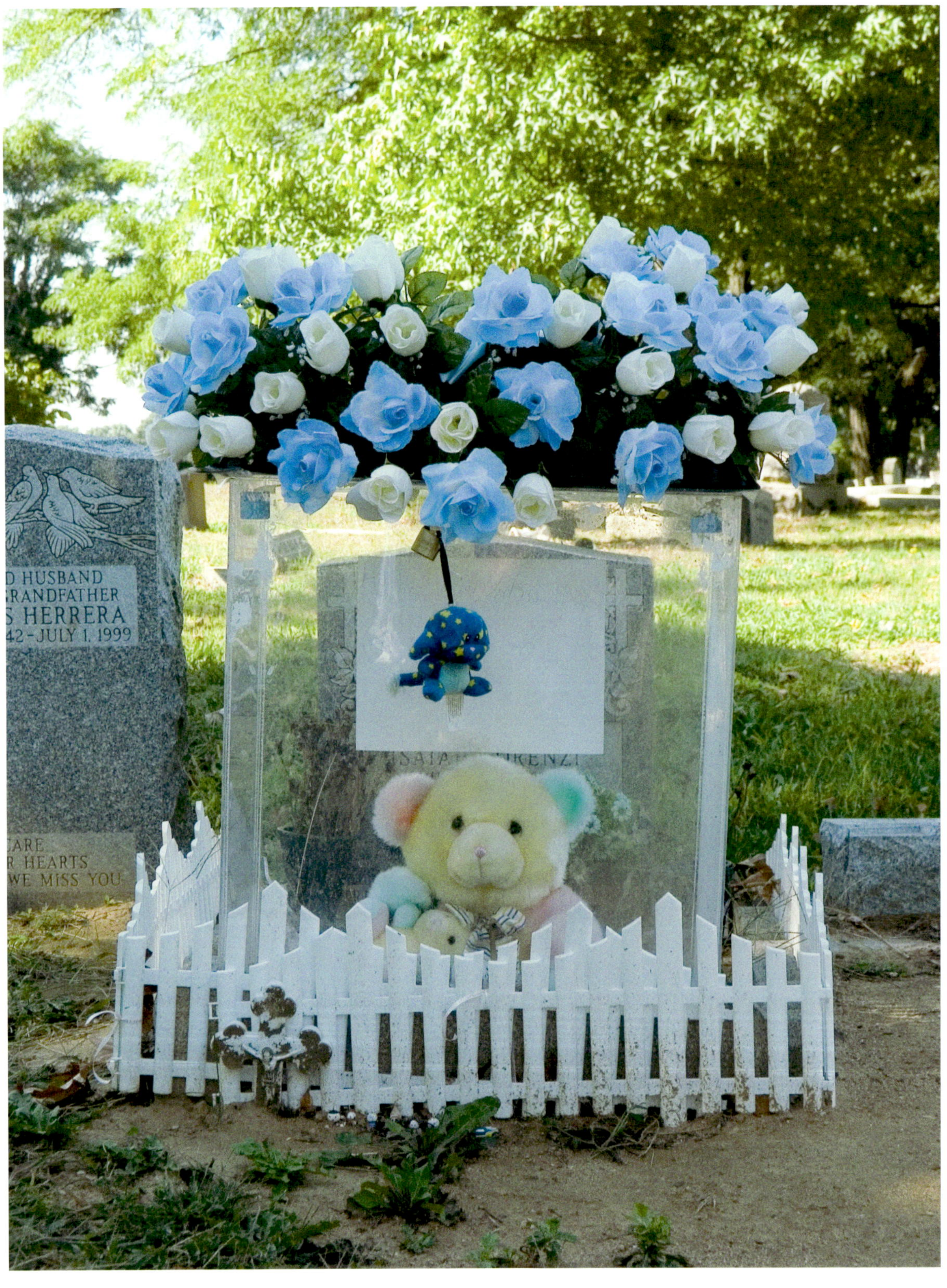

#93

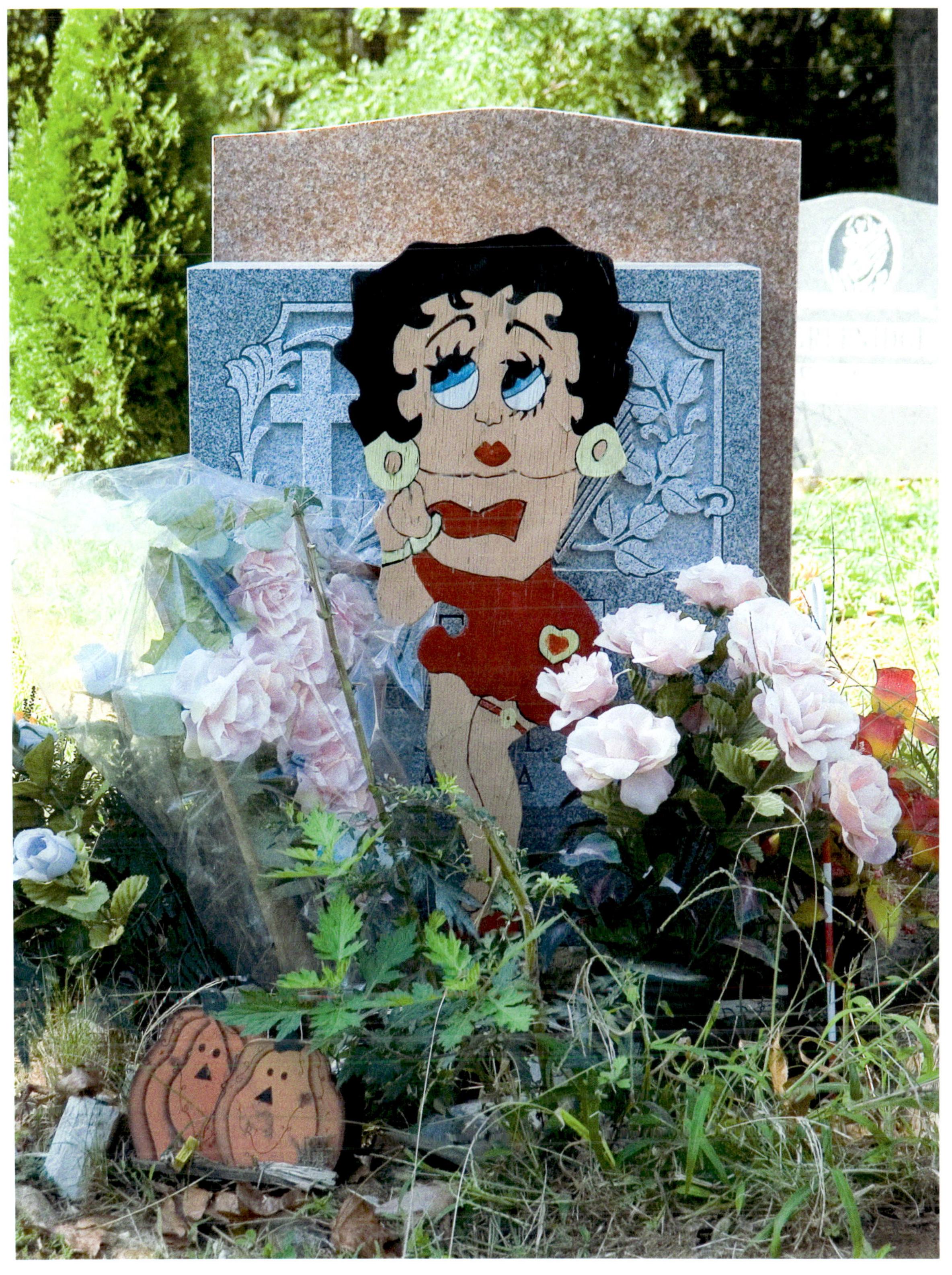

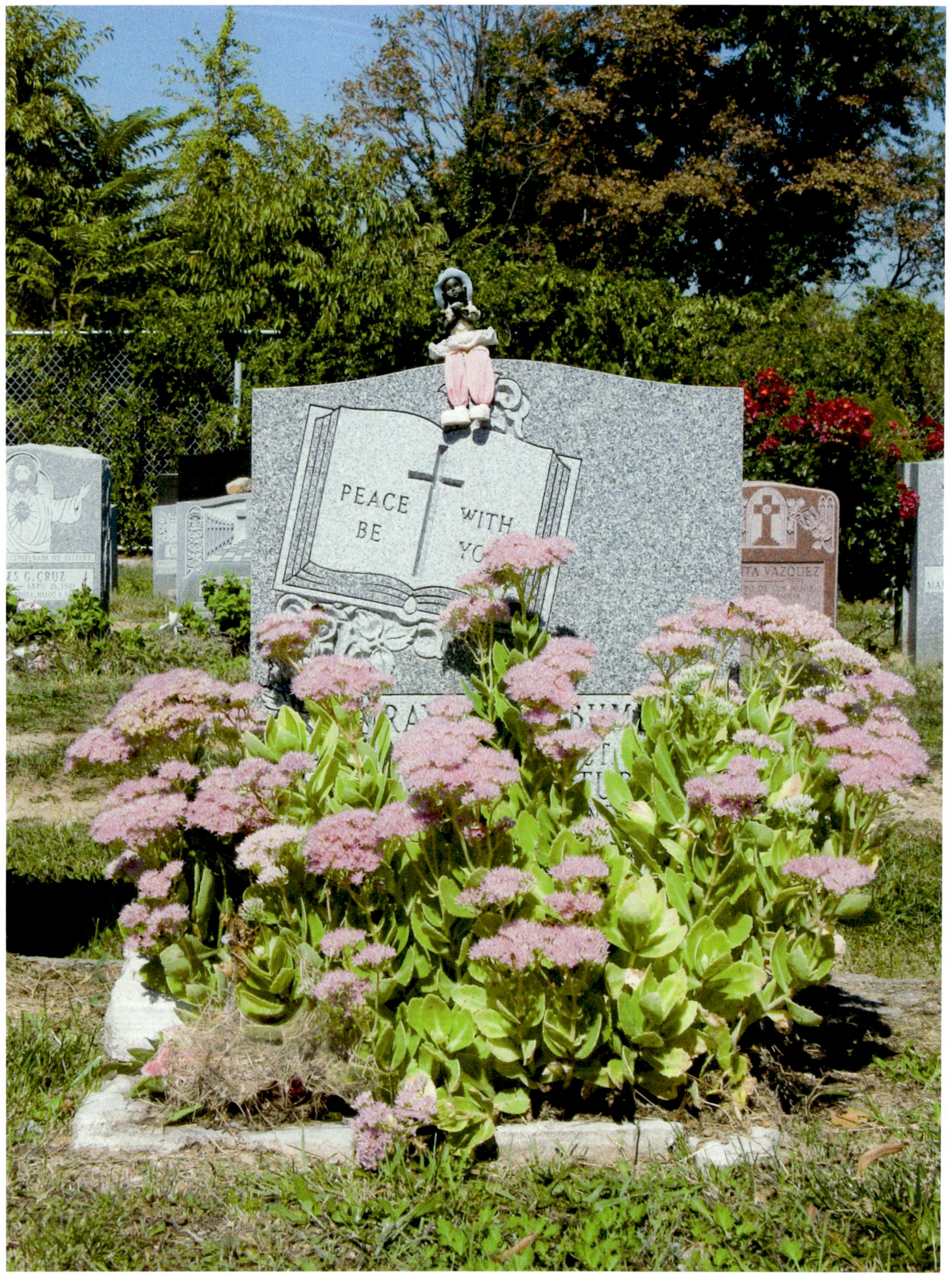

#95

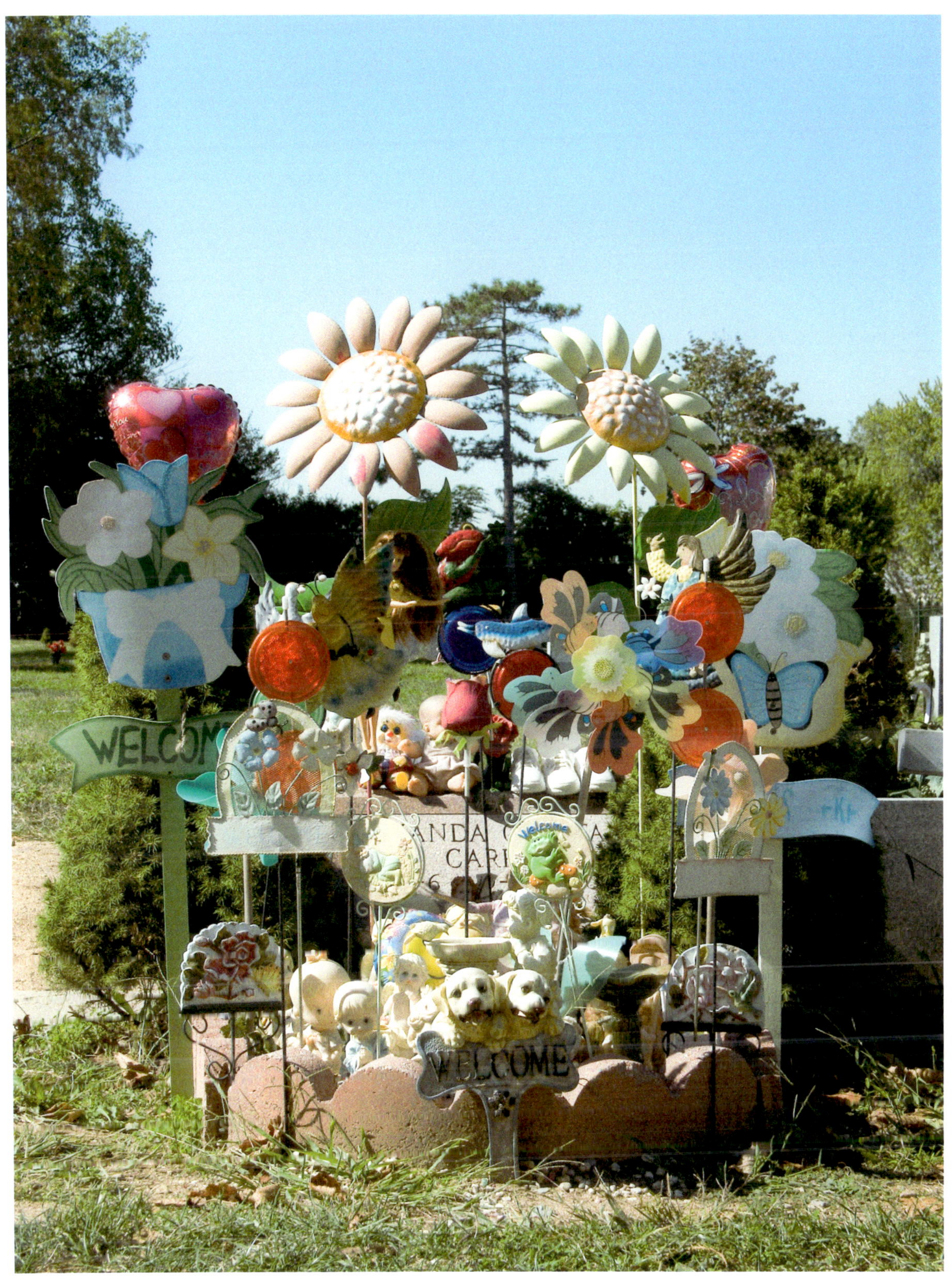

#96

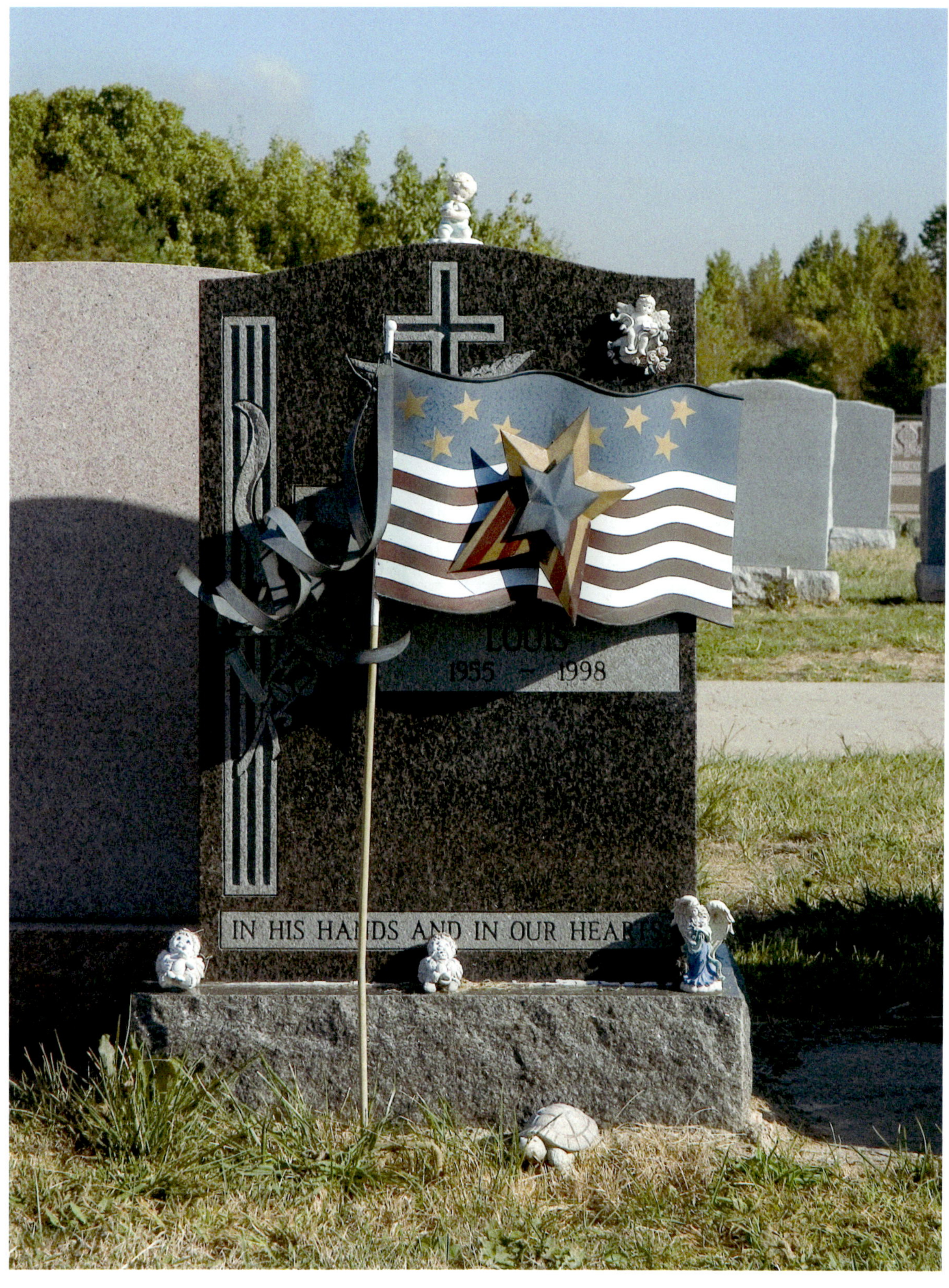

#97

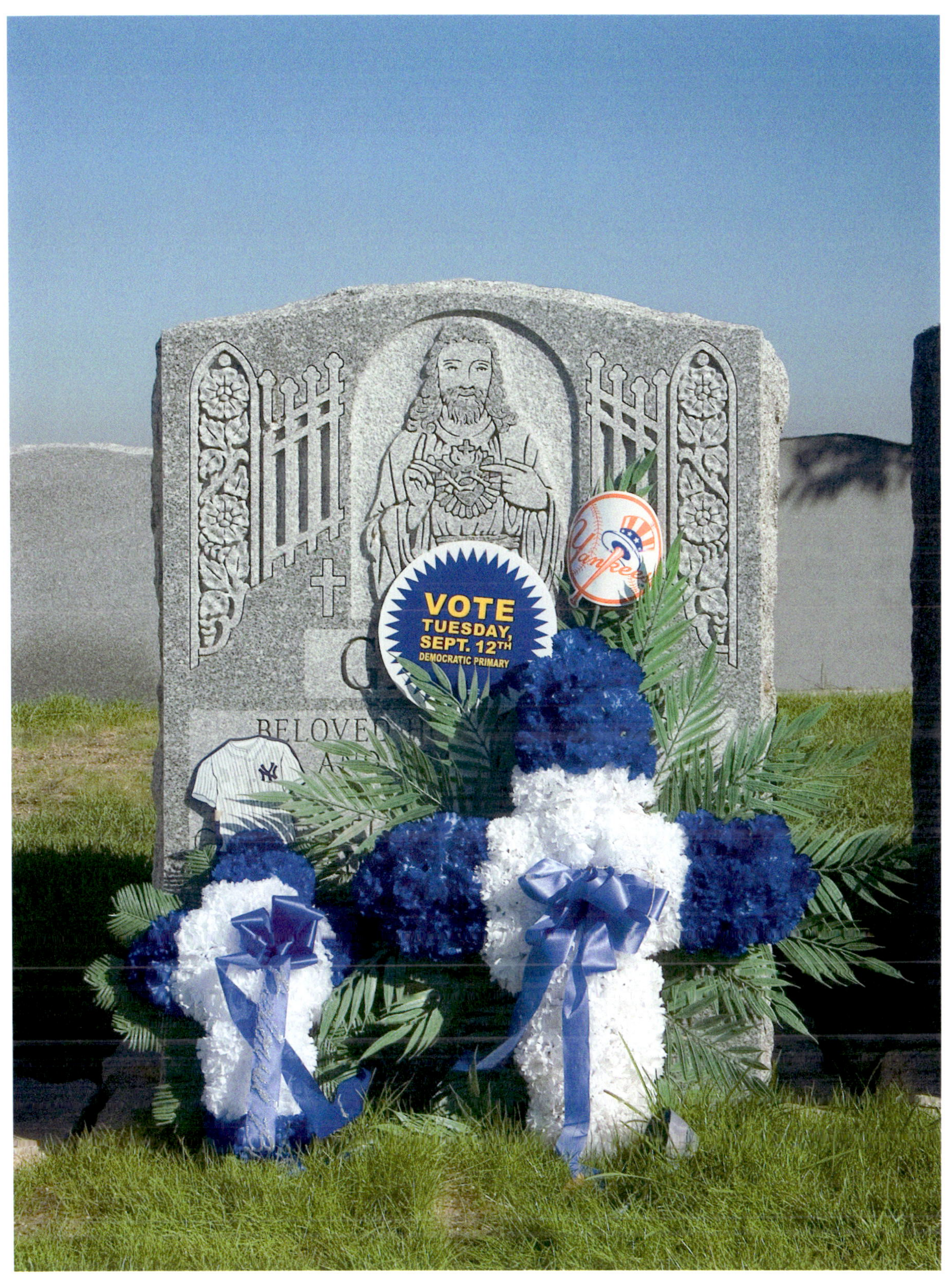

#98

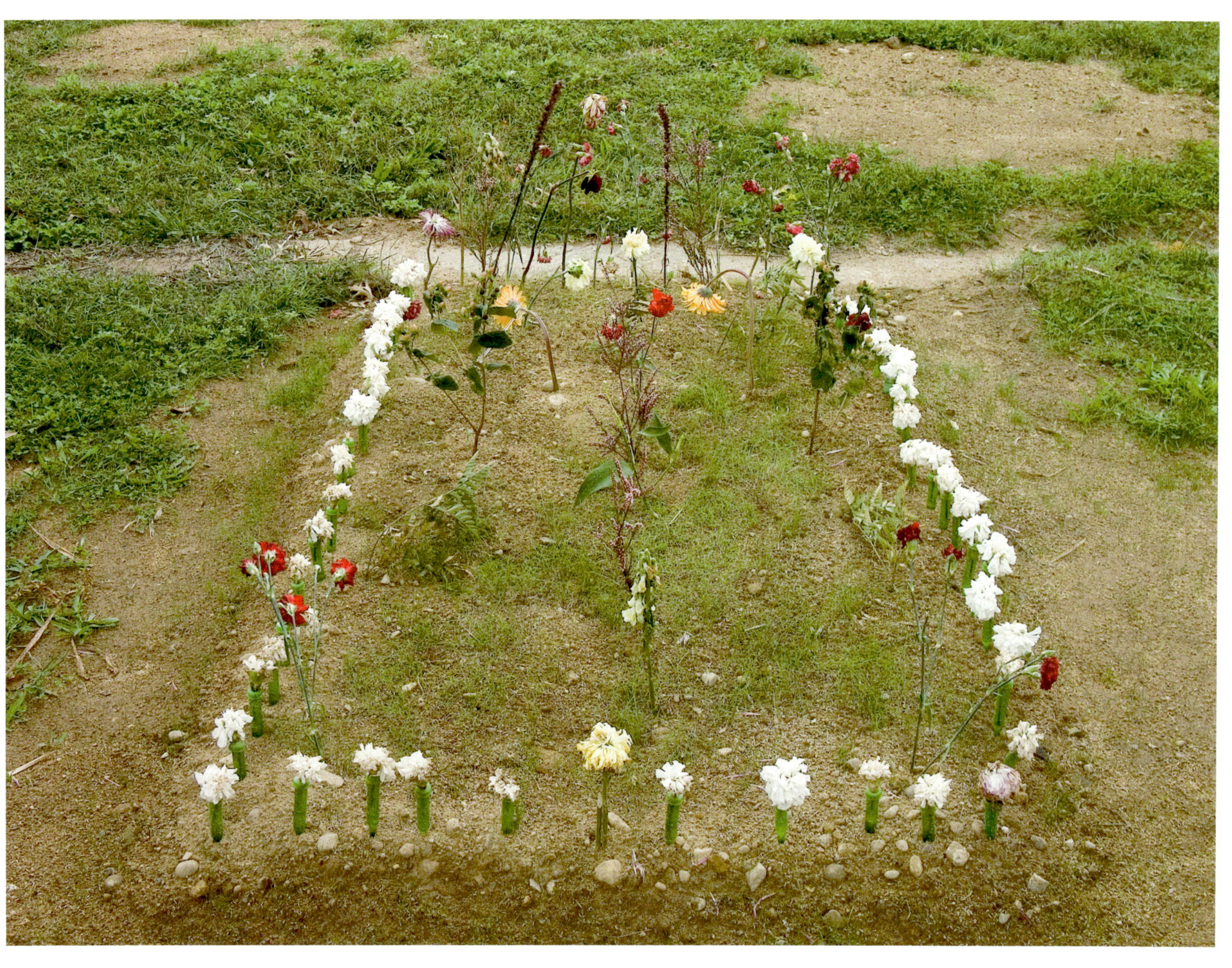

#99

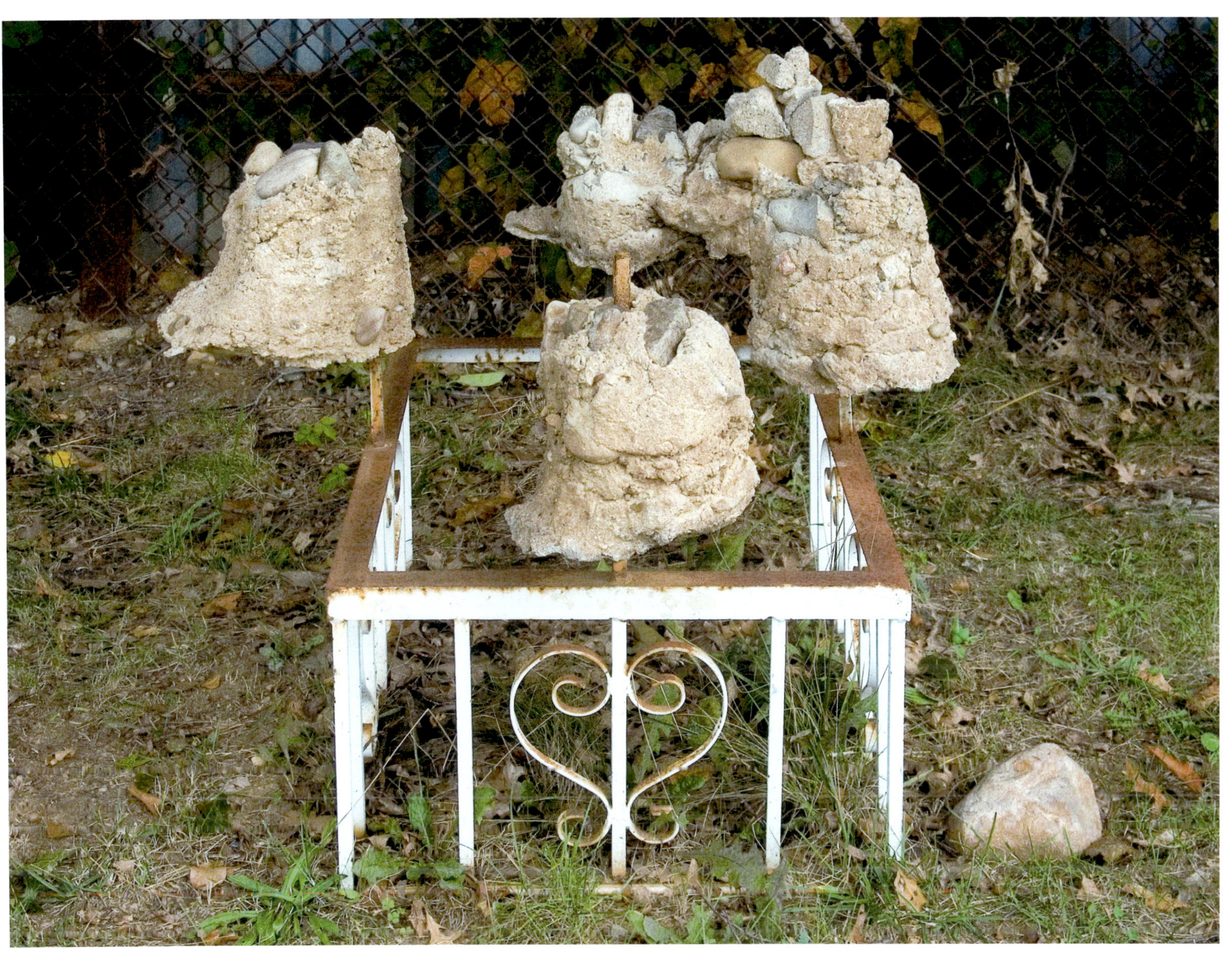

#100

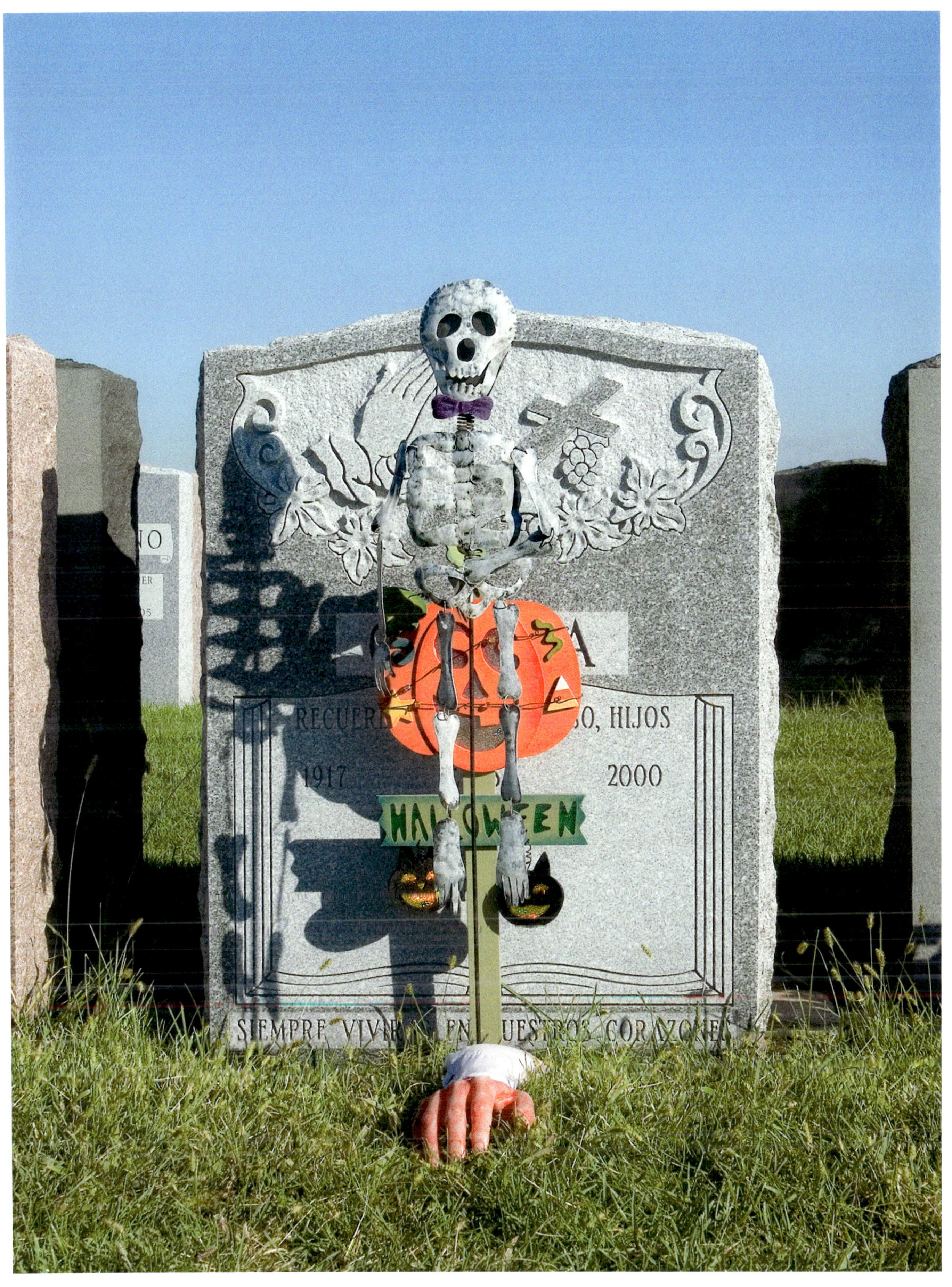
HIJOS
1917
2000
SIEMPRE

JULIAN J. G. CARUSO
DESTINY C. MORALES
DOMINICK A. TORMO
AMANDA S. ISALES
TIJANI OSUMANU
RAMA ANN OSUMANU
DENNIS J. O'CONNELL
DYLAN J. O'CONNELL
AUGUSTA J. SPENCER
RENNY CUFFY
ANGELINA ORTIZ
BABY LOPEZ
ALLISON A. HARKINS
FRANKIE GIOIA
JULIAN

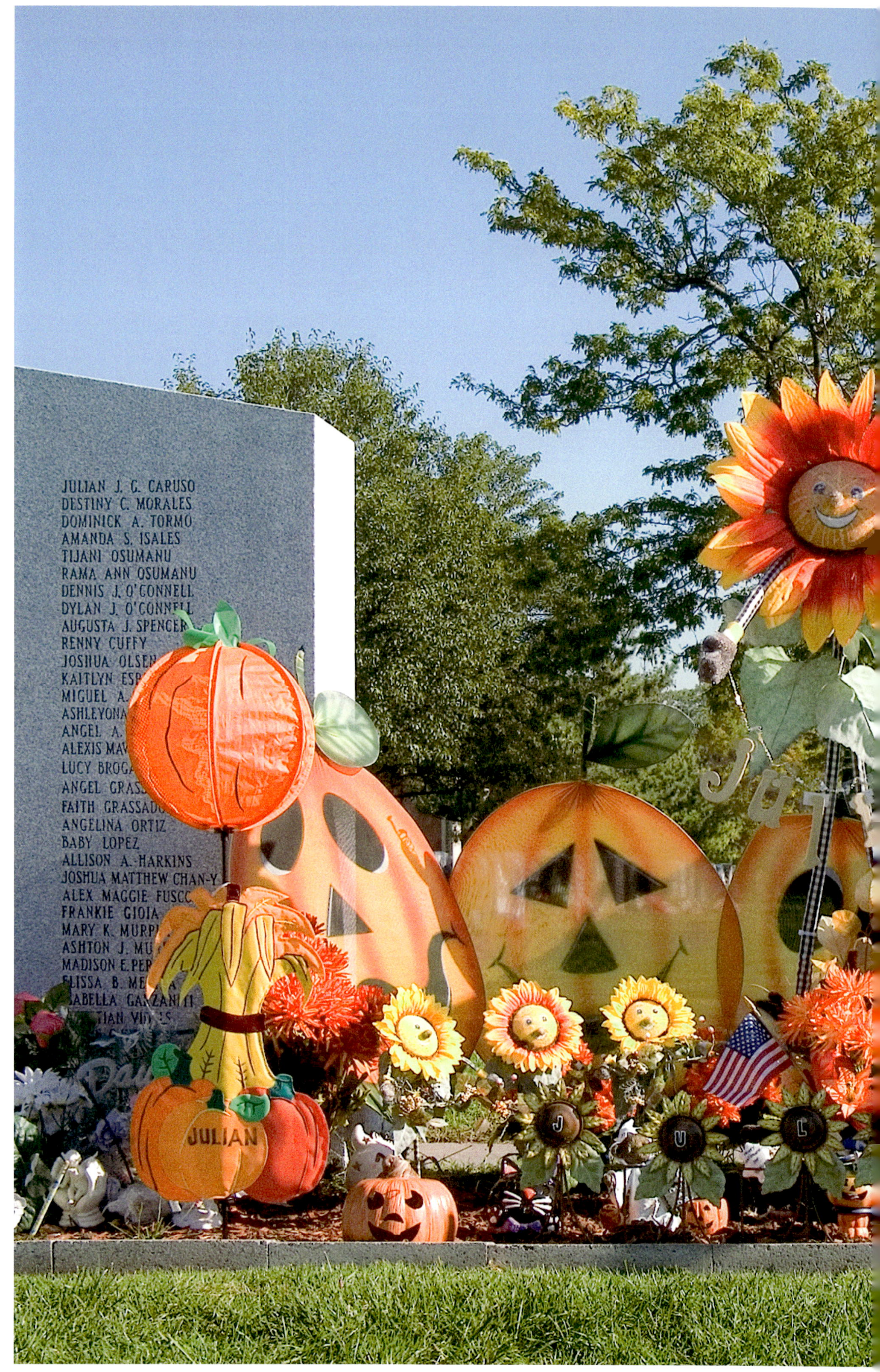

#56C

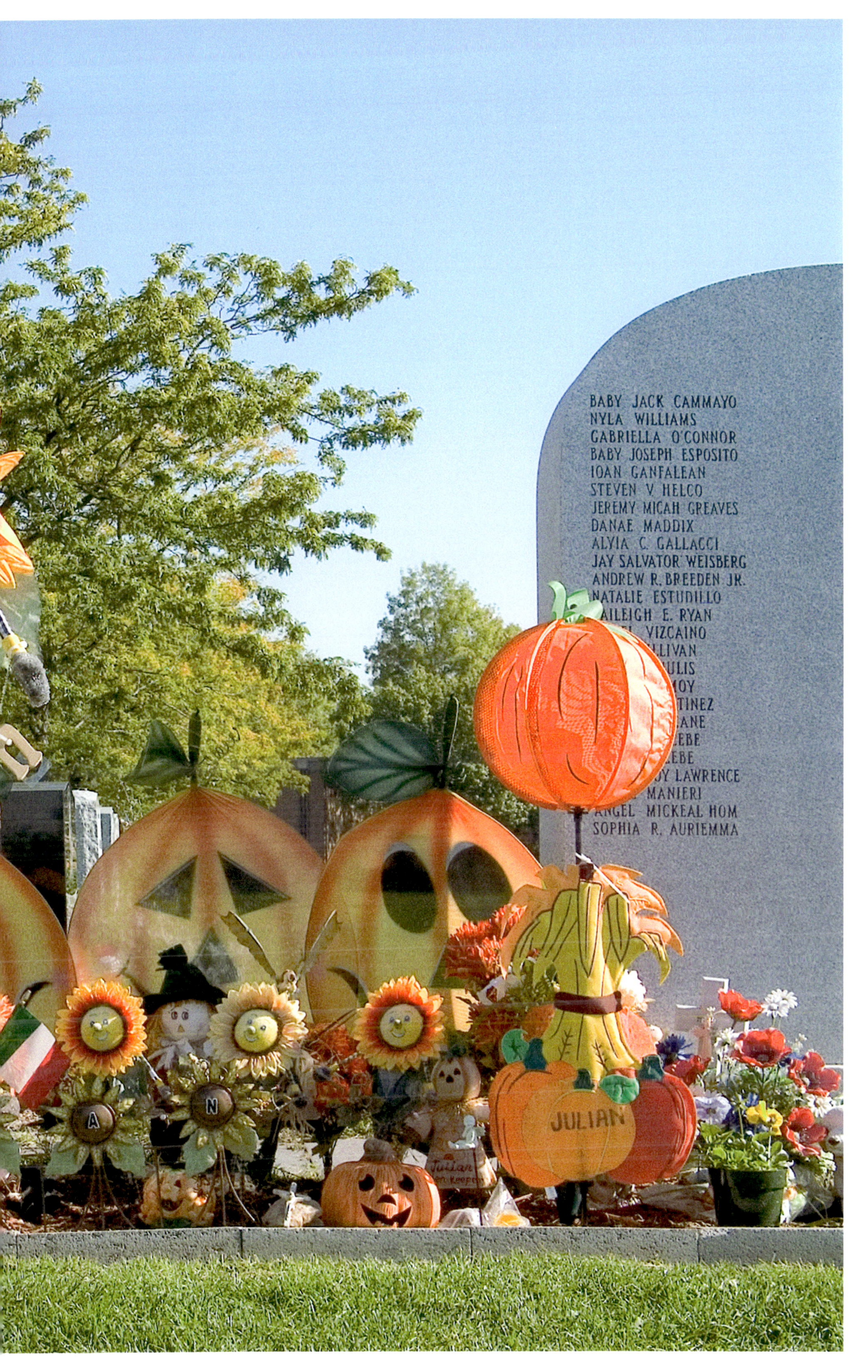
BABY JACK CAMMAYO
NYLA WILLIAMS
GABRIELLA O'CONNOR
BABY JOSEPH ESPOSITO
IOAN GANFALEAN
STEVEN V HELCO
JEREMY MICAH GREAVES
DANAE MADDIX
ALYIA C. GALLACCI
JAY SALVATOR WEISBERG
ANDREW R. BREEDEN JR.
NATALIE ESTUDILLO
SOPHIA R. AURIEMMA
JULIAN

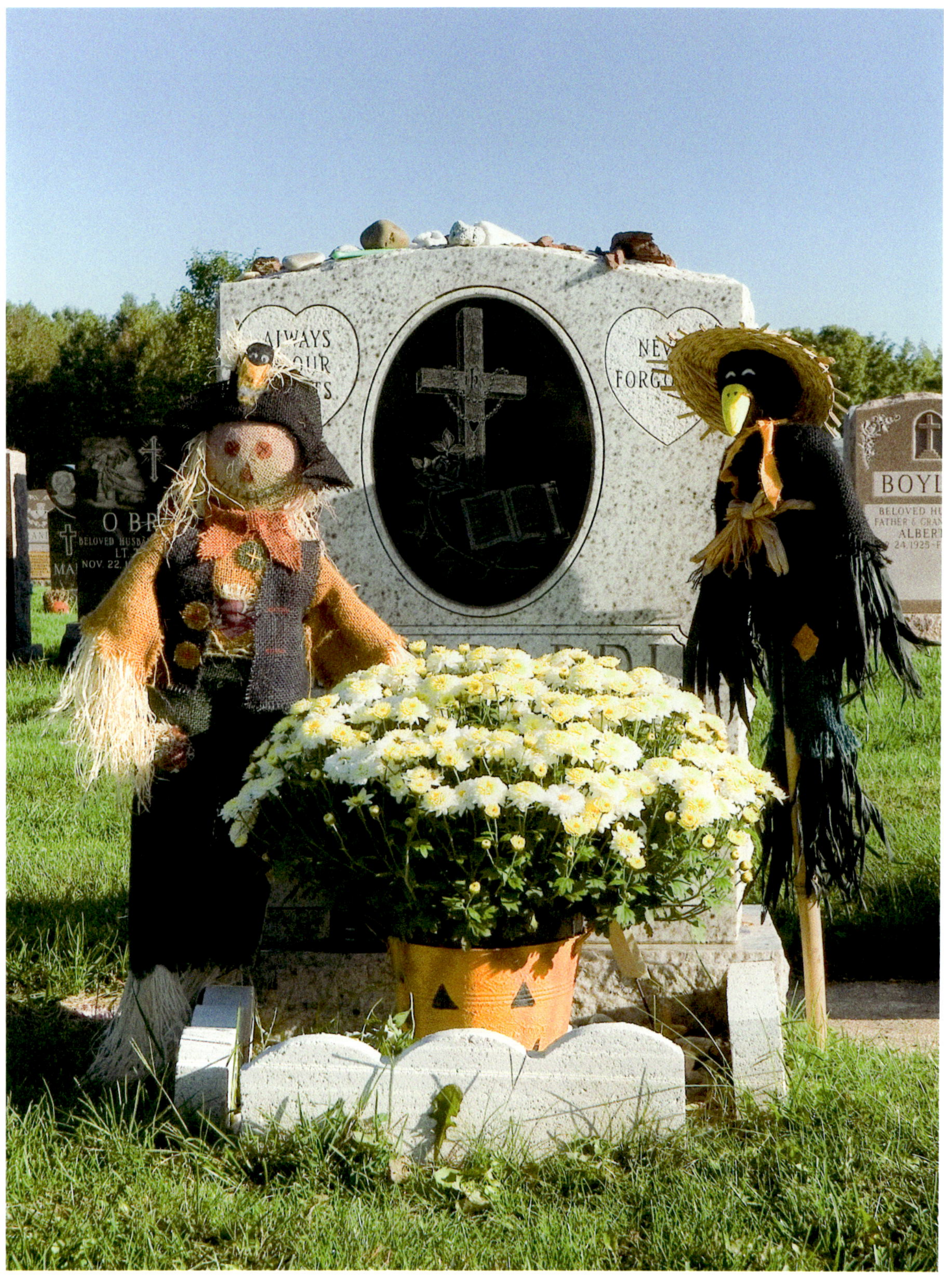

#102

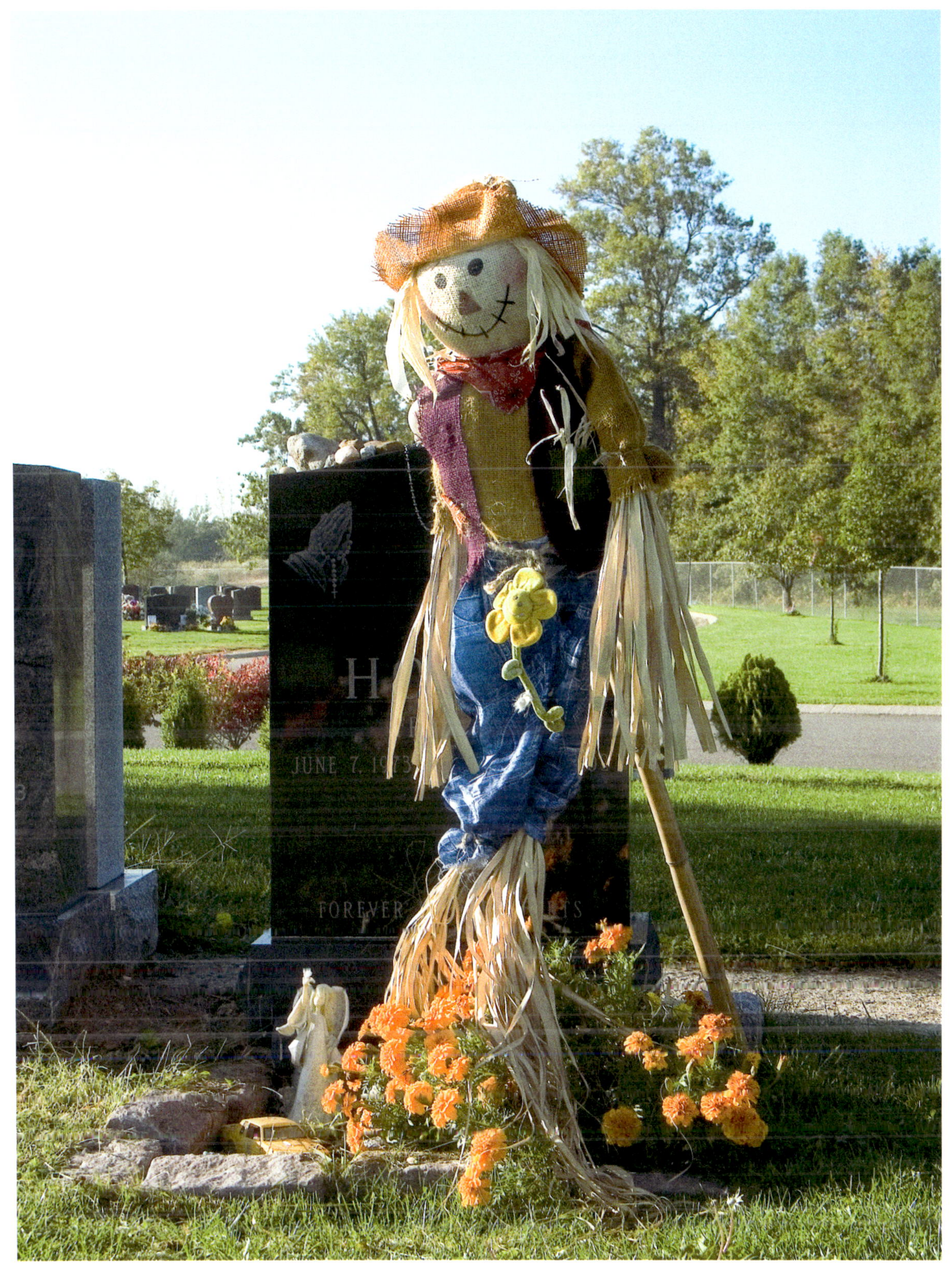

#103

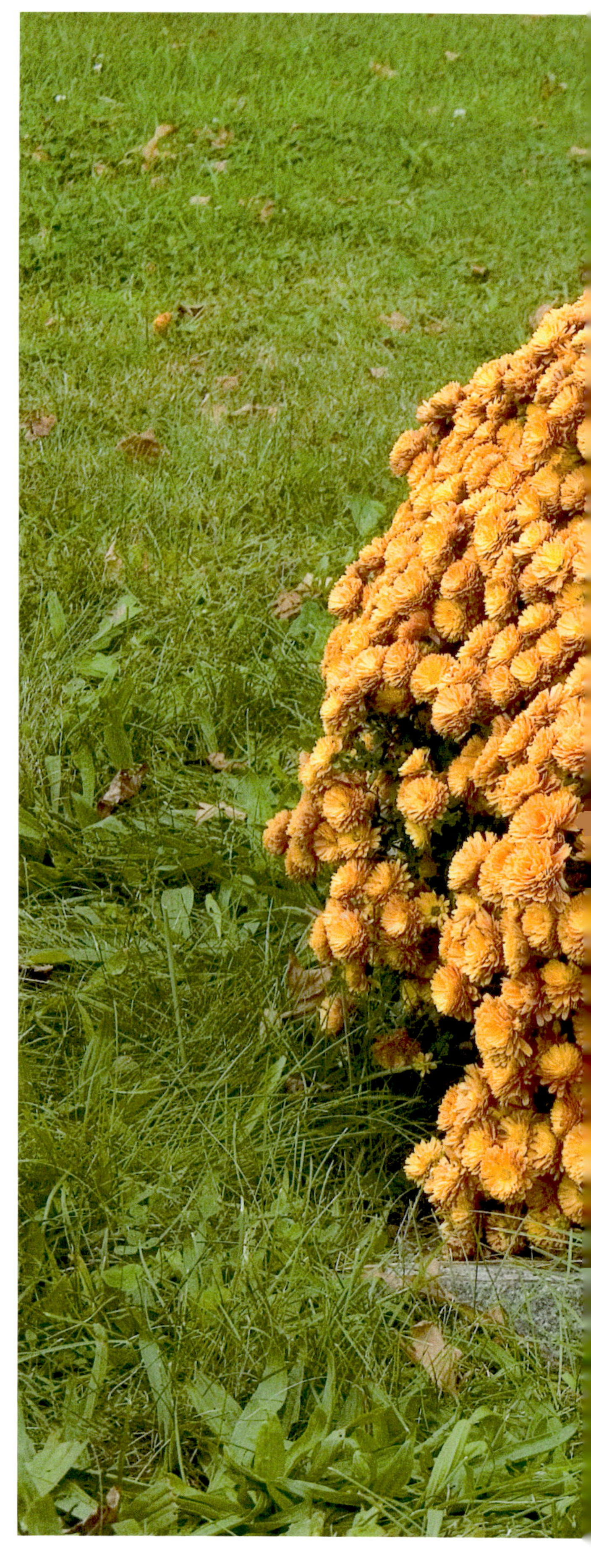

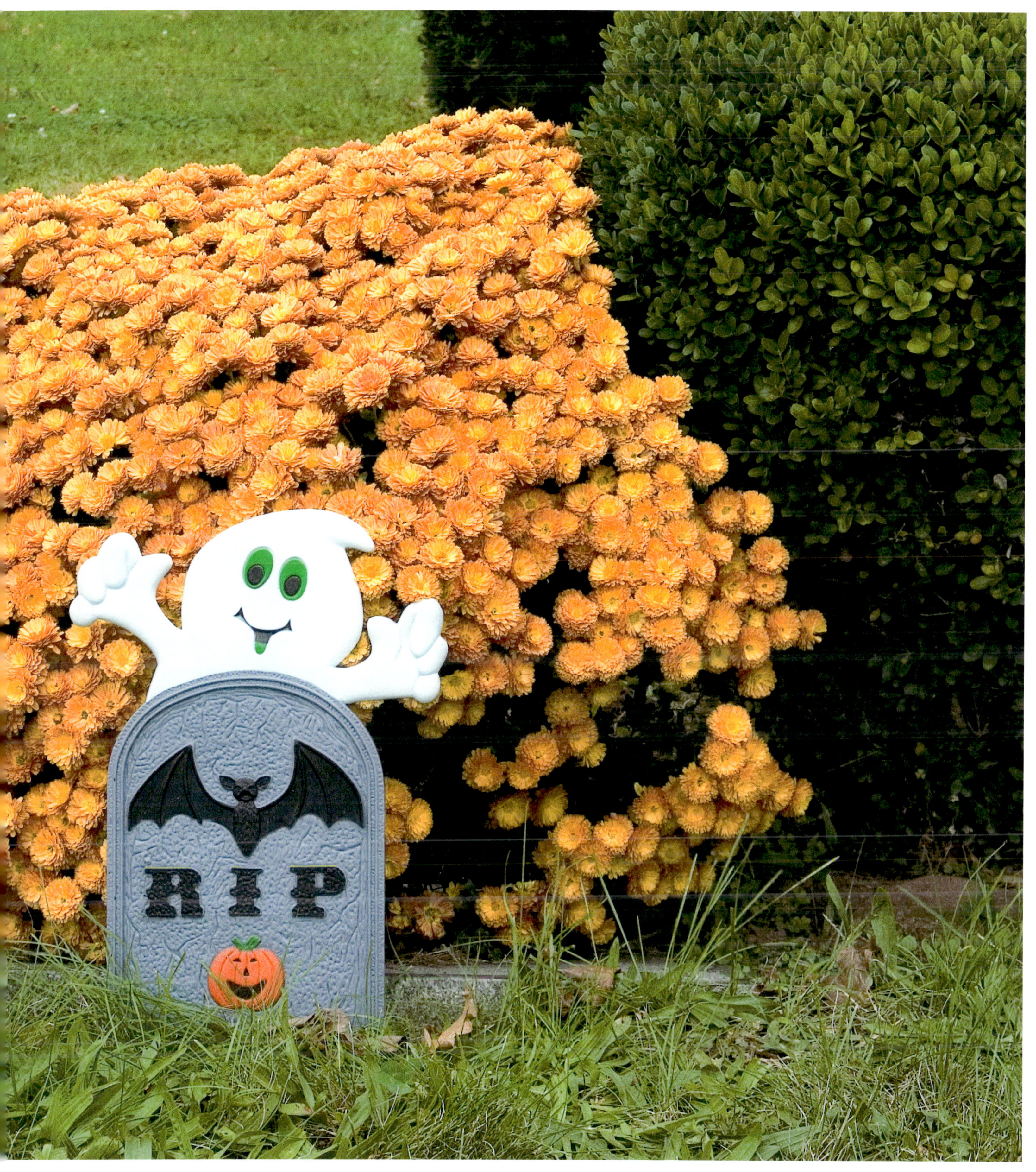
RIP

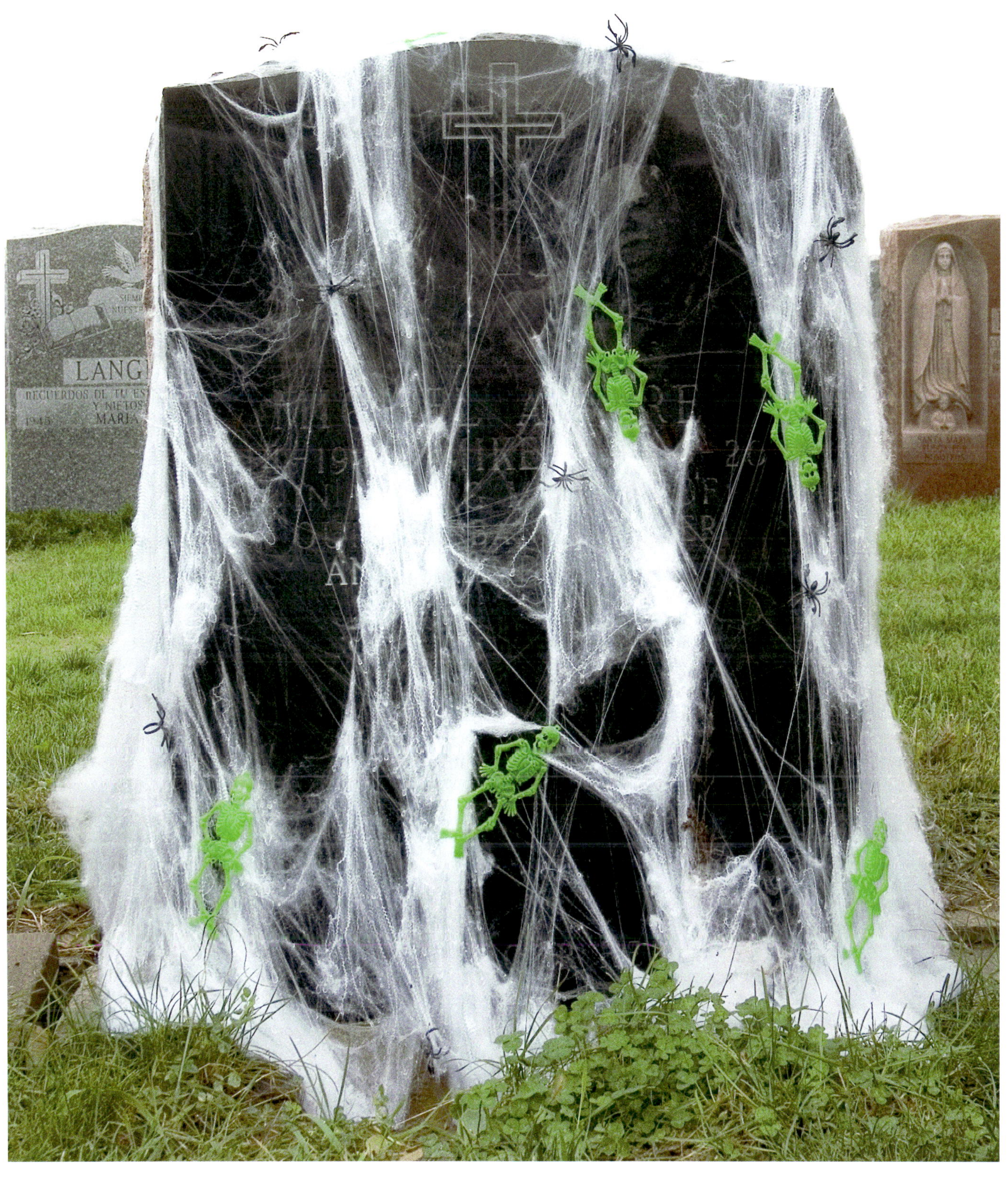

ALWAYS IN OUR HEARTS
BELOVED DAUGHTER AND MOTHER
CELESTE AMANDA RIDGEWAY
MAR. 6, 1958 – JULY 25, 2000
FOREVER IN OUR HEARTS
JOHNSON

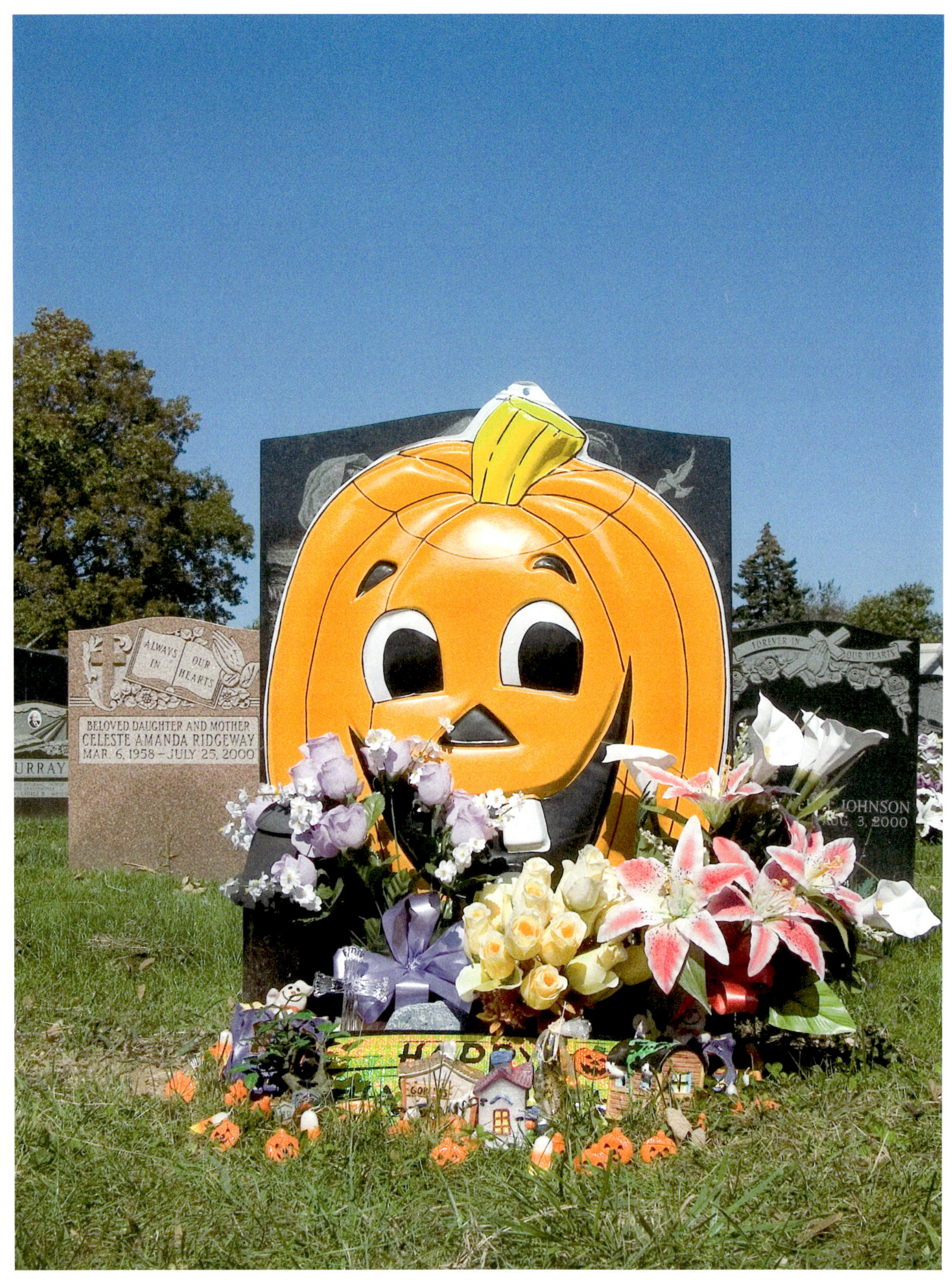

#106

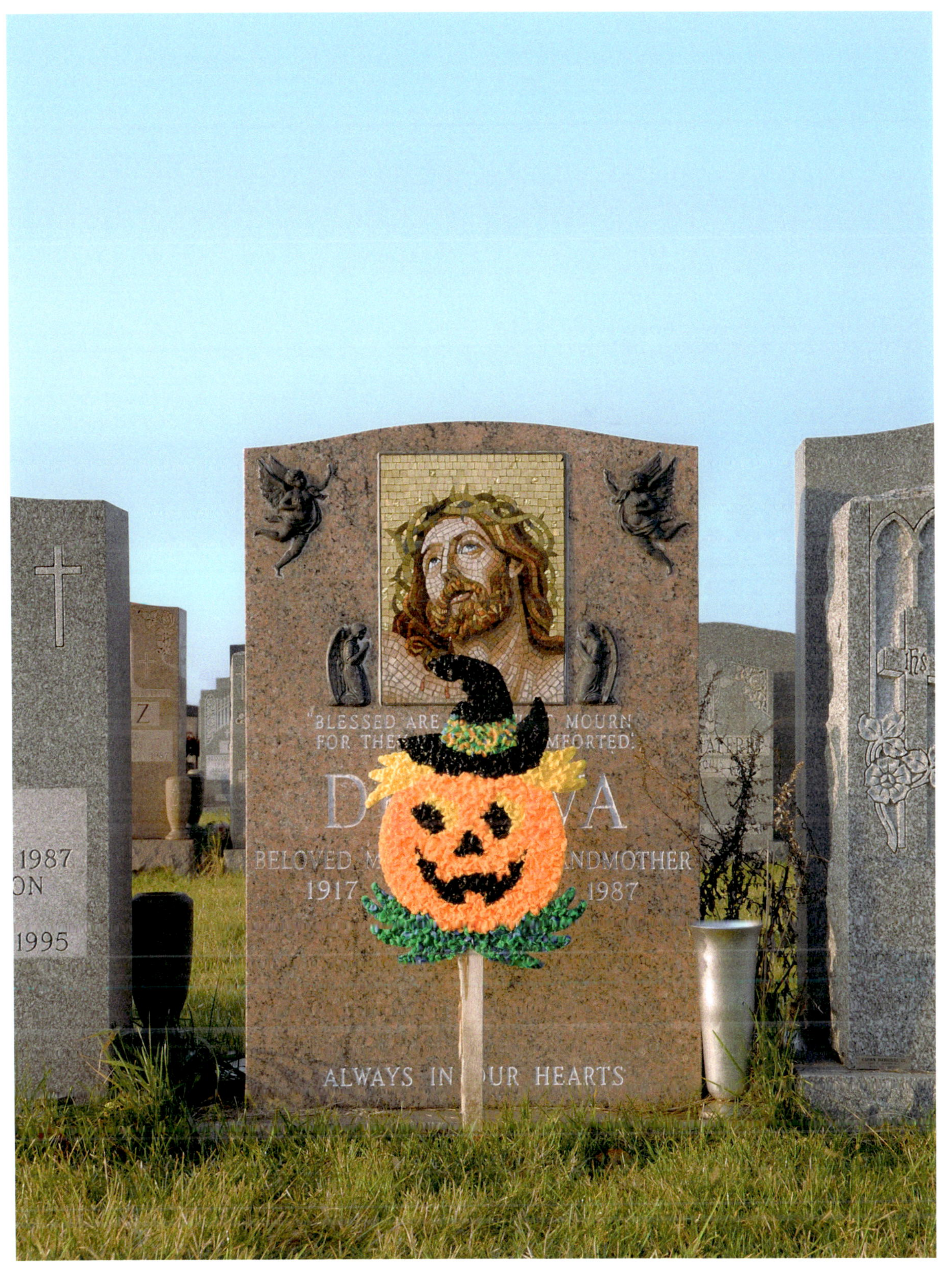

#107

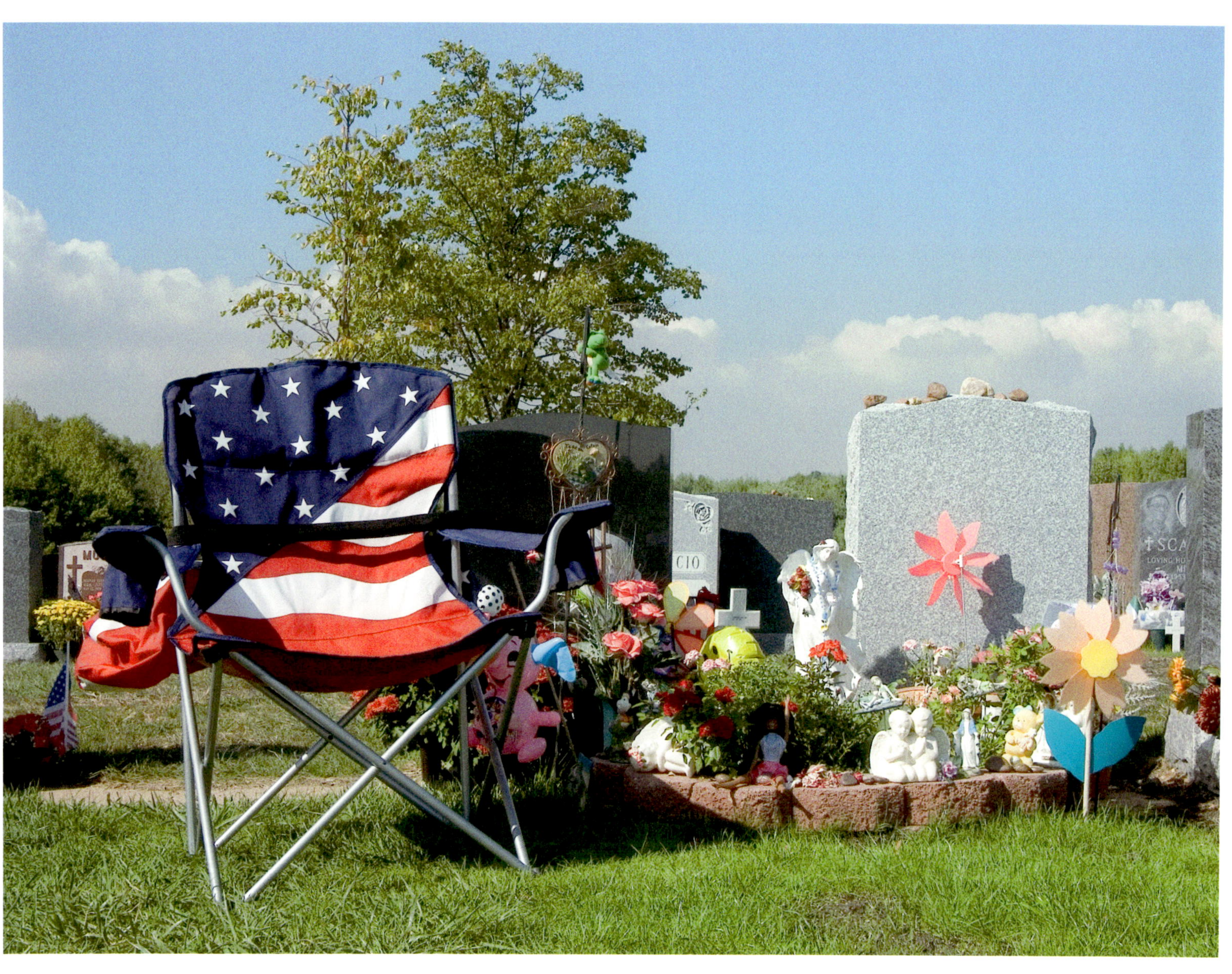

#108

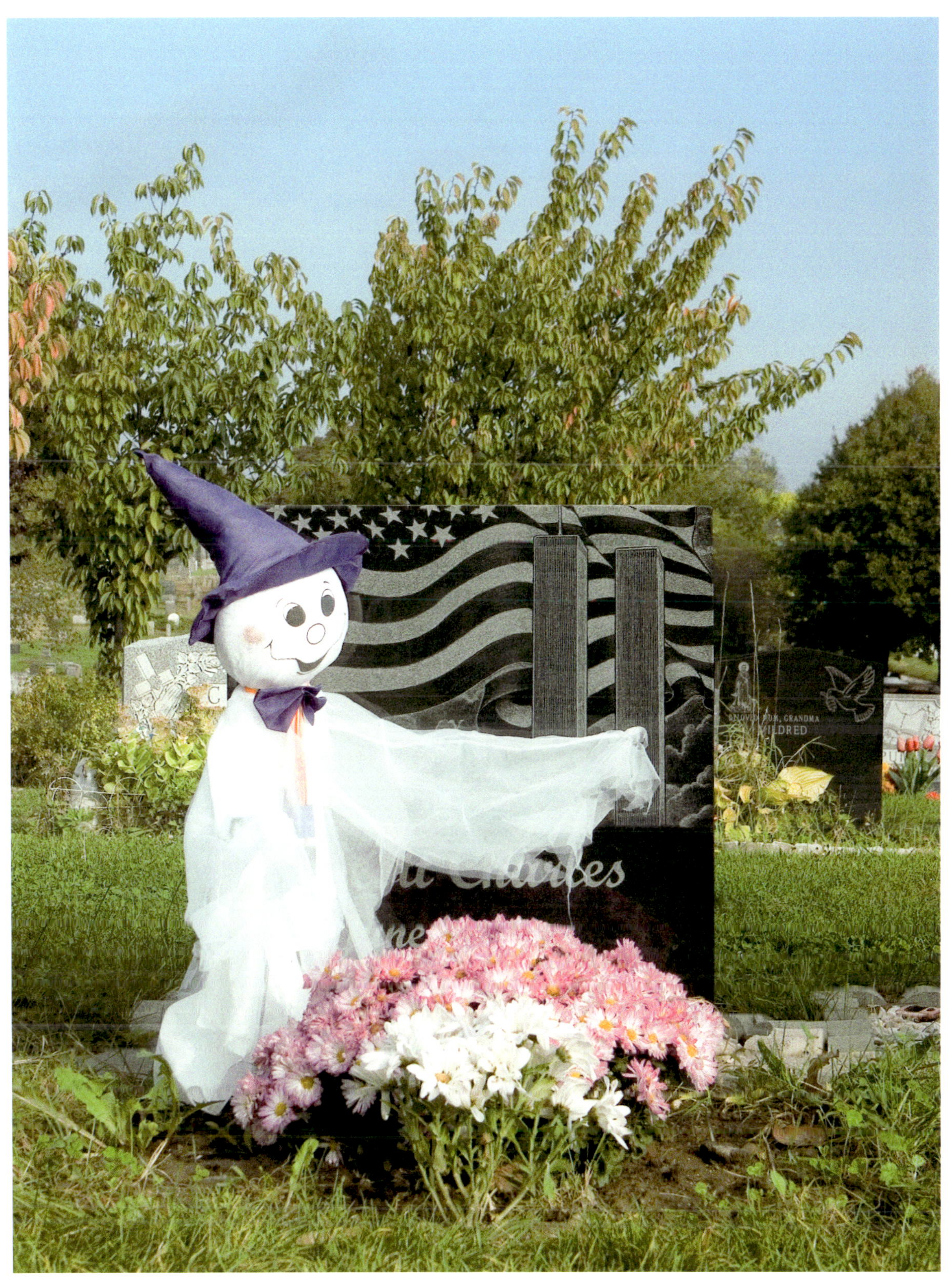

#109

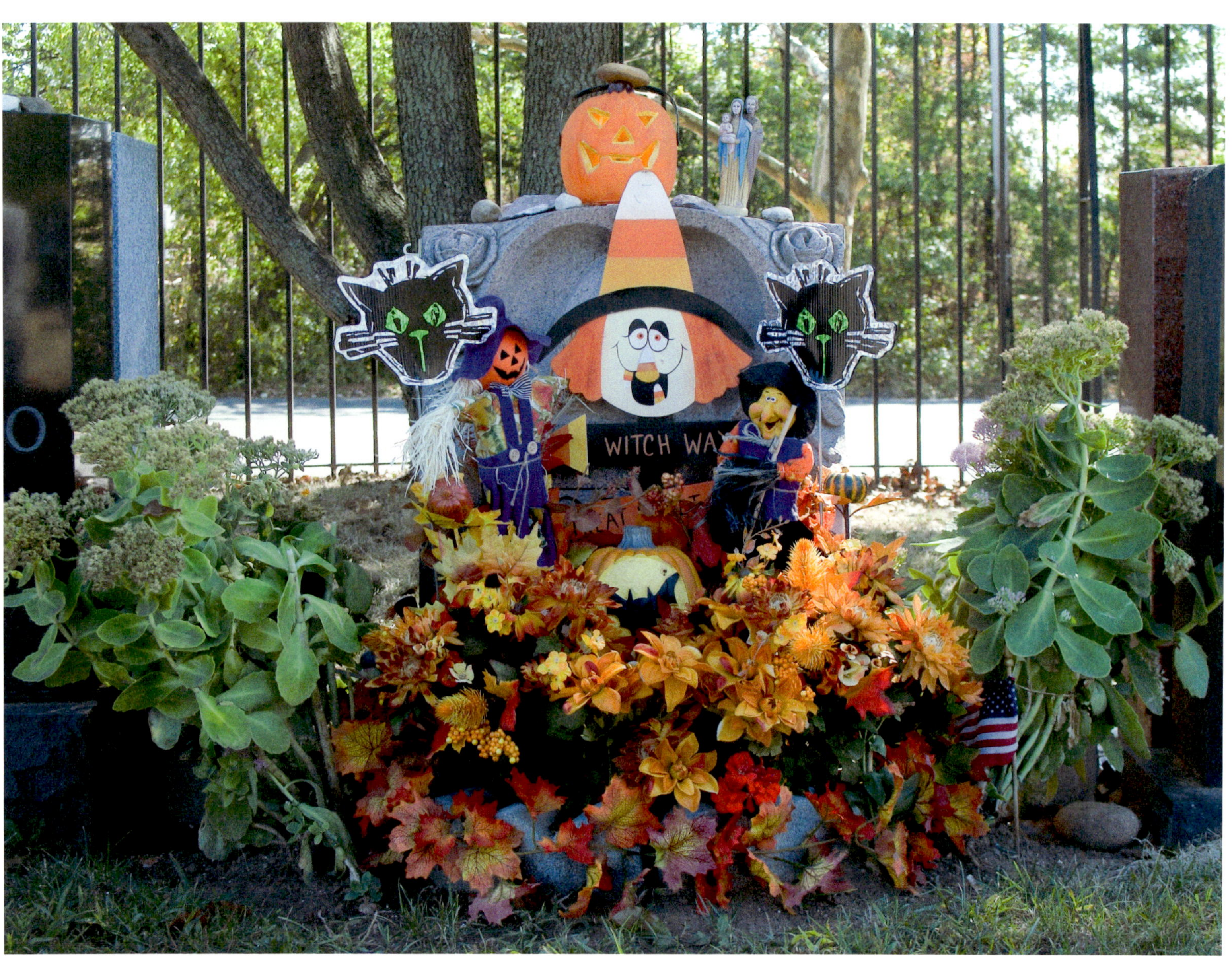

#110

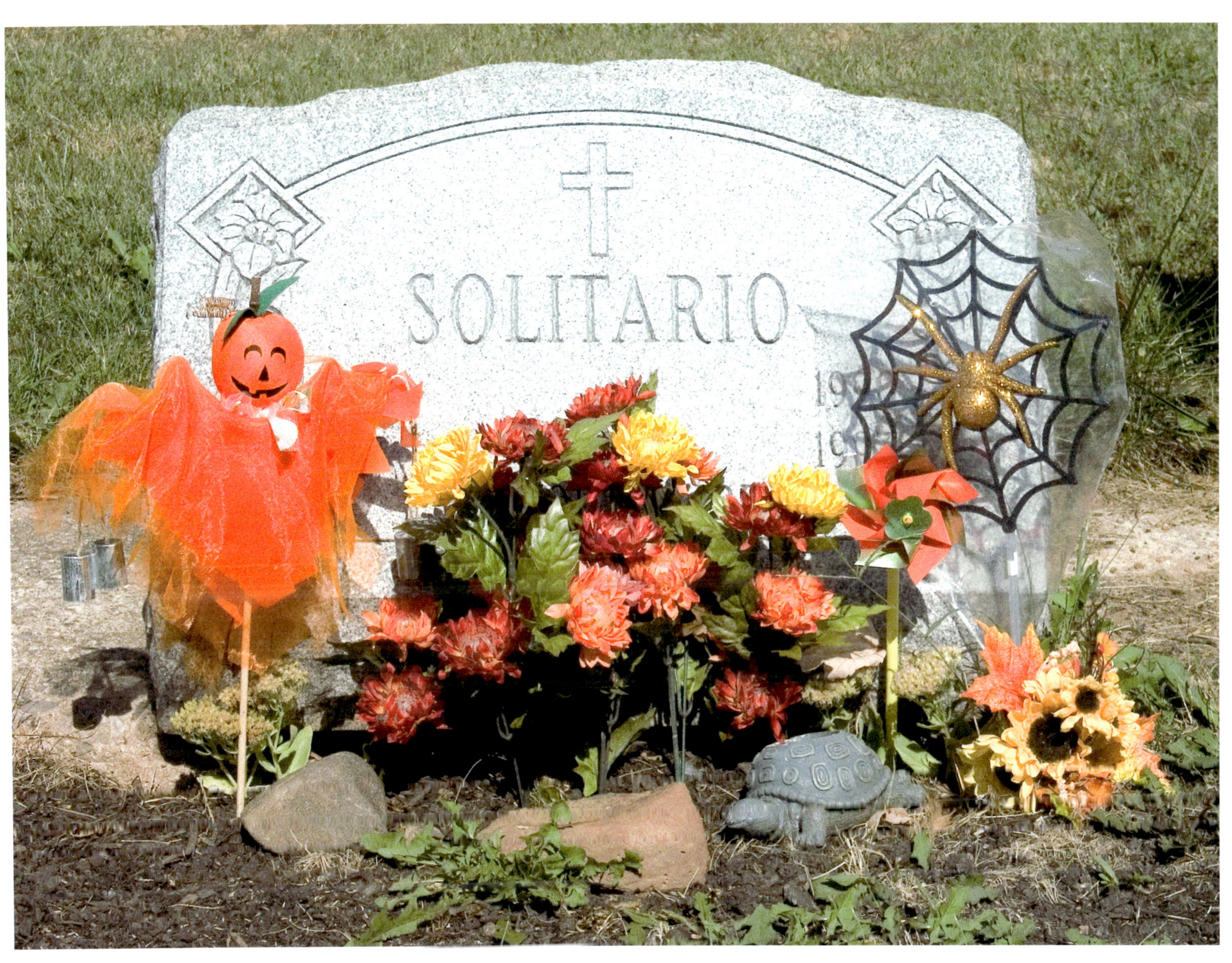
SOLITARIO

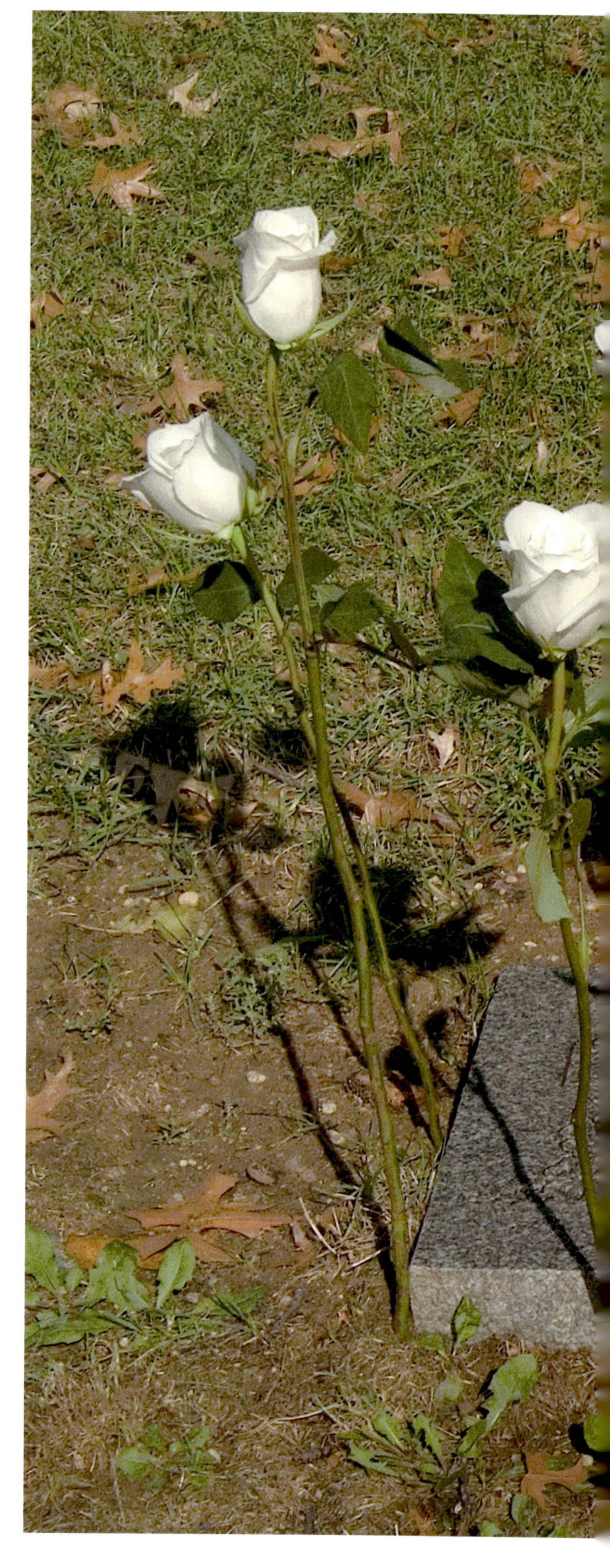

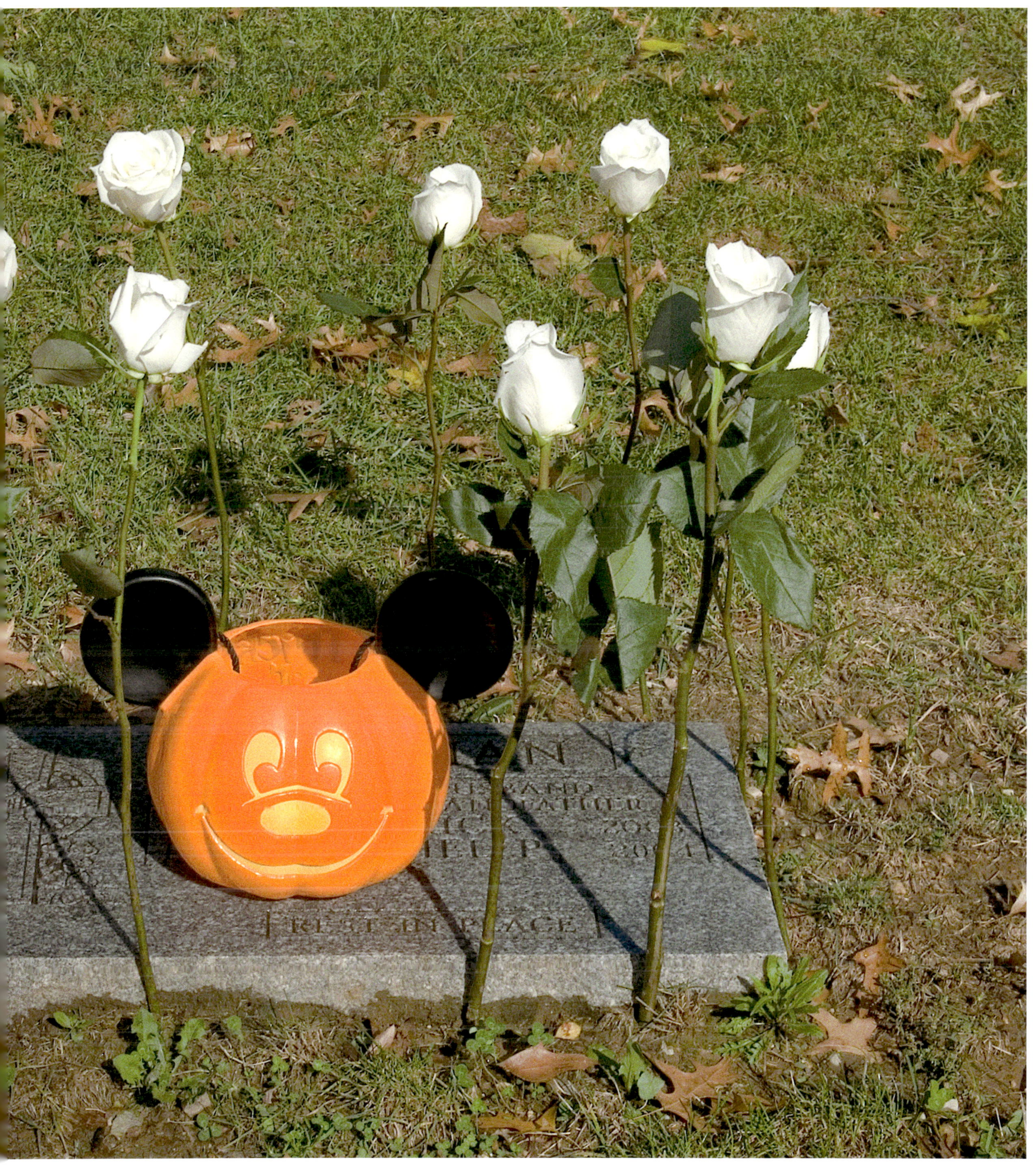

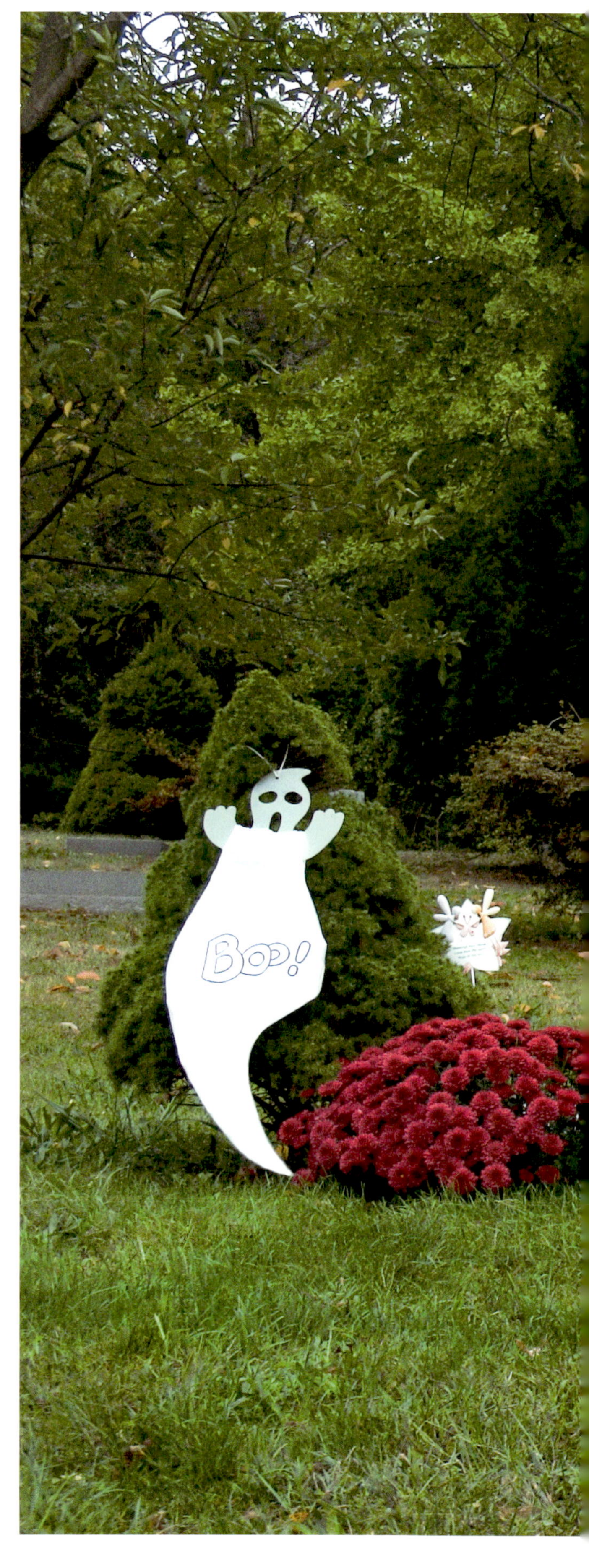

#113

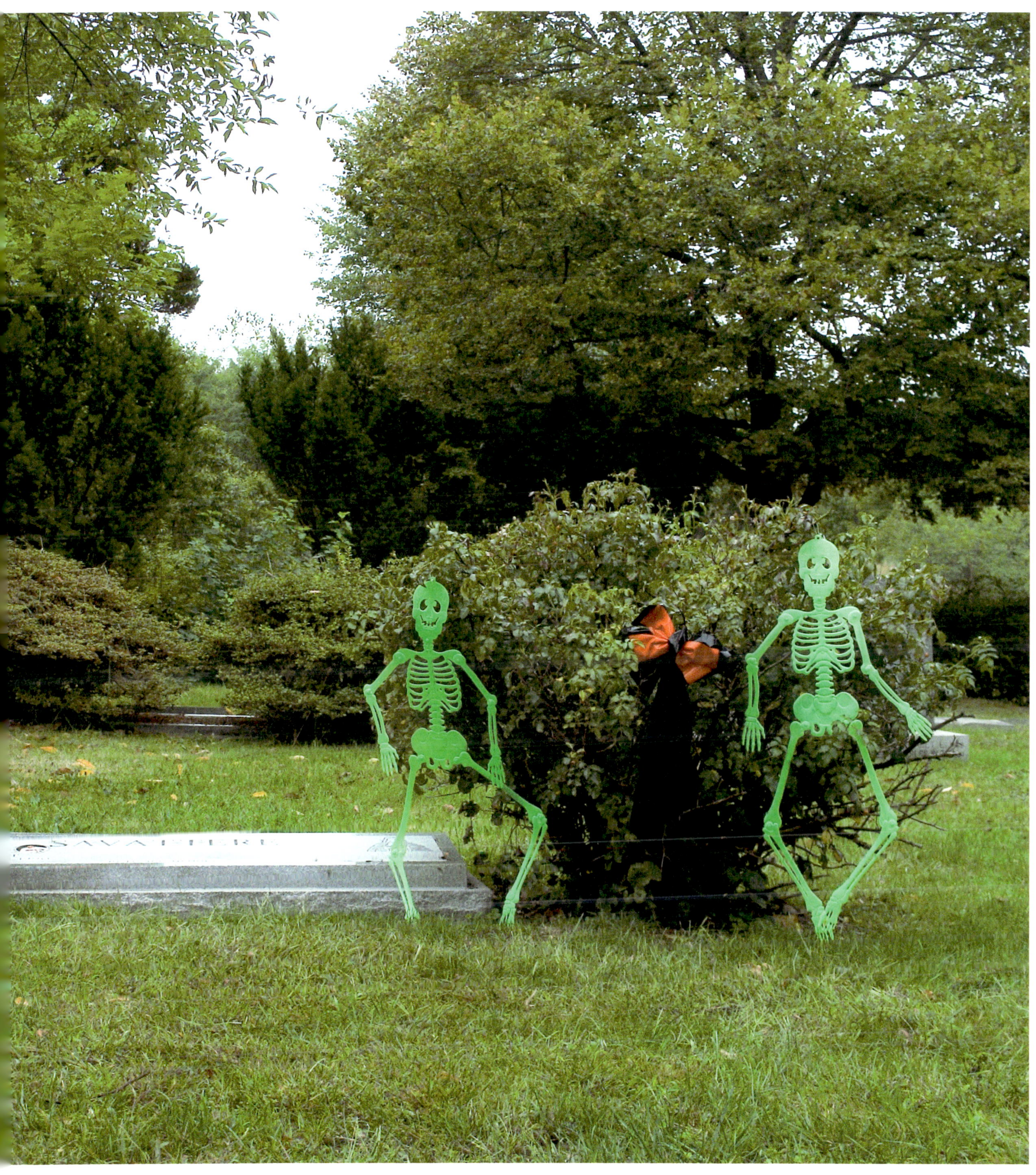

RON
FATHER
DFATHER
NDRO
SEPT. 21, 1996
EARTS
Z
IS PADRES,
1996
BEI
1919

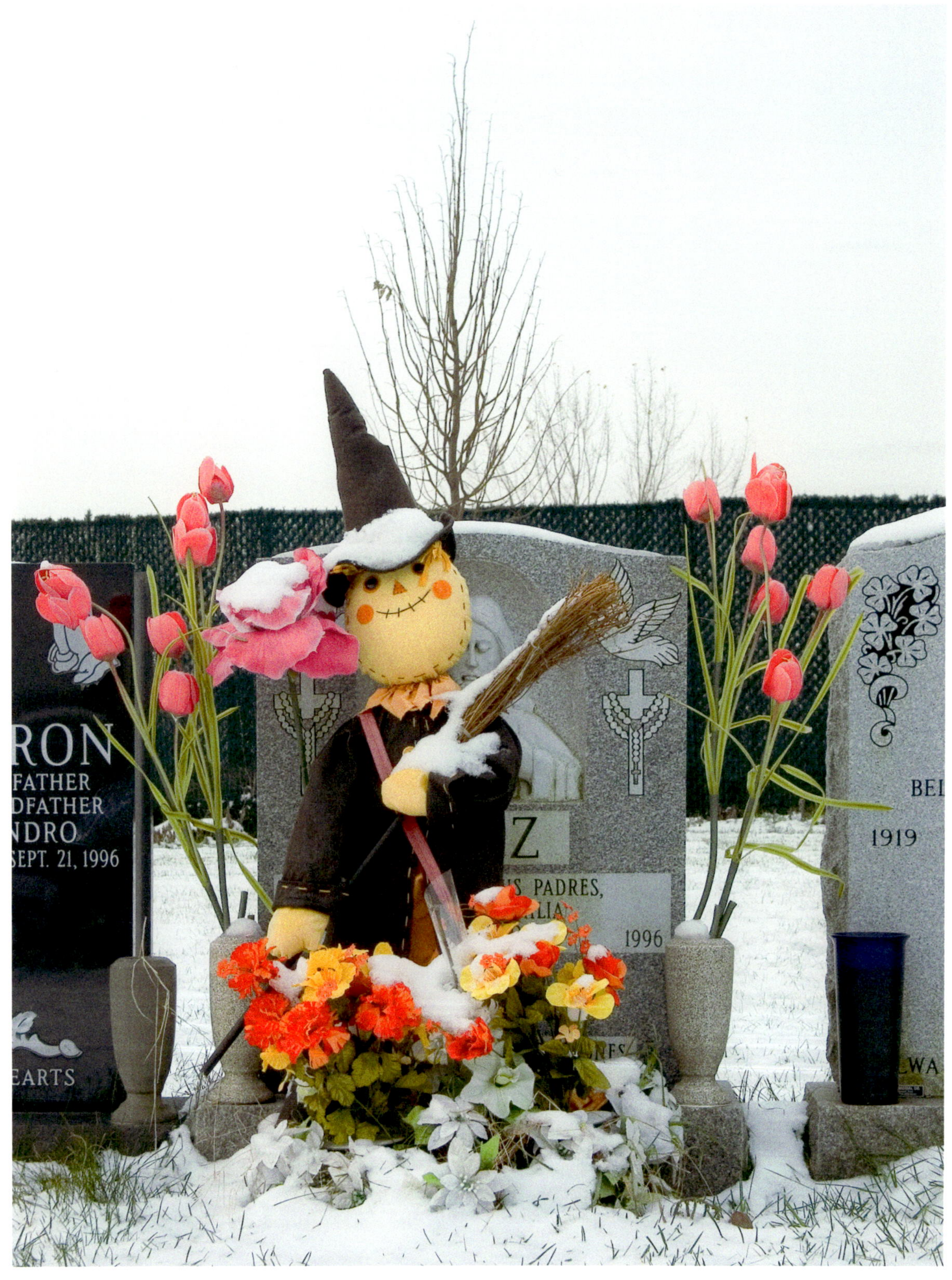

#114

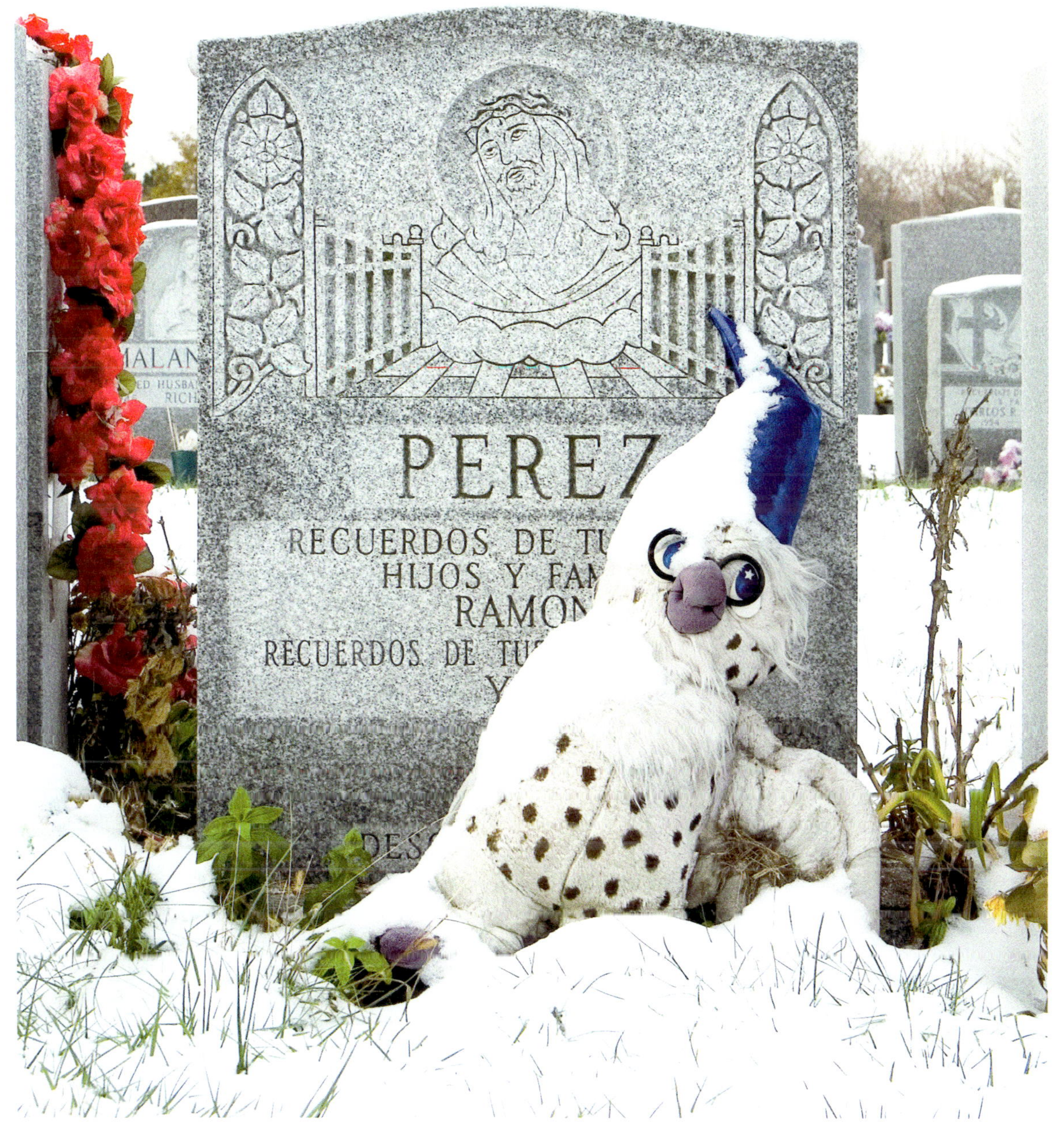
PEREZ
RECUERDOS DE TU
HIJOS Y FA
RAMON
RECUERDOS DE TU

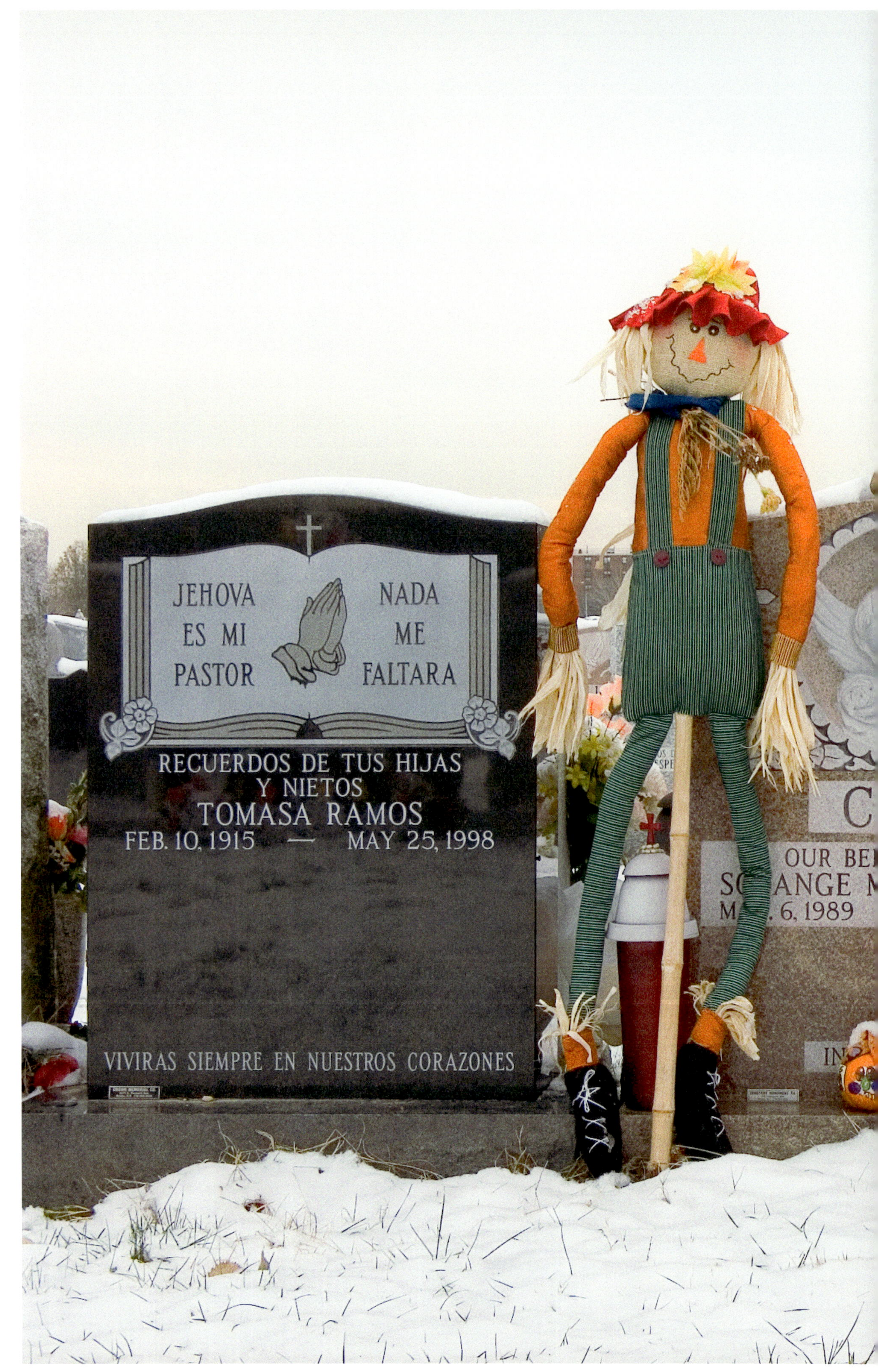
JEHOVA
ES MI
PASTOR
NADA
ME
FALTARA
RECUERDOS DE TUS HIJAS
Y NIETOS
TOMASA RAMOS
FEB. 10, 1915 — MAY 25, 1998
VIVIRAS SIEMPRE EN NUESTROS CORAZONES

#116

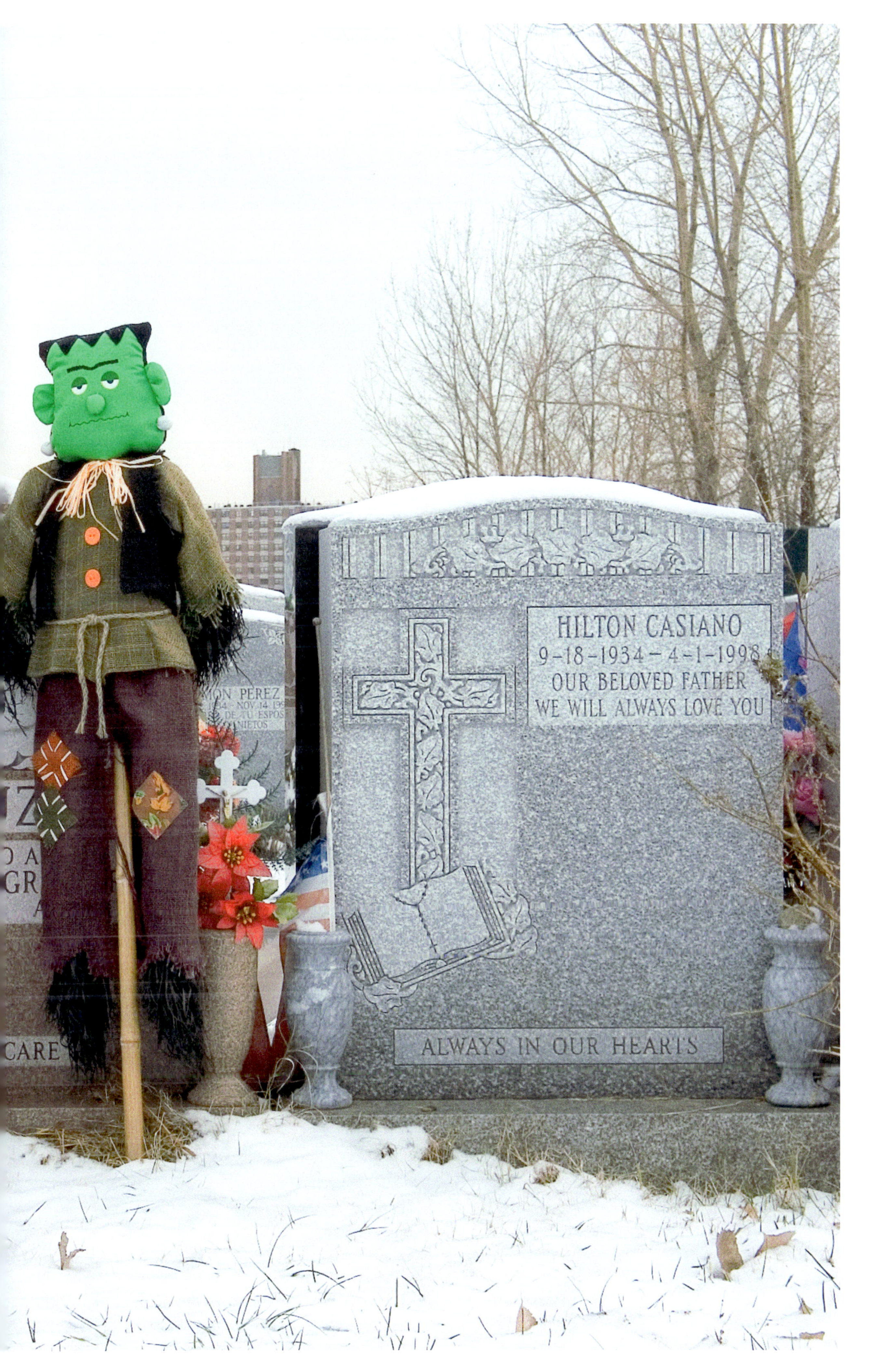
HILTON CASIANO
9-18-1934 - 4-1-1998
OUR BELOVED FATHER
WE WILL ALWAYS LOVE YOU
ALWAYS IN OUR HEARTS

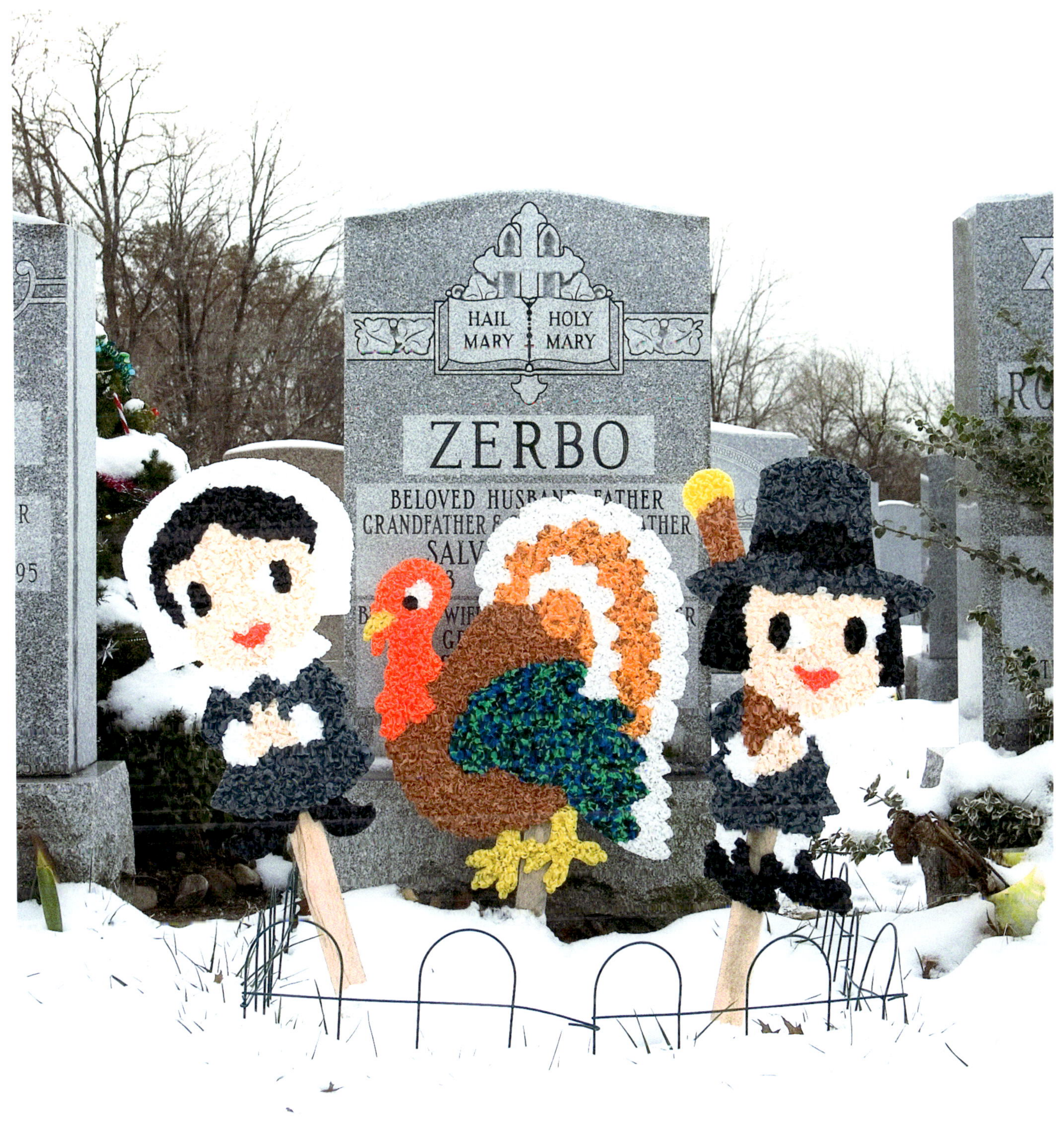
HAIL MARY
HOLY MARY
ZERBO
BELOVED HUSBAND FATHER
GRANDFATHER

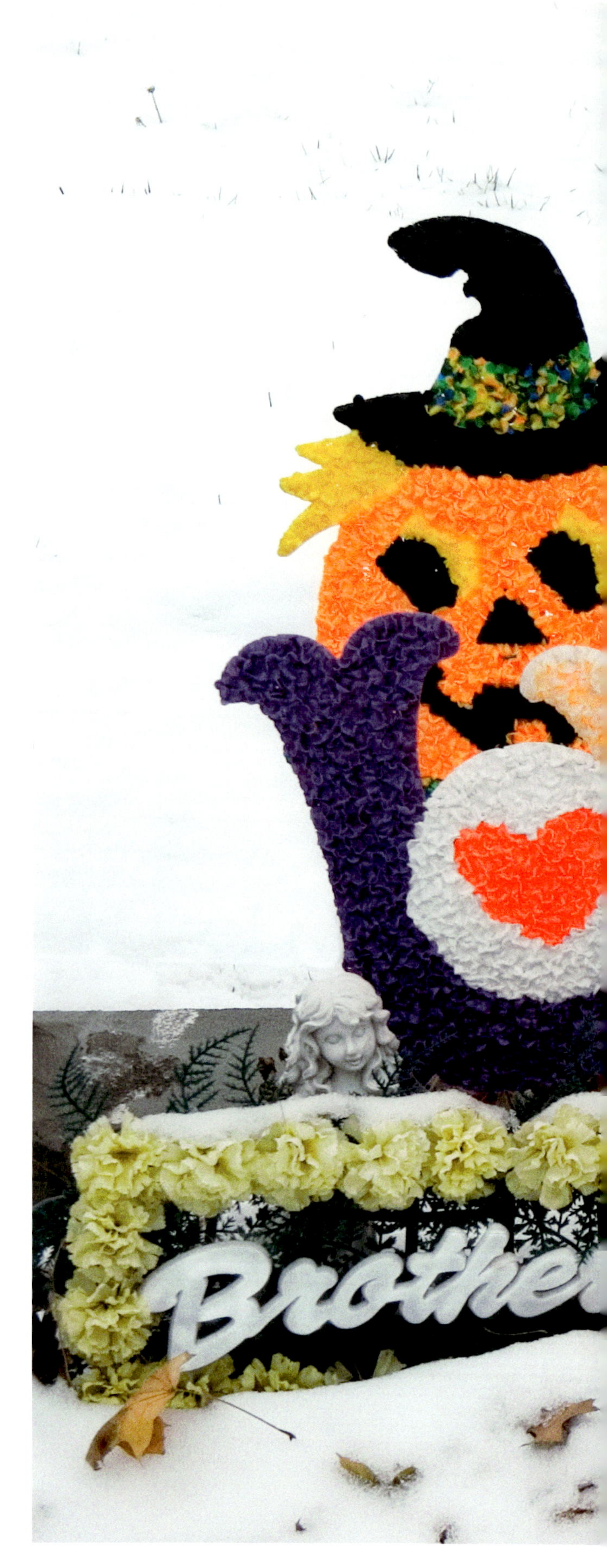

#118

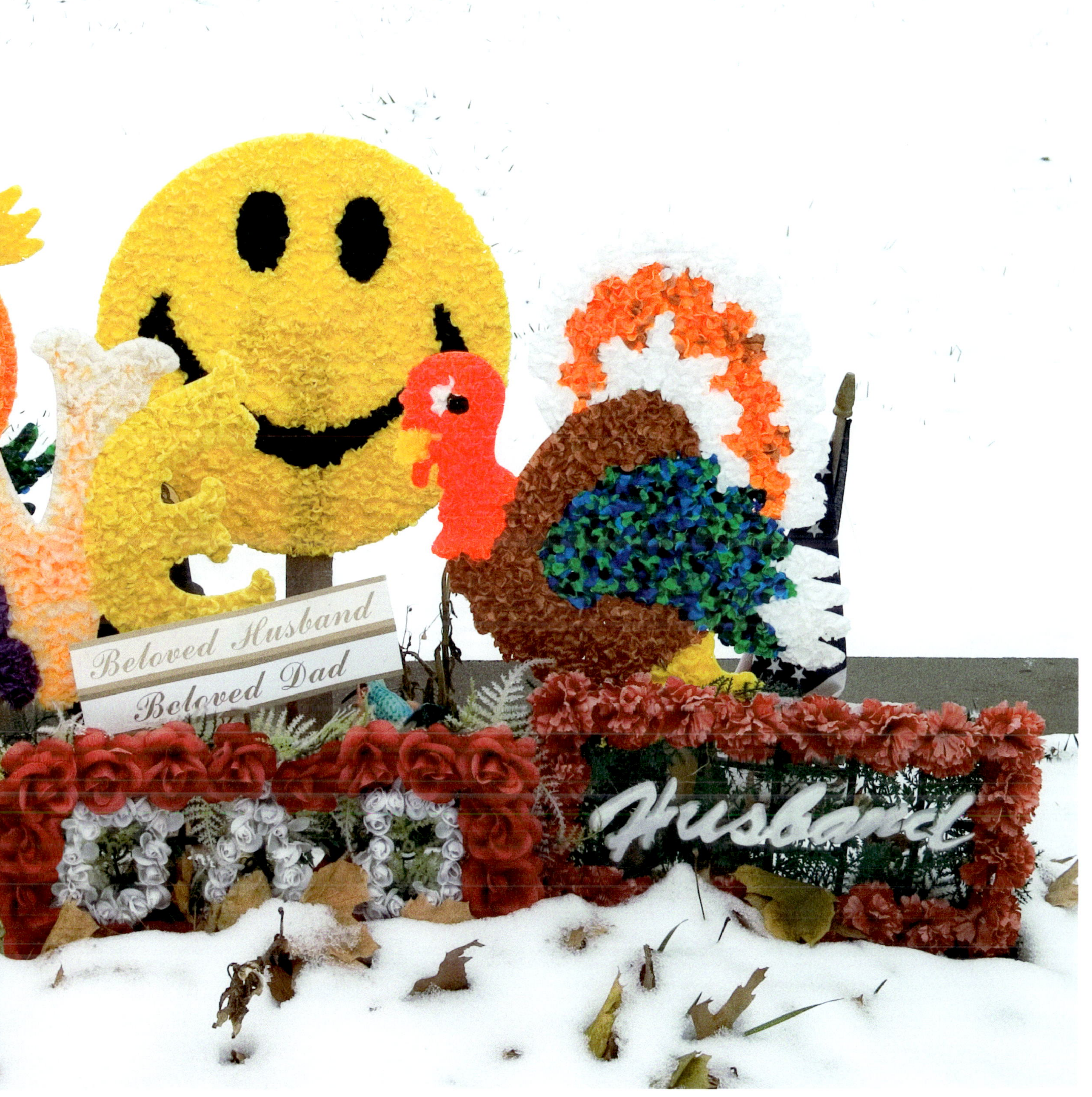
Beloved Husband
Beloved Dad
Husband

HAPPY
THANKSGIVING
1947
1991
1941
HENRY
1995
DESCANSE EN PAZ

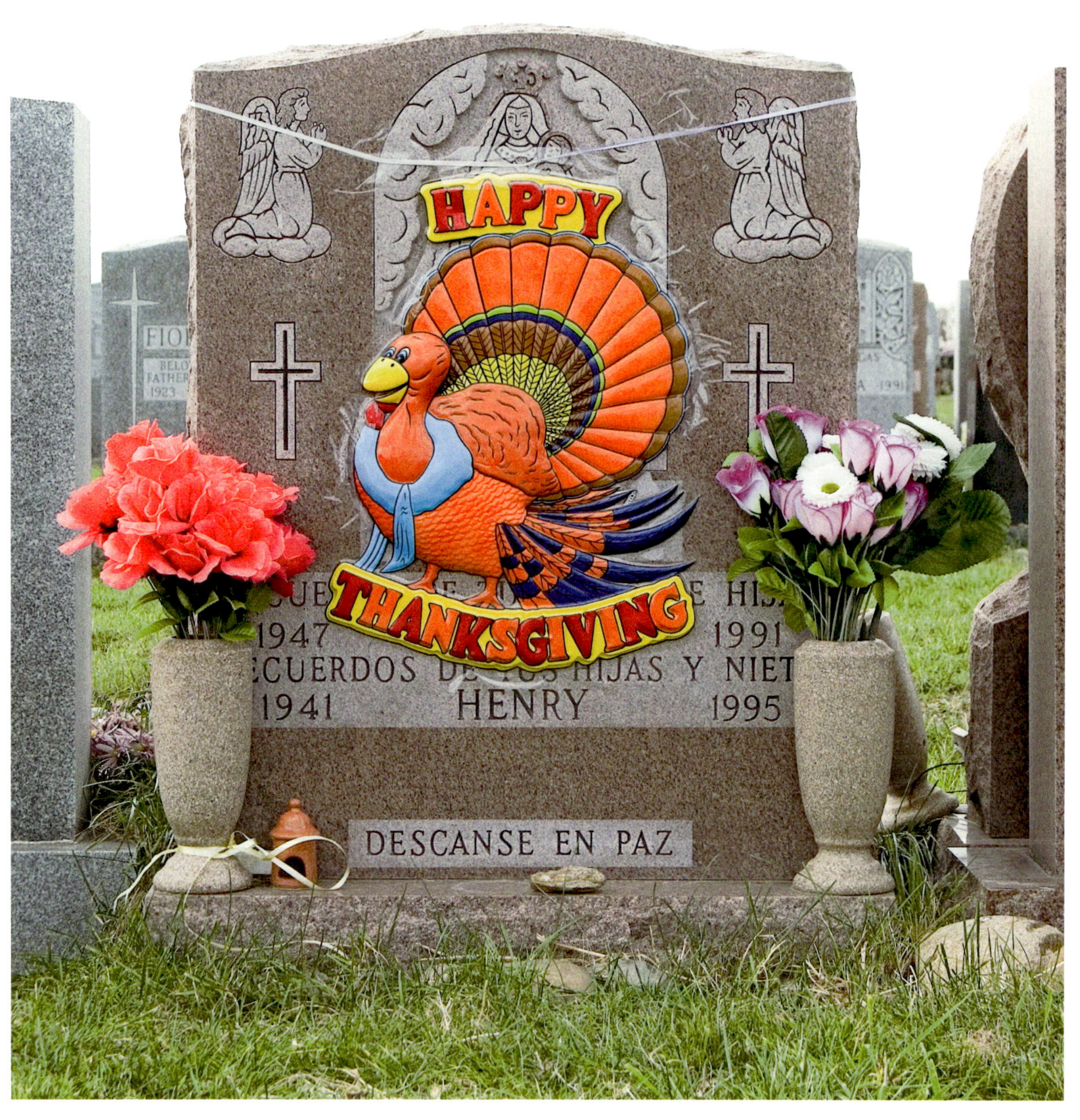

#119

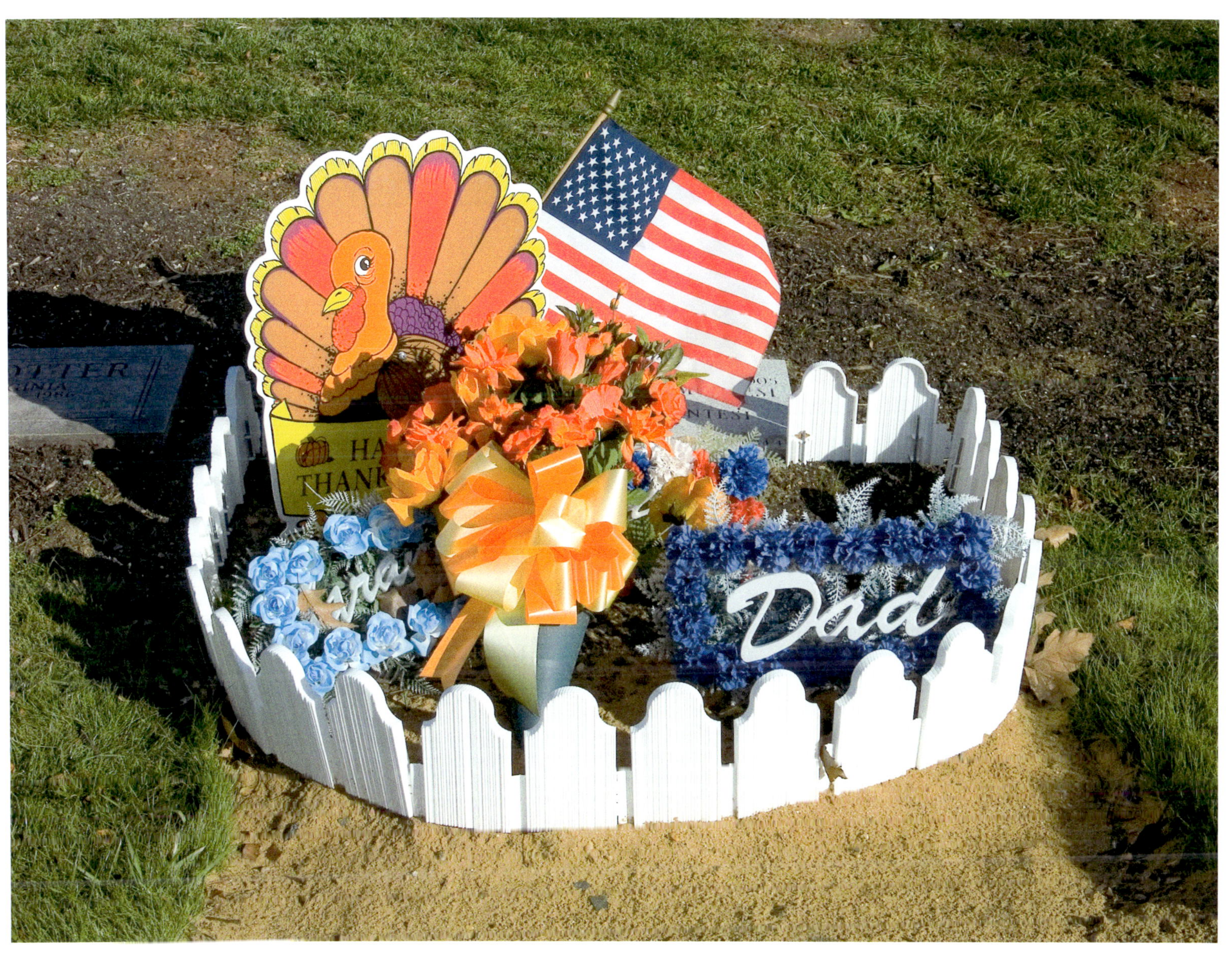

#120

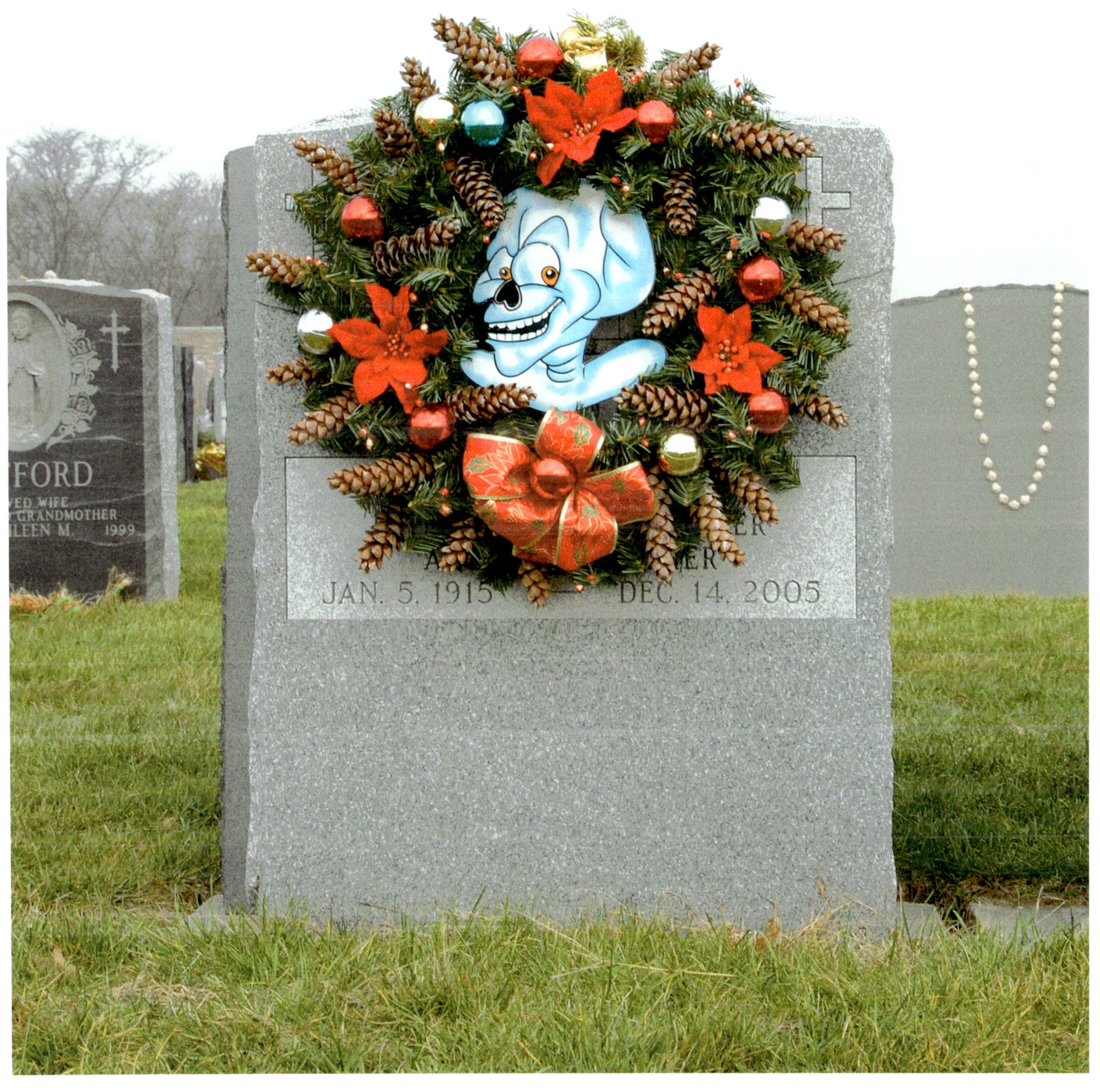
FORD
VED WIFE
GRANDMOTHER
ILEEN M. 1999
JAN. 5. 1915
DEC. 14. 2005

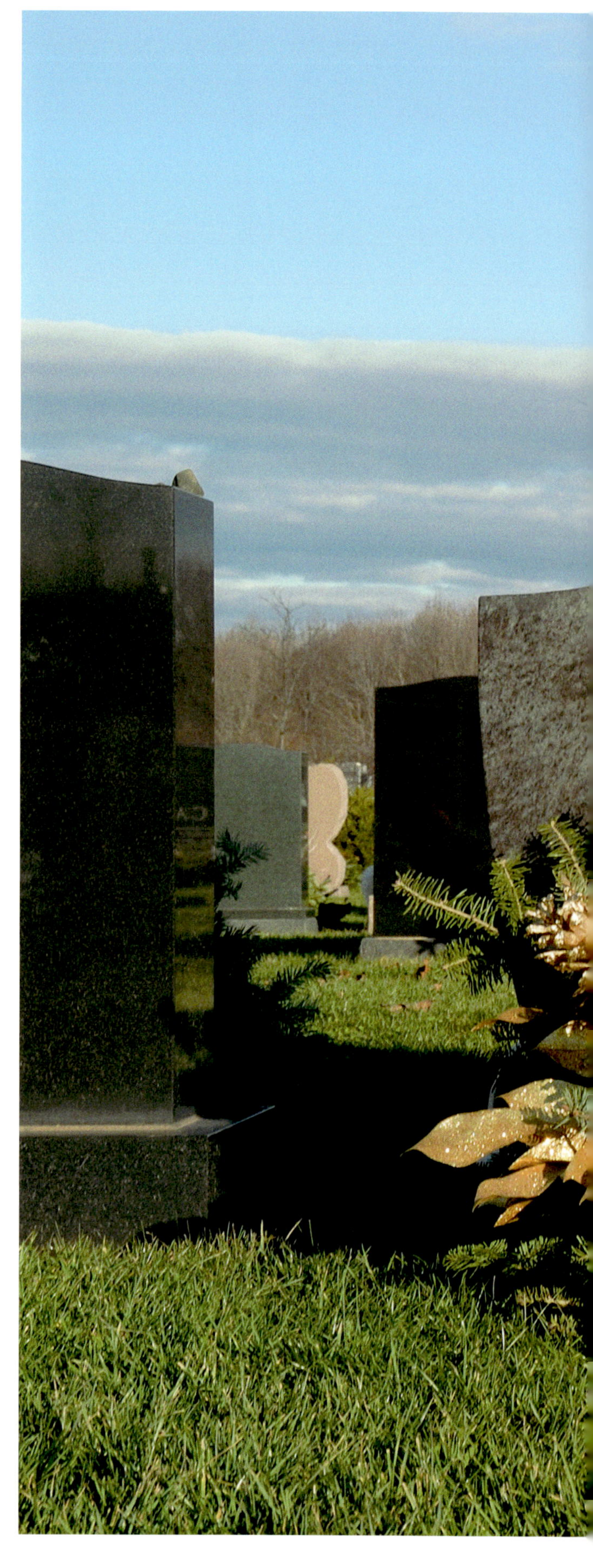

#122

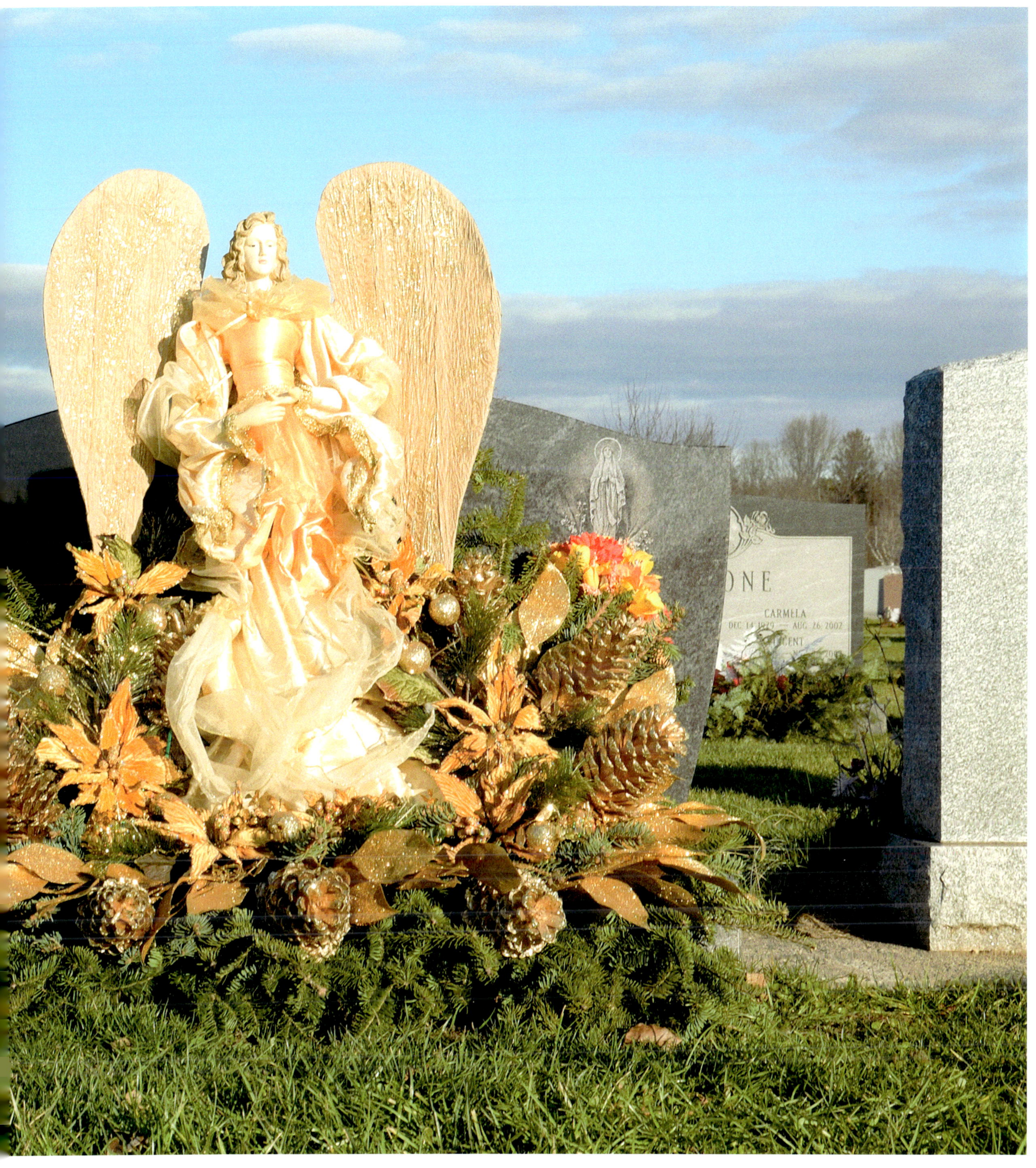
ONE
CARMELA

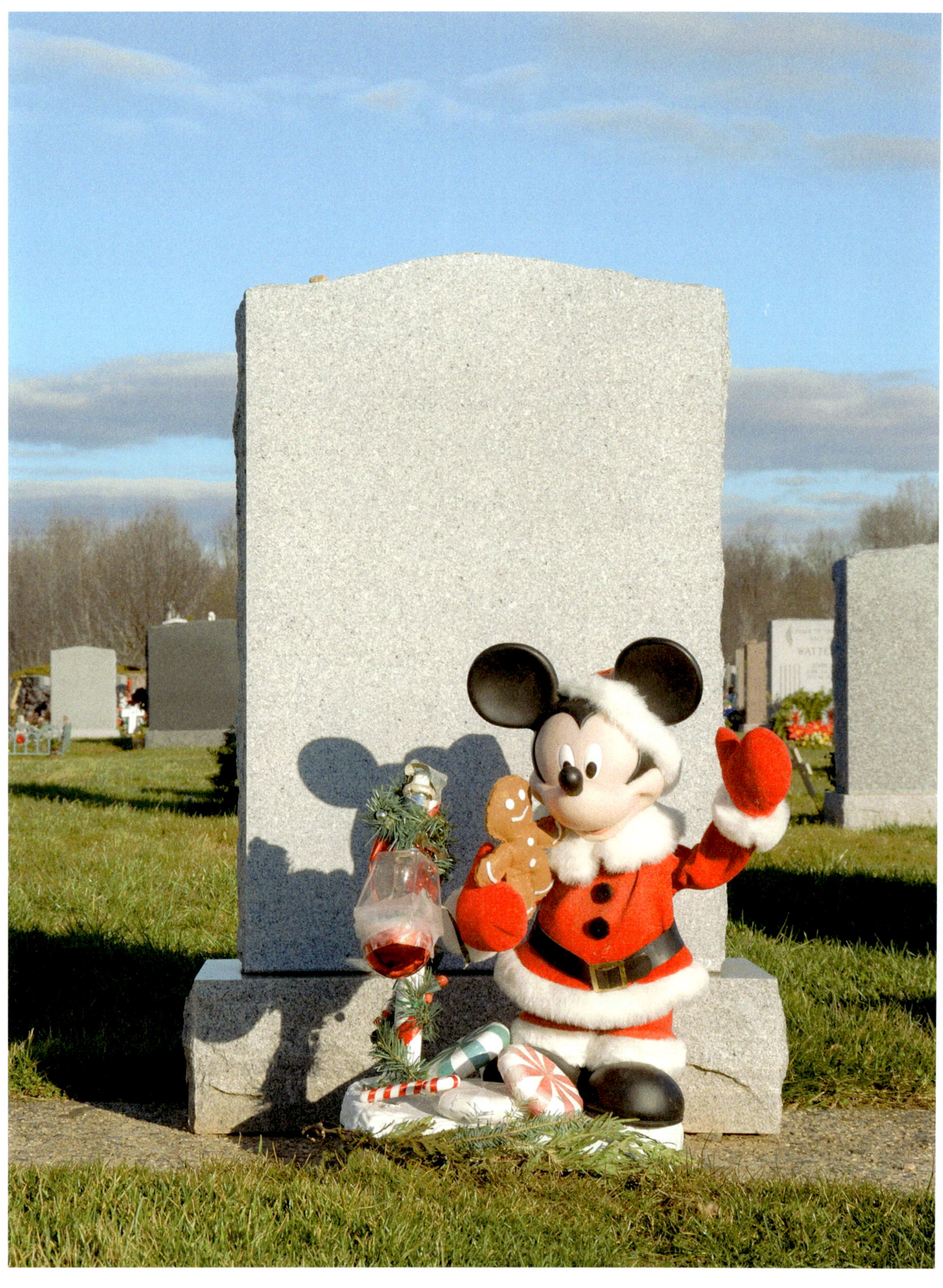

#123

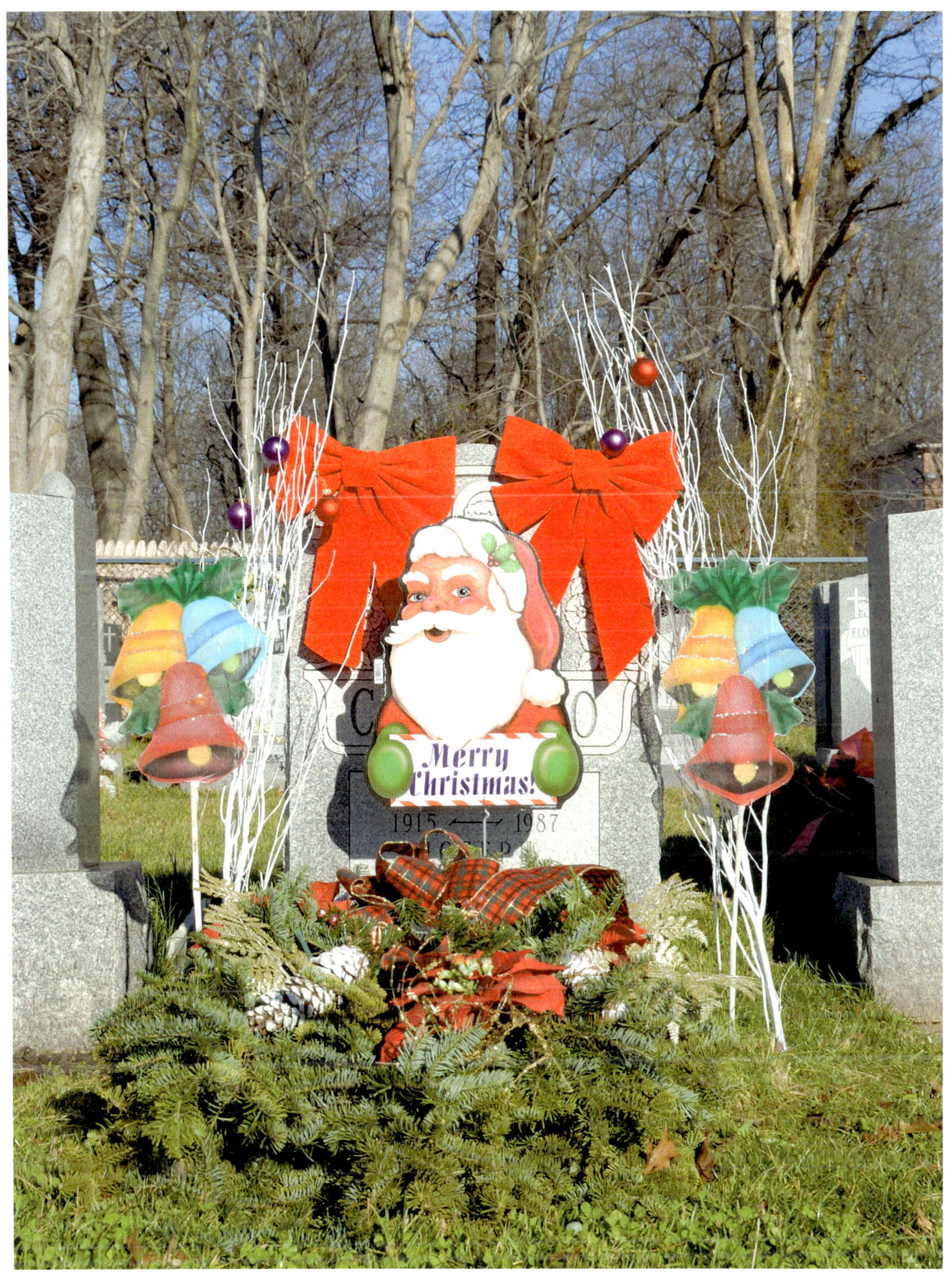
Merry
Christmas!
1915
1987

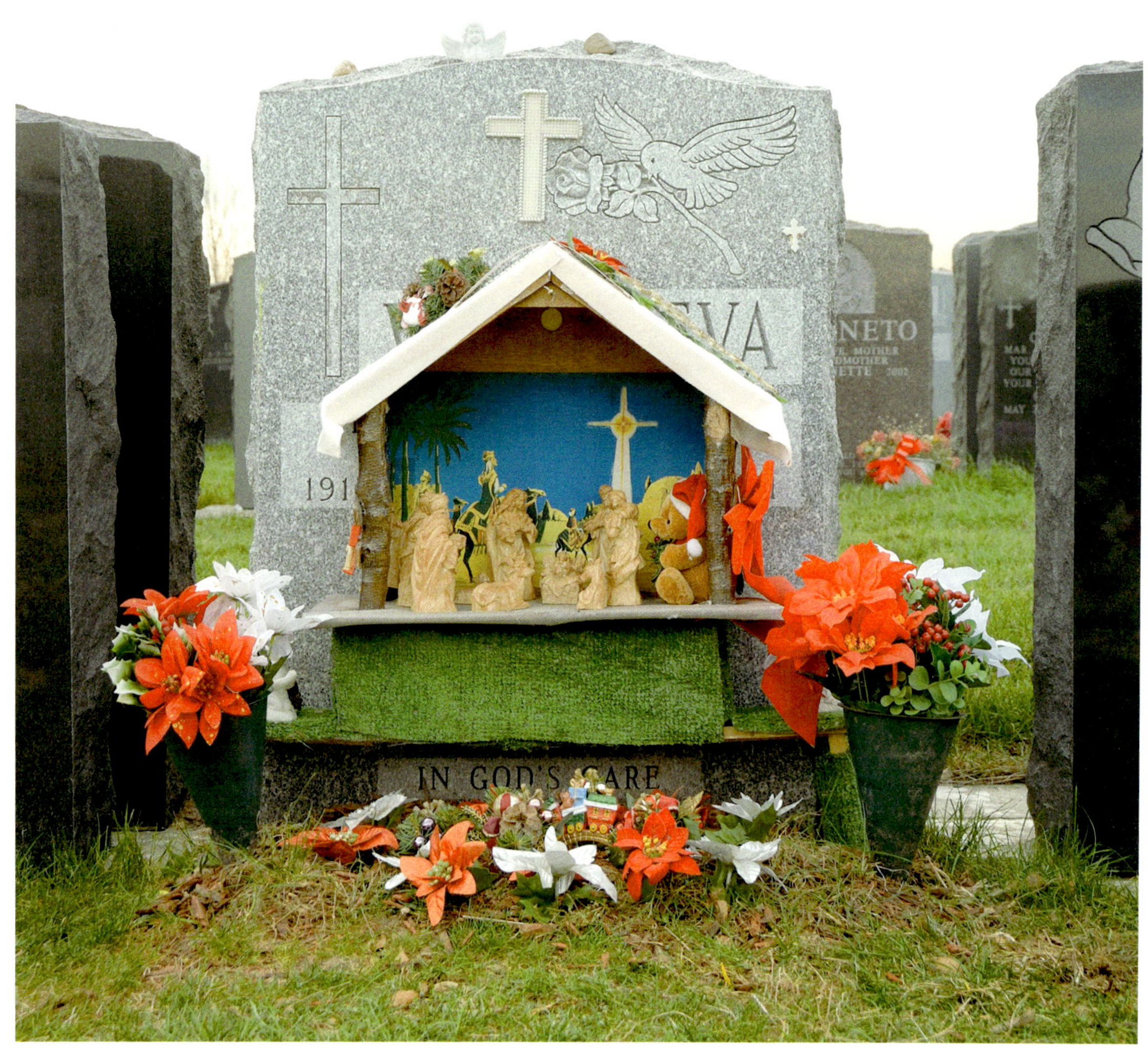

#125

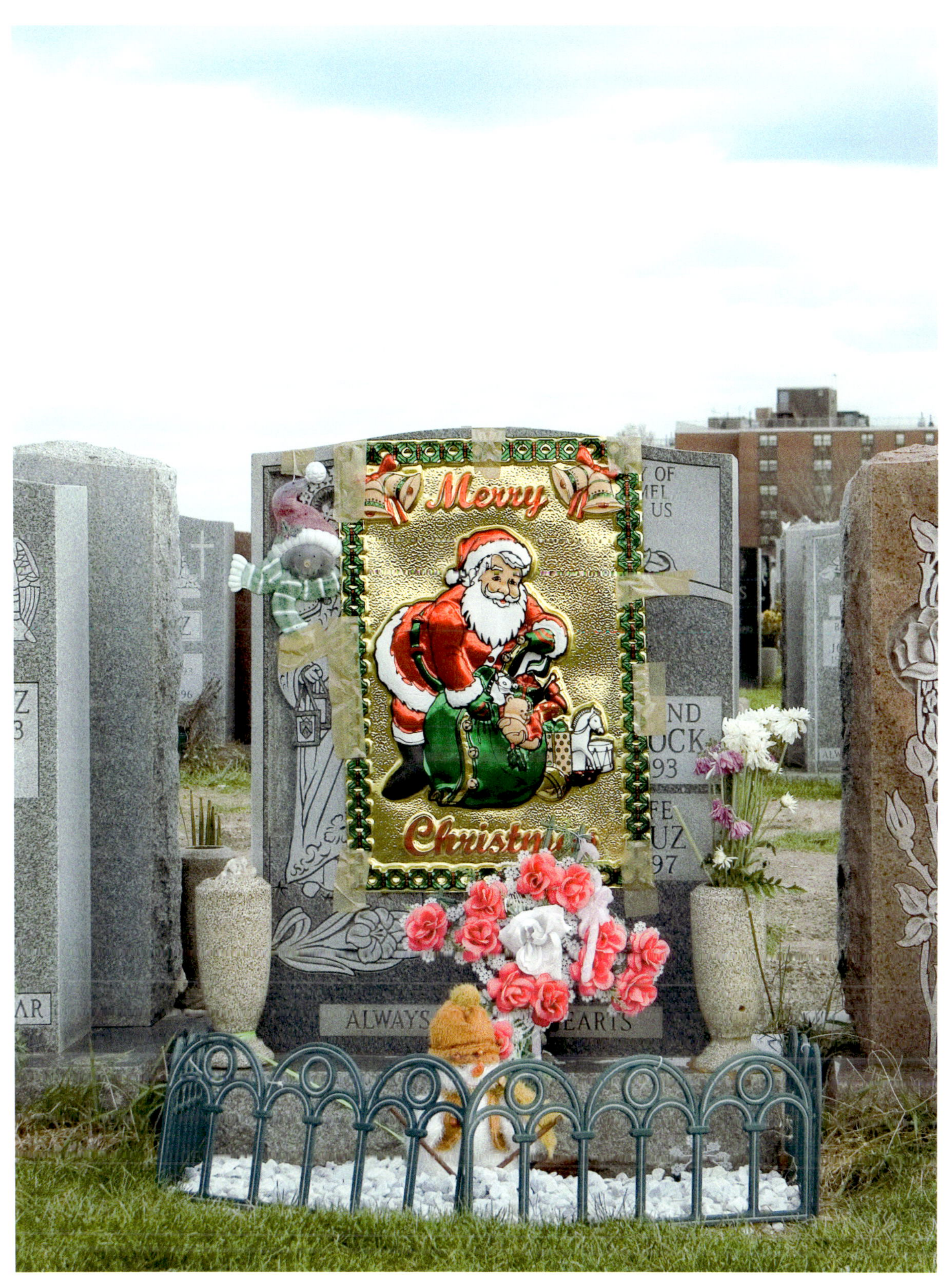

#126

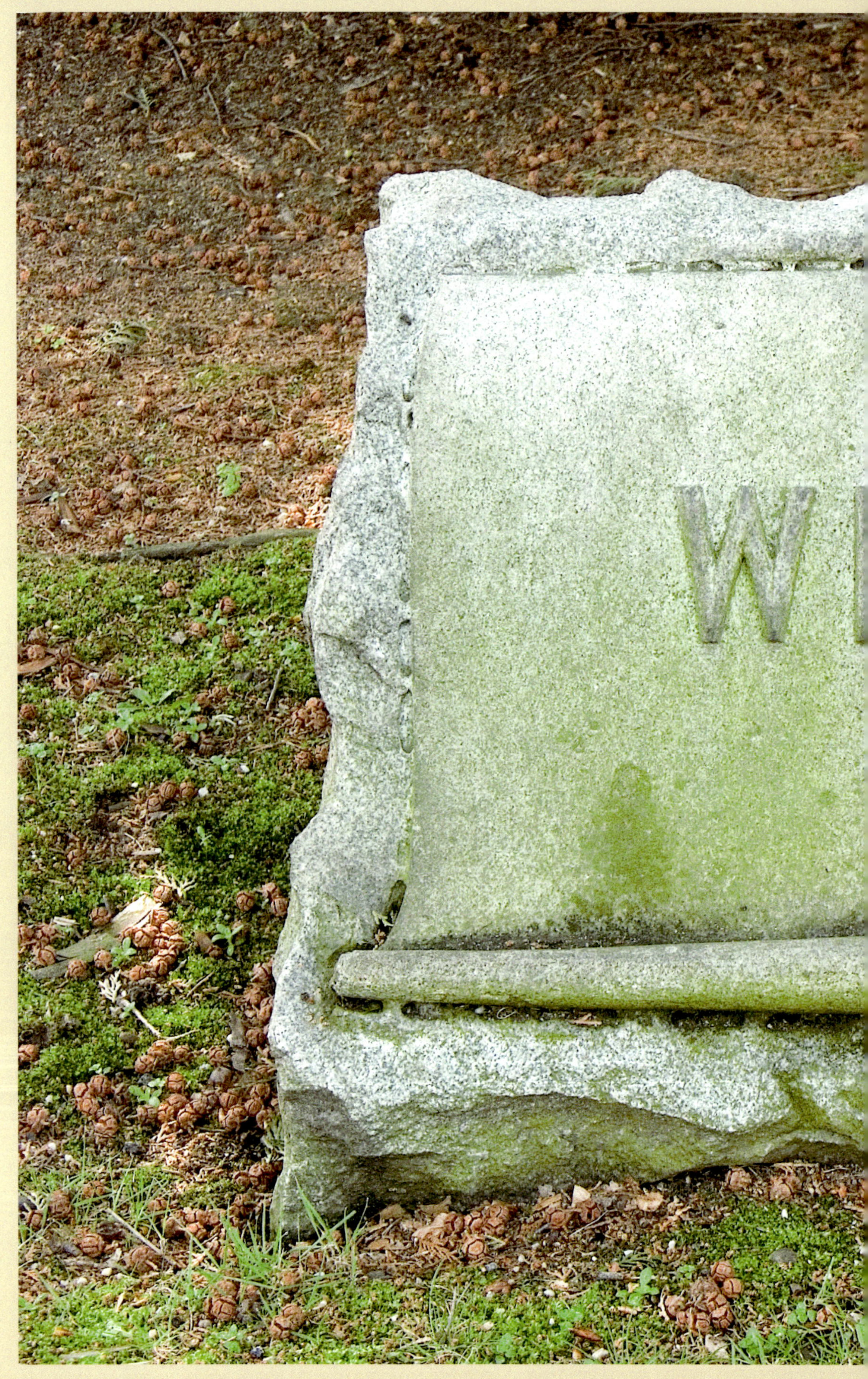

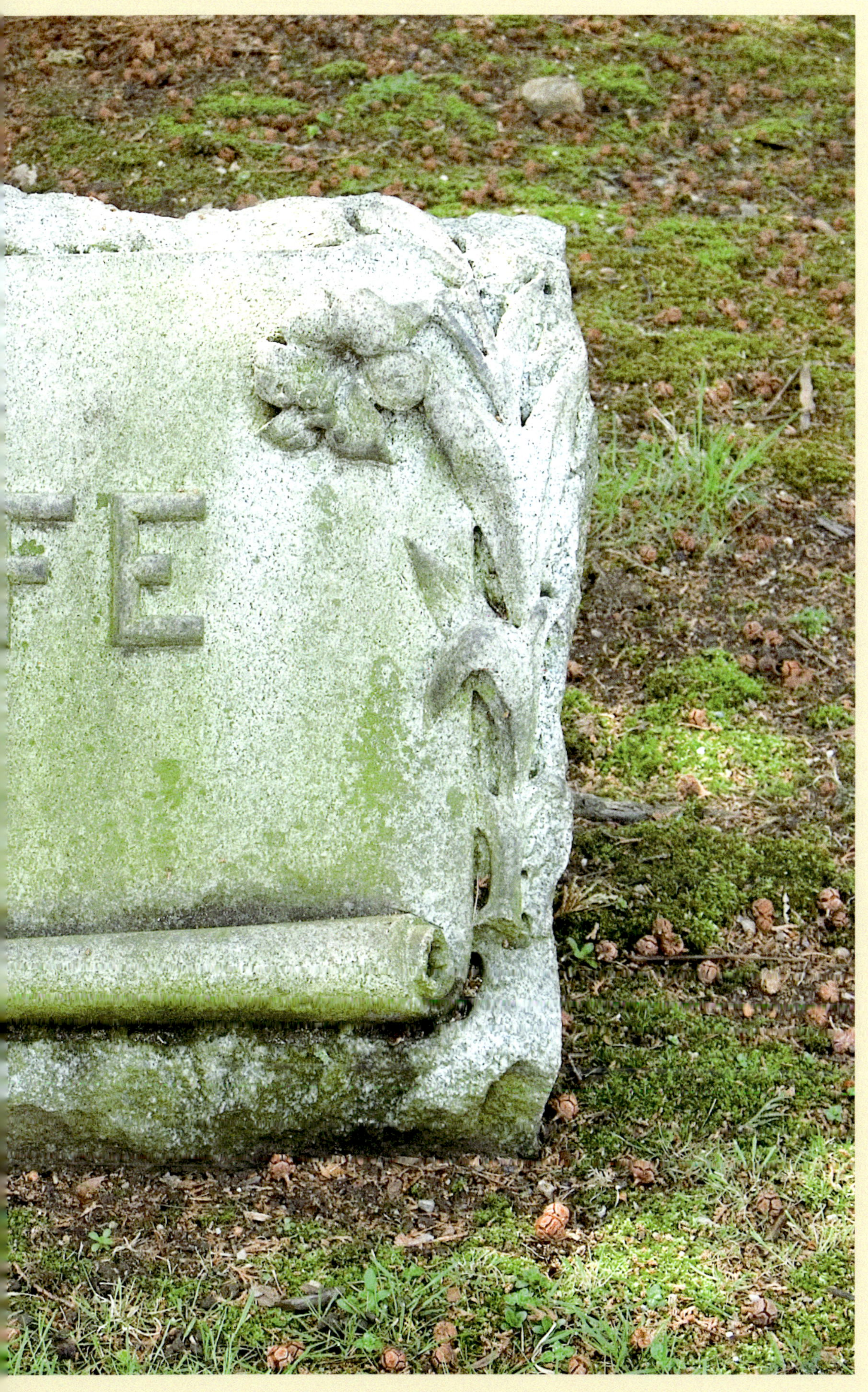
FE

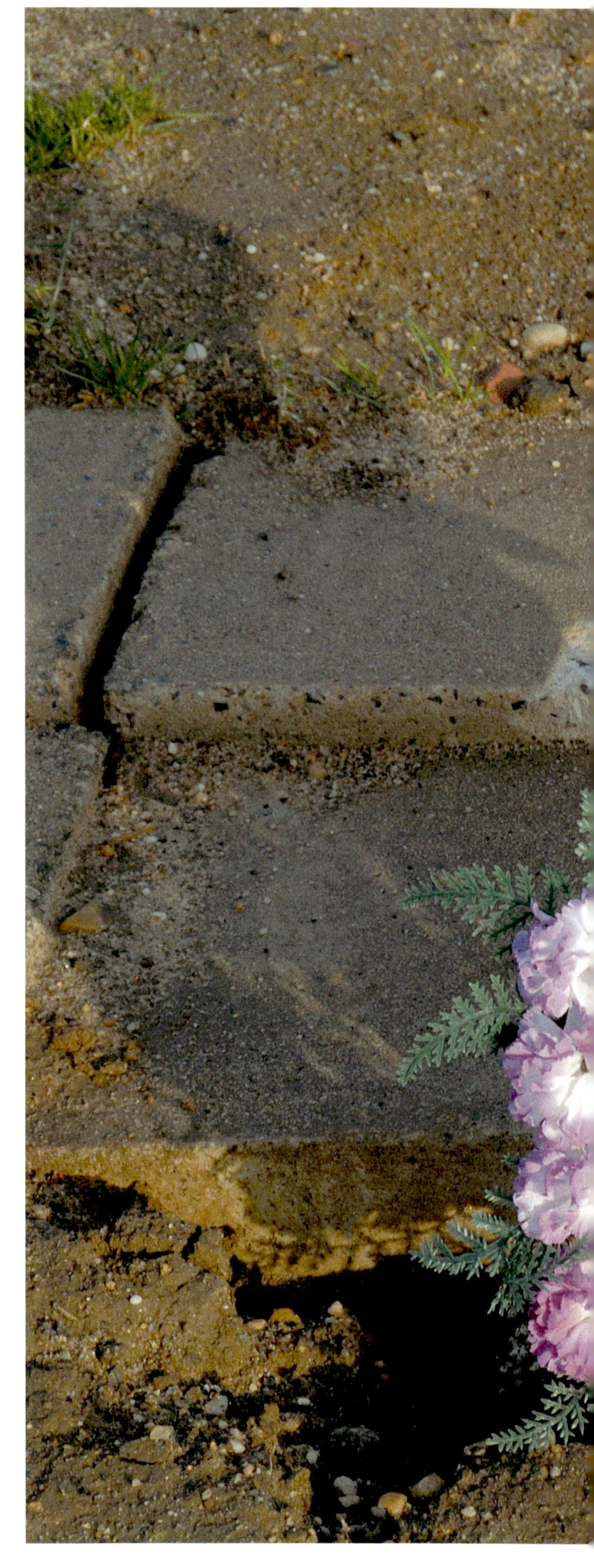

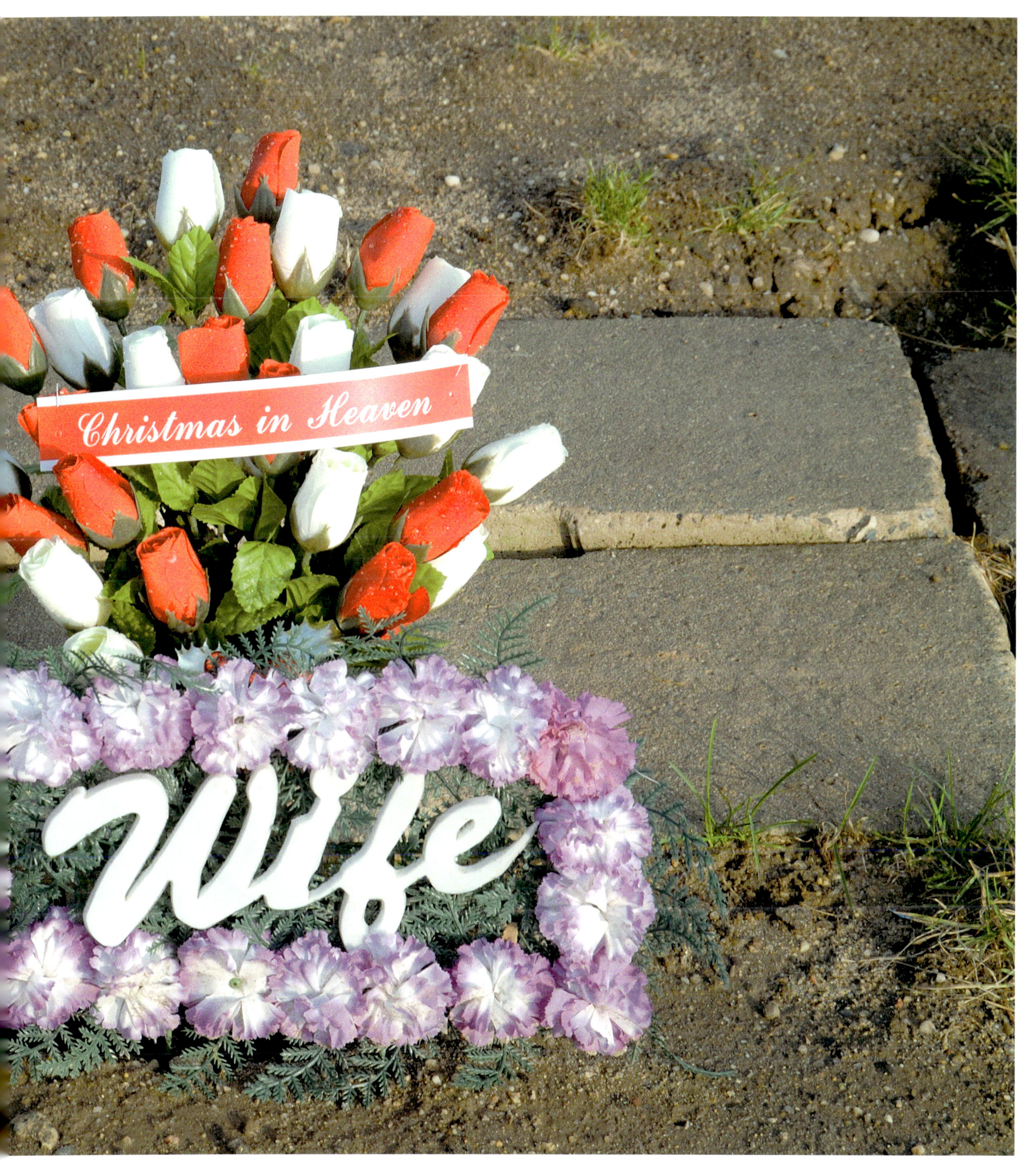
Christmas in Heaven
Wife

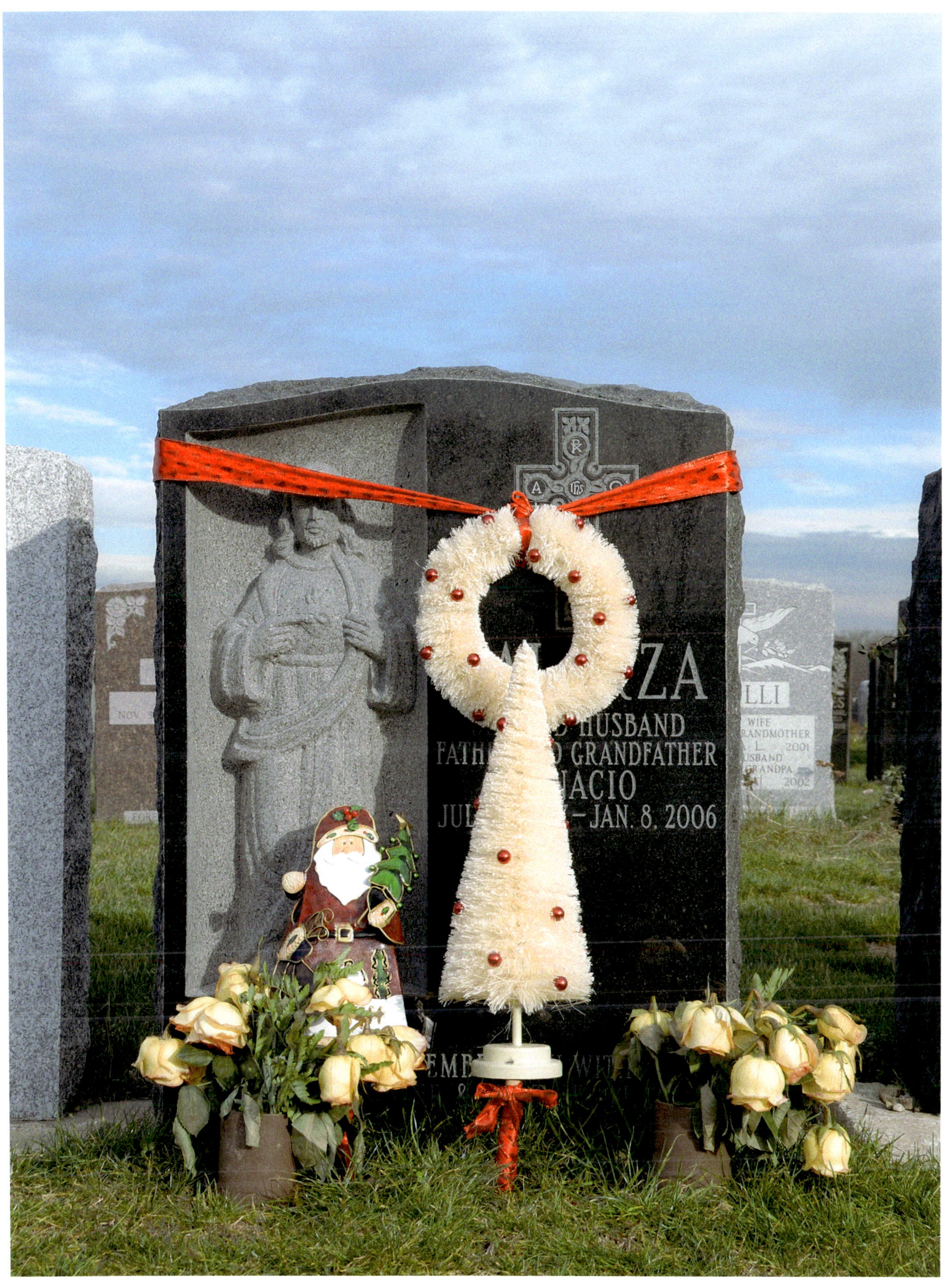
HUSBAND
GRANDFATHER
JAN. 8. 2006

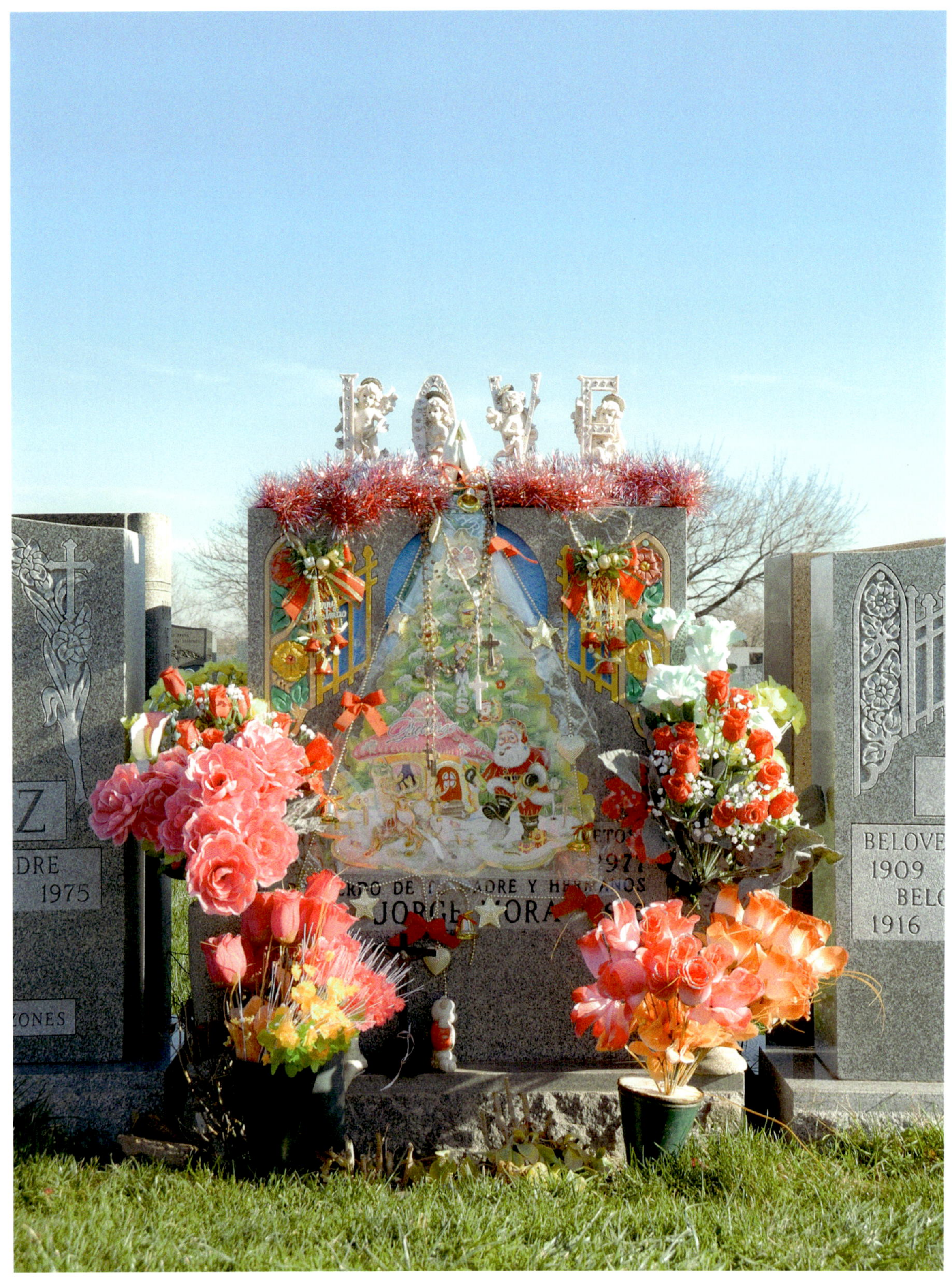

#129

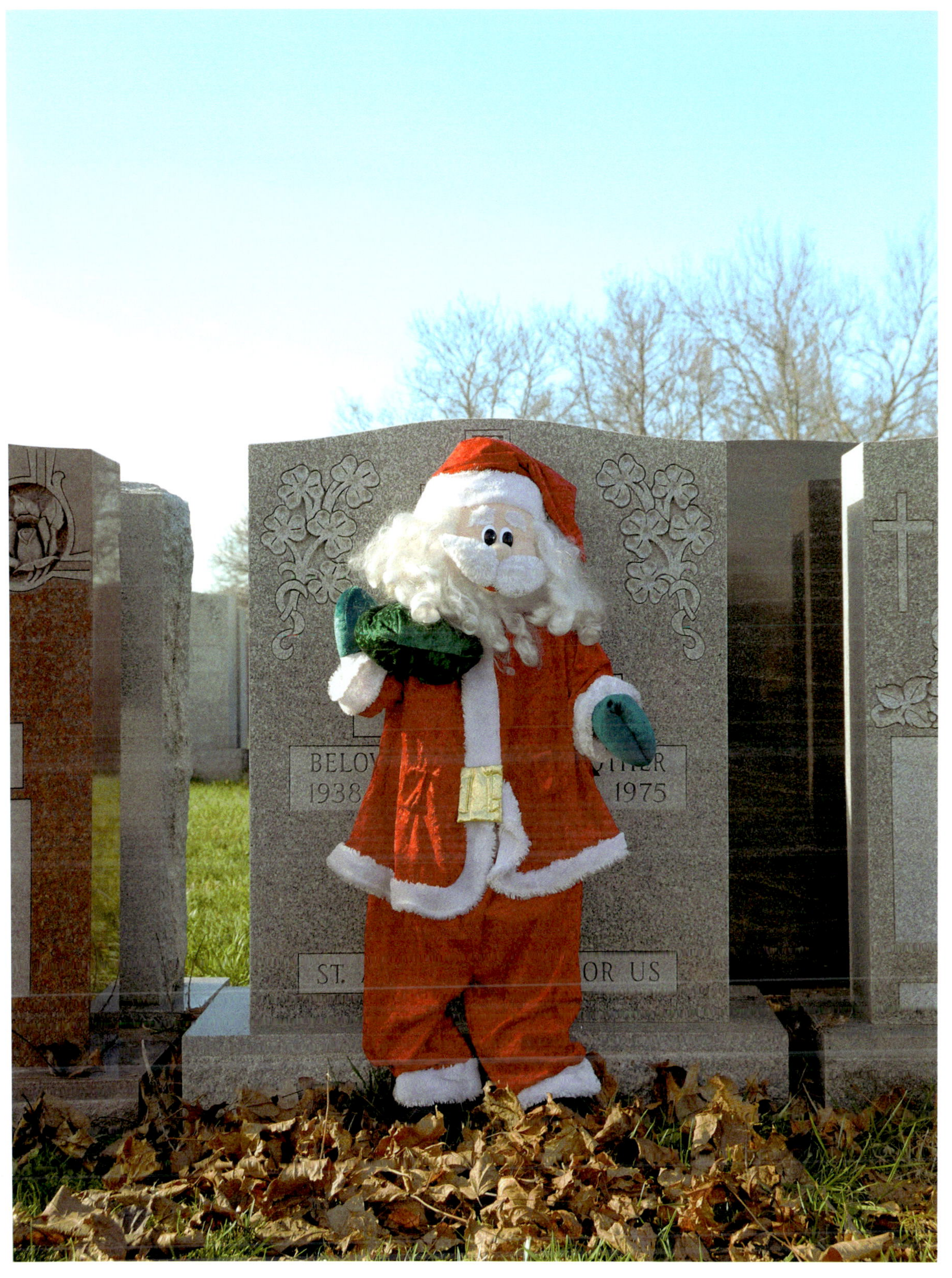

BELOV
1938
1975
ST.
OR US

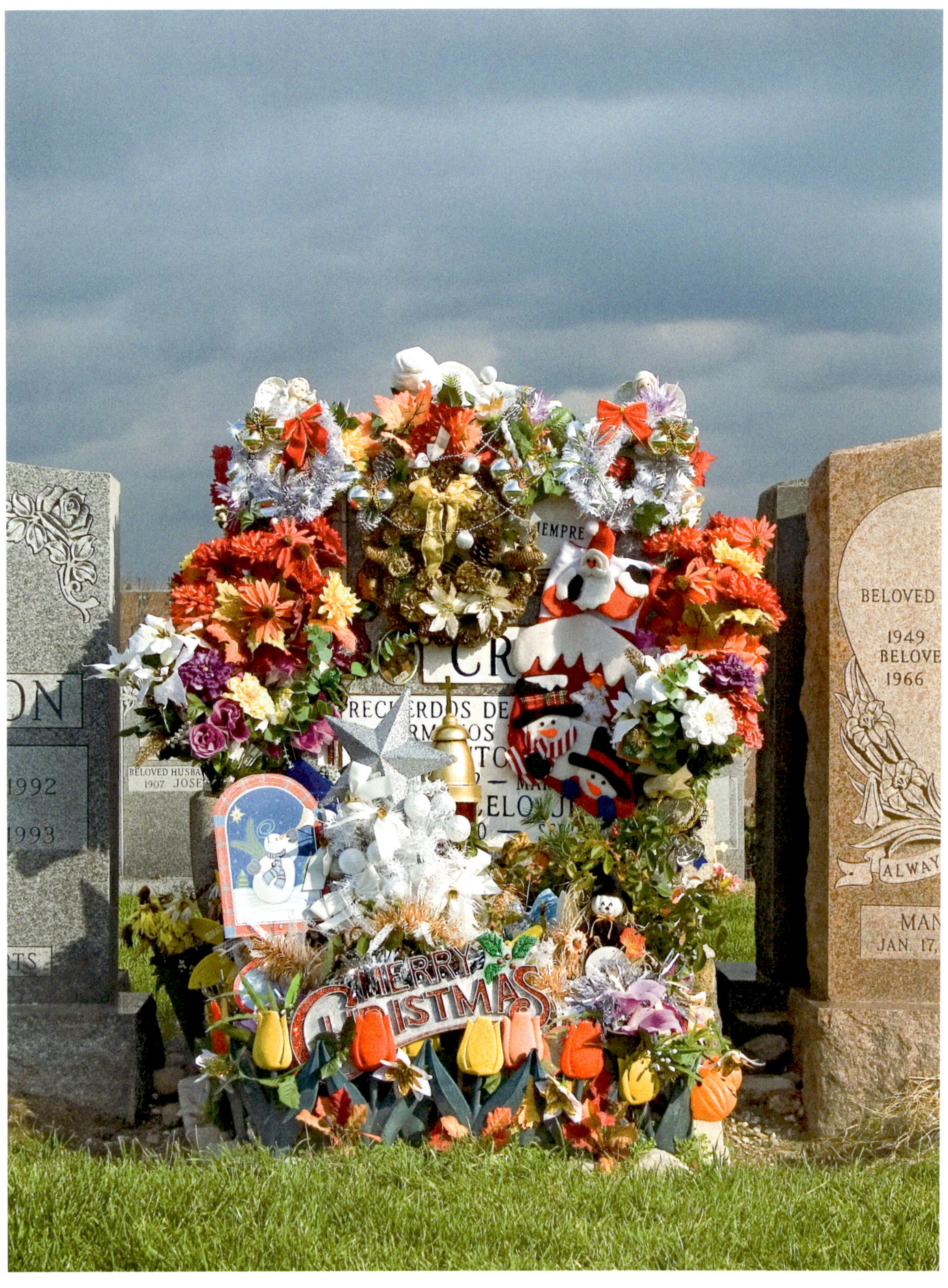

#131

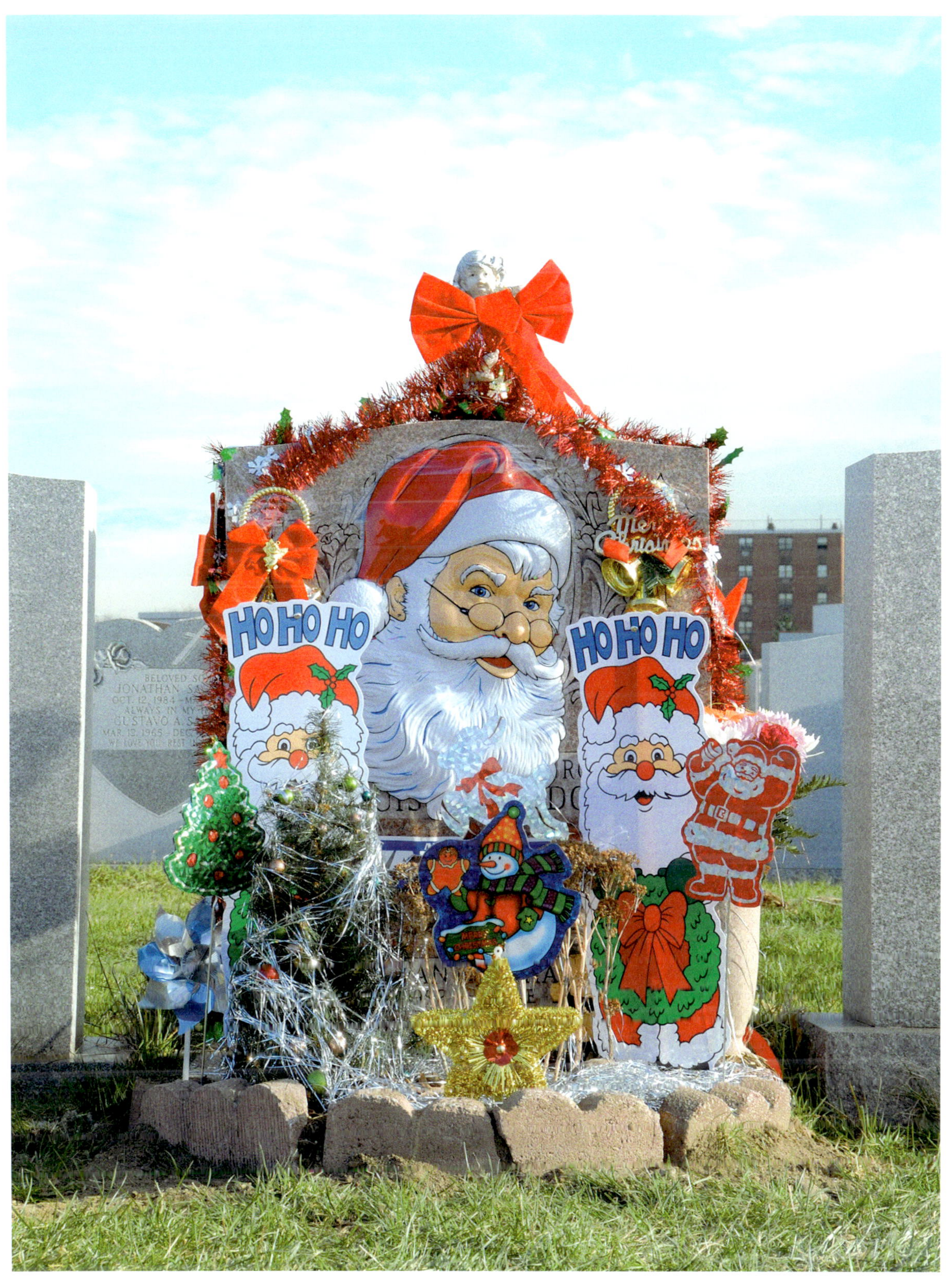
HO HO HO
HO HO HO

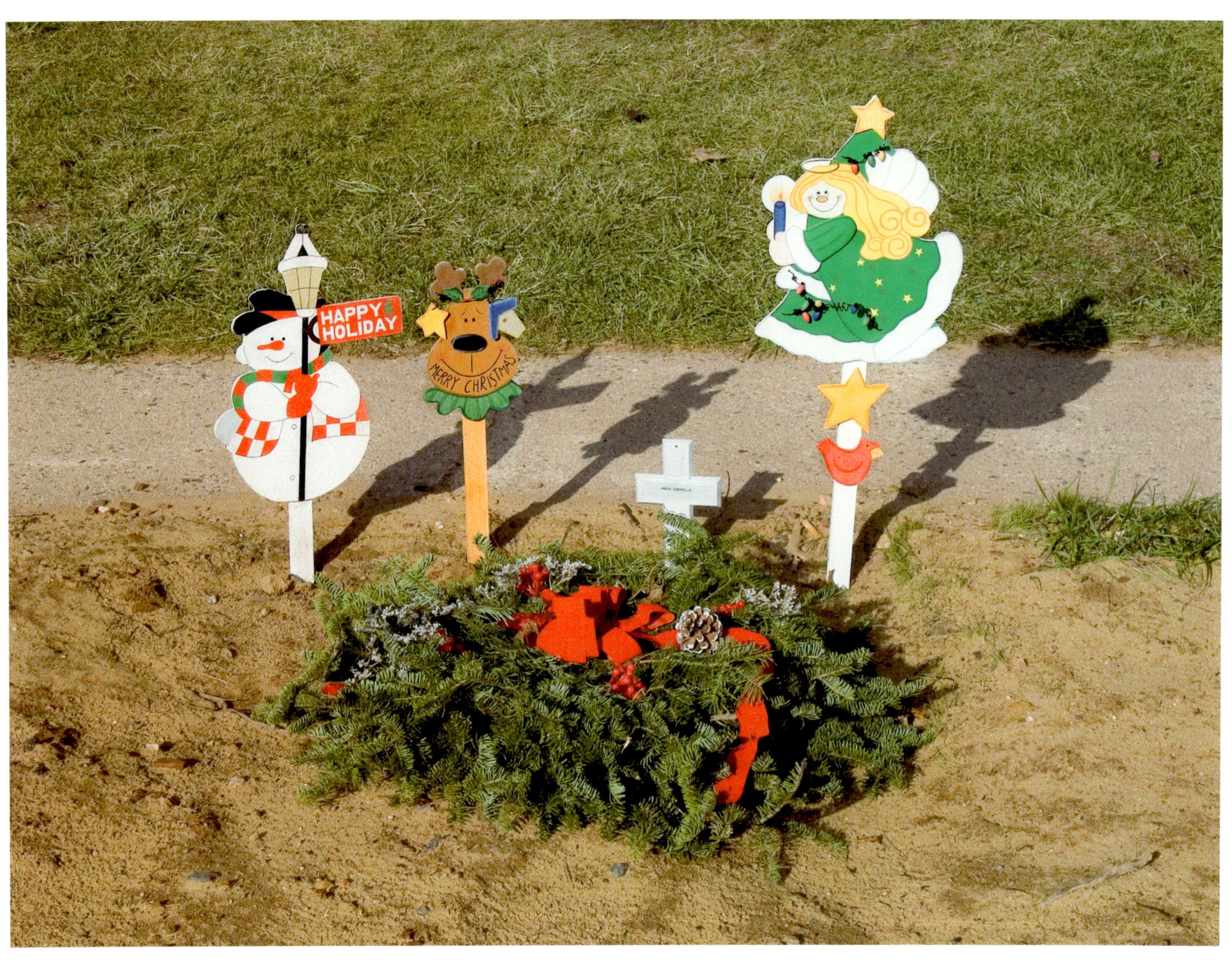

#133

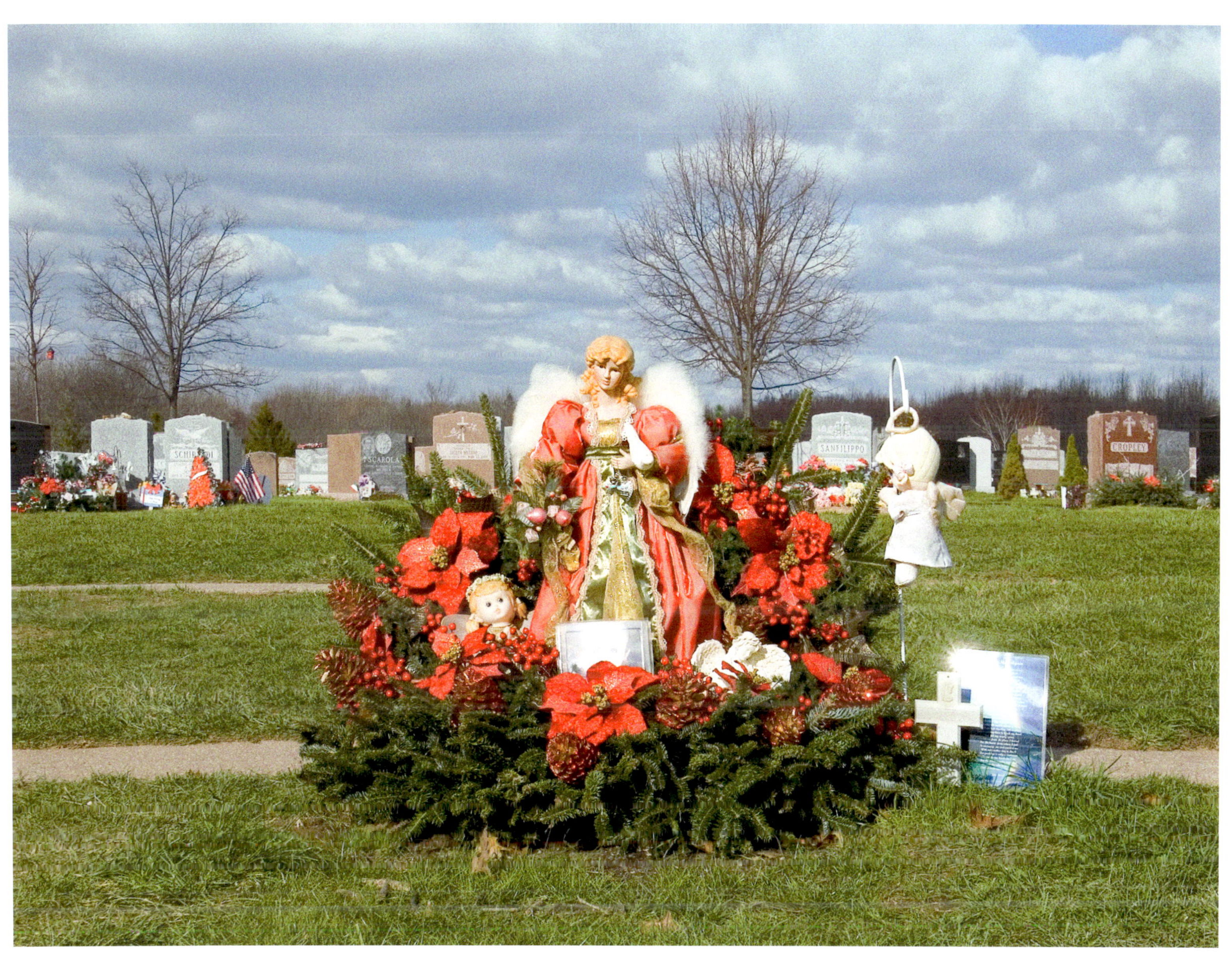

#17B

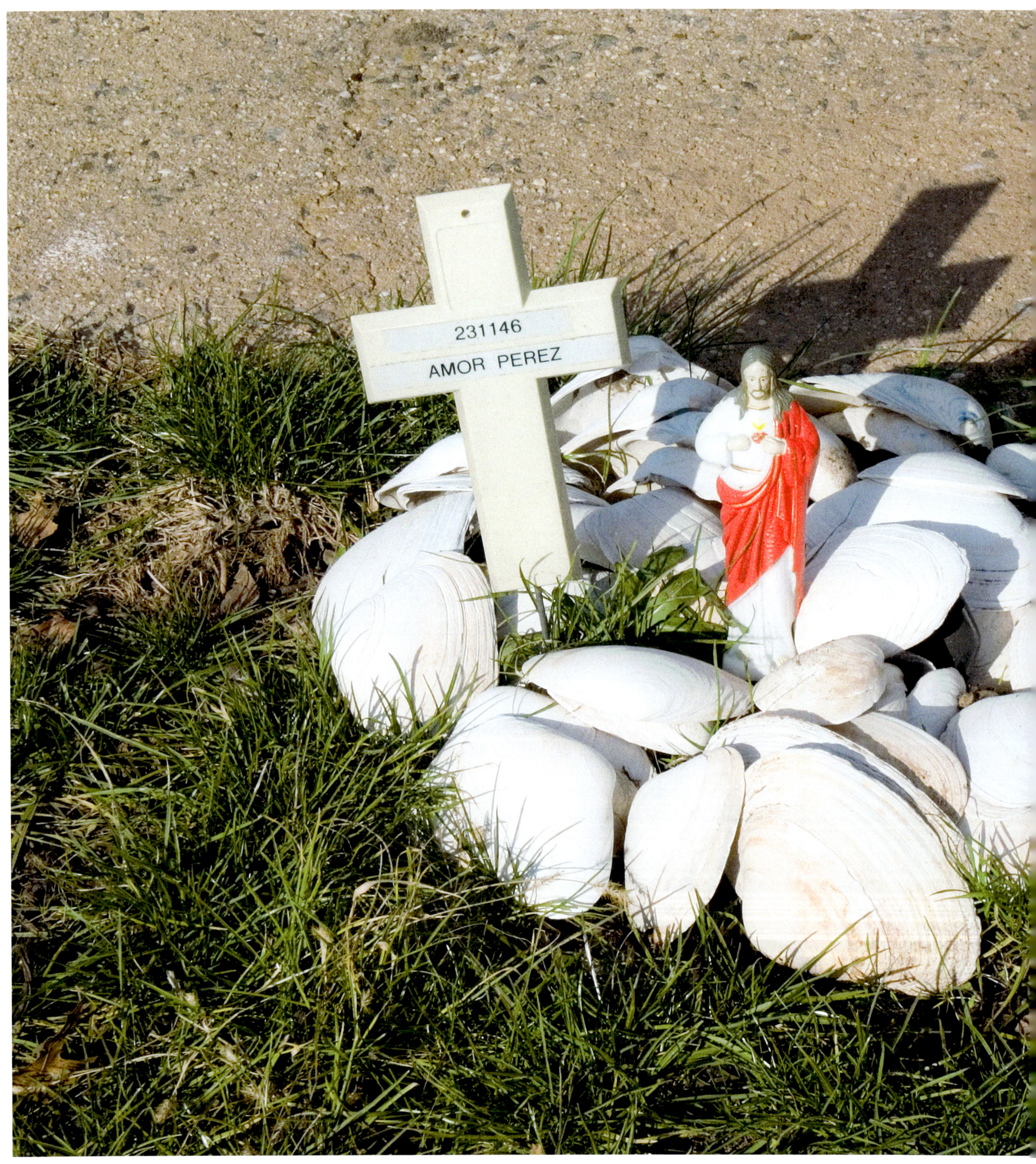
231146
AMOR PEREZ

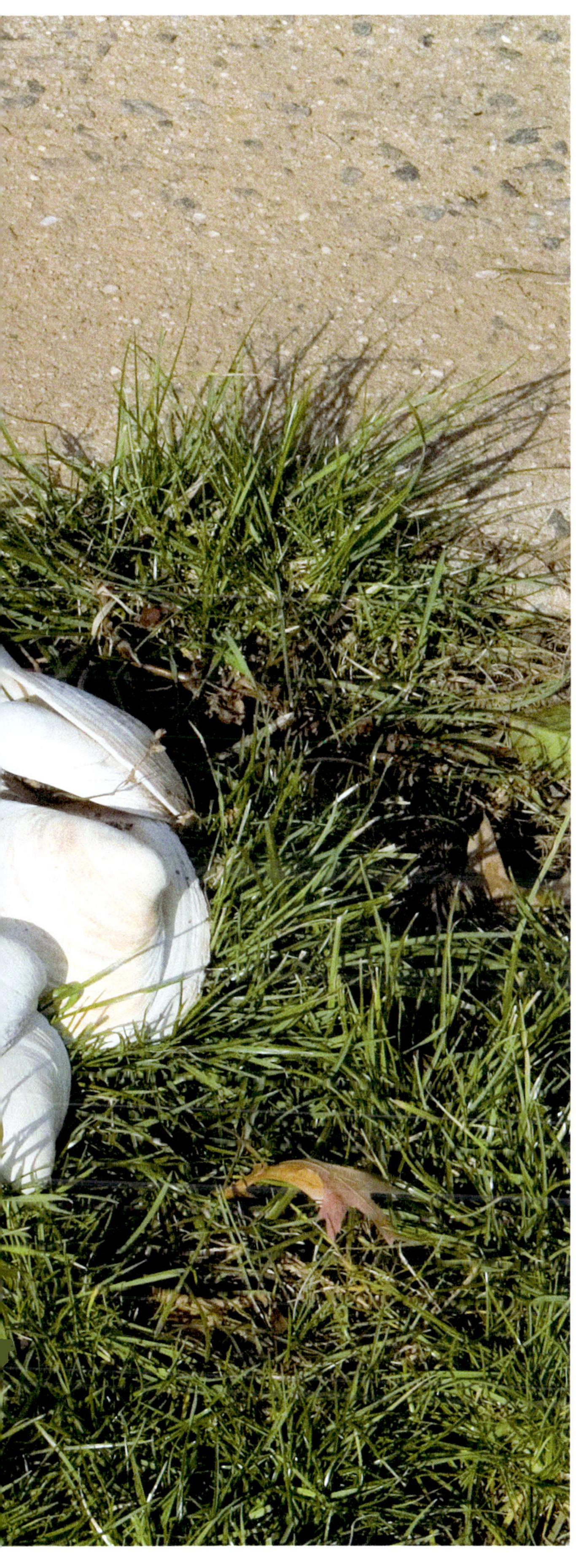

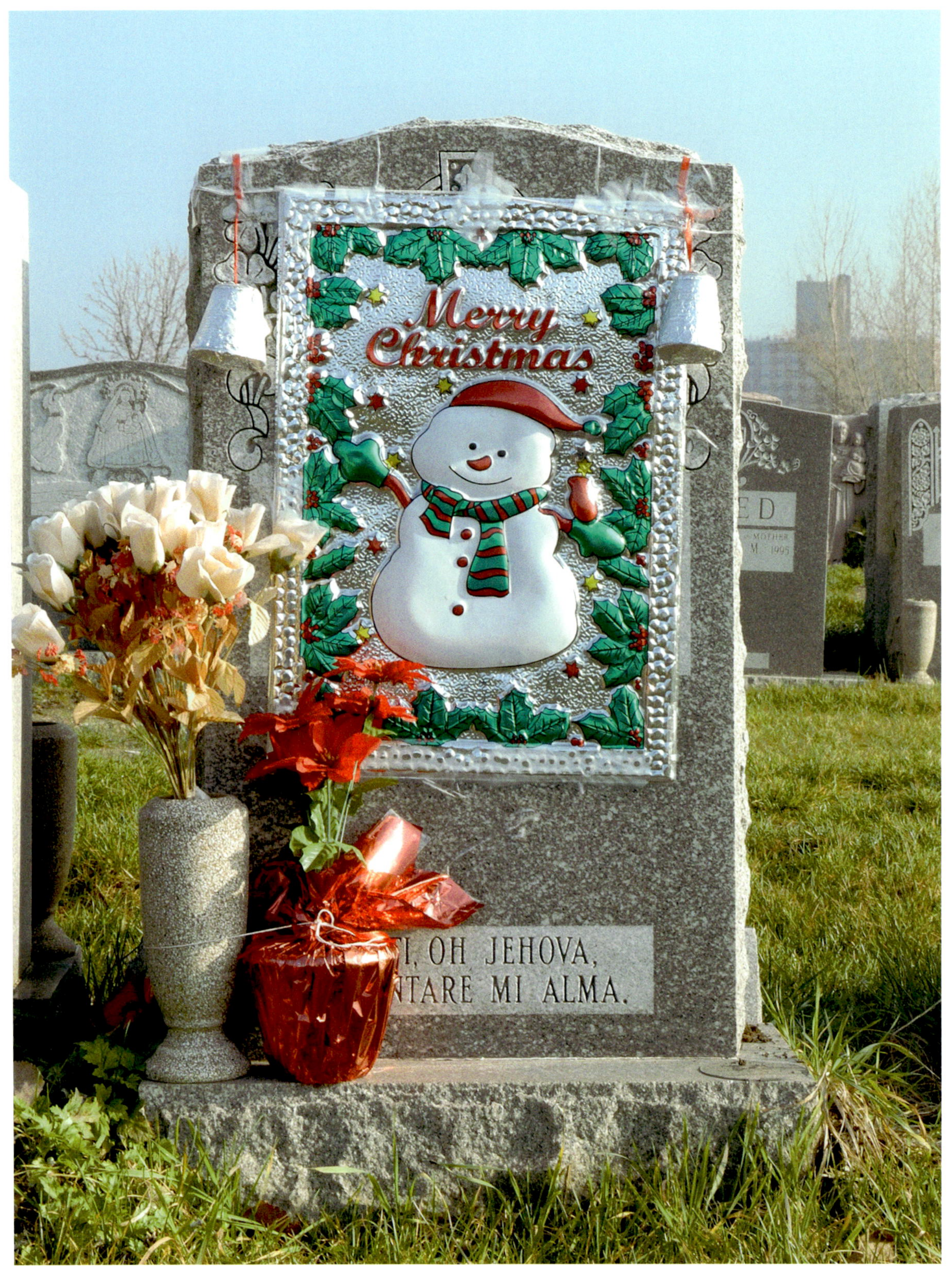

#135

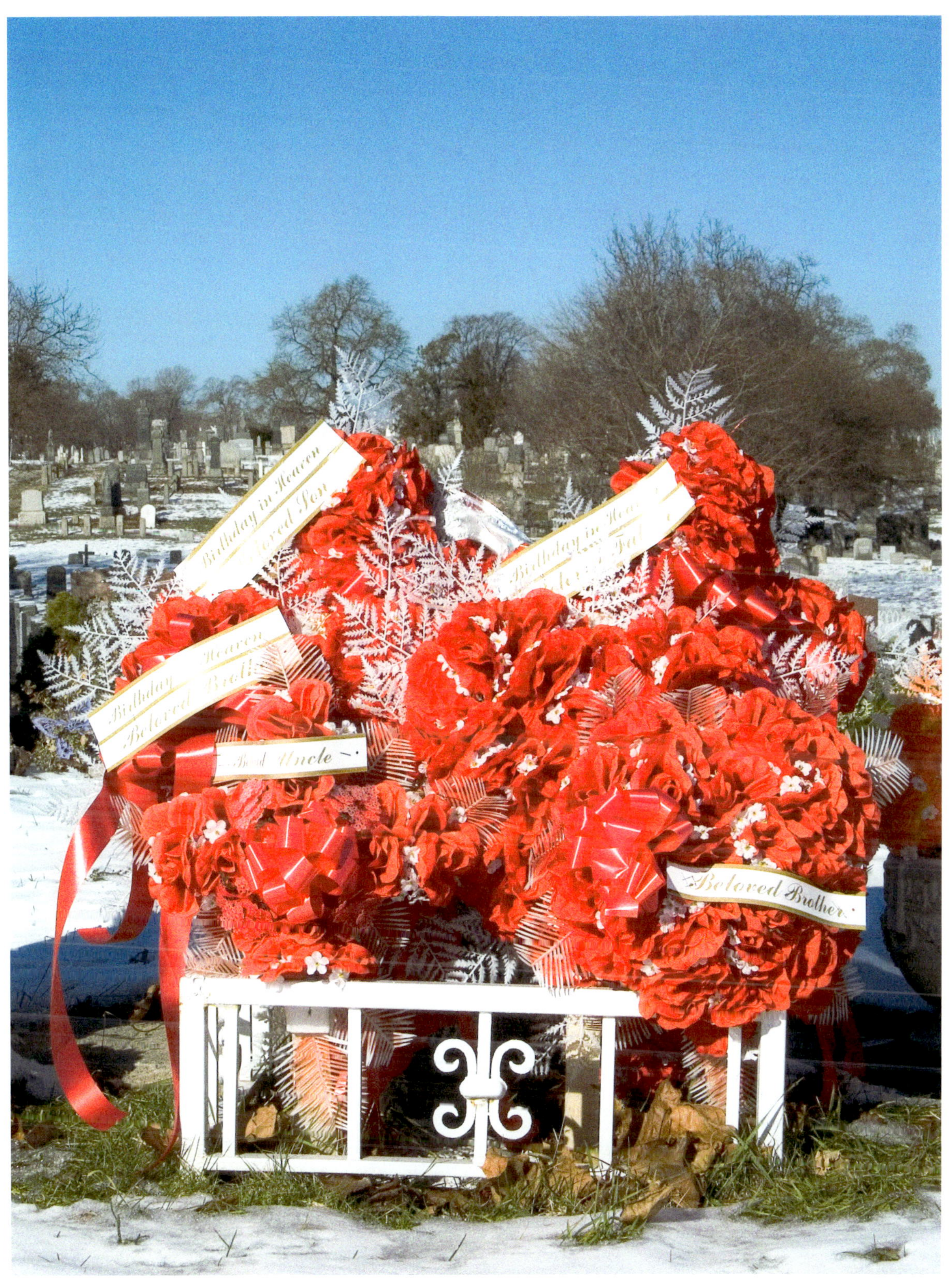
Birthday in Heaven
Birthday in Heaven
Uncle
Beloved Brother

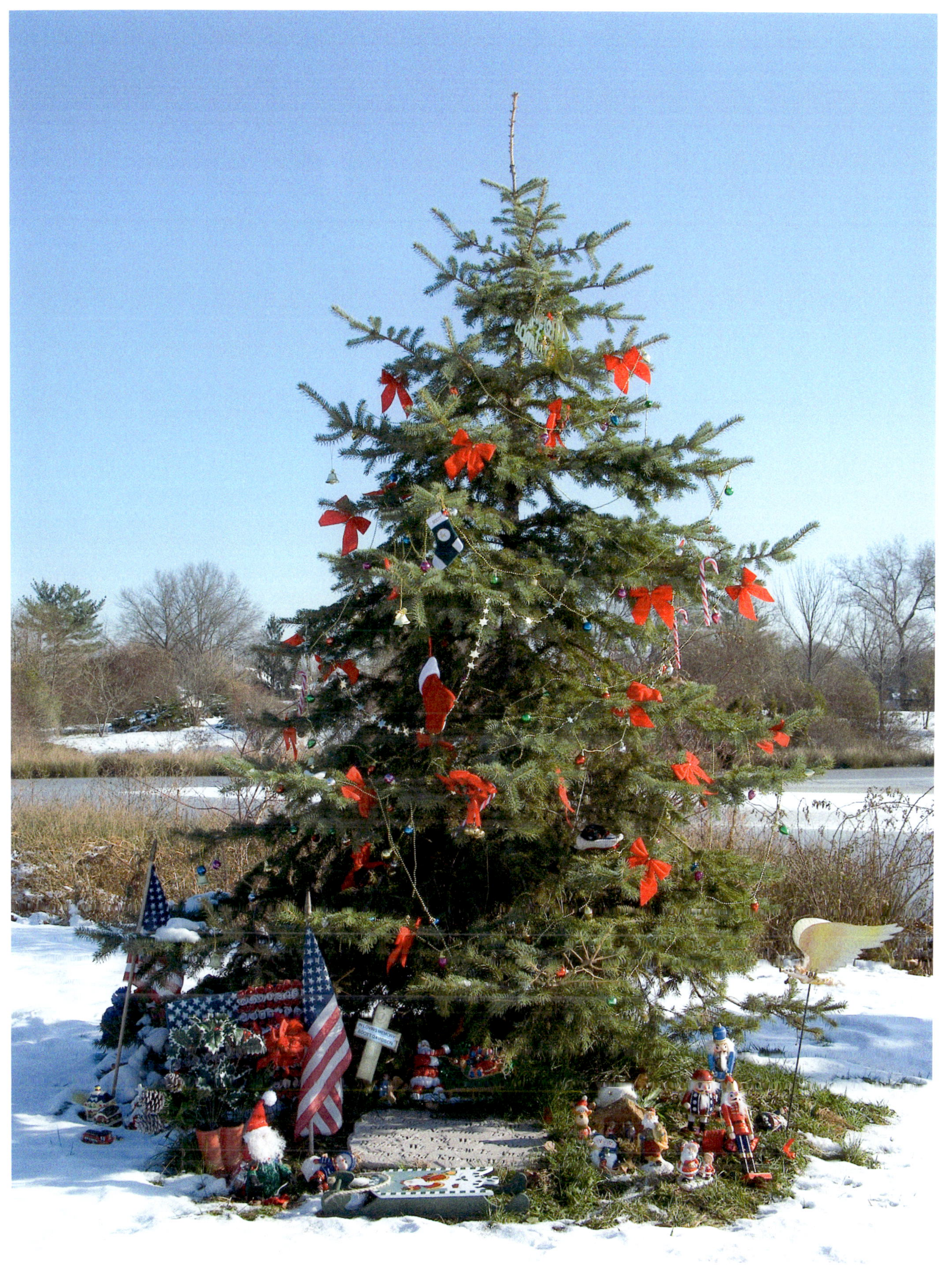

#137

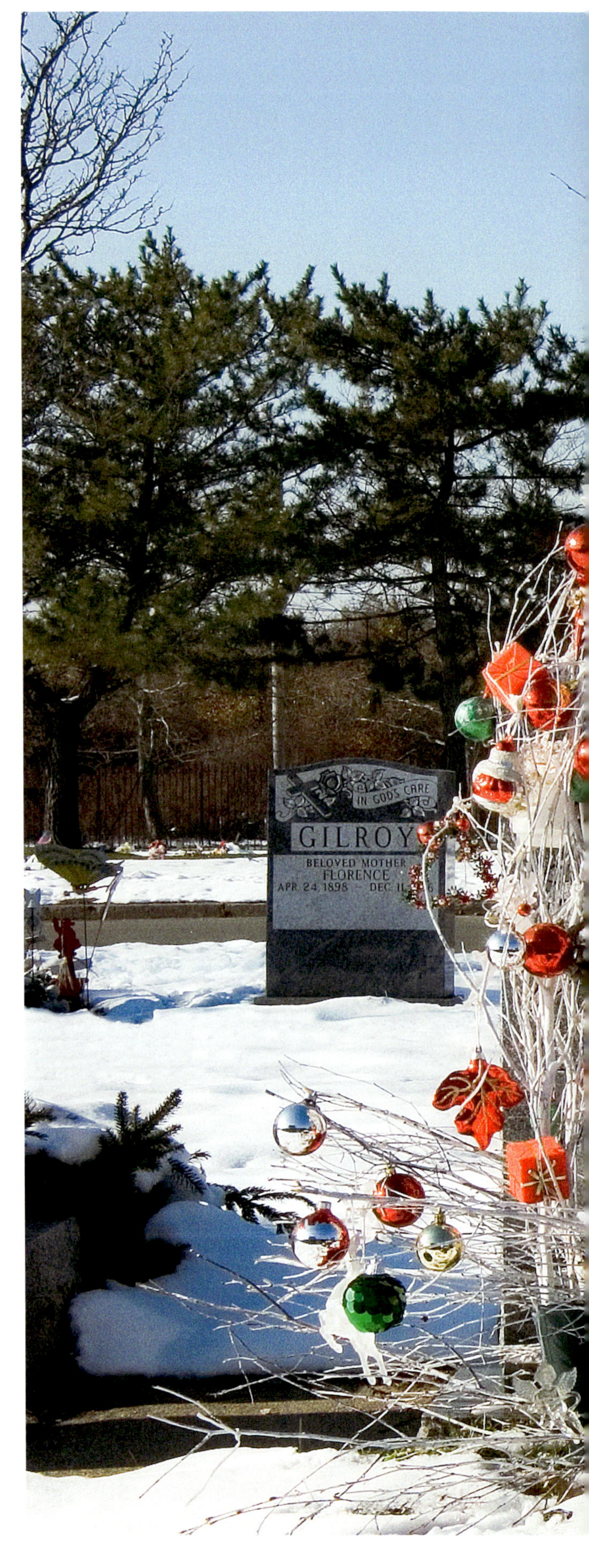
IN GODS CARE
GILROY
BELOVED MOTHER
FLORENCE
APR 24 1898 — DEC 11

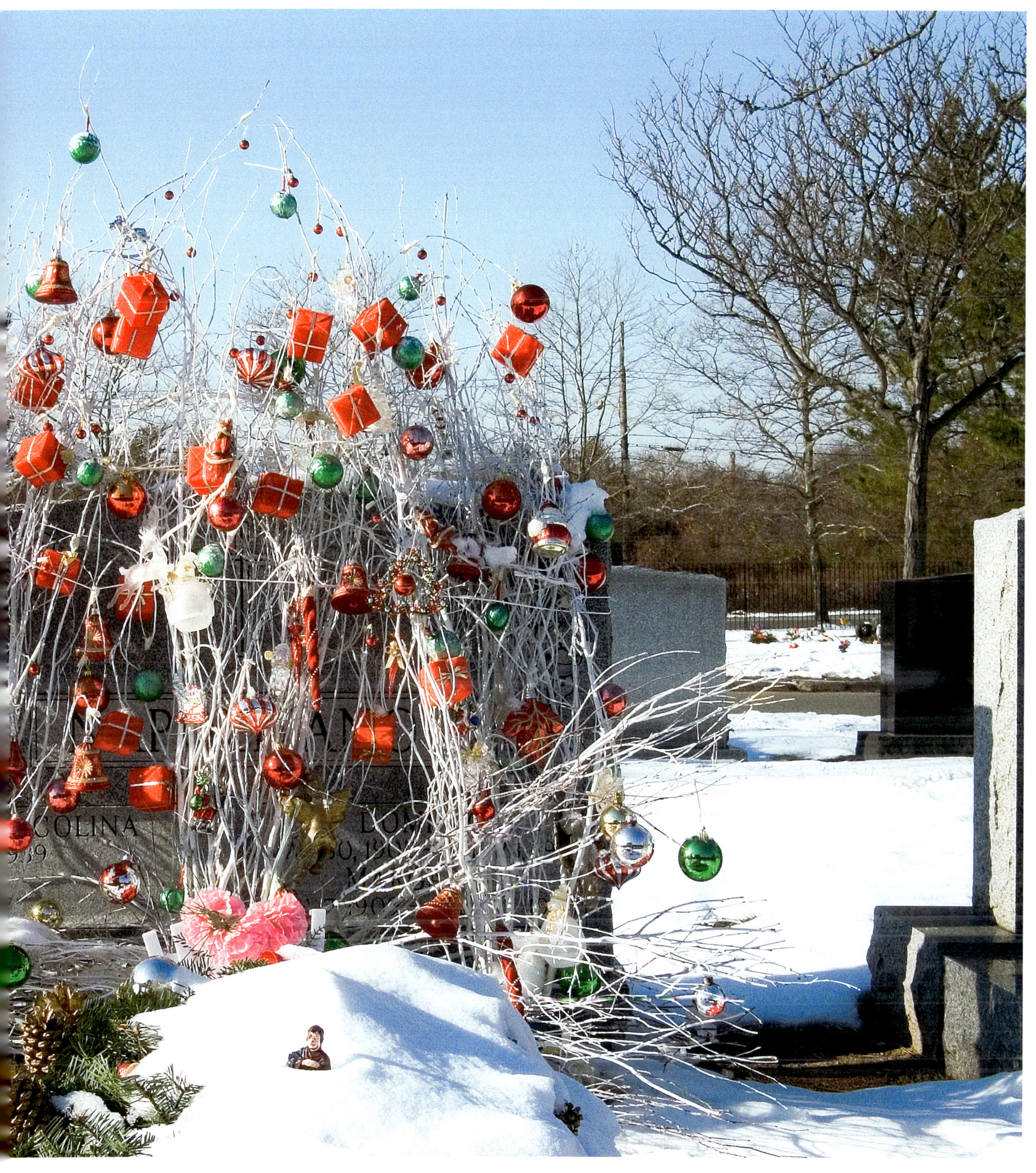
COLINA

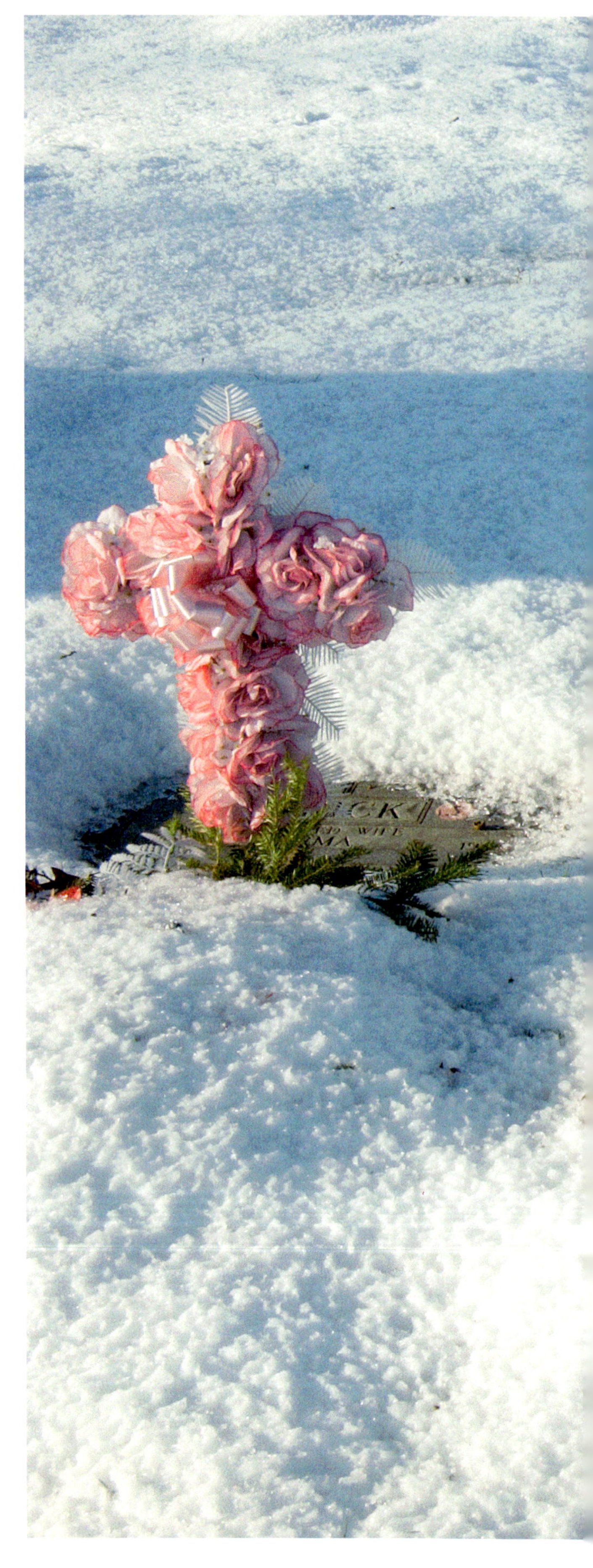

#139

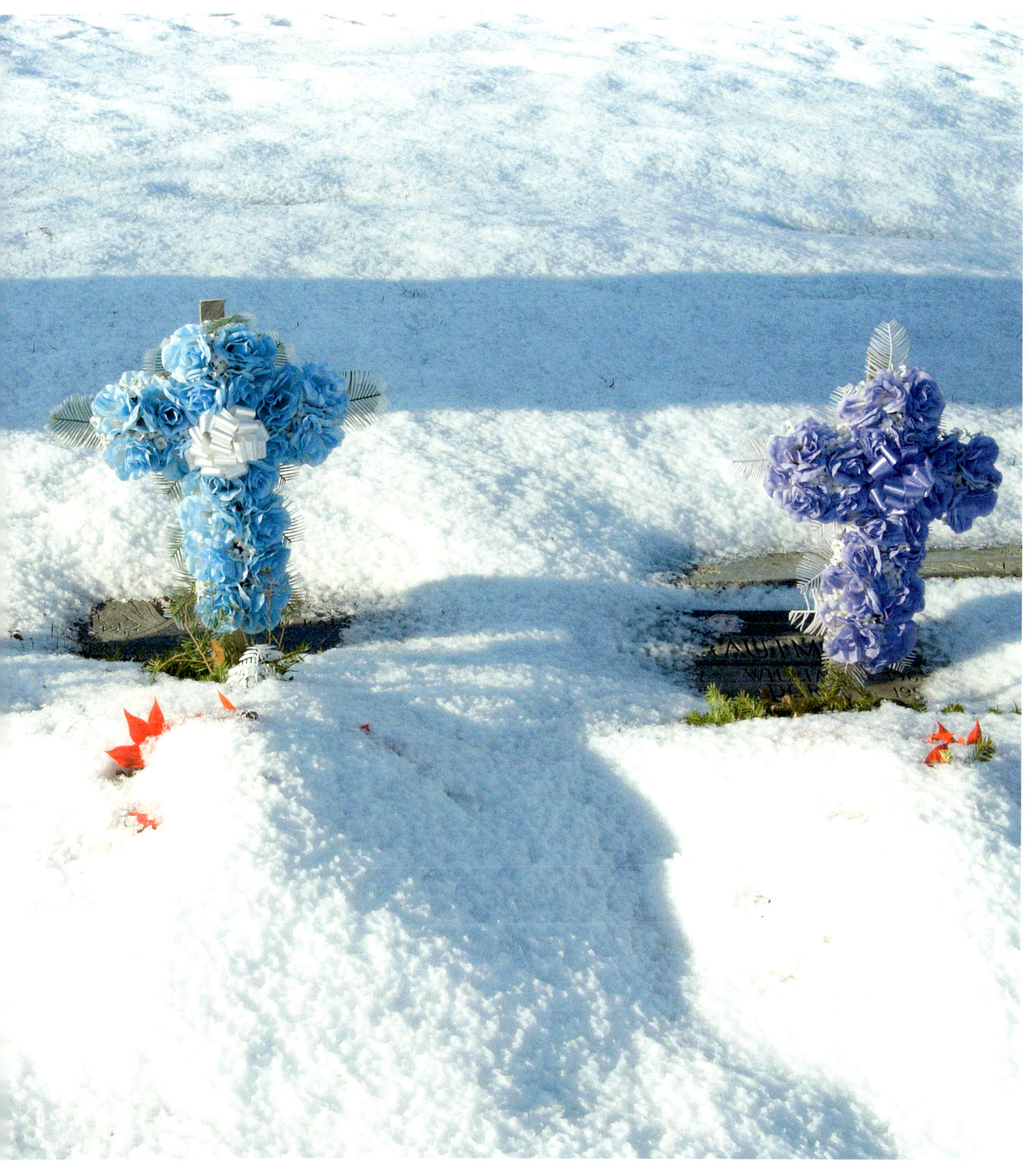

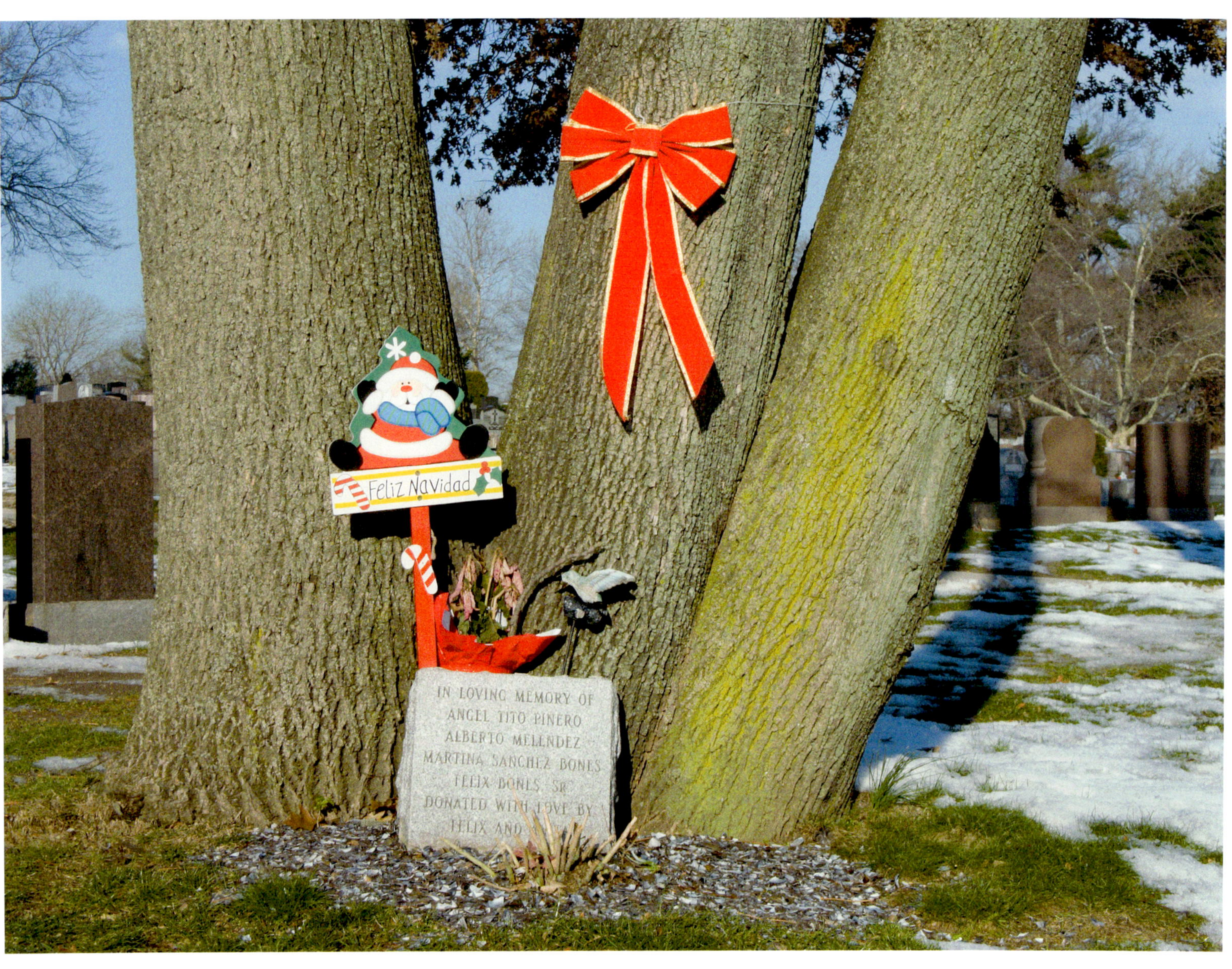
Feliz Navidad
IN LOVING MEMORY OF
ANGEL TITO PINERO
ALBERTO MELENDEZ
MARTINA SANCHEZ BONES
FELIX BONES, SR.
DONATED WITH LOVE BY
FELIX AND

#140

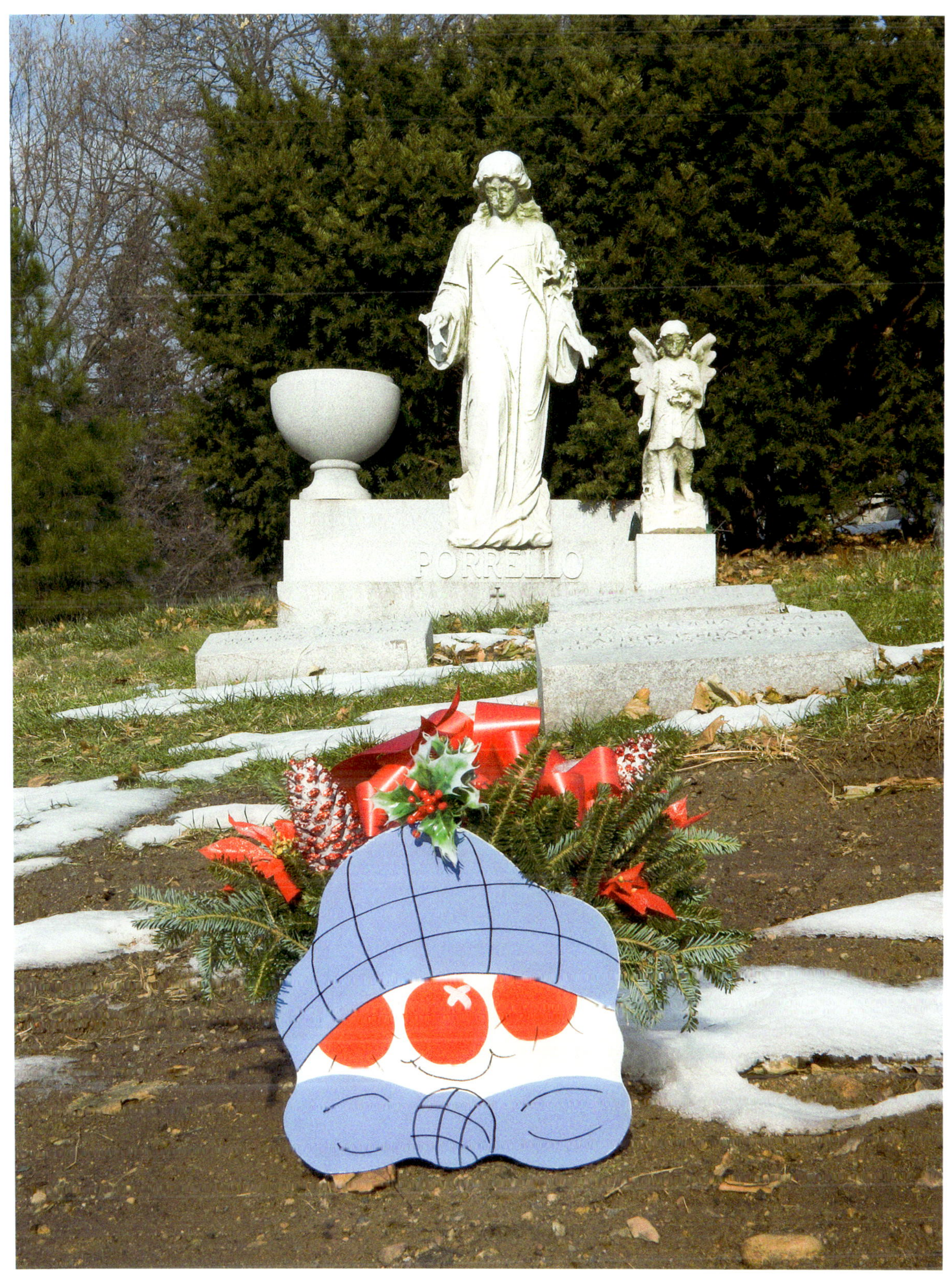

#141

J. G. CARUSO
C. MORALES
K A. TORMO
S. ISALES
OSUMANU
NN OSUMANU
J. O'CONNELL
J. O'CONNELL
J. SPENCER
UFFY
OLSEN
ESPOSITO
A. MARRERO
NA G. MARRERO
A CRAWFORD
AWU-ELOM BUBB
OGAN
RASSADONIO
ASSADONIO
Julian

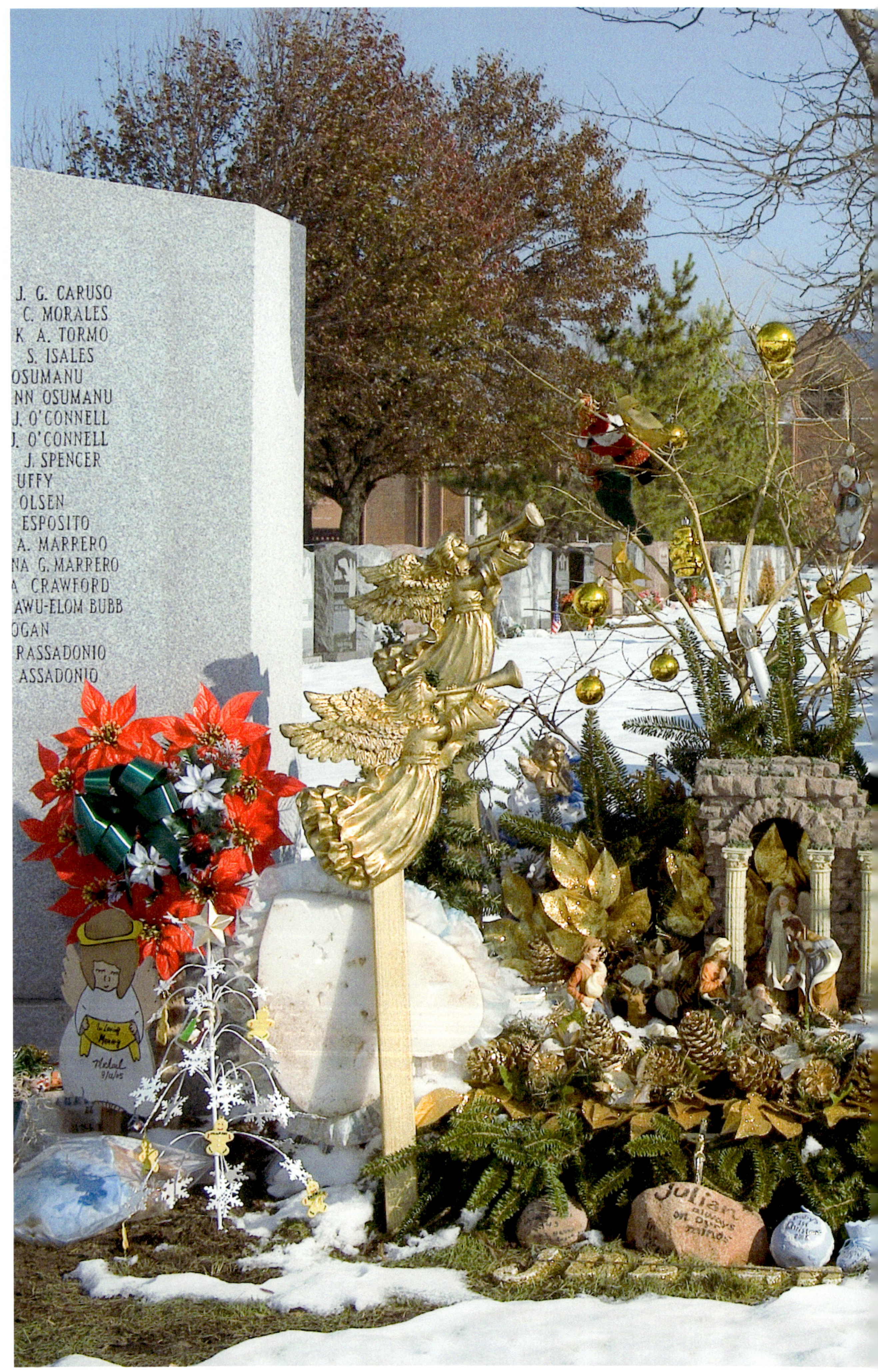

#56D

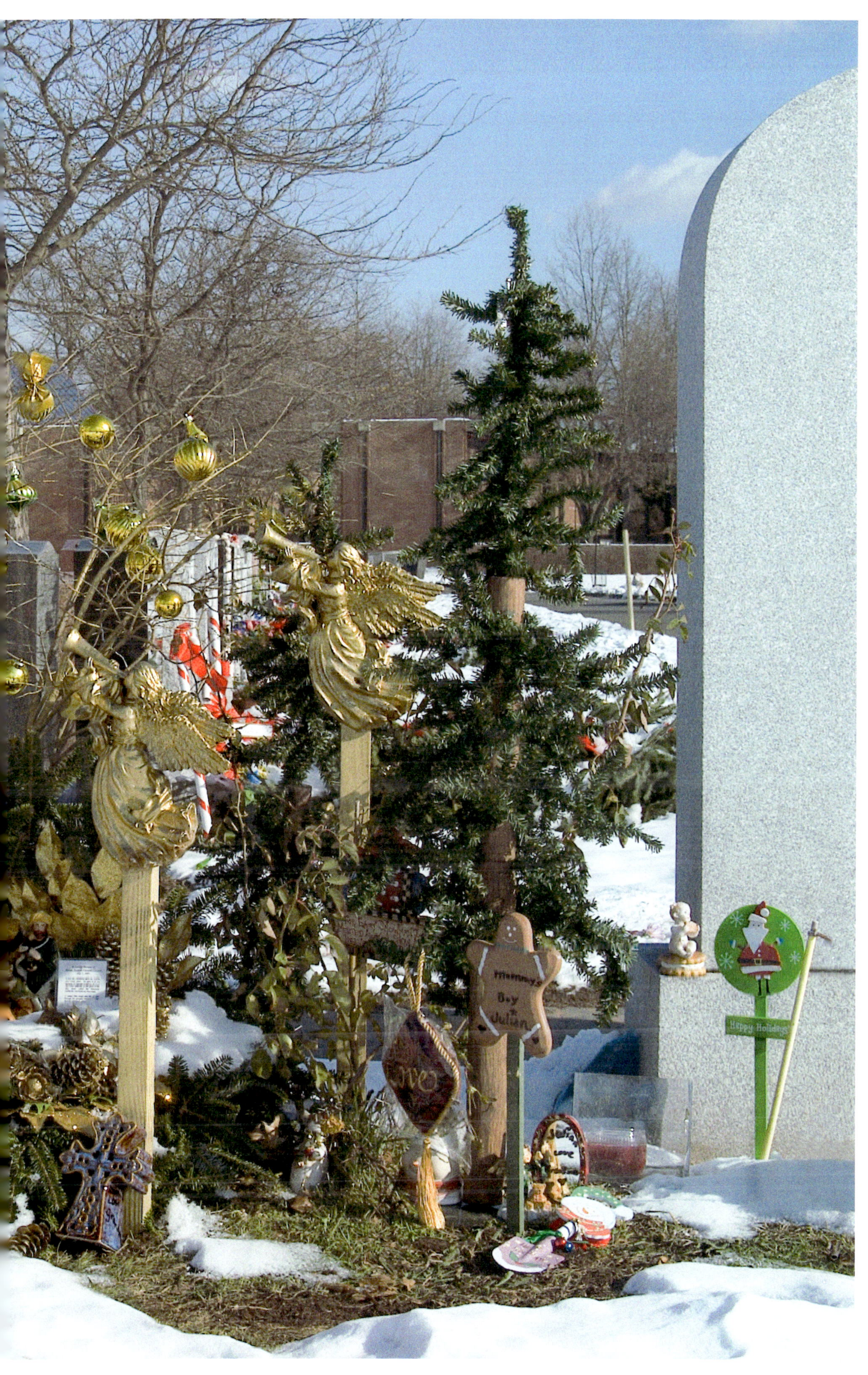
Mommy's
Boy
Julian
Happy Holidays

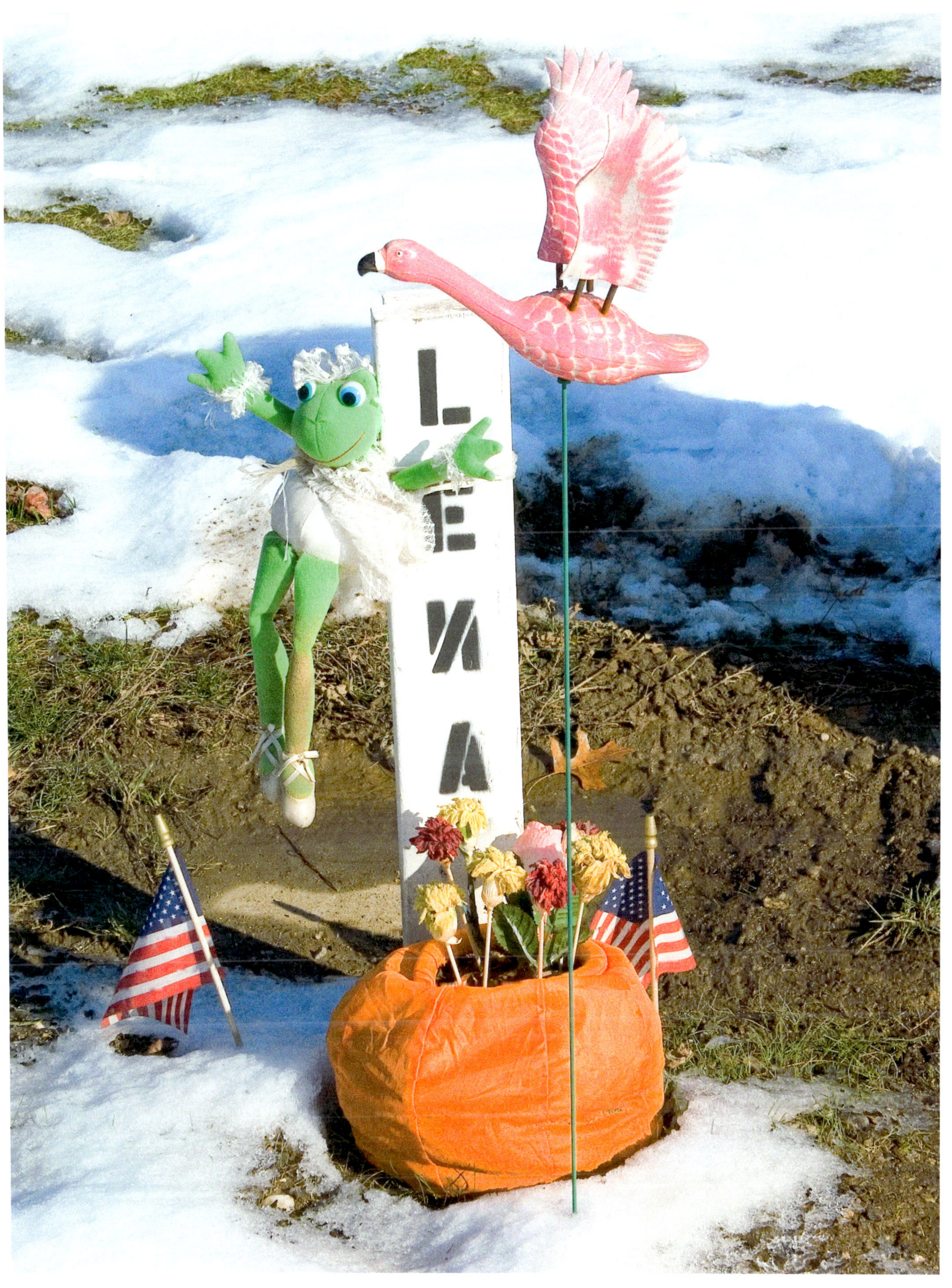

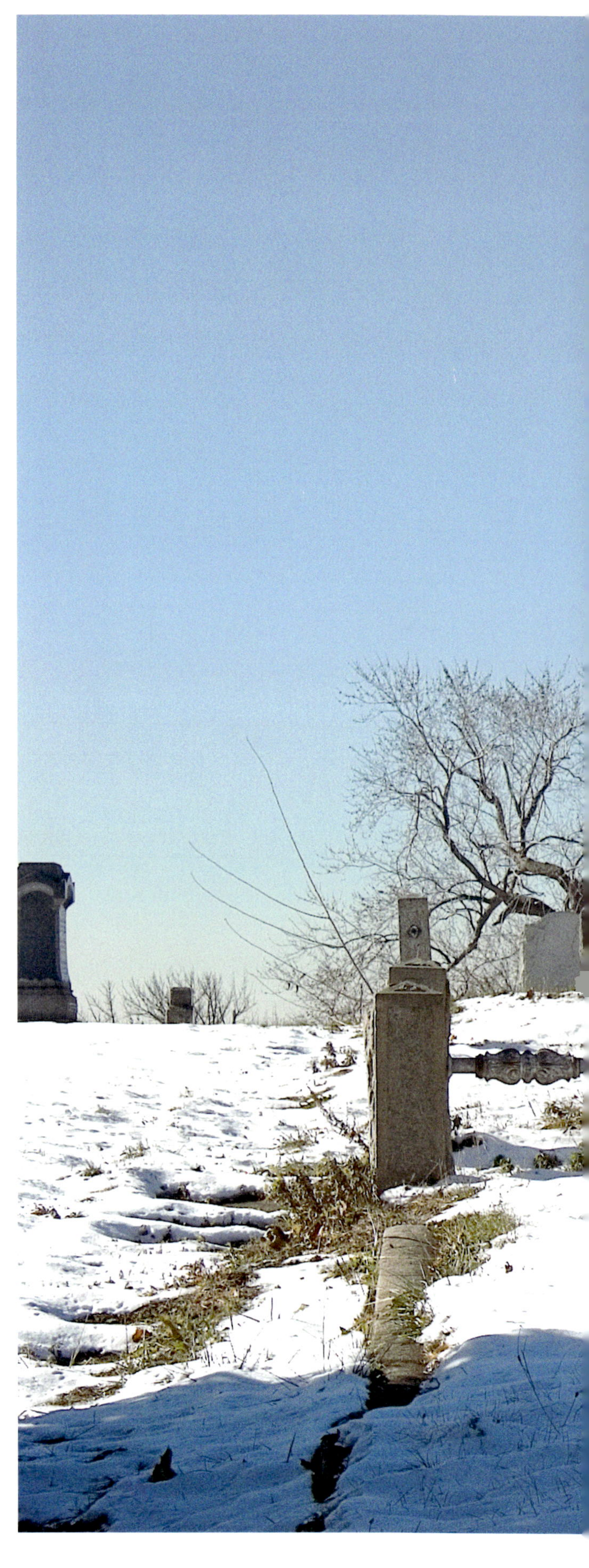

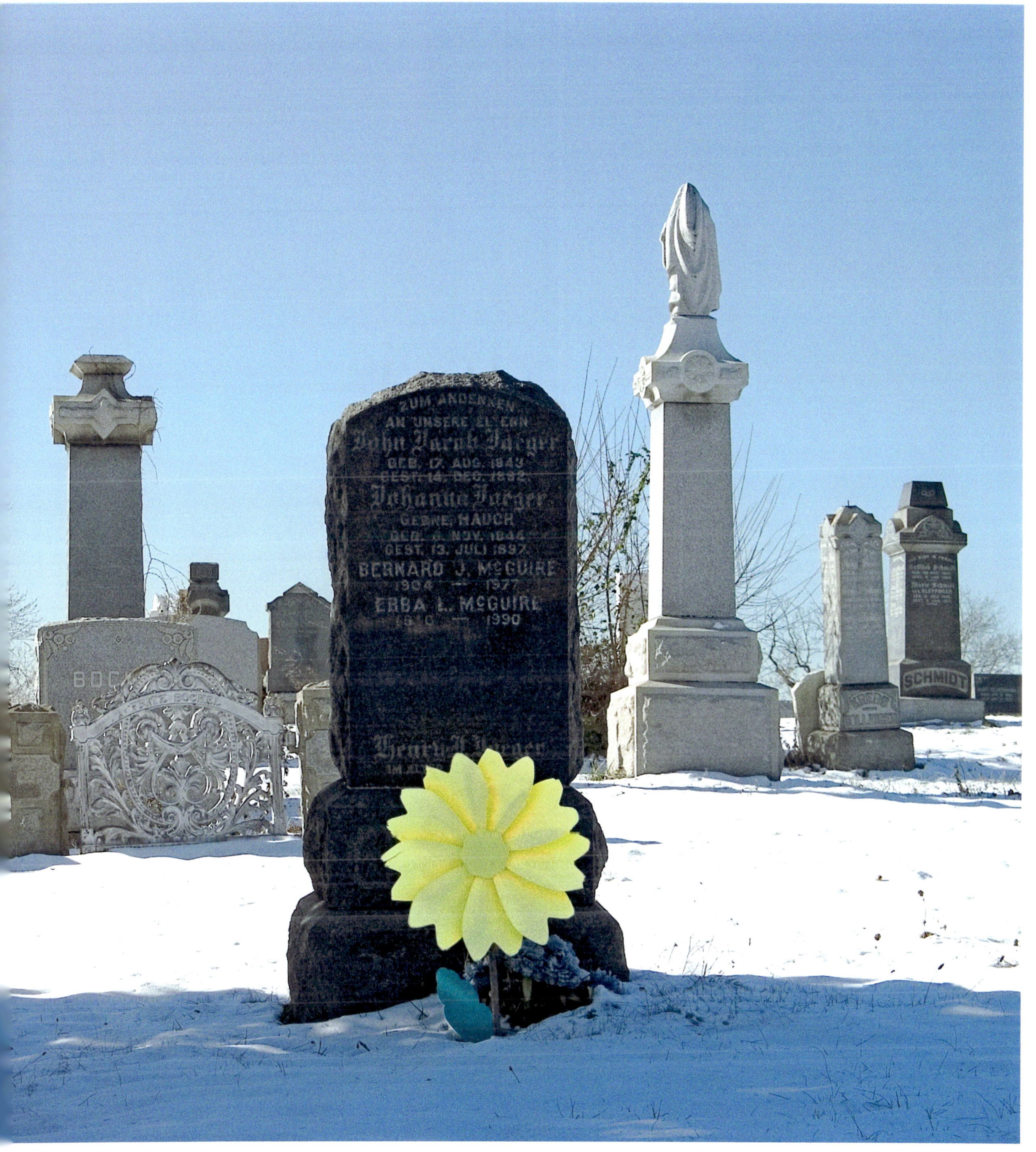
ZUM ANDENKEN
GEB. 17. AUG. 1843
GEST. 13. JULI 1897
BERNARD J. McGUIRE
1904 — 1977
ERBA L. McGUIRE
1990
SCHMIDT

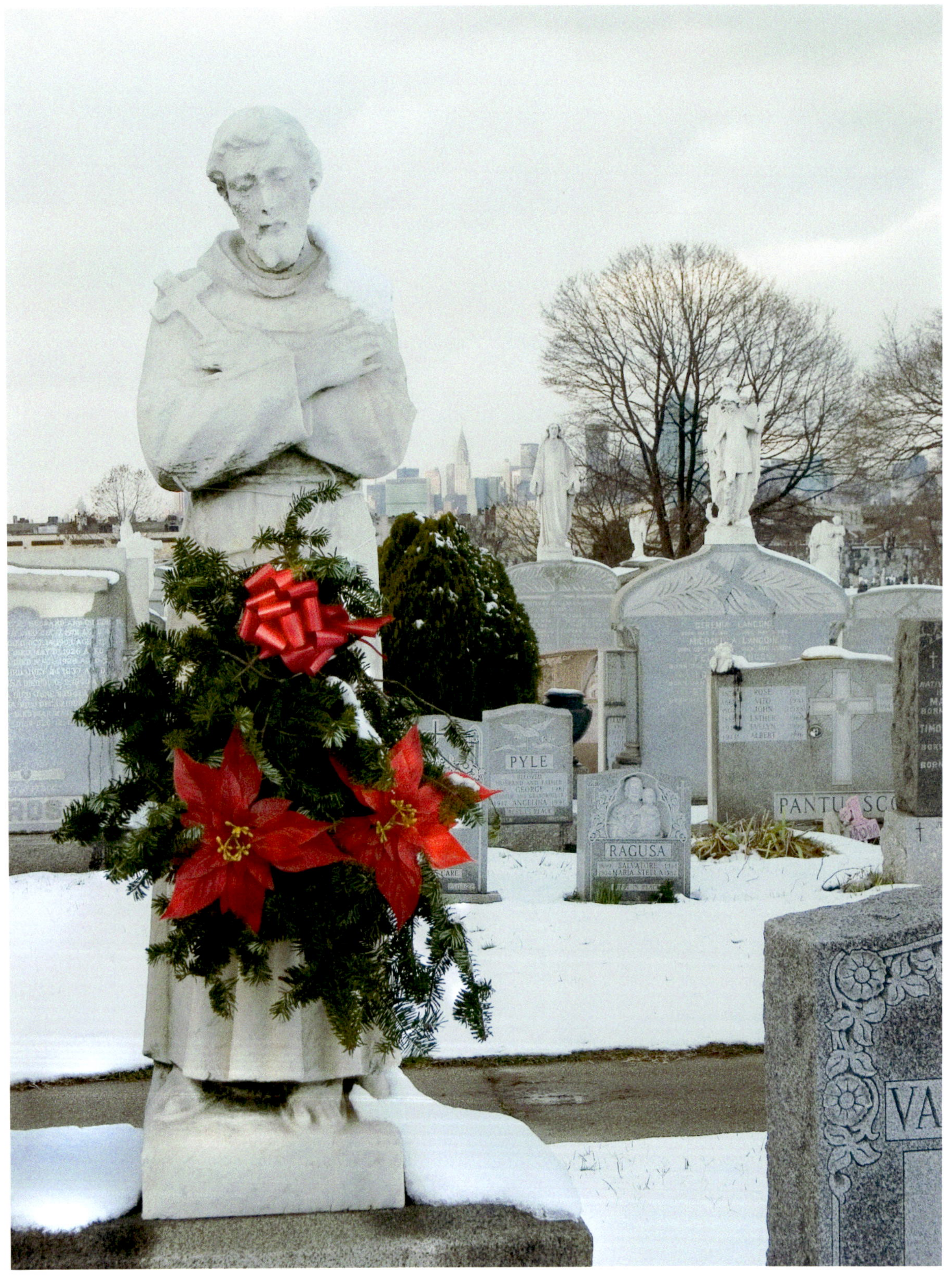

#32B

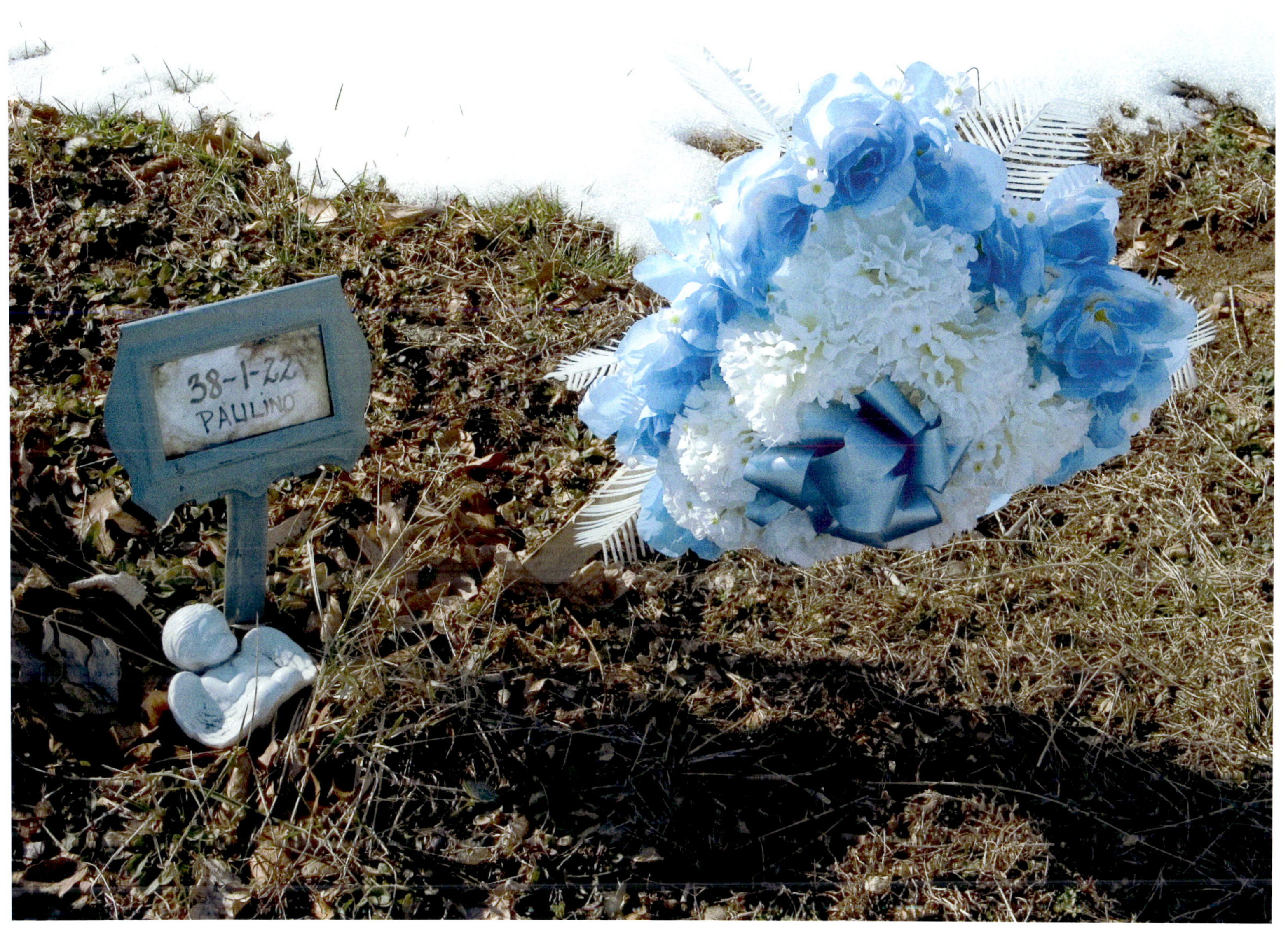
38-1-22
PAULINO

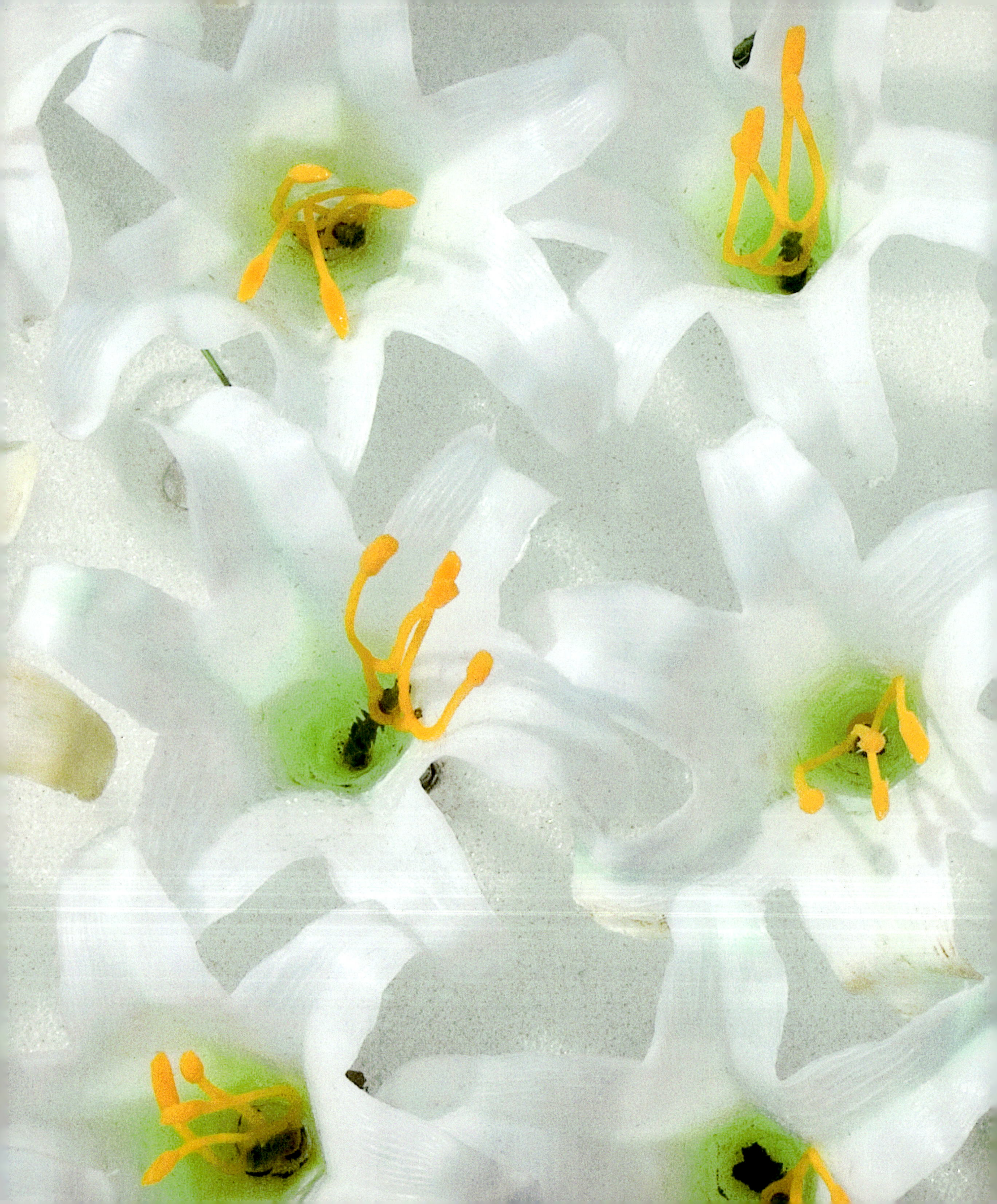

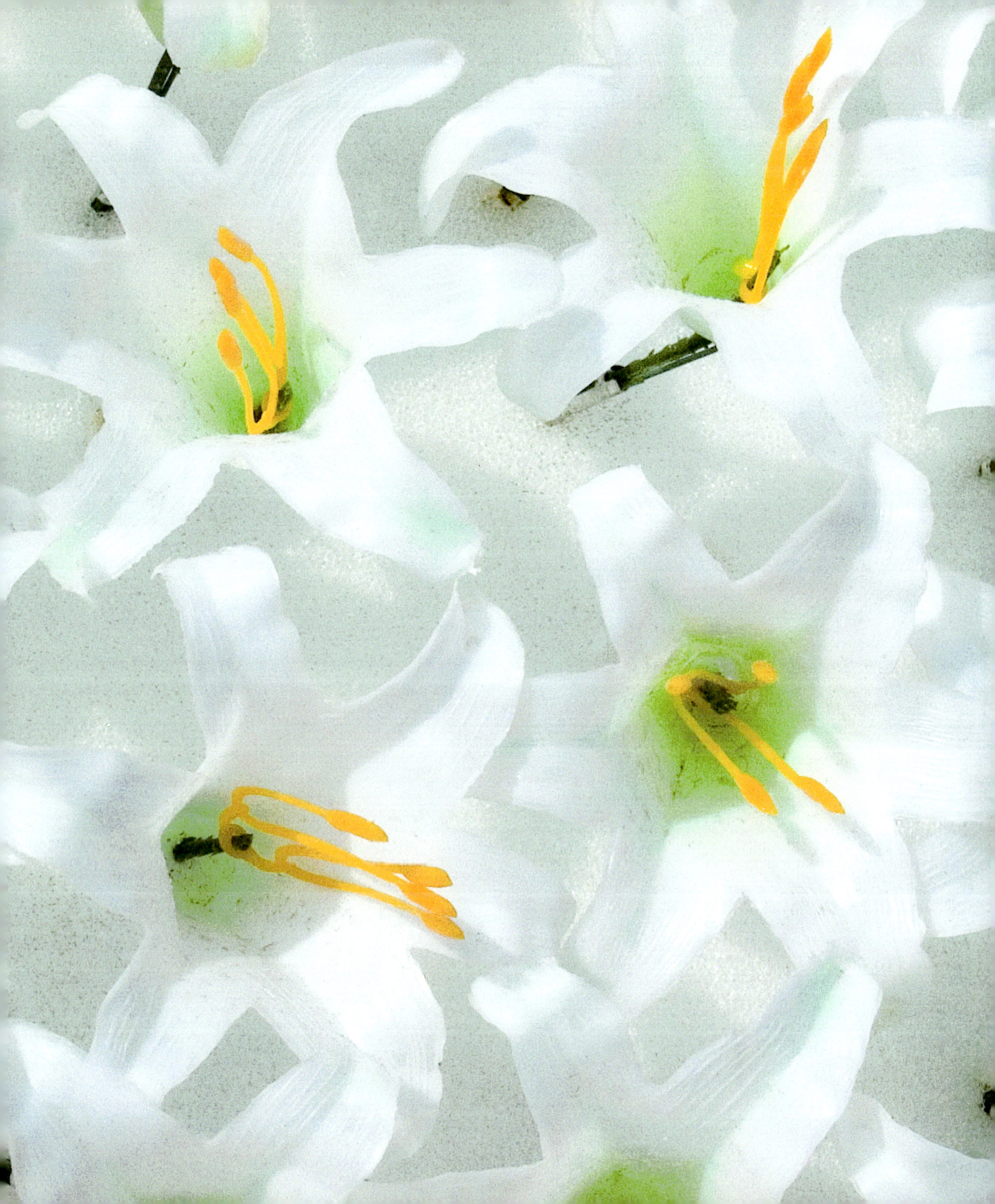

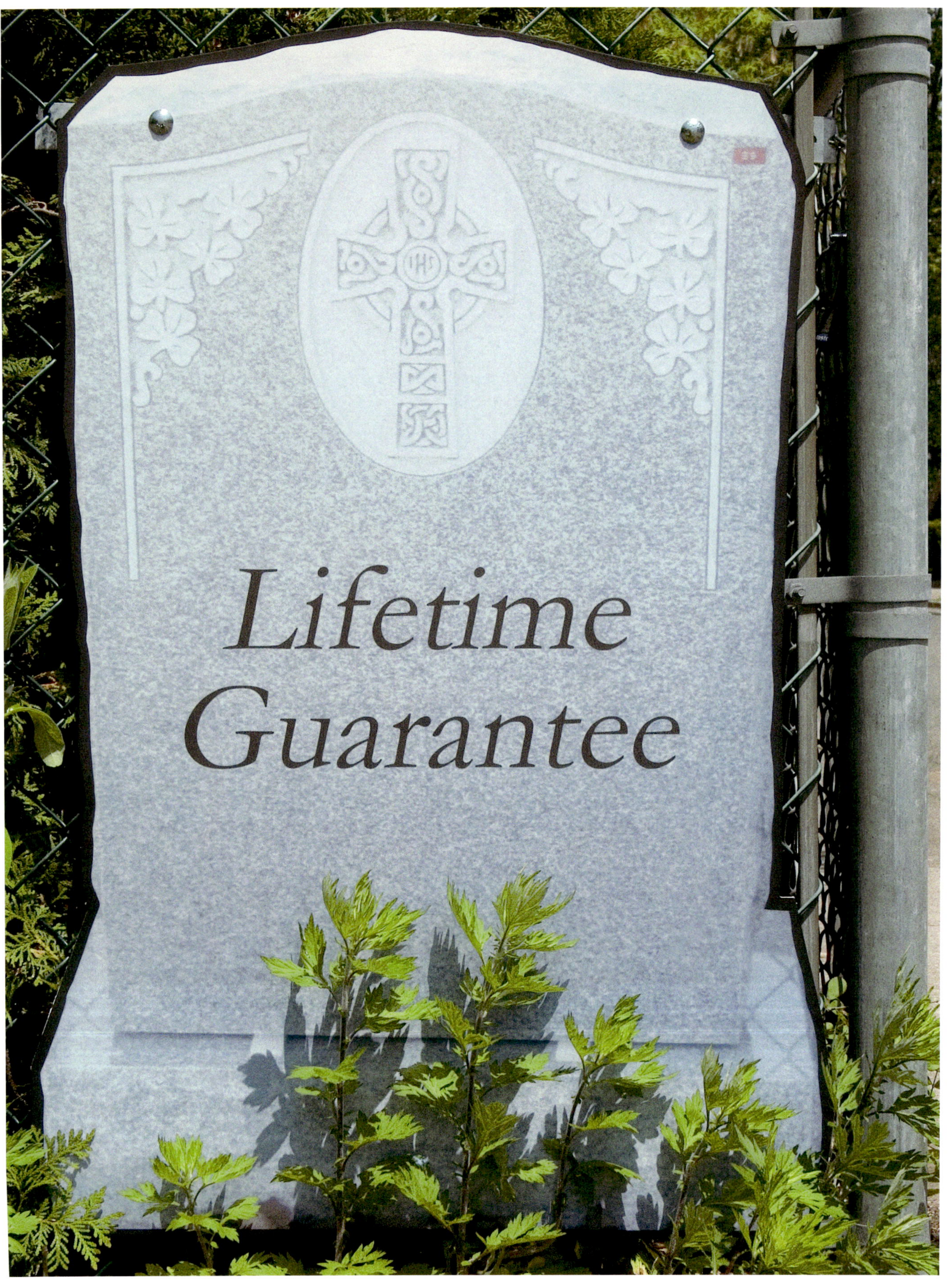
Lifetime
Guarantee

THE FAMILIES AND FRIENDS OF THE DEAD

AND

ADAM AND EVE
ROBERT AMMERLAAN
MARTIN ANGIONI
FONS ASSELBERGS
GREGORY A. CLARICK
PETER COX
DAVID FRANKEL
RUDI FUCHS
HOWARD GARDNER
MARK HOLBORN
MAX KISMAN
MARIE-JOSÉE KRAVIS
CATERINA PAZZI
FRANCESCA PIETROPAOLO
LIZ SAVAGE
IDA SIPORA
ROBERT STORR
KAREL JAN TUSENIUS
ASTRID VOSTERMANS

Acknowledgments

This book is set in Gill Sans, a typeface designed in the late 1920s by the English sculptor, graphic artist, and type designer Eric Gill. In designing the font, Gill was inspired by Johnston, the typeface designed in 1916 by the innovative British letterer and teacher Edward Johnston for the signage of the London Underground. Gill's alphabet, however, is more classical in proportion. The capital letters are modeled on monumental Roman capitals, like those of Trajan's Column, and on the Caslon and Baskerville typefaces. The capital M is based on the proportions of a square, with the middle strokes meeting at the center; the uppercase also contains Gill's signature flared R. The lowercase letters are modeled on lowercase Carolingian script, an influence most noticeable in the two-story a and the eyeglass g. (Following the humanist model, the lowercase italic a becomes single story.) The italic e is highly calligraphic; the lowercase p has a vestigial calligraphic tail. Rooted in pen-written letters, Gill Sans is a humanist sans serif font, very legible in quality.

About the type

Concept and photography: Jan Christiaan Braun
Essays: Howard Gardner, Cambridge, Mass.; Robert Storr, New York
Editor: David Frankel, New York
Designer: Rick Vermeulen, Rotterdam
Lithographer and printer: Drukkerij Lecturis BV, Eindhoven
Publisher: Stichting Over Holland, the Netherlands

Available in North, Central and South America through
D.A.P./Distributed Art Publishers, Inc., 155 Sixth Avenue, New York, NY 10013, USA
T +1 212 627 1999 F +1 212 627 9484 E dap@dapinc.com

Available in the rest of the world through
Thames & Hudson Ltd, 181A High Holborn, London WC1V 7QX, England
T +44 (0)20 7845 5000 F +44 (0)20 7845 5050 E mail@thameshudson.co.uk

Printed and bound in the Netherlands

ISBN 10: 90-78850-01-9
ISBN 13: 978-90-78850-01-4

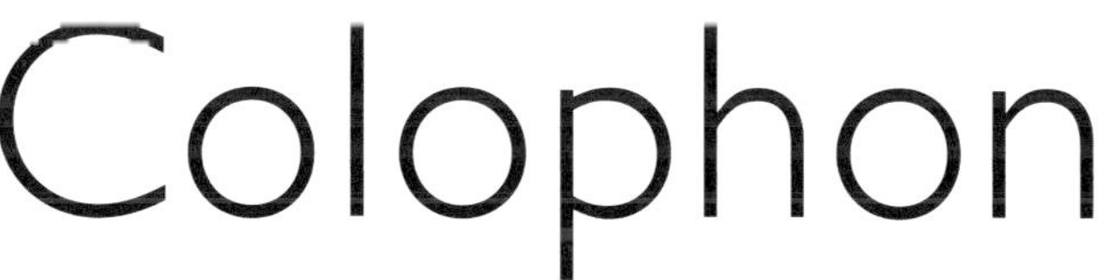

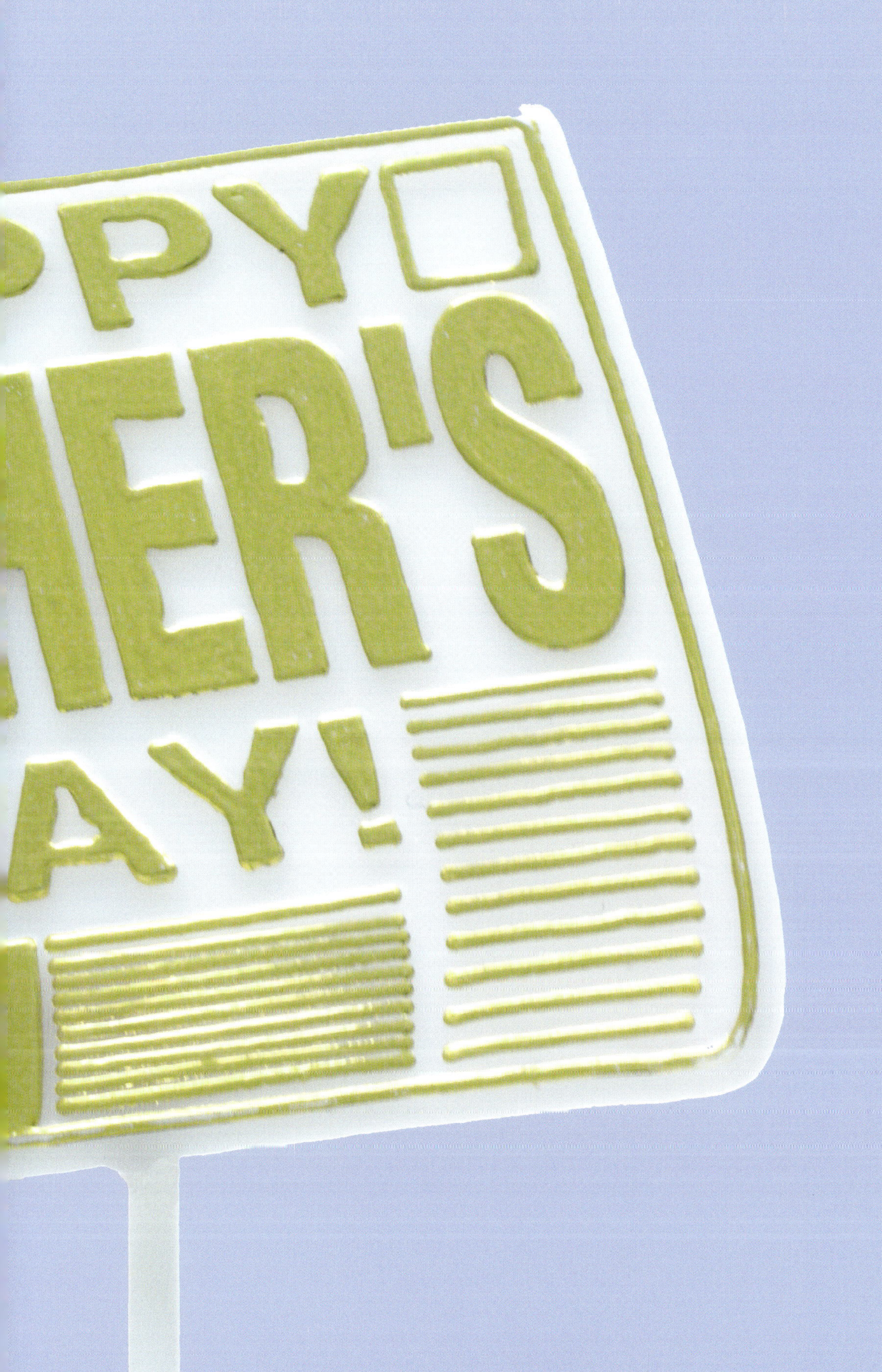

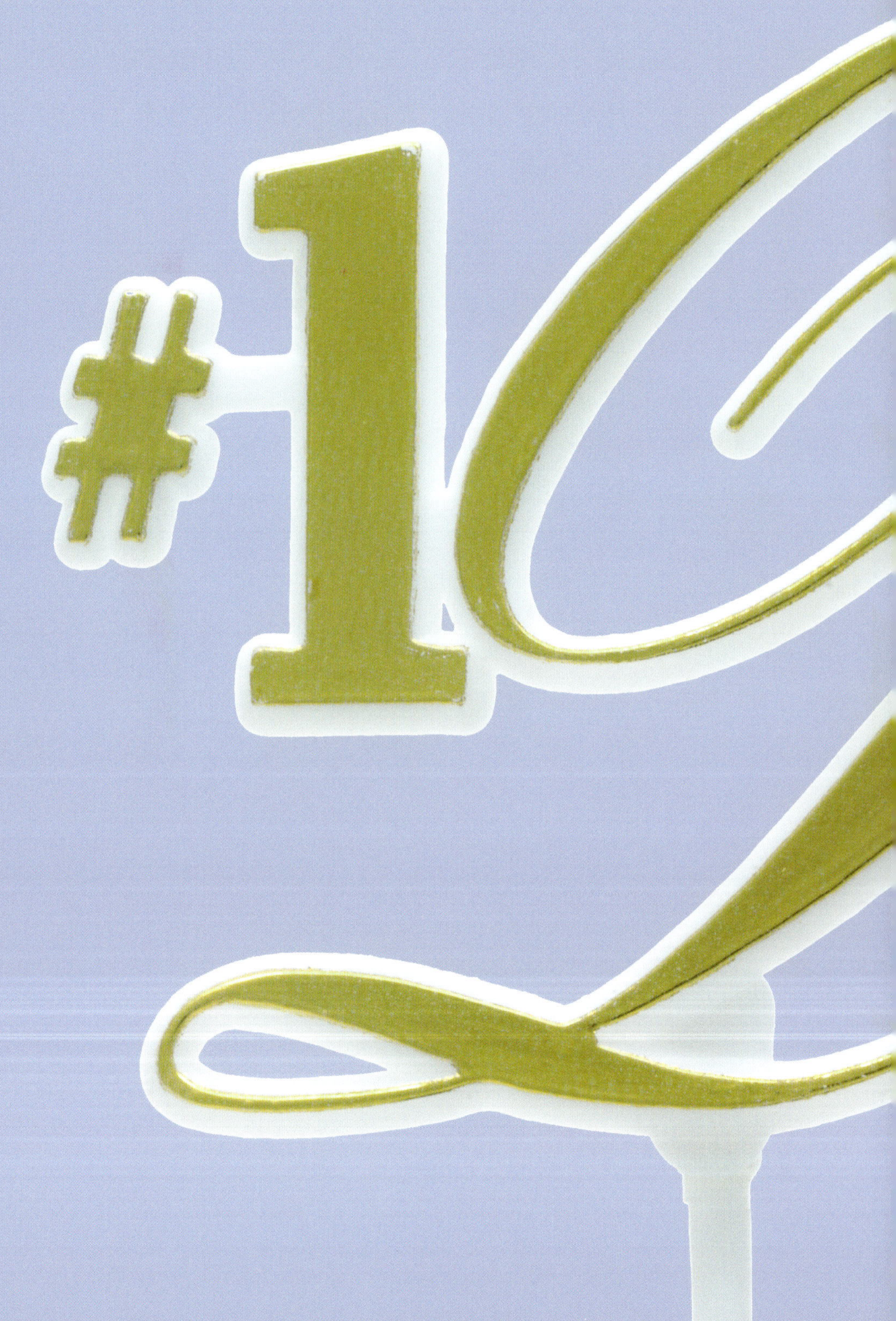
#1

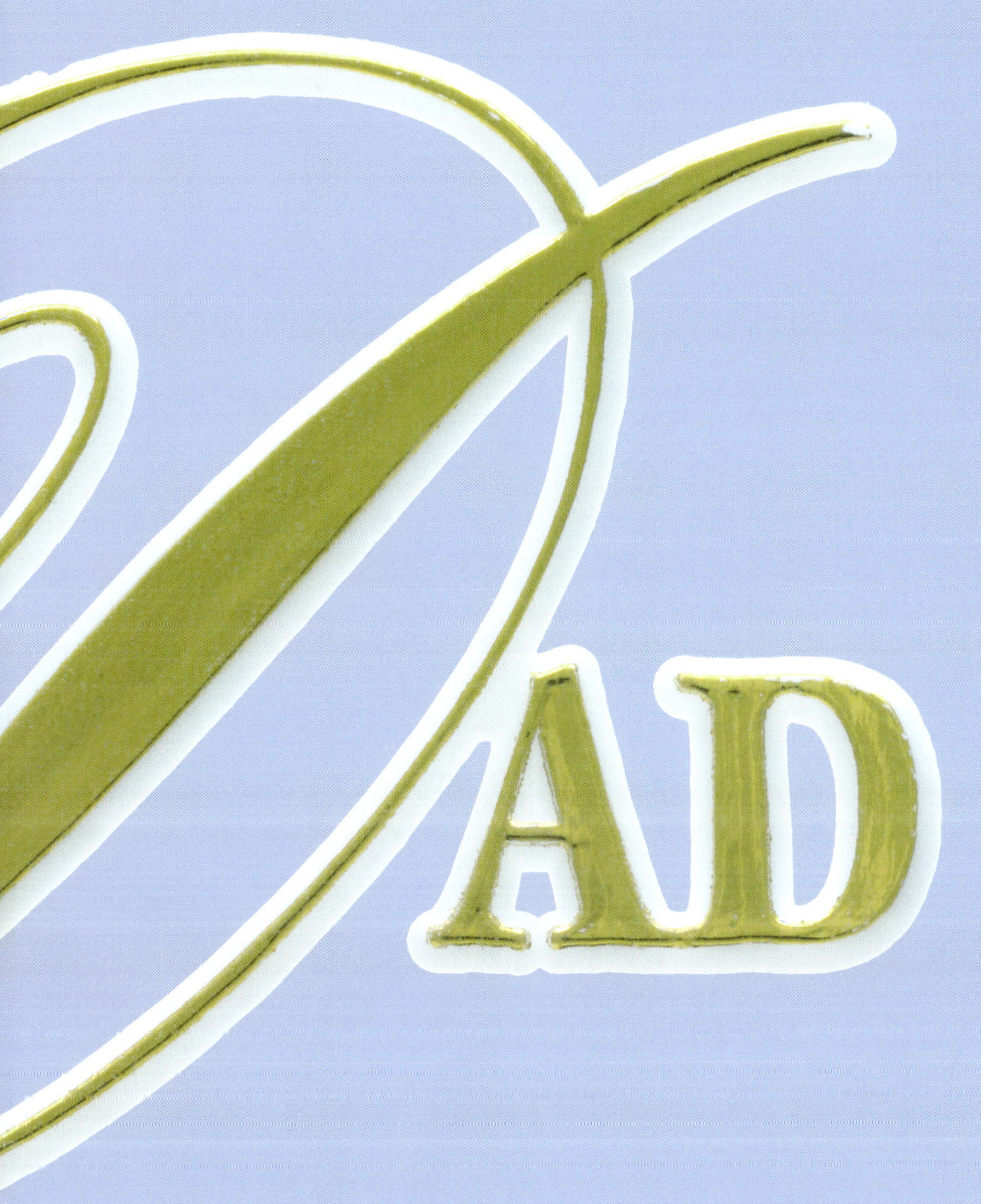
AD

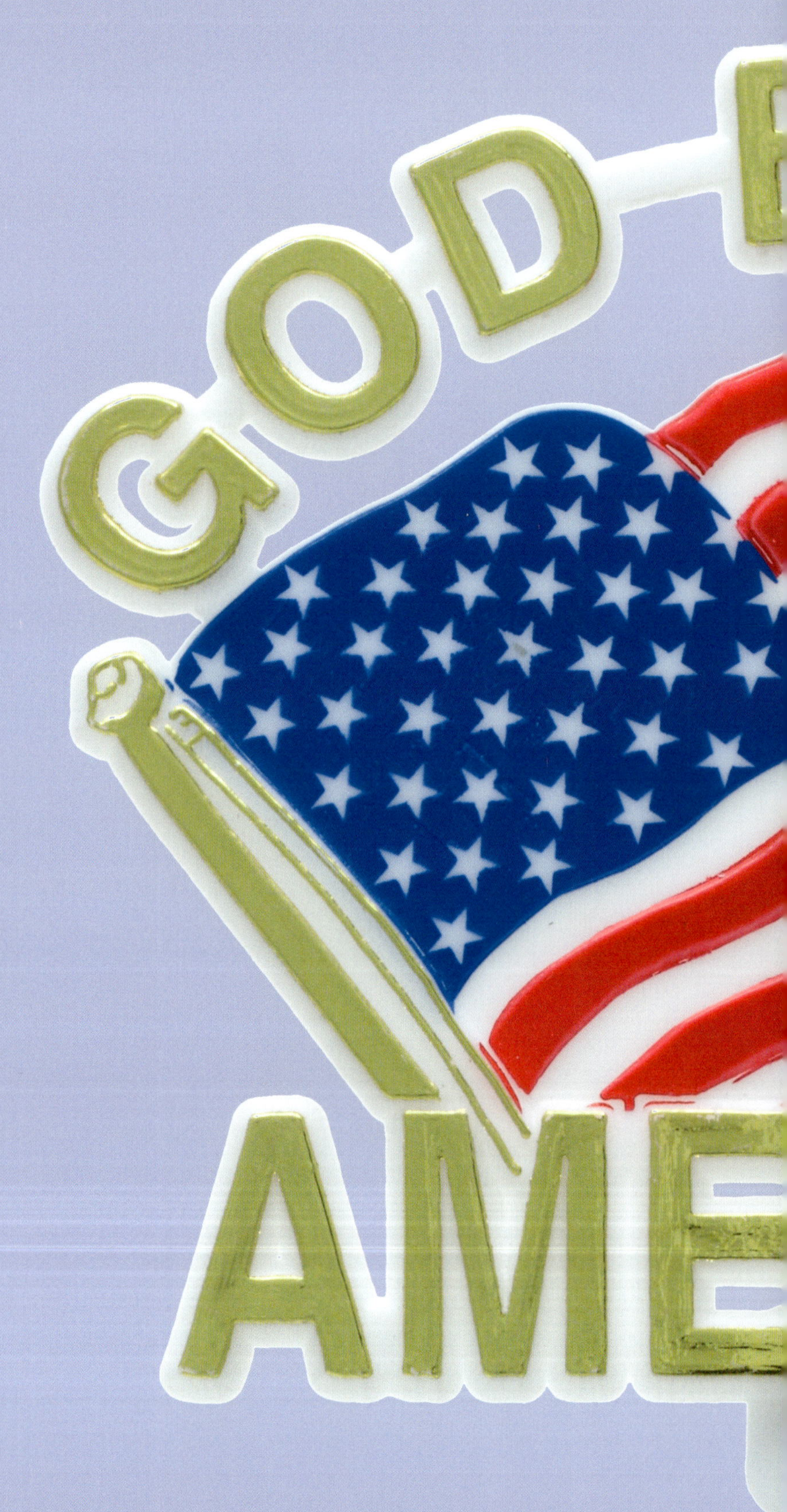
GOD

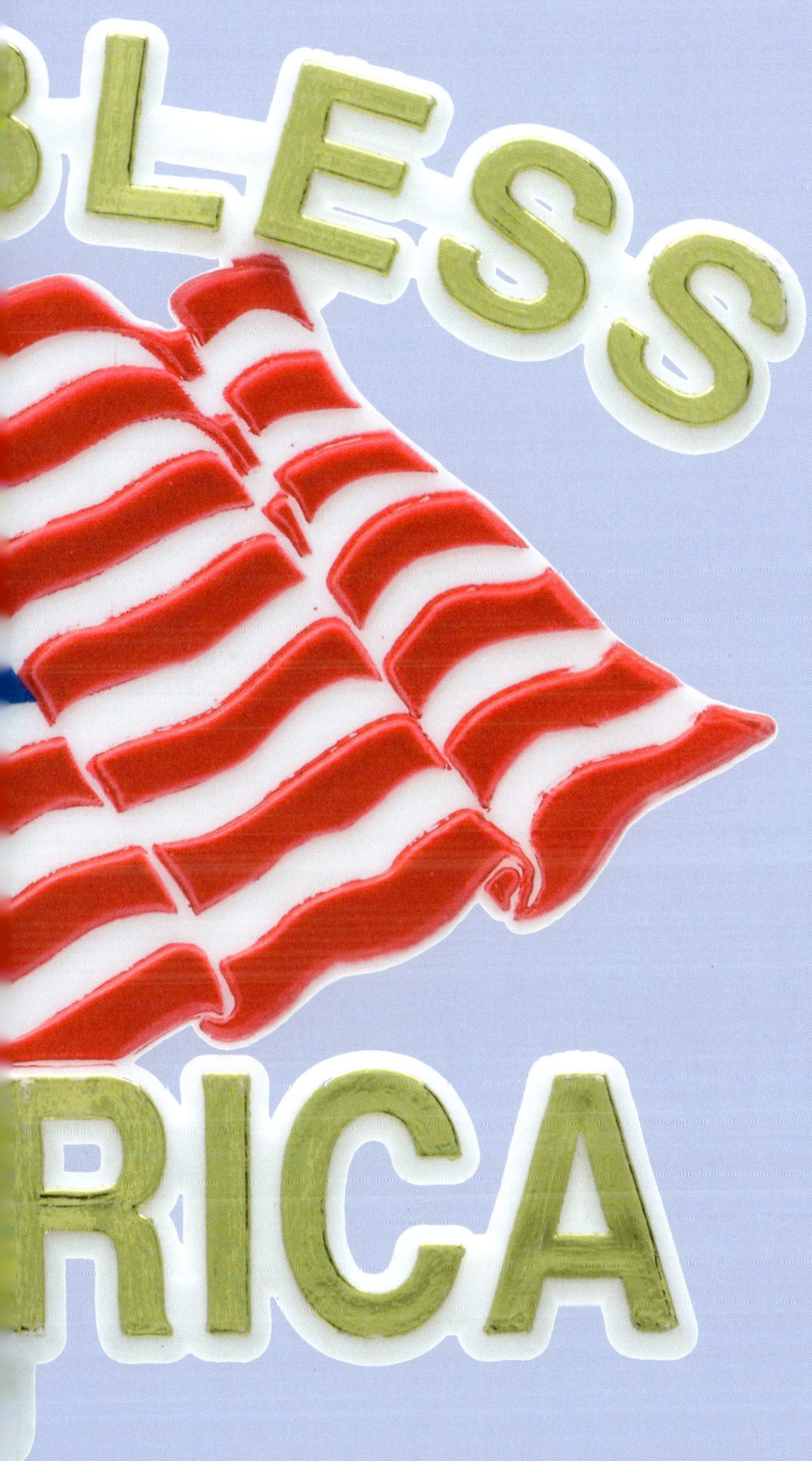
BLESS
RICA

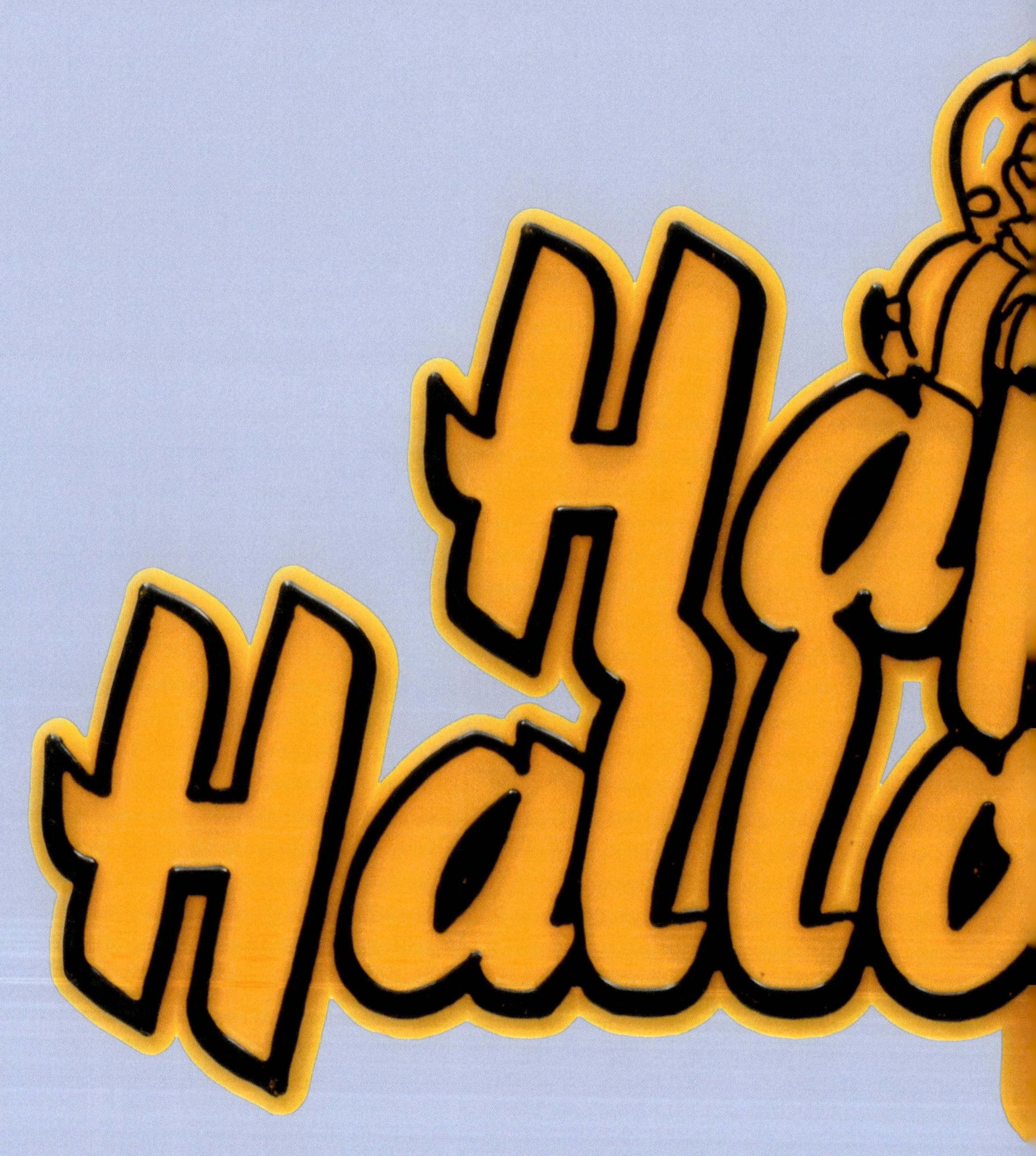

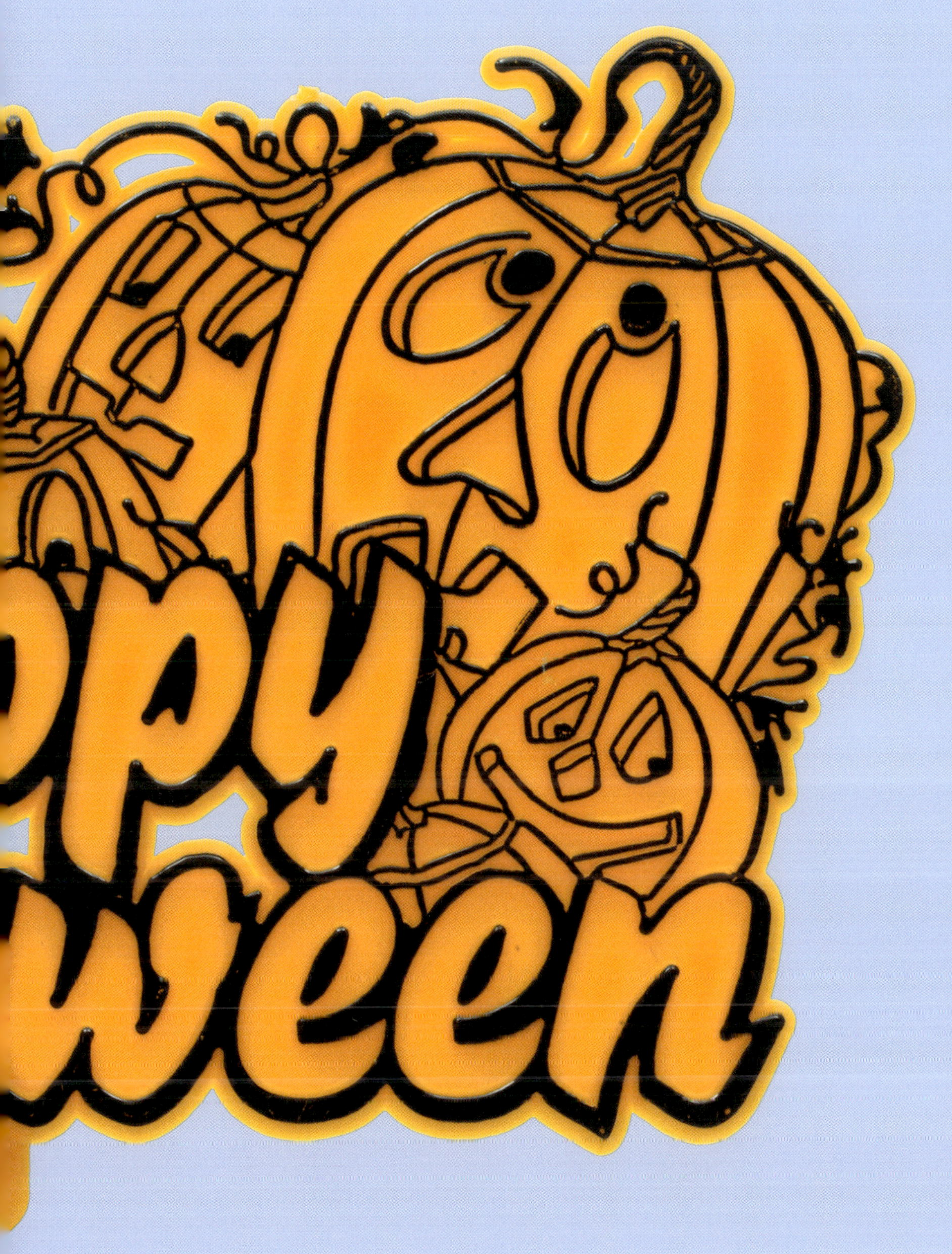

ppy
ween

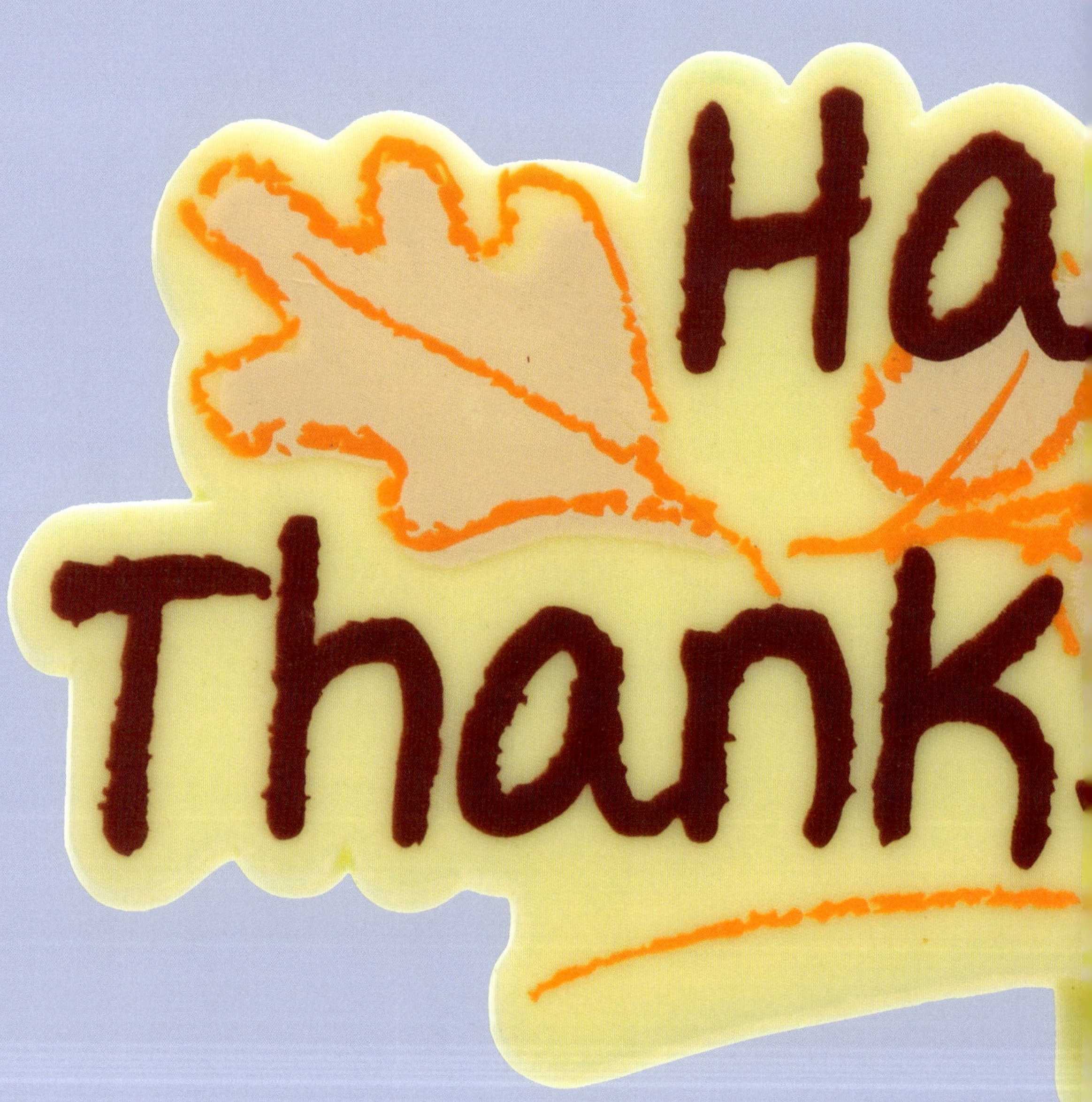
Ha
Thank

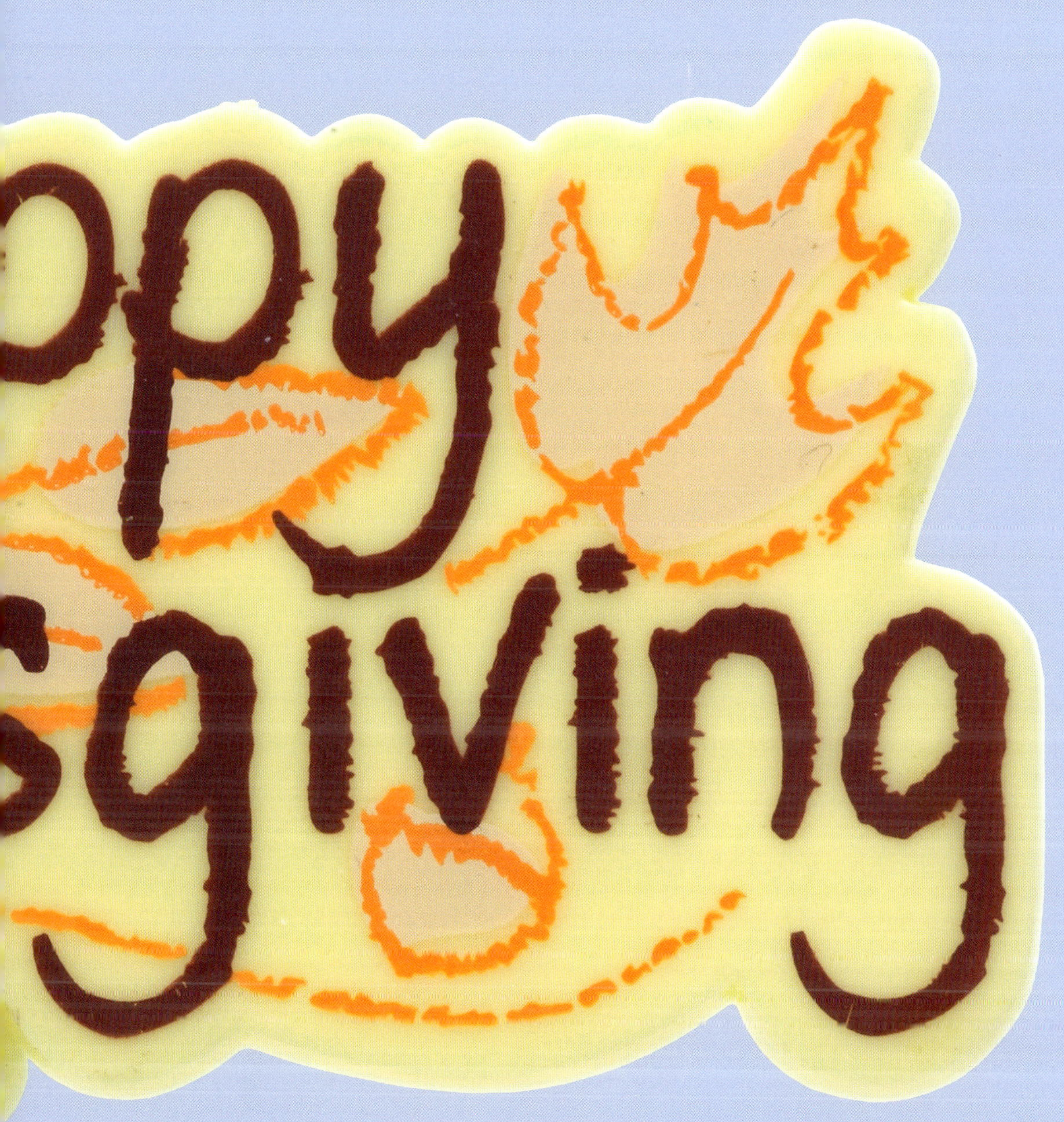

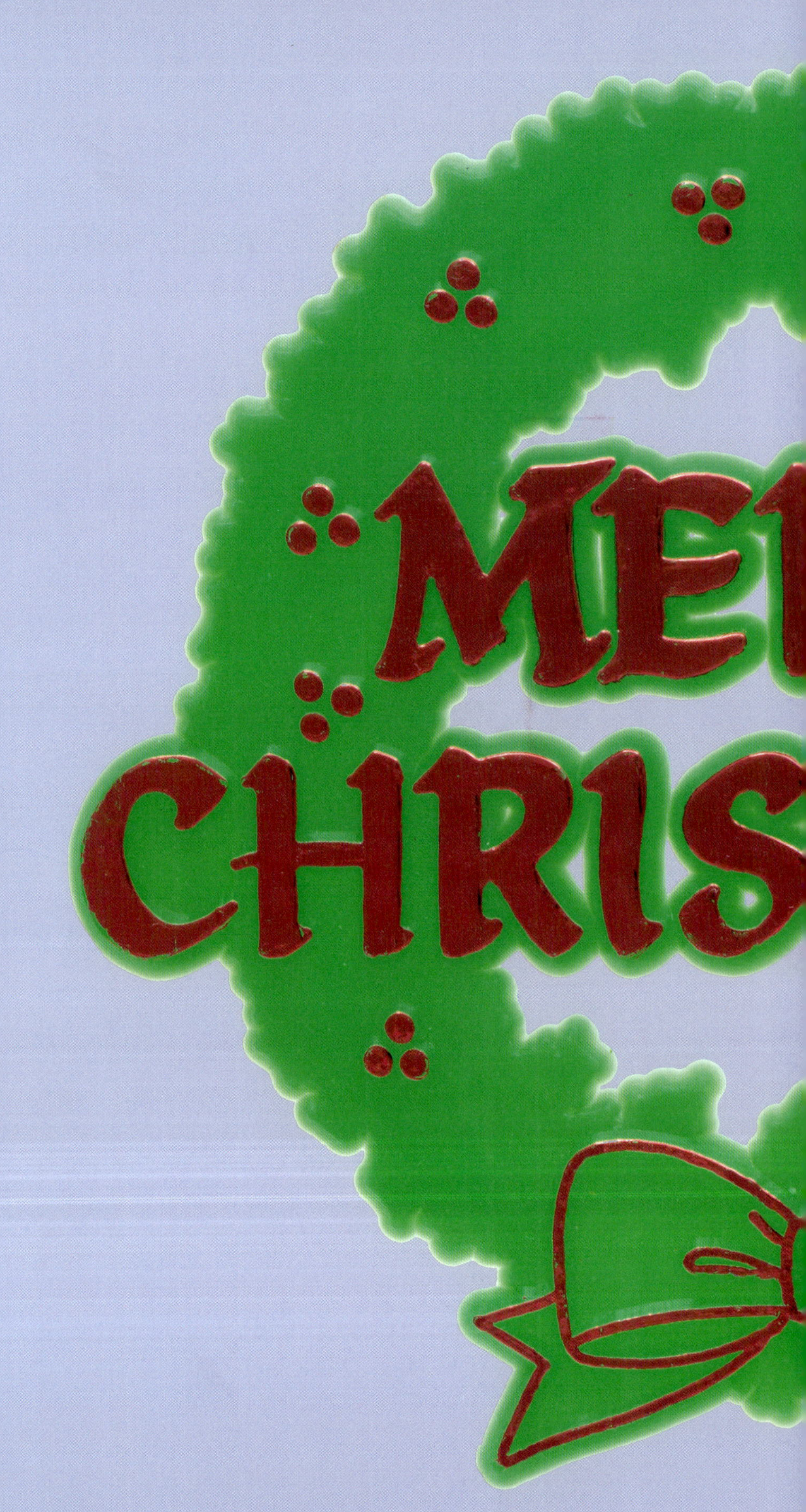